A HISTORY
OF EXPLORATION

" One of the thinges most naturally desired of noble hartes is to heere reade of comon or straunge contries, and espetiallie of contreis that we have had no knoweledge of, being farre aparted from us, and of there commoditees, behaviour and customes wch are very straunge to owres."

BARLOW, *A Brief Summe of Geographie.*

" For as Geography without History seemeth a carkasse without motion, so History without Geography wandreth as a Vagrant without a certaine habitation."

JOHN SMITH, *Generall Historie of Virginia.*

"ISABEL" ENTERING THE POLAR SEA THROUGH SMITH SOUND, MIDNIGHT AUGUST 26TH, 1852.

From a drawing by Commander E. A. Inglefield, 1852.

[Front.]

A HISTORY
OF EXPLORATION

FROM THE EARLIEST TIMES
TO THE PRESENT DAY

By
BRIGADIER-GENERAL
SIR PERCY SYKES

K.C.I.E., C.B., C.M.G.

*Gold Medallist of the Royal Geographical and
Royal Empire Societies
Author of " A History of Persia ", etc.*

GREENWOOD PRESS, PUBLISHERS
WESTPORT, CONNECTICUT

Library of Congress Cataloging in Publication Data

Sykes, Percy Molesworth, Sir, 1867-1945.
A history of exploration from the earliest times to
the present day.

Reprint of the 1949 ed. published by Routledge &
K. Paul, London.
Includes index.
1. Discoveries (in geography)--History.
2. Explorers. I. Title.
G80.S9 1975   910'.09   75-35031
ISBN 0-8371-8576-9

This edition originally published in 1949 by Routledge & Kegan
Paul, London

Reprinted with the permission of Routledge & Kegan Paul, Ltd.

Reprinted in 1975 by Greenwood Press,
a division of Williamhouse-Regency Inc.

Library of Congress Catalog Card Number 75-35031

ISBN 0-8371-8576-9

Printed in the United States of America

Dedicated to

THE ROYAL GEOGRAPHICAL SOCIETY

IN GRATEFUL APPRECIATION OF ITS ENCOURAGEMENT

OF MY HUMBLE EFFORTS IN THE FIELD

OF EXPLORATION

CONTENTS

CONTENTS

LIST OF ILLUSTRATIONS

LIST OF ILLUSTRATIONS

COMPLETE LIST OF MAPS

COMPLETE LIST OF MAPS

PREFACE

EXPLORATION and travel have constituted the chief interests of my life and I count myself fortunate to have been able to wander far and wide. I have also listened to many great explorers, beginning with Sir Samuel Baker, when a boy of ten; and some of them I can reckon among my friends.

In this work, which is written for the general reader, I have made no attempt to include every explorer or every journey. This would be impossible with the limited number of words at my disposal; indeed the overflowing abundance of material has constituted a serious difficulty. My plan has been to set the stage when necessary and, as far as possible, to allow the chief actors to speak for themselves. I have touched lightly on the better-known countries and have devoted the greater part of my space to the more remote lands of the world.

I have received much help from my friends. Lieutenant-Colonel Kenneth Mason, Professor of Geography at Oxford, has read through practically the whole of my proofs, while I am also deeply indebted to Mr. E. Heawood and Mr. G. R. Crone, of the Royal Geographical Society, in whose library this work was mainly written. Chapters dealing with subjects on which they are leading experts have been read by Sir Percy Cox, Sir William Gowers, Dr. Hugh Mill, Colonel C. H. D. Ryder, Colonel T. E. Lawrence, Mr. J. M. Wordie, Dr. T. G. Longstaff and Mr. John Baddeley. This valuable assistance I would gratefully acknowledge. I am deeply indebted to Mr. J. N. L. Baker's standard work and for the permission of Messrs. George Harrap & Co., to use his excellent sketch maps, which incidentally show the routes of various travellers whom I have been unable to mention. I would also thank my two daughters who have industriously typed the chapters, and the many corrections and additions.

Apart from acknowledgements made in the text, I would thank Messrs. Jonathan Cape for permission to quote from *Arabia Felix*, and the proprietors of the Argonaut Press for permission to quote from their *Varthema* and *Cabot*. Messrs.

Thornton Butterworth have granted me similar permission for *The Lost Oases*, and Messrs. Constable & Co. for Mr. Philby's works. Finally, I would express my thanks for any other quotations that I may have made from other works.

The number of books consulted has been great, but, instead of a bibliography, I have given the chief works in footnotes as they were consulted by me. I have, as a rule, referred to explorers by their surnames only in the text but, in the index, their initials are shown. Thirty-six maps illustrating the journeys of explorers have been provided, but I also take it for granted that my readers use their atlas.

In conclusion, for nearly two years I have been enjoying the company of the great explorers, past and present, and if this epitome of their heroic achievements affords my readers one tithe of the pleasure that I have experienced in writing it, I shall deem myself richly rewarded.

PREFACE TO THE THIRD EDITION

" The thirst for adventure is the vent which Destiny offers, a war, a crusade, a gold mine, a new country, speak to the imagination and offer swing and play to the confined powers."

EMERSON.

BEFORE dealing with recent exploration, I would express to the Royal Empire Society my deep gratitude for the award to me, in 1934, of its gold medal, which, hitherto, I have been unable to acknowledge in this work.

Over a decade has elapsed since the second edition of my *History of Exploration* was published, and the period has been a busy one. In this edition an appendix has been added, in which the latest journey of that veteran explorer St. John Philby is noted, together with those of men and women, who have also won distinction in the field, from Central Asia to Central Africa, and from the Antarctic to the land of the reindeer-riding Tungus.

Once again, I would thank Doctor Hugh Mill, the veteran historian of the Antarctic and Mr. G. R. Crone, the Librarian of the Royal Geographical Society. I would also thank Mr. Charles E. Denny of its Map Department.

A HISTORY OF EXPLORATION

CHAPTER I

EARLY EXPLORATIONS

" He stretcheth out the north over the empty place, and hangeth the earth upon nothing."

Job xxvi. 7.

EXPLORATION in the widest sense of the word was undoubtedly undertaken all over the world by its primitive inhabitants. They depended for their food partly on berries and roots, but more especially on hunting, and must have travelled far and wide in search of the game on which, in the colder regions at any rate, they depended not only for food but also for their pelts ; in the coastal regions they relied on shell-fish and fishing. After such early " food gathering " came agriculture, which was probably " invented " in the valleys of the Euphrates and Nile. The early agriculturists lived a partly pastoral life, as they still do in countries where grazing is scanty owing to insufficient rainfall. Persia is a typical case in point, where nomad tribes, like the Kashgais, move in the spring 200 miles from the warm districts near the Persian Gulf to the bracing uplands of Fars, and a similar distance in the autumn back to their winter pastures. The army of Cyrus the Great consisted chiefly of the shepherds of Fars, Media, and Elam.

On reaching historical times, inscriptions tell us mainly of the wars that were waged and the temples that were founded. Yet here and there we find mention of exploration. In the legend of Gilgamesh, one of the earliest old-world stories of Sumer, we read how the hero set out with a companion to attack the King of Elam, who had invaded Sumer. " Hearing that their enemy was concealed in a sacred grove, they pressed on, and stopped in rapture before the cedar-trees ; they contemplated the height of them, they contemplated the thickness of them." It is clear that the writer of the legend was a dweller in the plains of Iraq, which, save for the date groves, are treeless, and had travelled to the mountains of Elam, where the magnificent trees especially struck him.

I

The earliest campaigns of Sumer were with these mountaineers of Elam, but Sargon, the founder of the dynasty of Akkad, conquered Elam and many districts to the north, as well as Syria to the west, while Naram-Sin conquered Lulubi, a country in the neighbourhood of the modern Kermanshah, this conquest being recorded in the famous stele of Naram-Sin.

Trade was active from very early days, even in the fourth millennium B.C. As Leonard Woolley [1] points out, the wealth of Sumer was purely agricultural, and its imports included copper from Oman, silver from Elam, limestone from the Upper Euphrates Valley, and diorite from Magan in the Persian Gulf; lapis-lazuli was imported from distant Badakshan. All these raw materials were paid for by the exquisite goldsmiths' work, the sumptuous tissues and other manufactures that were sought throughout the Near East. About the time of the First Dynasty, we find in Egypt stone maceheads, cylinder seals and other objects which prove conclusively the existence of trade connections between the Euphrates and the Nile valleys. Nor is this all. Recent excavations at Mohenjo-daro have brought to light a very early civilization akin to that of Sumer. Not only are its seals similar in form, subjects and style, but a likeness is also traceable in terra-cotta figures. Indeed, it is evident that these two civilizations have a common source, which is probably to be found in Persia. A variety of objects discovered in the Indus Valley, Elam, and Iraq, prove the existence of considerable intercourse at the close of the fourth millennium B.C., the period when Mohenjo-daro was at its zenith.

Sumer and Akkad were succeeded by the first empire of Babylon, which reached its zenith under Hammurabi, the famous lawgiver. He was possibly the Amraphel of Genesis xiv., who raided Palestine with the Kings of Elam, of Larsa, and of the Hittites, carrying off Lot, who, according to the account, was rescued by his uncle Abraham.

But Assyria, throughout her existence, was the most warlike of the old Powers, and conquered provinces in every direction. About 1100 B.C. Tiglath-Pileser marched to the source of the Tigris, where an inscription still standing describes the campaign. Eastwards he invaded Media, a list being given of the places he captured, while to the west he defeated the Hittites and reached the Mediterranean, embarking at Arvad for a cruise on the sea. Sargon II in the eighth century

---

[1] *The Sumerians*, by C. Leonard Woolley, p. 45 *et seq.*

annexed the country of the Hittites, captured Samaria, and led Israel captive to the plains of Iraq and to distant Media. His successor Sennacherib gives a detailed account of a naval expedition that was despatched against certain Chaldaeans who had taken refuge in the coast-lands of Elam. The Assyrian monarch describes how his fleet was constructed on the upper reaches of the Tigris and Euphrates, the ships built on the former river being dragged on rollers from Opis to the Euphrates. From the port of Bab-salimeti [1] near its mouth the fleet sailed to the Ulai or Karun River, where the surprise of the Chaldaeans was complete. Their settlements were destroyed, and the expedition returned in triumph to its base. It is to be noted that at this period the three rivers reached the Persian Gulf independently, the land having advanced well over a hundred miles since the date of Sennacherib's expedition, which unquestionably added to Assyrian geographical knowledge.

Esarhaddon, who succeeded his father, conquered Egypt. He also penetrated into Media as far as Mount Demavand, which he considered to be the boundary of the world. Assyria reached the zenith of her power under this monarch, while in 645 B.C. Assurbanipal captured and sacked Susa, and Elam as a kingdom disappeared. Not long after, Cyaxares of Media and Nabopolassar of Babylon captured Nineveh, and Assyria disappeared in its turn to make way for the empires of Media and Persia.

Throughout this long period of some 2,000 years we have no definite information as to intercourse with China, but Grousset [2] proves clearly, if only by his illustrations, that, at the dawn of history, a common civilization existed extending from Egypt to the Hwang-Ho or " Yellow River " and the Indus, the ideals, processes, and subjects of its art being of a decidedly similar nature. We are therefore justified in concluding that the horizon and the commerce of the peoples gradually extended, while we realize from the exchange of letters and gifts between the rulers of these ancient monarchies that they were well informed regarding the politics and trade-routes of the Near and Middle East.

We next come to what may be termed the Aegean area, which is remarkably favourable for navigation. The earliest maritime empire was that of Crete, founded about 2800 B.C., and known as the Minoan, after its great historical dynasty,

---

[1] This name is almost identical in form with modern Arabic and signifies " The Gate of Safety ".

[2] *The Civilization of the East*, by Réné Grousset, 1932, Vol. I, p. 25.

which, in later ages, became legendary in Greece. Throughout its long existence, Crete was closely connected with Egypt, and the two empires waxed and waned together down the centuries. At Cnossus, I have seen what was undoubtedly the throne of Minos.

Owing to the fact that the many Cretan tablets that have been found cannot be read, our knowledge of the Keftui and their history is mainly obtained from Egyptian annals. We know that they were a sea-faring people, who established their influence over the neighbouring islands, whence it spread to the mainland of Greece, Mycenae finally taking the place of Crete. Ships figure on their seals. They were single-masted, with high sterns, and were propelled by oars. The splendid palaces of Cnossos and the luxury of their occupants prove the extent and importance of their sea-borne commerce, which undoubtedly extended to Sicily and Southern Italy. We also read of a contract made by Thotmes III with these seafarers for the transport of timber from Lebanon to Egypt in 1467 B.C.

The Minoan Empire fell about 1450 B.C., and it is generally believed that it was the Achaeans who overthrew the sea-power of Crete, and established the hegemony of Mycenae.

Their successors were the Phoenicians of Byblus, Arvad, Tyre, and Sidon, who developed a remarkable aptitude for seafaring, and, beginning at about 1200 B.C., founded trading stations at many points in the Mediterranean and even farther afield, where they sold their fine linens, their dyed woollen goods and their glass wares. Carthage, their chief colony, was founded about 840 B.C. Their fleets traded in the Red Sea, and opened up commercial relations with India. In this connection Ezekiel, who was a priest of the Temple at Jerusalem, wrote a most interesting account of the trade relations of Tyre early in the sixth century B.C. Beginning with timber for the ships and oars from Senir (Mount Hermon), Lebanon, and Bashan, he refers to the fine linen with embroidered work from Egypt for the sails; while blue and purple work were imported from the isles of Elishah in the Aegean Sea. He continues: "The inhabitants of Sidon and Arvad were thy mariners, thy wise men were thy pilots." The Prophet then deals with the caulkers, and mentions that the Persians, the Lydians, and the men of Phut (Libya) were the fighting men. Returning to commercial matters, Tarshish (probably a port in India) traded in silver, iron, tin and lead; Javan (the Ionian Greeks), Tubal (the Balkans) and Meshech (the port of Dhufar or Ophir) dealt in slaves and brasswork. The house of

Togarmah (Armenia) brought horses and horsemen and mules. Syria traded in emeralds, purple, and broidered work, fine linen, coral, and agate. Damascus dealt in Tyrian manufactures, while Dan and Javan imported bright iron, cassia and calamus. Arabia supplied sheep and goats, while the merchants of Sheba (Yemen) and Raamah in Hadramaut dealt in various spices, in every description of jewellery, and in gold. Finally Haran in Iraq, Canneh in Chaldaea, and Eden (the modern Aden), as well as the merchants of Sheba, Assur and Chilmad in Media, are mentioned. Altogether we have a most valuable, even detailed, account of the commercial relations of Tyre with the surrounding countries. It is, however, to be noted that the Phoenicians—whose chief exports were timber and purple dye—never produced either jewellery or pottery of an artistic nature, and this was probably one reason for the success of their Greek rivals. Like the Venetians, they were chiefly carriers, and not manufacturers.

There is a story told by Herodotus that Necho, King of Egypt about 600 B.C., sent out an expedition manned by Phoenicians, who sailed round Africa from east to west, keeping the sun on their right hand, and returned safely to Egypt by way of the Pillars of Hercules, after taking three years over the voyage. It is in this connection that the Atlantic Ocean is so named for the first time by Herodotus. It might be thought that such an exploit was beyond the range of possibility in those early days. But is this so certain? Many years ago, when I first visited Maskat, I was amazed to learn that a branch of the ruling family reigned as Sultans of Zanzibar, which is distant some 2,000 miles. On making inquiries it appeared that the regular north-east wind that blows during the winter and the steady south-west monsoon of the summer furnished the explanation. It also helps to solve our present problem.

The ships of the Phoenicians were craft of much the same kind as the modern Arab *baggala*, and their seamen were experienced navigators who were also skilled shipwrights, while the question of supplies would be managed by sowing a crop and waiting for it to ripen. Consequently it is not improbable that this great feat was actually accomplished.

However this may be, Carthage despatched an expedition at about this period with the object of founding colonies on the west coast of Africa. Indeed, Carthage displayed amazing energy in the foundation of trading posts, which stretched westwards to the straits of Gibraltar and down the African coast. The scale on which she worked is proved by a statement that 30,000 men and women were sent to found the posts in Western Morocco. Again, we hear of exploration northwards along the coast of Spain, and expeditions were undoubtedly despatched to bring back tin from the " Tin Islands ", though apparently no posts were founded there.

Generally speaking, the Phoenicians, unlike the Greeks and Etruscans, did not colonize in the sense of settling down to till the land with trade as a secondary consideration. For the Phoenicians, commerce came first throughout, and where they held land it was almost entirely cultivated by slaves. Not that they did not build fine cities on the coast of Africa, in the west of Sicily and on the island of Sardinia. In Africa, apart from sea-borne commerce, they were deeply interested in the caravans that traded across the Sahara to the Middle Niger. The eastern route to Lake Chad ran directly south from the Greek colonies of Cyrene and Barca, and consequently lay outside their sphere. Finally, in Spain, where Gades (Cadiz) was a very old settlement, they were able to prevent Greek adventurers from penetrating into the Atlantic, or indeed from settling elsewhere in Spain.

Another powerful race of seafarers were the Tyrrhenians, brothers of the Lydians, who settled on the Italian coast, mainly between the Tiber and the Arno, and were known to the Romans as " Tuscans " or " Etruscans ". They reached Italy possibly in the ninth century B.C., and by the sixth century had formed a league of twelve leading communities which represented the strongest power in Italy, but waned after the Latins and Sabines of Rome expelled their Etruscan masters in 510 B.C. These Tyrrhenian pirates, as they were generally called, were friendly to the Carthaginians, and hindered Greek activities by every means in their power.

No introduction to Greek sea-voyages would be complete without mention of the *Odyssey* of Homer. In this chapter reference has already been made to the rise of Mycenae, the capital of an Achaean confederacy which ruled the South Aegean. Her rival was Troy, situated on the Dardanelles, which had arisen on the ruins of the Hittite Empire and was supported by a powerful confederation of tribes. Homer's immortal theme was the siege of Troy by the Achaean league about 1200 B.C., an undertaking which, until the spade of the archaeologist set matters right, was considered to be entirely legendary. So far as concerns the geographical side of

6

the poems of Homer, a correct knowledge of the Aegean area is shown, as we should expect, but when Odysseus on his journey home from the Trojan War visits Egypt and tells of the lotus-eaters, or is almost killed by the Cyclops of Sicily, or again when he just escapes from Scylla albeit with the loss of six heroes, and eludes Charybdis, he gives rein to the delightful genius which has enthralled mankind down the ages.

> "Now through the rocks, appall'd with deep dismay,
> We bend our course, and stem the desperate way;
> Dire Scylla there a scene of horror forms,
> And here Charybdis fills the deep with storms;
> When the tide rushes from her rumbling caves,
> The rough rock roars, tumultuous boil the waves."

The wily Odysseus stands out as the type of the hardy mariners of the Mediterranean, who defeated Persia at the battle of Salamis, and I suffered bitter disappointment on being informed during a passage through the Straits of Messina that an earthquake had caused historical Charybdis to disappear beneath the waves.

The Greeks came later into the field, and were vigorously opposed by the Phoenicians, who sank all foreign ships in the Western Mediterranean at sight, as well as by the Tyrrhenians. However, as time went by, Greek colonies were planted on the east and south coasts of Sicily, while Carthage occupied its western and northern coasts, and also Sardinia.

The products of Greece, which were more valued than those of Carthage, helped to support Greek commercial ventures, and in spite of Carthaginian hostility, Greek adventurers successfully founded Massilia (Marseilles) in the Western Mediterranean and Cyrene in Northern Africa, both of which colonies flourished. In the Black Sea the Greeks had settled from early times, choosing sites for their cities at the points where trade routes ended and at the mouths of rivers.

To Anaximander of Miletus, who lived in the sixth century B.C., we owe the first map of the world. He regarded it as a section of a cylinder of considerable thickness, suspended in the heavens, just as Job describes it in the motto to this chapter. The Aegean Sea formed the centre of this circular disc, with a vast ocean flowing round it. Hecataeus, who lived more than a generation later, displayed an intimate knowledge of the lands bordering on the Mediterranean Sea as far west as Sardinia, and was generally acquainted with the

7

provinces of the Persian Empire. He had also travelled in Egypt, which he was the first to describe as " the gift of the Nile". His book, entitled *Periodos*, is the earliest known work on geography.

Hecataeus lived during the reign of Darius, the great organizer of the Persian Empire. Realizing the importance of communications, Darius had constructed the Royal Road, running from Sardis to Susa, through the heart of Asia Minor, crossing the Euphrates at Samosata and the Tigris at Nineveh, and so to the winter capital of the Great King, a distance of more than 1,500 miles. This was considered a three months' journey for a man on foot, but, with relays of horses at each stage, it could be traversed by couriers in about a fortnight. As might be supposed, the construction of this road widened the horizon of the provinces through which it ran, and generally opened up Persia to the Hellenic world and especially to the Ionian Greeks.

Herodotus, the Father of History who flourished in the fifth century B.C., was an explorer and an eminent geographer. He travelled far and wide in the Black Sea, Greece, and Magna Graecia. He visited Tyre and Gaza, and spent a long time in Egypt. He also travelled along the Royal Road to Susa and Babylon. As a result of his extensive voyages and studies, Herodotus realized that the theory of the world as a circular disc was untenable, and he divided the lands which enclose the Mediterranean Sea into the continents of Europe, Asia and Africa. Europe he takes as bounded by the Atlantic on the west, but as stretching indefinitely across Northern Asia. He possesses but little knowledge of Central and Northern Europe, and shows Pyrene —presumably an echo of the Pyrenees—as a town, while similar echoes of the Alps and Carpathians appear as tributaries of the Ister or Danube, which he considered to be the chief river of Europe. In Asia his knowledge extends to the India of the Indus Valley, and thanks to Scylax, whose expedition is described in the next chapter, he knows of the Erythrean Sea.

In Africa he has heard of Meroe, the capital of Ethiopia, but the Nile is shown as corresponding with the Danube, owing to the Greek passion for symmetry. Although he has heard of stages in the caravan route to the west, and lays down the outline of the northern coast of Africa, his knowledge of the interior of that continent is as vague as in the case of Northern Europe. Yet he mentions a story which

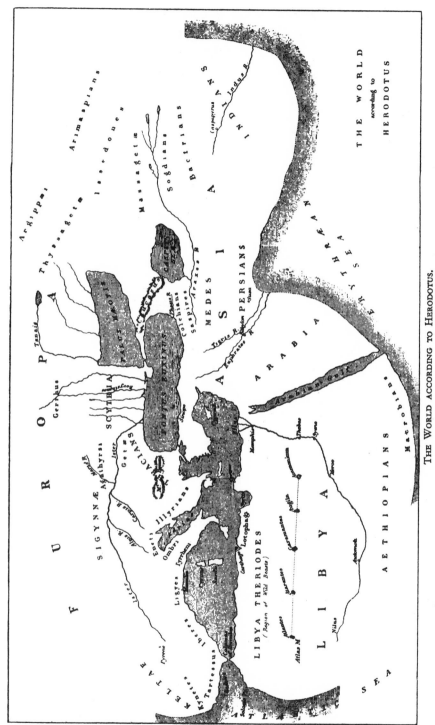

THE WORLD ACCORDING TO HERODOTUS.

(*From E. H. Bunbury's "History of Ancient Geography", by permission of Messrs. John Murray & Co., Ltd.*)

9

had reached him from the Siwah Oasis of a great river far away to the south-west, swarming with crocodiles, which is obviously the Niger, but which he took to be the upper reaches of the Nile.

Such, then, was the position of exploration in the fifth century B.C.

CHAPTER II

THE EXPEDITION OF ALEXANDER THE GREAT

> " His city there thou seest, and Bactra there ;
> Ecbatana her structure vast there shows,
> And Hecatompylos her hundred gates ;
> There Susa by Choaspes, amber stream,
> The drink of none but Kings."
>
> MILTON, " *Paradise Regained* ".

ALEXANDER THE GREAT, both in his character and his achievements, represents the culminating point of Greek civilization.[1] He had the good fortune to be educated by Aristotle, who, among his other claims to immortality, was the first scientific geographer, and proved that the earth was a sphere by the circular shadow thrown on the moon during an eclipse, and by the shifting of the horizon as one travelled from north to south and lost familiar stars, while new stars rose into view. Alexander, the greatest conqueror of all time, was also a great explorer, and thanks to the record that was kept of his campaigns, he initiated an epoch of geographical discovery.

But before we follow him across Asia to the Jaxartes (Syr Darya), it is interesting to examine the position of Greek knowledge of Asia at this period.

We may begin our survey by a reference to the campaigns of Darius, who in 512 B.C. annexed large districts of the Punjab and of Sind. The Great King took advantage of the situation to despatch Scylax of Caryanda with a flotilla to explore the Indus. Scylax not only reached the Indian Ocean, but apparently sighted the coast of Oman and the Persian Gulf, and his account of this voyage was undoubtedly read by Alexander.

A century later, in 401 B.C., Cyrus the Younger marched from Sardis with a considerable force of Greek mercenaries to fight his elder brother Artaxerxes for the throne of Persia. Thanks to the admirable account given by Xenophon, we can follow the adventurous expedition across Phrygia and Mysia to the famous Cilician Gates in the Taurus, which they traversed unopposed and descended into Cilicia.

---

[1] This chapter is mainly based on Sykes, *History of Persia* (3rd ed.), Chaps. XXI–XXIV.

Cyrus now experienced considerable difficulty in persuading his Greek troops to advance, but the promise of an increase of pay overcame their objections, and he marched swiftly through the Gates of Syria opposite Cyprus and reached the Euphrates at Thapsacus. Once more there was no opposition, and, fording the Euphrates, the army proceeded rapidly southwards, hoping to meet the Great King before he was fully prepared. Suddenly, during the fourth stage, a scout informed Cyrus that the huge Persian army was on its way to attack him. The battle of Cunaxa ended in a victory for the Greeks, who broke and pursued the Persian left wing, but Cyrus, charging at the head of his cavalry, was struck in the eye by a javelin and killed.

The situation was entirely changed by the death of Cyrus, and the victorious Greeks finally agreed to return to Hellas up the valley of the Tigris. In spite of the treacherous seizure of their chief officers, the immortal " Ten Thousand " under the leadership of Xenophon shook off the half-hearted attacks of the Persians, and marched steadily north, marvelling by the way at the half-ruined cities of Assyria. The Persians left them when they entered the uplands, where they were harassed by the attacks of the Carduchi, the ancestors of the virile Kurds. But the Greeks were past-masters in hill tactics, and marched on undaunted, obtaining supplies at times with difficulty but yet never losing heart. They passed to the west of Lake Van and across the main range of Asia Minor, suffering from bitter cold, until one happy day, having climbed a pass from which the Euxine was visible, they arrived at Trapezus, the modern Trebizond, after accomplishing a magnificent feat of exploration, which is worthily described by their great leader. At Trebizond I was shown the pass where the Greeks shouted " *Thalassa! Thalassa!* ", as well as the site of their camp outside the city, which is still called *Campos*. Some, at any rate, of the older Macedonians must have met veterans of the Ten Thousand, and there is no doubt that the proved superiority of the Greeks over the myriads of Persians on the plain of Cunaxa must have encouraged Alexander and his soldiers to aim at the lordship of Asia.

Alexander started on his famous campaign in the spring of 334 B.C. His father, Philip of Macedon, had trained the heavy cavalry whose charge won every battle, and the irresistible phalanx. He had also conquered and annexed Thrace as far as the Dardanelles, and a Macedonian garrison held

Abydos on the Asiatic side, to which city the army was safely transported.

Alexander then marched north to attack a powerful Persian force which was drawn up on the right bank of the Granicus. The infantry portion of the Persian army consisted of 20,000 Greek mercenaries, who were most unwisely kept in reserve. The Persian cavalry offered a desperate resistance, but their short javelins were no match at close quarters for the lances of the Macedonians, and they were finally defeated, after which the Greek mercenaries were cut to pieces. The prize of this victory was Lydia with Sardis. Alexander immediately re-organized its administration, thus showing that he intended his conquest to be permanent. He gradually annexed the various provinces of Asia Minor, meeting with a stubborn resistance from the chief Greek cities on the coast. The Greeks, indeed, were the backbone of the opposition that was offered throughout, and the death of Memnon, who was organizing an invasion of Macedonia on behalf of the Great King, must have been a source of intense relief to the Macedonians.

Alexander marched across Phrygia to Gordion, where he cut the knot of the waggon of Gordius, thereby fulfilling the oracle which promised to whoever should perform this feat, the lordship of Asia. After arranging for the administration of the various provinces included in Asia Minor, he made a forced march to the Cicilian Gates, which he passed without any opposition, and occupied Tarsus. He then went on to the Syrian Gates, expecting to meet Darius Codomannus in the open plains to the east of the " Gates ". But to his amazement he heard that the huge Persian army had crossed a pass to the north, and was actually encamped in his rear at Issus. Alexander marched back and, in the battle that ensued, his charge drove the craven Darius in headlong flight, Issus being the decisive battle of the campaign.

After Issus, the next objective of the Macedonians was the capture of the ports of Phoenicia, the bases of the Persian fleet. Tyre, relying on its immense strength, defied Alexander, but was finally captured, while the squadrons belonging to Sidon and other cities deserted from the Persians and made terms with the conqueror. After Tyre, Gaza was captured, and Alexander then marched across the desert to Egypt, where he treated priests and people with the utmost consideration. In Egypt he founded Alexandria, which rapidly became a great port. Impelled by the strain of mysticism in his blood, he also crossed the desert to the mysterious temple of Amen-

Ra, known to the Greeks as Zeus Ammon, situated in the remote Siwah oasis. There the priests assured him that he was the true son of the god. He is consequently portrayed with horns in his portraits, and obtained as a result in later years the title of *Zulkarnain* or "Lord of the two Horns", by which name he is still remembered throughout the Moslem East. During this expedition he received envoys who offered the submission of Cyrene. We are lost in admiration at the exploits of this great conqueror, who in so short a time had laid low the might of Persia and annexed so many of her richest provinces.

Alexander organized his march into the heart of the Persian Empire from Tyre, where he met his fleet and reinforcements. Finding that the country beyond the Euphrates was held only by a small force of Persian cavalry, he had ordered the construction of two bridges of boats, which were ready, and the army crossed the river without delay. No opposition was offered in the vast open plains of Iraq, where, some three centuries later, Crassus met his fate at the hands of Parthian mounted archers. Again, at the swift Tigris, crossed with considerable difficulty, no engagement took place, and Alexander marched down its left bank to find Darius awaiting him at Gaugamela, near the ruins of Nineveh, situated some seventy miles north-west of Arbela, which latter town has given its name to the battle. The battle of Issus had been the decisive encounter, and at Arbela the *coup de grâce* was administered. Darius again played the craven, and was thenceforth practically a refugee. The victor marched on Babylon, where, like Cyrus the Great, he was welcomed, and "took the hands of Bel". The Babylonians, who had been severely treated by the later Persian monarchs, served Alexander loyally.

From Babylon Alexander advanced on Susa, which the Greeks regarded as the capital of the Great King, and here treasure of inestimable value was seized.

Alexander then determined to invade Pars (now Fars) the homeland of the dynasty and the classical Persis. Crossing the Karun at the modern Ahwaz, he entered the mountains, where the Uxii, who were accustomed to take toll of the Great King, demanded the like from Alexander. He bade them come to the defiles to receive it, and following a hill-track, fell on their rear and held them at his mercy. Marching swiftly, he again repeated the Persian tactics of Thermopylae, and having cut to pieces the defenders of the "Persian Gates",

ALEXANDER THE GREAT AS "LORD OF THE TWO HORNS"
(*Through the courtesy of the Hellenic Society*)

seized Persepolis, the Great King's spring capital, where he was accustomed to receive the tribute of his subjects on March 21, the Persian New Year, as the bas-reliefs show. Here again incredible wealth was seized, for it was the custom of each Achaemenian monarch to add to the gold reserve of his ancestors ; and the favourable effect of the dispersal of this treasure on commerce was extraordinary.

Alexander was now in possession of Babylon, Susa, Persepolis and of Pasargadae, the capital of Cyrus the Great, a stage to the north. Darius had fled from Arbela direct to Ecbatana, the ancient capital of Media. Alexander spent some four months at Persepolis, and then prepared to start in pursuit of the fugitive. At Pasargadae he visited the tomb of Cyrus the Great and gave orders for it to be carefully preserved, and, hearing that Darius was organizing a new army, made a forced march on Ecbatana. Darius fled before his arrival, and as Ecbatana was situated on the main line of communication from his main base at Tyre, Alexander decided to make it his advanced base. He accordingly garrisoned it with 6,000 troops, in whose charge he left his enormous treasure.

Darius had fled towards Bactria, and was moving slowly, apparently not expecting to be pursued. Alexander took a picked body of men and made forced marches to Ragae, the Rhages of the book of Tobit, the ruins of which lie a few miles south of Teheran. But Darius had already passed through the Caspian Gates, a long march east of Ragae. Accordingly the conqueror rested his men for a few days, and then continued the pursuit. He was now following the caravan route which runs east to Khorasan and Central Asia, and he finally overtook the hapless Darius, who had been assassinated by Bessus, the Satrap of Bactria, in the vicinity of modern Damghan, which later became Hecatompylos, the capital of Parthia, mentioned by Milton.

With the death of Darius all national resistance ceased, and in his future campaigns Alexander was faced with only local opposition, albeit stubborn resistance was offered in Central Asia and in India.

Under the new conditions Alexander decided to conquer and annex the provinces as he passed. To the south of his route was the great desert of Persia, whereas to the north lay fertile Hyrcania. Crossing the main range, which runs from Mount Ararat to loftier Demavand, and so eastward across Northern Afghanistan, he received the submission of the leading men of the province at Zadracarta, which occupied a site near modern Astrabad. He then followed up the Gurgan Valley. When exploring in that neighbourhood some years ago, I heard a legend to the effect that Alexander grazed his horses in the meadow of Kalposh. I visited this meadow, and found that it undoubtedly lay on his route, and that from it he entered the valley of the Kashaf Rud near Susia, the medieval Tus. Here he heard that Bessus had assumed the title of Great King, and he decided to pursue him. Traversing Areia, now the Herat province of Afghanistan, he restored it to its Satrap, Satibarzanes, who had submitted. He was well on his way to Bactria (now Badakshan) when he heard that Satibarzanes had rebelled and had killed the Macedonian representative and his escort. Nothing daunted, Alexander made a long forced march back to Artacoana, the capital of Areia, and the rebellion collapsed. Alexander now decided to attack Barsaentes, Satrap of Drangiana, which includes modern Sistan, probably in order to protect his long and vulnerable lines of communication. No resistance was offered, Barsaentes, who had been one of the murderers of Darius, fleeing to join Bessus.

To the south lay the Lut desert, and Alexander accordingly struck the Etymander and marched north-east, intending once again to take up the pursuit of Bessus. Marching through Arachosia and then up the Argandab River, he founded another Alexandria, the Kandahar of to-day. Thence he turned almost due north, along what has been a caravan route from time immemorial, to Kabul, the modern capital of Afghanistan. Two thousand years later another European force, under Lord Roberts, was to march in the opposite direction to relieve Kandahar. Alexander was now close to India, which he undoubtedly meant to conquer, little realizing its enormous extension to the south. Accordingly he decided to found another Alexandria *ad Caucasum* at a point where the three passes over the Indian Caucasus or Paropanisus met. He then crossed the range, suffering from bitter cold and lack of supplies, and descended into Bactria, where Bactra, the medieval Balkh, known as the " Mother of Cities ", was occupied without a contest. Bactra was the last of the great cities of the Persian Empire to fall to the Macedonians.

Alexander crossed the Oxus on rafts, and after receiving the surrender of Bessus, who was betrayed by his own officers, marched north to Maracanda, now Samarkand. After resting his troops at the future capital of Tamerlane, he beat the boundaries of the Persian Empire by advancing to the Jaxartes or Syr Darya, where he founded Alexandria Eschate or " the Extreme ", on the site of modern Khojand—a city situated some 3,500 miles east of Hellas. What that signified before the era of modern communications can hardly be grasped by the European of the twentieth century. Yet the Macedonians considered the Jaxartes to be the same river as the Don !

Alexander suffered his only disaster during the course of his campaign in Sogdiana, where the virile chiefs fought bravely to expel the invaders. Stronghold after stronghold was captured, and among the prisoners was Roxana, whom Alexander married. In no part of Asia is the fame of Iskandar *Zulkarnain* so high, even the chiefs of distant Hunza claiming descent from the great conqueror.

Nearly two years had been spent in Central Asia fighting and exploring, and at last Alexander was free to invade India, the attraction of which was irresistible. He had entered into relations with various chiefs, which resulted in the submission of King Taxiles, whose capital has recently been excavated in the vicinity of Rawal Pindi. Alexander ordered the main body to march by the trade route to the north of the Khyber Pass, while he undertook a campaign in the Swat Valley, culminating in the capture of Aornos, which Sir Aurel Stein has recently discovered in a bend of the Indus.[1] Crossing the Indus, Alexander was opposed by Porus on the banks of the Hydaspes, now the Jhelum, where his tactics excite profound admiration. He gained a complete victory and captured Porus, whom he reinstated on his throne. He crossed the rivers of the Punjab, and when halting on the right bank of the Beas, began to prepare for a march into the Ganges valley. But his way-worn veterans mutinied, and Alexander consented to march back down the Indus to Persia.

Constructing ships on the Jhelum, the force started off on a march nearly 1,000 miles in length, which included the conquest of various tribes and strong places, one of which, identified with Multan, offered a stubborn resistance and nearly cost Alexander his life.

Sailing on the Indian Ocean, Alexander despatched Nearchus with orders to coast westwards to Persia. He himself, realizing that the fleet might suffer from starvation, resolved to march across the entire length of Gedrosia, now Makran, hoping thereby to keep in touch with Nearchus and victual the fleet. For perhaps 100 miles this arrangement worked fairly well, but at this stage Ras [2] Malan forced the

---

[1] *On Alexander's Track to the Indus*, 1929.   [2] *Ras* signifies a headland.

troops to turn inland, and, to quote Arrian, "the blazing heat and want of water destroyed a great part of the army . . . tortured alike by raging heat and unquenchable thirst".

Alexander regained the coast near Pasni, where fresh water can be obtained by digging wells on the sea-shore. He followed the coast to Gwadur, whence, although very anxious about the fleet, he marched inland to Pura, now termed by the Baluchis Pahra and by the Persians Fahraj, and situated in one of the few fertile valleys of Persian Baluchistan. Here Alexander regained touch with his Persian officials, and his worn-out troops, whose losses had been very severe, were rested and refitted.

The question of the route followed in the onward march was settled by me in 1894. Rejecting the previous opinion, which made Alexander march to another town named Fahraj to the north-west, I explored a westerly route which followed down the river of Pura to a large *hamun* or inland lake, termed the Jaz Morian, into which it discharged. Continuing westwards up the Halil Rud, which also discharged into the Jaz Morian, Alexander made a standing camp in the modern district of Rudbar. One of my greatest treasures is an alabaster unguent vase dug up in this valley which may well have belonged to Alexander. It was at this standing camp, where an Alexandria was founded which may be identified with the modern Gulashkird, that Nearchus appeared in rags. Alexander feared the total loss of his fleet, but the intrepid Admiral reported that it was safely drawn up at Harmozia, on the Anamis, now the Minab River.

Nearchus deserves immense credit for his successful conduct of this voyage. Not only did he suffer from the hostility of the natives, but both supplies and sweet water were hard to procure. As they still do to-day, the "Ichthyophagi", who lived on fish, as their name implies, inhabited a desert where not a tree grew, and where there were not even wild fruits. Yet in spite of these anxieties, Nearchus kept a careful log of the distances traversed, and gave the harbours their local names, which have changed very little. To give but one instance, Hormuz was the medieval form of Harmozia.

Craterus, who had been sent in charge of the elephants and baggage, rejoined the army after a march down the Helmand in Rudbar, so wonderfully did Alexander's plans work out.

The march to Susa was then resumed, Nearchus rejoining the fleet, with Hephaestion marching along the coast in touch with it. Alexander traversed the districts of Sirjan and Baonat to Pasargadae, where we read of his distress upon finding that the tomb of Cyrus had been desecrated. At Susa the greatest of all exploring expeditions ended in rejoicings and in weddings between the noblest Macedonians and Persian women of high degree. Shortly afterwards Alexander, while preparing an expedition for the exploration and conquest of Arabia, died at the early age of thirty-two in the plenitude of his splendid powers.

We have seen what valuable additions Alexander made to Greek knowledge of Asia, and it is interesting to reflect on his conception of the world. He had no idea of the enormous size of the Indian peninsula, nor of the existence of the Malay peninsula, nor indeed of the huge area of China. He still believed that the world was very much smaller, even as regards the continent of Asia, than it actually is, and that the Ganges flowed into the Ocean to the east, which washed the northern coasts of Scythia and of which the Caspian formed a bay. Had he lived another decade, the position would have been very different. Of his successors, Seleucus Nicator gained considerable information about the Ganges valley from Megasthenes, whom he despatched on an embassy to the Maurya monarch at Patali-putra (Patna), where he lived for many years, and wrote an account of his experiences, in which the earliest reference is made to the monsoon. Moreover, under the patronage of Ptolemy Euergetes, Erastosthenes, who laid the foundations of mathematical geography, gave the world the first approximate knowledge of the size of the globe. Euergetes also despatched expeditions which explored parts of Arabia.

To conclude this chapter, we may mention that the earliest Greek explorer beyond the Mediterranean was Pytheas of Massilia (Marseilles), who in 330 B.C. determined to visit the countries which produced tin and amber. Coasting Iberia and the Bay of Biscay, the island of Uxisama (Ushant) was reached. He then sailed up the English Channel to Cantion (Kent), where he resided for a considerable period and visited the tin mines of Cornwall. Later, he followed up the east coast of Britain to the north of Scotland, where he heard of a distant land called Thule. As if this adventure were not enough, in a second voyage he apparently sailed the Baltic, visiting the coasts where amber was found, and finally returned to Massilia in safety. Pytheas took five observations of the lengths of the longest days, by which he fixed his latitudes. His works are unfortunately lost, but he ranks among the greatest of the ancient explorers.

CHAPTER III

EXPLORERS OF THE CHINESE EMPIRE

" The Tien Shan mountain of ice forms the northern angle of
Pamir.   It is most dangerous, and its summit rises to the skies.
From the beginning of the world the snow has accumulated on
it, and has turned into blocks of ice, which melt neither in
springtime nor in summer.   They roll away in boundless
sheets of hard, gleaming white, losing themselves in the
clouds."

HSUAN-TSANG.

THE civilization of China does not compare in antiquity with
those of Sumer and Egypt.   Yet we have good reason to
believe the evidence of ancient records, according to which
the Chinese had emerged from the pastoral stage in the third
millennium B.C., and were tilling the soil in the valley of
the Hwang-ho.   In the second millennium the Chou dynasty
was founded, and one of its members, about 1000 B.C. made
a royal progress to a province of the empire which may
perhaps be identified with Khotan.

The great teacher Confucius flourished in the sixth century B.C., and was a contemporary of Cyrus the Great.   At this
period China was far advanced intellectually, but, owing to her
feudal system she was split up into a number of weak states, and
was unable to withstand the raids of barbarian tribes from the
north, or to end the constant civil wars.   As elsewhere in early
times, the contest lay between the " desert and the sown ".

In the third century B.C. the unification of China was
accomplished by the founder of the Chin dynasty, who constructed the Great Wall, which, contrary to general belief,
afforded considerable protection to China and diverted the
migrations of the tribes westwards, with all its consequences
for the Middle East and for Europe.   To give an example
of these movements, in the second century B.C. the Hsiung-nu,
better known as the Huns, attacked and drove out the Yue-
chi, an Iranian tribe which inhabited the Kansu province and
the southern part of the Gobi,[1] thereby setting in motion a
series of human avalanches.   The Yue-chi crossed the Gobi

---

[1] *Gobi* signifies *desert*, and is particularly applied to the great waste which separates
China from Khotan or Hami.

to Kucha, and in their turn drove the Sakae from Kashgar in 163 B.C. and settled in their place, while the Sakae occupied Bactria, driving its Greek dynasty across the Hindu Kush. But, some twenty years later, the Huns again attacked the Yue-chi, who once more driving the Sakae in front of them, occupied Bactria. They then crossed the Hindu Kush and carved out an empire with Purushapura or Peshawar as their capital.

About 30 B.C. the Kwei Shang became the leading tribe of the Yue-chi. Antony sent ambassadors to this people, called by the Romans Kushan, and their envoys appeared before Augustus. Incidentally the peach and the pear were introduced into Persia from China through the agency of the Yue-chi, and reached Europe from Persia, the latter fruit proclaiming this fact by its name.

It is generally agreed that until 140 B.C. China had no knowledge of the West, but under the Emperor Wu-ti of the Han dynasty, who came to the throne in that year, missions were despatched in every direction. Wu-ti was most anxious to induce the Yue-chi to attack the Huns, his most dreaded enemies, and being ignorant of the fact of their second flight, in 138 he despatched Chang Kien, the earliest known Chinese traveller, to win them over to his wishes. The ambassador had hardly left China when he was captured by the Huns, whose prisoner he remained for ten years, after which he escaped and succeeded in reaching the state of Farghana. There he was well received, and reported that its inhabitants had heard of the power and wealth of China.

Chang Kien finally reached the Yue-chi, who had recently conquered Tokharistan and were occupying its capital. As was to be expected, the envoy was unsuccessful in his efforts to persuade the Yue-chi to return to their eastern possessions and engage the Huns. In 128 B.C., Chang Kien attempted to return to China *via* Tibet, only to be captured again by the ubiquitous Huns. Finally, in 126 B.C., this indomitable explorer reached China in safety, and was able to furnish the Emperor with much valuable information.

Eleven years later, Chang Kien was despatched on another embassy to the West, and gained much fresh information, besides sending agents to Farghana. It was probably from this journey that he brought back the vine to China, where, curiously enough, little wine is made. His reports resulted in the opening of the famous Silk Route which ran across the Gobi to Khotan, Yarkand and Farghana, with a northern alternative route *via* Hami and Kashgar. To make the former route safe, a chain of fortified posts was constructed across the Gobi, which were examined by Stein and yielded a rich harvest in 1907. The Huns were defeated, what is now Chinese Turkestan was occupied, and in 102 B.C. a Chinese army reached the distant province of Farghana, a fact which testifies to its efficiency as a fighting force. A southern route was also opened which crossed the mountains to India, and followed down the course of the Ganges.

Under the Han monarchy, more than one embassy penetrated as far as Parthia, which is named An-Sih, the Chinese form of Arsaces, the name of the royal dynasty. The ambassadors reported that An-Sih was a great country, producing rice, wheat and wine. Reference is made to silver coins bearing the effigy of the reigning monarch, while " they make signs on leather from side to side by way of literary record ". No mention is made of the Roman Empire by this embassy, which took place about 120 B.C. It is of especial interest to note that the reigning monarch of Parthia, Mithridates II, who received the embassy from China, was likewise the first Parthian monarch to open up relations with Rome. A century or more later Chinese envoys were again despatched to the West, and from their reports we learn that the eastern part of the Roman Empire now came within the ken of China.

Among the most famous conquerors and administrators of the Han dynasty was Pan Chao, who is credited with the conquest of fifteen kingdoms to the west of Kashgar. This period perhaps shows us the empire of China at its greatest extent, stretching from the Pacific Ocean to the Sea of Aral, and according to Chinese belief, to the Caspian Sea.

In A.D. 97 Pan Chao despatched his lieutenant Kan Ying on a mission to Parthia and Rome. This worthy duly reached Iraq, visiting Hecatompylos, the capital, on his way. In pursuance of his instructions he tried to reach Syria by the Persian Gulf, but, being informed that the voyage might take two years, he prudently decided not to make the attempt. At this period the route ran down the Persian Gulf and up the Red Sea and the Gulf of Akaba to Aelana, a matter perhaps of months, but the ships' captains evidently had every intention of preventing a Chinaman from gaining direct contact with the Roman Empire. Pan Chao died a few years later, and his memory is kept green at Kashgar, where he is buried in an artificial mound surmounted by a shrine.[1] As one result

---

[1] Vide *Through Deserts and Oases of Central Asia*, by Ella Sykes and Sir Percy Sykes, p. 67.

of these embassies, China equipped a mounted force on the model of the heavy Parthian cavalry, while the arts of both countries were mutually affected.

Chinese ambassadors again appeared in Persia, now called Po-sz, in the middle of the fifth century A.D., and the Persian monarch sent a return embassy with a gift of trained elephants. The Chinese account runs as follows :

> " Po-sz has its capital at Suh-li (Ctesiphon) . . . with over a hundred thousand households. The land produces gold, silver, coral, amber, very fine pearls and glass ; crystals, diamonds, iron, copper, cinnabar, mercury ; damask, embroidery, cotton, carpeting and tapestry. . . . The climate is very hot, and families keep ice in their houses. . . . They produce white elephants, lions and great birds' eggs ; there is a bird shaped like a camel,[1] having two wings which enable it to fly along but not to rise. It eats grass and flesh, and can also swallow fire."

An account is given of the king sitting on a golden throne supported by lions, with his magnificent crown, and even the titles of the chief Court officers are mentioned.

For China the silk trade was of the utmost importance, and for many centuries it was a monopoly, Roman ladies being obliged to purchase the luxury for its weight in gold. Virgil believed that silk was produced from the leaves of trees ; Pliny knew no better, nor did Ammianus, who wrote in the fourth century. But, as Yule points out,[2] there was a fluctuation of knowledge among the ancients, as in the case of the belief of Strabo that the Caspian formed a bay of the encircling ocean, whereas Herodotus knew that it was a small sea. Similarly, by Pausanias, who lived before Ammianus, silk was declared to be spun by worms which the Seres tended for the purpose.

China maintained her rich monopoly until, in the middle of the sixth century, Justinian commissioned two Persian missionaries, who had long resided in China, to bring him some of the precious " seed " concealed in a bamboo staff. This task, one of the great romances of commerce, was successfully accomplished, and on it was founded the important silk industry of Europe.

To turn to Chinese intercourse with India, Buddhism was introduced into China by the agency of the Yue-chi about the time of the Christian era, and the first expedition of which we have any account was despatched by the Emperor in A.D. 65 to obtain instruction in the doctrines of Buddha and to

---

[1] Curiously enough Persians term the ostrich the " camel bird ".
[2] *Cathay and the Way Thither*, Vol. I, p. 21.

bring back statues and manuscripts. This was but one of many such expeditions, and Indian monarchs, in their turn, sent missions to China. The policy of the Emperors who reigned for some two centuries from A.D. 220 interrupted this intercourse, but we hear of Fa-hsien who set off on a successful journey to India early in the fifth century, and there made an important collection of the Books of the Discipline.

Among the greatest explorers of the world was Hsuan-tsang and, by way of setting the stage for his appearance, I propose to give a brief account of the position in China at the time of his great journeys.[1]

Just as Europe, after the fall of the Roman Empire, was overwhelmed by waves of barbarian invaders, so China, on the overthrow of the Han dynasty, was afflicted by invasions of Turko-Mongol hordes during the fourth and fifth centuries. At the beginning of the fifth century, the Kings of Wei conquered the rival hordes, and adopting Chinese civilization, ruled over Northern China for nearly a century and a half. In 453 the Emperor was converted to Buddhism, which thus became the state religion.

Once again a period of anarchy ensued, which was ended by the rise of a great warrior, who ascended the throne in 626 as the Emperor Tai-tsung and founded the Tang dynasty. Under his virile leadership the Turks of Mongolia were crushed, Turkestan was conquered, and the suzerainty of China was recognized throughout Central Asia, and westwards as far as the Caspian Sea, thus restoring the ancient boundaries of the Chinese Empire.

At this point Hsuan-tsang appears on the scene. A fervent Buddhist, descended from a long line of *literati*, he realized after much study the existence of serious discrepancies in the sacred books, and determined to " travel in the countries of the West, in order to question the wise men on the points that were troubling his mind ". Hsuan and several other monks petitioned the Emperor for permission to leave China, but it was refused. However, in 629, fortified by a dream, Hsuan set out to cross the dreaded Gobi from Liang-chou, situated near the Great Wall.

Deserted by his companions and his guide, the Master of the Law, to give him the title by which he is best known, rode calmly into the desert. Finding the track by the bones of camels and their droppings, he suddenly saw the horizon

---

[1] *In the Footsteps of the Buddha*, by Réné Grousset ; also " The Desert Crossing of Hsuan-Tsang," in *G. J.*, Vol. LIV, p. 205, by Sir Aurel Stein.

covered with marching troops. "On one side were camels and richly caparisoned horses; on the other, gleaming lances and shining standards." This was of course a mirage. By a most remarkable coincidence, a Hindu merchant, who had certainly never heard of Hsuan-tsang, once described to me an identical vision of an army seen by him in the Takla Makan desert.[1]

Apart from the dangers of the Gobi, there was serious risk to be run in passing the forts that guarded the frontier. At the first the traveller was nearly wounded by arrows when drinking at the spring of water, but, entering the fort, he persuaded the officer by his eloquence to forward him on his journey. This he did, supplying him with provisions and introductions to officers at some of the other posts, but bidding him avoid the fifth and last watch-tower. To observe this strict injunction, Hsuan was obliged to leave the caravan route, and, "in order to find his way, endeavoured to observe as he walked the direction of his shadow". He not only lost his way, but dropped the skin of water given to him at the fourth post, and thus became a prey to thirst. For four nights and five days he had no water, but fortunately his horse scented a pool, and Hsuan, safe but exhausted, reached Hami, where he was welcomed by three Chinese monks.

The King of Turfan, at that time one of the most important states of Central Asia, received the Master of the Law with the highest honours and formed the design of retaining him permanently to grace his court. Indeed, only on threatening to starve himself to death, and actually beginning to do so, was he permitted to continue his journey. The ruler of Turfan was subordinate to the Great Khan of the Western Turks, and he not only furnished Hsuan with an escort, but also sent valuable presents to his suzerain to ensure his good-will.

Hsuan continued his journey through Kucha, and passing to the north of Kashgar, reached the camp of the Great Khan of the Western Turks early in 630, after crossing the ice-bound Tien Shan. He describes the cavalry of the Turks as being mounted on numerous horses, "carrying long lances, banners, and straight bows. Their ranks stretched so far that the eye could not follow them." The Master of the Law was treated with the greatest respect by the Great Khan, and arrangements were made for his onward journey to Gandhara.

From the camp of the Turks, Hsuan proceeded to Shash,

---

[1] *Through Deserts and Oases of Central Asia*, p. 197.

the capital (now Tashkent), and, crossing the Qizil Qum desert, he reached Samarkand, the Maracanda of Alexander, where the culture and religion were alike Iranian. Passing through the land which gave birth to mighty Tamerlane, and the " Gates of Iron ", Hsuan crossed the Oxus at Tirmiz and entered historical Bactria, which was ruled over by a son of the Great Khan. This Prince, who was a pious Buddhist, sent the traveller on to Balkh, destined later to be destroyed by the Mongols. From Balkh the Master continued his journey to Bamiyan, which could boast of ten Buddhist monasteries. To quote Hsuan's excellent description : " Bamiyan clings to the mountain-side and crosses the valley. . . . On the north side it leans against the rock." He visited the monastic cells cut out of the cliff, and mentions the two gigantic statues of Buddha which are still in existence.

From Bamiyan the Master swung due east, and entered fertile Kapisa, a district watered by the Panjshir, where he was welcomed by the King, who was also a devout Buddhist. After spending the summer of 630 in this upland resort, the Master descended to the plains of India, passing through a country which had become an important centre of Buddhism, with many relics of the Buddha. Among the great stupas Hsuan mentions one as measuring 300 feet, which was built by Asoka.

From the district of Nagarahara, Hsuan passed down the grim Khyber Pass to Gandhara, one of the most famous districts in India, which, under its modern name of Peshawar, is still the key to the chief land-gate of the North-West Frontier. As Grousset points out, it was in this district that the first statue of the Buddha had been chiselled by a Greek sculptor ; and the Master was taken to see the stupa erected by the great Kanishka. But a century previously the Huns had devastated a wide area in Central Asia, and Hsuan bitterly lamented their acts of vandalism. From Gandhara, Hsuan travelled up the Swat Valley and traversed the gorges of the Indus, which no European has yet seen.[1] " The roads were very danger- ous ", he wrote, " and the valleys gloomy. Sometimes one had to cross on rope bridges, sometimes by clinging to chains. Now there were gangways hanging in mid-air, now flying bridges flung across precipices."

In Swat, even more than in Gandhara, the Huns had ruined

[1] Sir Aurel Stein, bent on the discovery of the Aornos of Alexander the Great, referred to in the previous chapter, was also able to identify many of the sites mentioned by his " Chinese patron-saint " in the Swat Valley. See *On Alexander's Track to the Indus, passim.*

the Buddhist monasteries for which Udyana or " the Garden " was famous in distant China. Hsuan was not pleased with the monks of this valley, " who like reading this doctrine (of ecstasy), but do not seek to penetrate its meaning ".

Leaving the Swat Valley and following in Alexander's footsteps, Hsuan crossed the Indus and reached Taxila, where he found many monasteries, " but they are very dilapidated ". He next visited Kashmir, which he aptly describes as " a country with a circumference of 700 leagues, and its four frontiers have a background of mountains of a prodigious height. It is reached by very narrow passes." In this beautiful country Hsuan, to his great delight, found a teacher in a venerable monk aged seventy, who " was gifted with a profound intellect and his vast learning embraced every branch of knowledge ".

Two fruitful years, from 631 to 633, were spent in completing his philosophical training, after which the Master descended to the plains of India and travelled to the valley of the sacred Ganges, where at every centre he found doctors of the Law and great libraries full of the sacred books.

Hsuan travelled far and wide in the plains of India. Near the modern Allahabad he was captured by pirates, who prepared to sacrifice him to Durga. The Master, quite unmoved, asked for a short respite to permit him " to enter nirvana in a calm and joyous mind ". At this juncture a terrific storm arose, breaking trees, and raising waves which sank the boats. The pirates, attributing the fury of the elements and the loss of their boats to the power of Hsuan, fell at his feet and repented.

Benares, which had already become the sacred city of the Hindus, interested the Master, who was especially struck by a colossal statue of Siva " full of grandeur and awe ". Another site of great historical interest which he visited was Patali-putra (Patna), where the first Maurya emperor, " Sandrocottus ", had received Megasthenes, the ambassador of Seleucus Nicator. From this city, too, Asoka had governed his immense empire. As Grousset writes : " It was the real Holy Land of Buddhism."

Leaving Bodh-Gaya, where Buddha had attained enlightenment, Hsuan visited Nalanda, the great monastic city. There he found another saintly master, under whom he studied the philosophy of Idealism for over a year. Continuing his wonderful journey, Hsuan took the road to Bengal, " a low damp country where grain grows abundantly ", which he crossed to the port of Tamralipti. Thence, giving up the idea of a sea voyage, he decided to travel across the Deccan to Ceylon. He spent the year 640 in Dravida, the home of the Dravidians, but, hearing reports of civil war and famine in Ceylon, he reluctantly decided to renounce his visit to the sacred island.

He had travelled southwards along the east coast of the Gulf of Bengal, and he returned by the west coast. He now met and gave a good description of the warlike Mahrattas, of whose king he writes : " He has warlike tastes and puts the glory of arms before everything." Moving northwards Hsuan reached the peninsula of Gujerat, whose merchants traded with Persia, and he mentions that " the Persians can weave brocaded silk stuffs, and various kinds of carpets ". He also comments favourably on the Persian horses and camels.

Before starting on his long return journey, Hsuan accepted an invitation to visit Assam, of which he tells us that " the towns are surrounded by rivers, lakes and ponds. The bread-tree and the coco-nut flourish there." He ascertained that the frontiers of the Chinese province of Ssu-chuan were a two months' journey away, through forests infested by wild elephants. Accordingly he decided to visit Harsha, the Poet King of Northern India, and to return to China by Central Asia. Accompanying the King of Assam, he travelled up the Ganges with 20,000 elephants and 30,000 boats to Harsha's camp, where he was received with extraordinary honours. An assembly was convoked at Kanauj, at which Hsuan presided with much distinction, but his eloquence provoked the hatred of his opponents, who plotted to take his life, while Harsha was attacked by an assassin. It is interesting to note that Harsha had recently received an embassy from Tai-tsung, which proves the existence of diplomatic relations between India and China at this period.

In 643, the Master of the Law bade farewell to Harsha, who loaded him with gifts and sent an escort to protect him as far as the frontier. He traversed the Punjab without incident, but in crossing the Indus had the misfortune to lose fifty manuscripts and his collection of flower-seeds. Everywhere he was received with almost royal honours, and, bidding farewell to the King of Kapisa, the fearless Master decided to follow up the Oxus to the Pamirs and to visit Kashgar. In July 644, the Hindu Kush was crossed with much difficulty, and Hsuan traversed Tokharistan and Badakshan, where he spent a month with the Governor, who was a relation of the Khan of the Western Turks.

Provided with an escort, the Master reached Po-mi-lo, or the Pamirs, which he was the first traveller to describe.

> "The valley of Pamir is about a thousand *li* [1] from east to west, and a hundred *li* from south to north. It is situated between two snowy mountains. The cold is glacial, and the wind furious. Snow falls even in spring and summer, day and night the wind rages. Grain and fruit cannot grow there, and trees are few and far between. In the middle of the valley is a large lake, situated in the centre of the world on a plateau of prodigious height."

Descending from the Pamirs, while travelling through the gorge of the Tangitar, the Master was attacked by a band of robbers, and several of his elephants fell into the ravines and were killed. The travellers, however, reached Kashgar with their precious relics, manuscripts and statues unharmed.

Hsuan comments on the general desert nature of the country, but notes that in the oasis grain and fruit abounded. He also remarks that the eyes of the Kashgaris have green pupils, thereby, as Grousset remarks, proving their East Iranian strain.

From Kashgar the Master travelled to Yarkand and Kargalik, crossing a bay of the Takla Makan desert. Following the caravan route, Yutien or Khotan, the " Kingdom of Jade ", where Stein began his epoch-making archaeological researches, was reached. Here again the Master found an important Buddhist centre, boasting of one hundred monasteries. He arrived at Khotan in the autumn of 644, and spent several months awaiting the Emperor's permission to return to China. He then continued his long journey to Lop-nor and again waited at Tun-huang, which yielded such important documents, frescoes and paintings on silk banners to Stein and Pelliot. Finally, in 645, the obscure monk who had quitted his country against the orders of the Emperor was, upon his return, granted a magnificent official reception, and, with due solemnity, handed over to the Monastery of Great Happiness the relics, statues and manuscripts which he had collected with such loving care, and at the cost of infinite toil and risk.

How often, when following in the footsteps of the Master in the Pamirs or on the road to Khotan, have I referred to Hsuan-tsang, while during the night marches in the desert the universal feeling might be epitomized by Hsuan's

---

[1] Normally there are three *li* to a mile.

description : " The view was boundless, there were no traces of man or horse, and in the night the demons and goblins raised fire-lights as many as the stars ; in the day-time the wind blew the sand before it."

Hsuan-tsang, in short, was undoubtedly the greatest known traveller that the world had so far seen. One is always impressed by the accuracy and fairness of his distinctly critical mind, which seems to be almost that of a twentieth-century European. He was more highly educated, representing as he did a famous civilization at its zenith, than Marco Polo, and naturally understood the mentality and point of view of Asiatics infinitely better than the great Venetian. Moreover, the fact that for many years after his return he lived in close touch with the Emperor, his description of the countries he had visited and of the rulers he had met, must have been of considerable value to China. His services to the Buddhist religion, which, as Grousset writes, " had created a vast current of humanism, from Ceylon to the farthest isles of the Japanese archipelago ", were priceless.

Hitherto we have dealt with explorers by land, but, to complete the picture, a brief account will be given of the voyage of the monk I-Ching. In the autumn of 671 this intrepid explorer embarked on his voyage to India in a Persian ship, and wrote, " Long were we held over the immense abyss ; great waves, high as mountains, lay across the sea, over the whole of the vasty deep the waters rose, like clouds, to the heaven."

I-Ching duly reached Sumatra, where he remained for eight months, and was able to study Buddhism in its flourishing monasteries. He continued his voyage in a Sumatra ship, and, crossing the Bay of Bengal, coasted the Nicobar Islands, " the land of naked men ". He describes how these savages brought coco-nuts and bananas to exchange for iron, and added that " if one refuses. to barter with them, they immediately shoot with poisoned arrows ". In 673, I-Ching landed at the port of Tamralipti, where he studied Sanskrit for a year before penetrating into India. He then visited the sacred places and went back to Sumatra with more than 10,000 rolls of Sanskrit texts, which he set to work to translate. He finally returned to China, where he was granted the honour of a public reception, and he spent the rest of his life in completing his great literary work. He also wrote an interesting account of the eminent Chinese monks " who went to seek the Law in the countries of the West ".

The Chinese took a special interest in Ceylon, where the relic of relics, the tooth of Buddha, was carefully guarded. Indeed, it was the general belief that, if it were lost, the island would be swallowed up by demons. One of the earliest Chinese pilgrims to land in the sacred island attempted to steal it, but he was caught. Embassies were also exchanged with the court of China up to, and later than, the visit of Marco Polo to Ceylon.

The connection of China by sea with the West was primarily due to the courage and enterprise of the Arab seamen. We learn from Chinese sources that, in A.D. 166, " Antun (Marcus Aurelius Antoninus), King of Ta-tsin, sent an envoy by the parts beyond Jihan (Indo-China) with offerings of ivory, rhinoceros-horn and tortoise-shell ". This, if we may judge by the gifts, was no envoy, but probably a Roman merchant who hoped for better treatment by assuming the status of an ambassador. The earliest dated reference to the sea voyages of Chinese vessels is to be found in the pages of Masudi, who mentions that in the first half of the fifth century of our era ships from India and China were constantly to be seen in the Euphrates at Hira. Chinese annals of the seventh and eighth centuries describe the course taken by the junks from Canton to the Euphrates. From Ceylon they made for Malabar, and crossing the Gulf of Cambay they reached Diu. Mention is made of the great river Sinteu (the Indus), and, following unconsciously in the wake of Nearchus, in twenty days they reached the Straits of Hormuz, where it is interesting to learn that there was a great lighthouse, and so to Siraf and the Euphrates.

The Arabs established a factory at Canton in the seventh century A.D., or possibly earlier, and we are told that in 758 the Persians and Arabs were strong enough to burn and sack the city and then flee to their ships. But a century later we read that the foreigners resident at the Chinese ports were counted by thousands. In Chapter V an account is given of the relations between China and the Caliphate.

A most interesting branch of exploration was that conducted by the missionaries of the Nestorian church. According to the traditions of the Christian Church in India it was founded by St. Thomas the Apostle, and an anthem in the Chaldaean breviary of the Malabar church runs :

" The Hindus and the Chinese and the Persians, and all the people of the Isles of the Sea, and they who dwell in Syria and Armenia, in Java and Romania, call Thomas to remembrance. . . ."

After the condemnation and banishment of Nestorius in 431, his sect spread extensively in Persia and much further afield, Metropolitan sees being constituted at Herat, Samarkand, and in China during the seventh and eighth centuries. In the middle of the ninth century, we learn that the metropolitans of China, India, Persia, Merv, Syria, Arabia, Herat and Samarkand were excused from attending the quadrennial synods of the church on account of the remoteness of their sees.

The earliest reference to the Christian religion in China is an edict issued by the Tang Emperor in 745 in which it was declared that the religion of the sacred books known as Persian had originally come from the Ta-tsin and that its temples had become known as Persian temples. The edict enacted that these temples should in future be known as Ta-tsin temples.

The celebrated monument of Si-ngan-fu erected in the seventh century gives an abstract of Christian doctrine, with an account of the arrival of the missionary Olopun from Ta-tsin in 635, and of the decree of the Emperor commanding the construction of a church. In this church the monument was erected in 781.

The story of these Nestorian missionaries will be taken up again in Chapter VIII, but there is no question that there was communication, even if of an intermittent nature, between their sees throughout these centuries, and that the missionaries followed the trade routes.

Among the religions of the East which have profoundly influenced mankind was that founded by Manes. Born in A.D. 215, he proclaimed his mission at the coronation of Shapur I, the captor of Valerian, and for some years his influence was great at the Persian court. Later, falling from favour, he travelled to India, Tibet and China, from which latter country he brought back pictures which played a considerable part in the teaching of his dualist and pessimistic creed. Manes was put to death by a later Persian monarch, but Manichaeism spread over Central Asia and reached China, developing a wonderful art and was noted by the Polos, who mistook its followers for Christians. In Europe too it spread to the Albigenses in Aquitaine. St. Augustine of Hippo was a member of this sect before he embraced Christianity.

We have seen China emerging from a state of isolation under the Han dynasty and, later, under the Tang dynasty, becoming a world-empire which extended across Asia from the Pacific Ocean to the Caspian Sea, rivalling in wealth and importance the older empire of Alexander the Great and that which Rome had created. This chapter shows that no state was more anxious to explore neighbouring countries and open up diplomatic and commercial relations with them. Nor was any empire better served by its explorers. In return, China drew envoys, explorers and missionaries to her shores, to the great benefit of world exploration.

CHAPTER IV

GEOGRAPHERS OF THE ROMAN EMPIRE

*"I would examine the Caspian Sea, and see where and how
it exonerates itself after it hath taken in Volga, Jaxartes,
Oxus, and those great rivers. I would find out with Trajan
the fountains of Danubius, of Ganges and of Oxus."*
BURTON, *" Anatomy of Melancholy "*.

IN the previous chapter an account has been given of the
creation of a great empire by China. It is interesting to note
that when the Han dynasty set out on its wonderful career
of conquest, Rome had but recently overthrown Carthage in
201 B.C. In the case of both states a civilized power was surrounded by myriads of barbarians who were gradually conquered and civilized. Again, the introduction of Buddhism
into China coincided with the arrival of Christian missionaries
in Rome, each state respectively adopting the foreign religion.

Their final destinies lay far apart. The Han dynasty
disappeared, but China, which during the course of perhaps
2,000 years had gradually assimilated the aboriginal tribes,
and whose boundaries needed protection only from the north,
has survived to the present day, lamentable as is her condition
at the time of writing. Yet China alone can point to undoubted
lineal descendants of her illustrious teacher Confucius, whereas
neither in Persia nor in Europe do such connections with the
remote past exist.

The position of Rome in 201 B.C., after her decisive victory
at Zama, signified control, actual or potential, over the Central
and Western Mediterranean. Carthage was powerless, and it
only remained to annex her trading posts. Spain, too, was
included in the spoils of victory, and was annexed, though
not without much stubborn fighting. The supremacy of
Rome was firmly established in Italy south of the Po, and she
was mistress of Sicily, but had not conquered the Gauls of
Northern Italy.

As regards the East, Rome had had at this period no
contact with the Persian Empire, but in distant Parthia a
warlike chief had, in 250 B.C., founded a dynasty which was
gradually to annex provinces from the Seleucid power until

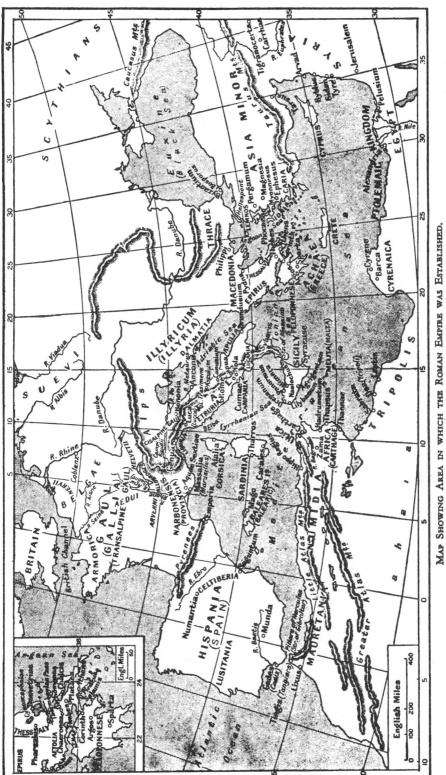

MAP SHOWING AREA IN WHICH THE ROMAN EMPIRE WAS ESTABLISHED.

(Reproduced from "The Universal History of The World", edited by J. A. Hammerton by courtesy of the publishers, The Educational Book Co. Ltd.)

Parthia became the protagonist of the East. As such she inflicted terrible defeats on the Roman armies, which time and again invaded Parthia, and for considerable periods made the Tigris, instead of the Euphrates, the boundary of the Parthian Empire.

The heirs of Alexander the Great were represented by Philip V of Macedon, by Antiochus III, who ruled over the vast empire of the Seleucids, and by Ptolemy V of Egypt, a boy-king who was under the protection of Rome. Arsaces III of Parthia was steadily annexing districts to the west when Antiochus appeared on the scene, and, following in the footsteps of Alexander, captured Hecatompylos and defeated Arsaces, who accepted his terms. He then marched through Bactria to the Punjab, where the successor of Asoka wisely bought off the invader with gifts of elephants and much gold. The Seleucid then followed the route taken by Craterus and probably wintered in the same valley of Rudbar in which Alexander had halted. He ended his expedition at Seleucia on the Tigris and assuredly well earned his title of " Great ". This beating of the bounds of his Empire undoubtedly added to Europe's knowledge of Central Asia and India, taking place as it did more than a century after the famous expedition of Alexander the Great.

Rome decided to crush Philip of Macedon, who had shown hostility to her during the Punic Wars and had foolishly stayed his hand when Rome was staggering under the weight of the blows delivered by Hannibal. Philip was defeated at Cynoscephalae in 197 B.C. Antiochus, who had not supported Philip, was finally overthrown at Magnesia in 190 B.C., while Macedonia was definitely crushed at Pydna in 168 B.C. Polybius dates the establishment of the Roman Empire from this last battle, which laid the Near East at her feet. Yet it is noteworthy that not an acre of land in Asia was annexed as the immediate result of these great victories.

Not until 133 B.C. do we find Rome appearing as a territorial power in Asia. The King of Pergamum had died without leaving a son, and bequeathed his state, the Lydia of Croesus, to the Roman people. The Senate accepted this valuable heritage, which made them the neighbours of Pontus, Armenia and Parthia ; and from this period, which terminates with the victory of Octavian at Actium in 31 B.C., Rome advanced from strength to strength. Simultaneously with this expansion in every direction, the lands surrounding the Mediterranean were explored, and to a certain extent surveyed, if only by the road-makers of Rome. Northwards, Western Germany and Gaul were annexed, while South Britain was reconnoitred. Eastwards, Asia Minor and Syria were absorbed, while Armenia and various provinces to the south of her mountains formed a bone of contention with Parthia.

This expansion was illustrated by a number of soldiers, merchants, explorers and geographers, whose reports formed the basis of the works of Polybius, Strabo and Ptolemy. The historian Polybius (204–122 B.C.) served on the staff of Scipio, who employed him to explore the coast of North Africa. He also explored parts of Gaul and Spain, while his knowledge of the geography of the Alps and of Italy was superior to that of any of his predecessors.

After Polybius came Strabo, who was born in Pontus about 63 B.C. He also travelled far and wide, and had penetrated into Egypt as far south as Syene and Philae. But his importance mainly lies in his work as a systematic compiler of accounts of other men's explorations. Basing himself on Eratosthenes and on Greek rather than Roman authorities, Strabo was the first writer to conceive the scheme of a work not only geographical, but also mathematical, physical, historical and political. He realized what a vast extension of geographical knowledge had taken place, but was struck by the comparative smallness of the known world, and acutely suggested the existence of hitherto unknown continents. Strabo reduced the width of the world to less than the estimate of Eratosthenes, from 3,750 to 2,872 geographical miles, and unwisely rejected the explorations of Pytheas.

The great geographer of the Roman Empire was Claudius Ptolemaeus, commonly known as Ptolemy, who flourished during the second century A.D. His *Geographike Syntaxis* was the most considerable attempt of the ancient world to place the study of geography on a scientific basis.[1] The point which chiefly affects us in this work is the increased knowledge of the world which Ptolemy displays. To the north Thule is placed in latitude 63° N., which is not far from the true position of the Shetland Islands. With it are the northern parts of Europe and the unknown lands of Northern Asia. In the reign of Nero a Roman knight led an expedition to the Baltic to purchase amber. In this he was successful, and he reported that the amber coast was situated about 600 miles

---

[1] Ptolemy divided the world by parallels of latitude reckoning from the equator, and by parallels of longitude reckoning from the island of Ferrol the most western point that he knew.

north of Carnuntum on the Danube, just below modern Vienna, which estimate for the caravan route was accurate. Again, Corbulo's map of Armenia and of the neighbourhood of the Caspian, which is mentioned by Pliny, shows the latter as a sea with the Volga and other rivers, including the Oxus, flowing into it; albeit he does not name the rivers, and the width of the Caspian is considerably exaggerated.

Arabia in ancient times was a relatively fertile country, with at least three great rivers flowing from the western mountains across the huge peninsula to the sea. Of these great rivers there are distinct traces in dry *wadis* traversing the modern *Arabia Deserta*, though to-day there is no perennial river in the peninsula. The question of rainfall is of great importance in Arabia. For instance, the visitor to Aden is

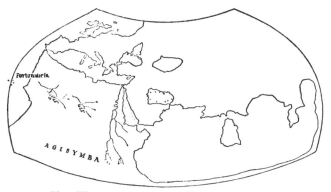

THE WORLD ACCORDING TO PTOLEMY, A.D. 150.

shown magnificent reservoirs, mainly hewn out of the solid rock, on which the inhabitants of this ancient port, which is mentioned in the book of Ezekiel, undoubtedly depended for their water-supply. Since the British occupation in 1839, these reservoirs have never been more than one-eighth full: indeed, they are generally empty. It is therefore clear that there has been a marked movement towards desiccation in Arabia, at any rate throughout the Christian era.

Sabaean inscriptions date back to the ninth or tenth century B.C., and in the Book of Kings we have an account of a Queen of Sheba who came to prove Solomon " with hard questions ". This visit would have taken place about 950 B.C. The Sabaeans lived in North Arabia at this period, and, so far as is known, they moved southwards during the ninth and eighth centuries.

The story of Job, " a man in the land of Uz ", is the subject of an interesting theory advanced by Bertram Thomas, who, with reference to his comforters, would identify Eliphaz the Temanite with the Bani Teman, Bildad the Shuhite with the Shihuh (who inhabit the country round Daba in the neighbourhood of Cape Musandam), and Zophar the Naamathite with the Naim tribe. All these tribes inhabit the Oman district, while Uz is found in Azd, the ruling tribe of Maskat. To quote his summing up : " The Book of Job is held by many to have been written not earlier than the time of the Babylonian captivity, and it would appear not unreasonable to suppose that it was Musandam . . . upon which a Babylonian author of the book drew for his local colour." [1]

The Sabaeans conquered the Minaean dynasty and established themselves in Yemen. We hear of a second dynasty of " Kings of Saba ", who began to rule about 550 B.C. with their capital at Marib. In 115 B.C. they were succeeded by the Himyarites, who constructed the celebrated dam of Marib. The Abyssinians overthrew the Himyarite dynasty early in the sixth century A.D., and established Christianity in parts of Arabia, but in 575 a Persian expedition despatched by Noshirwan restored a scion of the Himyaritic family, who ruled for a short period under the overlordship of Persia.[2]

The prosperity of Arabia was due to the fact that the Indian trade in spices, drugs, and perfumes reached Ophir, probably the modern Dhufar, and was thence carried by caravans through Mecca, Medina and Petra to the Mediterranean. Dhufar, too, it will be remembered, produced frankincense and possibly gold. Arabia remained a rich, mysterious land to the inhabitants of the Roman Empire until Augustus despatched an expedition under Aelius Gallus which in 25 B.C. landed in Hejaz with Yemen and Hadramaut as its objectives. Their route lay through Negrana (the modern Nejran), and the army reached Marib, the capital of the Himyarite kingdom. Thence it was not very far to the Incense Land of Hadramaut, but the Roman general, disillusioned as to the reputed wealth of *Arabia Felix*, marched back to the coast and left the Arabs to themselves. This expedition enabled Ptolemy to enumerate the towns and villages of *Arabia Felix* with some accuracy, while various caravan routes were outlined.

In Africa exploration followed up the valley of the Nile, passing the junction of the Blue Nile and continuing as far as the *Sadd*, which is described. Ptolemy shows that the

---

[1] *Alarms and Excursions in Arabia*, by Bertram Thomas, pp. 230-1.
[2] *History of Persia* (3rd ed.), Vol. I, p. 455.

source of the Blue Nile was in a lake in the east, and that the White Nile had its origin in important lakes, which were fed by the snow waters of the " Mountains of the Moon ". It is probable that this information, which was finally proved to be correct, was gained from traders in touch with the east coast of Africa rather than from dwellers in the Nile Valley. The Romans also undertook an expedition against the Queen of Ethiopia in 25 B.C., which added to their knowledge of the borders of that country.

In view of the importance of Ptolemy's opinions, which influenced explorers down to the eighteenth century, I quote him at some length. " The uninhabited part of the earth is bounded on the East by the unknown land which lies along the region occupied by the eastern nations of Asia Major, the Sinae and the nations of Seres, and, on the South, by the unknown land which shuts round the Indian Sea, and encompasses that Ethiopia to the south of Libya and Europe ; and on the North by that continuation of the same ocean which encircles the Britannic Isles." In this summary we have the theory of the existence of a great southern *Terra Incognita*, which made the Indian Ocean an inland sea. The eastern extension of Asia was also enormously exaggerated, a fact which will be referred to later in this work. There is, however, a distinct recognition of the sea route to China, and a comparison with the map of Herodotus will show how considerable was the advance in geographical knowledge of the world since he wrote in the fifth century B.C.

At the same time these errors and the belief that the habitable world of the north temperate zone was separated from a similar temperate zone in the south by an impassable area of deadly heat, hindered the progress of exploration for more than 1,000 years.

To turn to the question of commerce, at no period was the Mediterranean Sea so free from pirates, while the enormous empire could be traversed in every direction with reasonable safety. It produced every requisite in its provinces except perhaps spices and incense, and this fact made for a flourishing internal trade, which was encouraged by the stable and uniform currency.

Under Augustus the navigable canals of Egypt were cleaned out, and military operations were conducted on both sides of the Red Sea to check raiding and piracy. Trade with India flourished, and Strabo reported that 120 ships were engaged in it. About the middle of the first century A.D., a sea-captain named Hippalus discovered that voyages could be made from the Red Sea to India out of sight of land, thanks to the steady monsoon winds. As a result of this discovery trade with India increased to such an extent that Pliny bewails the huge sums spent upon eastern luxuries. Large quantities of Roman coins have been discovered in Southern India, whence came spices and pearls, while silk, perfumes and ivory also reached Rome in considerable quantities.

Hippalus left no record of his epoch-making discovery, but a book by an unknown author giving commercial information was published about A.D. 60 under the title of *Periplus Maris Erythraei*. In it a description is given of the east coast of Africa almost as far south as Zanzibar; the south coast of Arabia and the west coast of India are also treated with some accuracy, while the silk trade is described as following the routes mentioned in Chapter III. In the next century traders reached Zanzibar, while, as we have already mentioned, Roman merchants penetrated to China.

Julius Caesar, the only Roman who can be compared with Alexander the Great, resembled the illustrious Macedonian as a great explorer. He not only conquered Gaul, but made the first reconnaissance of Britain. A brief account of both these enterprises will be given.

We first hear of Gaul at the foundation, about 600 B.C., of the Greek colony at Massilia, whose citizens are known to have opened up relations with the Gallic tribes inhabiting the Rhone Valley. Rome took her first forward step in the country by annexing the hinterland of Massilia in 121 B.C., which, with its port of Narbo Martius (Narbonne), constituted the province of *Gallia Narbonensis*. Later followed the campaigns so well described in Caesar's *Commentaries*. His first very serious task was due to movements of tribes which, as already mentioned, have played a decisive part in world history. The Teutonic tribes on the right bank of the Rhine were pressing in on the Celtic Helvetii, occupying the western portion of modern Switzerland,[1] with the result that the Helvetii decided to initiate a tribal migration westwards, a movement that would have constituted a serious menace to Gaul. The year 58 B.C. was consequently spent in attacking the Helvetii and driving them back to their mountains. The German tribe of the Suevi (Swabians) had next to be dealt with. They had crossed the Rhine and attacked the Aedui, who lived on the northern borders of the Roman province.

---

[1] Their capital, in Roman times, was called Aventicum. It is now Avenches.

Accordingly Caesar marched to help his allies and defeated the Suevi with crushing losses. This defeat alarmed the Belgae of North-East Gaul, whose leading tribe, the Nervii, Caesar attacked in the following year. The Roman army was very nearly overwhelmed, but Caesar's personality finally won a great victory. He then led, or sent, columns through the south-west (Aquitania) and the north-west (Armorica), and gradually annexed the country. In 55 B.C. a fresh invasion of German tribes was hurled back, and Caesar himself crossed the Rhine and raided their country, but wisely decided that that great river should constitute the boundary of the Roman Empire. Caesar was the conqueror and explorer, and Augustus organized his uncle's conquests. Caesar and Augustus thus laid the foundations of the greatness of France, which owes to Rome both its civilization and its language.

To turn now to Britain, in the late summer of 55 B.C., Caesar organized an expedition at Portus Itius, now Boulogne. As he himself wrote in *De Bello Gallico* : [1] " He understood that in almost all the Gallic campaigns succours had been furnished for our enemy from Britain ; and he supposed that if the season left no time for actual campaigning, it would still be of great advantage to him merely to have entered the island, observed the character of the natives, and obtained some knowledge of the localities, the harbours, and the landing-places."

Acting on information gained by a tribune who had reconnoitred the coast in a galley, Caesar landed his force on the beach between Walmer and Deal. The invaders were strenuously opposed by the British, who drove their chariots into the sea, until, aided by the galleys which enfiladed the British, the landing was successfully accomplished and the Chief sued for peace. While negotiations were in progress, Caesar's fleet was partially wrecked, and the British resumed hostilities ; finally, however, terms were made, hostages were given, and Caesar, who had narrowly escaped disaster, returned to Gaul.

In the following year he landed near Sandwich at the head of a powerful army, and, marching inland, defeated the British near Durovernum, later Canterbury. He was recalled to the coast by a report that many of his ships had been wrecked, and this retrograde movement encouraged the British to resist more stoutly. Their chief leader was Cassivel-

[1] Translated by H. J. Edwards for the Loeb-Library, 1917.

launus, whose dominions became the Roman objective. After again defeating the British, Caesar crossed the Thames not far from Brentford. The bed of the river was staked, as was its left bank, but the legionaries would not be denied, and Cassivellaunus was defeated. He retired on his capital Verulamium (St. Albans), which was carried by assault. Cassivellaunus realized that he was beaten, and, as an attack on the naval camp had been repulsed with heavy loss, he sued for peace, which was granted on the terms of payment of tribute and the surrender of hostages. When the pledges had been handed over, the Roman army marched back to the coast and returned to Gaul.

Caesar estimated the circumference of Britain at 3,000 miles, a very accurate calculation. Moreover he noted that the Britons, generally speaking, did not grow much wheat, but lived on milk and flesh; they did not make cheese. He also referred to the use of woad, " which produces a blue colour, and makes their appearance in battle more terrible ".

" Caesar ", Plutarch writes, " was the first who brought a navy into the western ocean, or who sailed into the Atlantic with an army to make war; and by invading an island, the existence of which was a matter of controversy among historians, he might be said to have carried the Roman Empire beyond the limits of the known world."

The ultimate conquest of Britain was inevitable, if only because of the racial connection of its people with Gaul. Augustus seriously considered it, but it was not actually undertaken until, after the death of Cunobeline, who was friendly to Rome, his son Caractacus headed an anti-Roman party and expelled a brother of his, who appealed for aid to the Emperor. Taking advantage of this pretext, in A.D. 43 a powerful force, 40,000 strong, landed in Kent and marched on London. The Emperor Claudius himself took part in the expedition, which crossed the Thames and captured Camulodunum (Colchester). Using London as their base, three columns swept the south, the midlands, and the east with such success that, in four years, the country south of the Humber and east of the Severn was annexed without any particularly stubborn resistance being encountered, except from Caractacus in the west. That king was finally defeated on the borders of Wales in A.D. 50, and was betrayed to the Romans in the following year.

The revolt of Boadicea, whose husband ruled the Iceni of East Anglia under Roman suzerainty, was caused by Roman injustice at his death. His dominions, which he had be-queathed to Rome, were taken over with great brutality, and Boadicea, " bleeding from the Roman rods ", rose in revolt. The inhabitants of South-East Britain joined in the insur-rection and destroyed Verulamium (St. Albans), Colchester and London, massacring the Romans settled in the country and nearly annihilating the ninth legion. Rome, however, quickly reasserted her authority, and practically the whole of lowland Britain was explored and annexed, as was Southern Scotland. The latter territory was guarded by a wall built by Antoninus Pius from the Firth of Forth to the Clyde.

In 120 Hadrian began the construction of the celebrated wall which still runs from Wallsend to Bowness near Carlisle, a distance of eighty miles. This, the most important Roman work in Great Britain, consisted in its final form, as rebuilt by Septimius Severus in 207, of a strong stone wall defended by seventeen forts with castles and towers at close intervals. The terrain reminded me of the celebrated *Chemin des Dames*.

As to the important question of communications, Ermine Street, which connected London with York, and Watling Street, which ran *via* Uriconium (Wroxeter) to Chester, to-gether with the south-west road to Silchester, Caerleon and Exeter, were of primary importance. Indeed, the road-makers of Rome were her chief explorers. Again, the Romans introduced the walnut, beech, elm, chestnut, syca-more, cherry, peach, pear and fig; also the deer, the hornless sheep and the pheasant. Under their influence the mining industry was greatly developed, tin, iron, lead, copper, gold and salt being all produced in increased quantities. The chief exports were slaves, tin, cattle, iron and skins, with which chains, amber, glass and metal goods were purchased.

Britain owed much to Rome, whose hegemony lasted for a period as long as that which separates the present generation from the Tudors. Education made considerable progress, trade flourished, the upper classes were civilized to some extent, and the poorer people at least had their horizon widened and their food supply improved and better assured.

CHAPTER V

EXPLORATION UNDER THE CALIPHATE

*" The King of Sarandib gave me a cup of ruby a span high ;
and a bed covered with the skin of a serpent which swalloweth
the elephant, and whoso sitteth upon it, never sickeneth, and
a slave-girl like a shining moon."*

Sindbad the Sailor.

THE rise of Mohammed, the Prophet of Arabia, is one of
the most stupendous events in history. He appeared at a
time when both the Byzantine and Persian empires were exhausted by a long series of desperate campaigns, which seriously weakened Byzantium and created a state of anarchy
in Persia. The Arabs, fervent believers in the creed which
united them, and perhaps attracted still more strongly by
the lure of rich spoils, once again swarmed from the desert
to the sown, and founded the greatest empire that the world
had seen, stretching from the borders of China on the east
to Morocco, which is washed by the waves of the Atlantic
Ocean, on the west, a distance of some 7,000 miles.

The early campaigns of the Moslems, who attacked the
two neighbouring empires simultaneously, displayed an utter
lack of strategical knowledge, but their valour was irresistible.
The fruits of victory included Syria, taken from the Byzantine Empire, while, at the battle of Cadesia in A.D. 636, which
ranks with Issus in its decisiveness, the great Persian Empire
was overthrown. At the battle of Nahavand, fought on the
Iranian plateau in 642, the *coup de grâce* was given. Like the
unfortunate Darius, Yezdegird, the last monarch of the Sas-
sanian dynasty, fled eastwards. He sought help from China
in vain, and was finally murdered at Merv in 652 for the
sake of his jewels.

Mohammed died in A.D. 632, and was succeeded by his
staunch supporter Abu Bekr, who thus founded the Caliphate.[1]
During his short rule of two years the Arabs continued their
advance, but Omar, who succeeded him, was the greatest
Soldier Caliph, capturing Damascus, Antioch and Jerusalem,

[1] The correct title of the Caliph is *Khalifa Rasul Illah* or " Successor of the Prophet
of Allah ".

feats of arms soon followed by the annexation of Egypt and the advance of the Moslems along the coast of North Africa to Barca. Omar was assassinated in 644, and his successors Othman and Ali also met violent deaths, the latter, who was the son-in-law of the Prophet, being assassinated in 661. His son Hasan retired in favour of Moawiyah, the Governor of Syria, who founded the Omayyad dynasty.

It is of considerable interest to note that in the annals of the great Tang dynasty, whose power was acknowledged to the south of the Hindu Kush and whose influence extended to the Caspian Sea, we read that "Ta-tsin has, in later days, been called Fu-lin". This is the Greek word πόλιν or "the city", by which term Constantinople was known. A description is given of the city, surrounded by a continuous belt of towns and villages, with its Golden Gate 200 feet high, its palaces with "colonnaded porticoes and parks with rare animals", and of the dazzling costume of the monarch. Of still greater interest is a reference to Moawiyah: "The Ta-shi (Arabs), having overrun kingdom after kingdom, at last sent their General-in-Chief, Moi, to lay siege to the capital of Fu-lin. . . . The negotiator of the peace which followed made it one of the conditions that the Ta-shi should every year pay tribute consisting of gold and silk-stuffs." We know from other sources that Moawiyah's fleet was destroyed by "Greek fire", and that his army was defeated, with the result that he was obliged to sue for peace and paid tribute. This is, so far as I know, the earliest reference in the Chinese annals to a great historical event in Europe.

In 742 we hear of a mission "composed of priests of great virtue" visiting China, and then, since the Moslems formed an impassable barrier between the two nations, there was a cessation of friendly intercourse for centuries.

The Moslems under the Caliphate penetrated deeper and deeper into Asia, where, it must be remembered, they considered themselves as explorers. During the years 705 to 714, Bokhara, Samarkand, Farghana and finally Kashgar fell into their hands. Alexander had penetrated only to the Syr Darya, whereas the Moslems advanced across the Tian Shan hundreds of miles farther east. A curious story has been preserved relating to this campaign. The Arab general had sworn an oath to take possession of the soil of China, whereupon the "king"—probably the local governor—released him from his oath by the despatch of a load of soil on which he might trample, a bag of Chinese money to symbolize tribute, and four royal youths on whom he imprinted his seal. We learn from other sources that the Tibetans became allies of the Arabs, whose support they received in Chinese Turkestan —so wide was the range of the Arabs at this period.

We hear of an Arab embassy to China in 713. The envoy demanded exemption from the *kotow*, stating that he " bowed only to Allah, never to a Prince ". At first it was decided to kill the bold Arab, but wiser counsels prevailed, and the emperor graciously pardoned him. Relations between the two countries were not always friendly. Indeed in 709 a force commanded by the Emperor's nephew had joined in the coalition against the Arabs who were invading Bokhara. There were also appeals for help against the Arabs from Tabaristan, one of the Caspian provinces of Persia, whose rulers maintained their independence for a century after Nahavand. Later, embassies, including one from Harun-al-Rashid, were received at the court of China.

At this period a Moslem force marched through Makran to Sind, where Multan was captured, yielding wealth beyond the dreams of avarice. Almost perforce, so long as the tribute was paid, the Arabs permitted the worship of idols, in direct violation of the orders of Mohammed.

Under Abdul Malik and his son Welid, who ruled successively from 692 to 714, the Caliphate reached its zenith. Not only had Arab armies marched across the frontier of China and to the Indus, but the conquest of Spain constituted a third splendid achievement. In 717 the Arabs made a second attempt on Constantinople, which again ended in disaster to their fleet and to their army.

The Saracens, as they are termed in Europe throughout the Middle Ages, had crushed the Visigoths and conquered Spain in two years, save for a few mountainous districts in the north-west. In 720, under Abdur Rahman they crossed the Pyrenees and besieged Toulouse. They were driven off by Duke Eudo, but retained Narbonne, and in 724 they raided Burgundy. In 732 Abdur Rahman reappeared in Aquitaine with a large force and drove Eudo across the Loire. Charles Martel came to the rescue, and after a hard-fought battle near Tours, in which Abdur Rahman was killed, the Moslems fled. Thus Islam had reached its limit, although the Riviera suffered for many generations from Saracen raids.

In 749 the Omayyad dynasty was overthrown by the Abbasid family, which was descended from the uncle of the Prophet. The Omayyad dynasty and Islam had been interchangeable terms, but after its fall, a refugee scion founded a dynasty in Spain which became very powerful, while the authority of the Abbasids was only intermittently acknow-ledged in Africa. The Abbasid capital was at Baghdad. Who has not been thrilled at the descriptions of the wealth and romance of that city under its famous Caliph, Harun-al-Rashid? It is of interest to note that Charlemagne despatched an em-bassy to the Caliph to arrange for easier access to the Holy Sepulchre and to foster trade relations. Harun was most cordial, and by a return mission presented the keys of the Holy Sepulchre to the Emperor of the West; he also gave him an elephant, the first to be seen in Western Europe for many centuries.

The earliest Arab to reach China of whom a record has been preserved was Sulayman the merchant, who, starting from the Persian Gulf, made several voyages to India and China about the middle of the ninth century. His descrip-tion of the latter country includes a full reference to the use of tea: "The people of China are accustomed to use as a beverage an infusion of a plant, the leaves of which are aromatic and of a bitter taste. It is considered very whole-some."

Under the Abbasid dynasty we have early geographers, beginning with a compiler of routes, followed by travellers who systematically describe each province in turn.[1] Of these worthies the earliest was Ibn Khurdadbih, who was postmaster of the Jibal province, the classical Media, in the ninth century. Khurdadbih describes the great Khorasan road, which, starting from Baghdad, crossed the Jibal province to Hamadan. Thence it took the same line as that followed by Darius in his flight to Rhages or Rei and to Damghan and continuing eastwards it reached Nishapur and Tus. From the latter place it went on to Merv, crossing the Oxus at Amul and passing Bokhara, and so "along the golden road" to Samarkand. Beyond Samarkand it made for Farghana, and finally ended at Uzkand on the borders of China, where it met the famous Silk Road. Khurdadbih compiled what would now be termed a Route Book, but a century later Istakhri, who travelled to India, and Mukaddasi, who wrote mainly from personal observation, provided much valuable informa-tion on the provinces of the Caliphate.

My own personal preference for many years has been for the encyclopaedia of Masudi, entitled in the French trans-

[1] *The Lands of the Eastern Caliphate*, by Guy Le Strange, p. 11 *et seq.*

lation *Les Prairies d'Or*. Masudi travelled all over the known world from Spain in the west to Turkestan in the east, while Sofala, Zanzibar, Sind and China are all mentioned by him. He was the first Arab explorer to visit the Sea of Aral. But Idrisi, although not the greatest of these Arab geographers, exercised more influence on Europe, both directly and indirectly, than any of his predecessors. Educated at Cordoba, he travelled widely in Europe, visiting France and England. He also journeyed over Asia Minor. Finally he settled at the court of Roger II, the Norman King of Sicily, and, working at Palermo, completed his famous map, which was engraved on a silver tablet in 1154.

Idrisi's map consisted in its original form of seven horizontal strips for the seven climates of the Arabs. It is especially interesting in view of the voyages of the Portuguese round Africa, with which we will deal very briefly. Idrisi, who was well acquainted with the map of Ptolemy, shows the Egyptian Nile as having its sources in lakes, but he depicts a great river, the Nil-al-Sudan, flowing from the central lake of the Egyptian Nile due west to the Atlantic. In other words, he creates a composite river, consisting mainly of the Niger and Senegal Rivers. To quote Idrisi:[1] " The towns are Mellil, Ghana, Shermi, Marasa, etc." Mellil, the Malli of Ibn Battuta, is described as belonging to the kingdom of Lamlam, " which touches the eastern boundaries of Wangara, the Land of Gold ". The gold of Ethiopia had been mentioned by Herodotus, who wrote : " Where the south declines towards the setting sun lies Ethiopia. There gold is obtained in great plenty, huge elephants abound . . . and the men are taller and longer-lived than anywhere else." Cambyses, the conqueror of Egypt, started off to annex these lands abounding in gold, but the expedition ended in disastrous failure. This delightful theme might be pursued further, but we will conclude by pointing out that, on the east coast of Africa, Idrisi mentions the ports of Malindi, Mombasa and the gold-lands of Sofala.

The *Arabian Nights*, the world's best story-book, underlying its marvels, gives a fairly accurate account of the voyages of the hardy Arab mariners. Seven voyages in all are recorded, each of which had for its objective a port or ports in the Indian Ocean. In the delightful company of Sindbad we visit the Spice Islands, we escape from whales, we see flying fish. Again we visit the east coast of Africa, and in Madagascar that fearsome bird, the roc, is made to carry our traveller to

[1] *Géographie d'Édrisi*, by P. Jaubert, 1836.

the Valley of Diamonds in Southern India. In a later voyage he visits Ceylon, where he receives the gift referred to in the motto to this chapter. Of him it might well be said :

> "I have gone so far towards the setting sun
> That I have lost all remembrance of the East,
> And my course has taken me so far towards the rising sun
> That I have forgotten the very name of the West."

It would be beyond the scope of this book to deal with these Moslem geographers in detail, but an example may be given of the great value of their work as epitomized by Mr. Le Strange. When occupying the post of Consul at Kirman, I read that the ancient capital of the province had been As-Sirjan, and utilizing the information he gave, I was able to discover this important site. It occupies a limestone hill, and constitutes a position of great strength with its walls and buildings in ruins. A stone pulpit [1] with a beautifully cut inscription in honour of Sultan Ahmad of the Muzaffar dynasty, bearing date 1387, was the most interesting find. This discovery was entirely due to the indications of the Moslem geographers.

Under Mamun, who was Caliph in the earlier part of the ninth century, Arabian science reached its zenith. Mamun " created the first school of geographical science ,which had been seen since the Antonines. . . . An observatory was founded at Baghdad, where attempts were made to determine the obliquity of the ecliptic. Once again, Mamun caused a simultaneous measurement to be taken, in Syria and in Mesopotamia, of a space of two degrees of the terrestrial meridian." [2]

It is indeed remarkable how · strong was the passion for travel at this period. To some extent this is proved by the distant centres from which Baghdad drew its most famous professors. The greatest of all Moslem philosophers, al-Farabi, came from the banks of the distant Oxus ; others hailed from still more distant Farghana, from Khwarizm (Khiva), and Sinna (in Kurdistan). It is well to recognize that what medieval Europe knew of Greek philosophy, chemistry, mathematics and astronomy, it learnt from indifferent Latin translations of Arabic manuscripts. They in their turn had for the most part been translated from· Greek into Arabic at the university of Nisibis, a Nestorian Christian institution.

---

[1] *Lands of the Eastern Caliphate*, p. 300 ; and Sykes, *History of Persia* (2nd ed.), Vol. II, p. 114, for illustration of the pulpit.
[2] *Dawn of Modern Geography*, by Sir Raymond Beazley, Vol. I, p. 409.

The last of the Arab geographers was Yakut. He flourished early in the thirteenth century, and compiled the famous *Dictionary of the Countries*. To this work I am myself deeply indebted for the identification of various Persian sites, more especially for the birthplace of Firdausi, the great epic poet of Persia.[1]

In conclusion, it is worthy of mention that one of the Seljuk monarchs, who reigned towards the end of the eleventh century, employed Omar Khayyám and other scientists to compute a new era, which was named the Jalali era after their royal master. As the Bard of Nishapur wrote :

> ." Ah, but my Computations, People say,
> Reduced the Year to better reckoning ?—Nay,
> 'Twas only striking from the Calendar
> Unborn Tomorrow, and dead Yesterday."

[1] Sykes, *History of Persia*, Vol. II, pp. 60-2.

CHAPTER VI

THE VIKINGS

" Floki, son of Vilgerd, held a great sacrifice and consecrated
three ravens which should show him the way to Iceland ;
for at that time no men sailing the high seas had lodestones
up in northern lands."

The " Hauksbok " on the Colonization of Iceland.

" But northward Hermod rode, the way below ;
And o'er a darksome tract which knows no sun,
But by the blotted light of stars, he fared.
And he came down to ocean's northern strand
At the drear ice, beyond the giant's home ;
Thence on he journeyed o'er the fields of ice
Still north, until he met a stretching wall
Barring his way."

MATTHEW ARNOLD, " *Balder Dead* ".

THE homeland of the Nordic races was unknown to the
ancient geographers. But while great events were taking
place in Asia and in the Mediterranean area of Europe, in the
long centuries before the Christian era, a race of men, with
distinctive mental and moral characteristics, was being developed on the northern shores of the Baltic Sea and on the
Atlantic coast of Scandinavia. Seamanship and courage were
being moulded by the stormy seas, while the scantiness of
their agricultural resources impelled these Norsemen to depend
upon their fisheries and to face the risks of the open sea as
the Mediterranean races never did. Their mode of life favoured
the development of ships more seaworthy than those of the
south, together with a spirit of adventure that has seldom
been equalled and never surpassed. We have seen how the old
navigators timidly hugged the coast and seldom left it willingly,
whereas the Norsemen were the first to make long voyages by
sea and to discover new countries in their sea-going ships.

The " Viking Age " indicates the period from about 750
to 999, during which the Norsemen began their raids on Europe
by sea, which resulted in their carving out more than one kingdom in fertile lands. So far, in the course of our survey of
the movements of peoples, their migrations were carried out
by land and were intended to be permanent settlements. In

consequence, these early immigrants were accompanied by their families, their cattle and their worldly goods. The Vikings, on the other hand, for at least a century, came to plunder and returned to their homes for the winter.

In 787, three of their vessels raided the south of England, and, according to the *Anglo-Saxon Chronicle*, this was the first of the Viking raids, which began an era of murder and destruction. Before this they had come as traders, spying out the land, but now they inflicted greater harm on Europe than ever the Saracens had done. It is told of Charlemagne that, not long before his death in 814, he was at a town near Narbonne when strange sails were observed, and it was questioned whether they were Jewish, African or British traders. Charlemagne, however, said, "No bales of merchandise are borne hither by yonder ships. They are manned by terrible enemies . . . and I grieve to think of the evils that they will bring on my successors."

In the ninth century the iron rule of Harold Fairhair of Norway drove out the wilder spirits of the land, who, in large numbers, emigrated to the Orkneys, the Shetlands, Scotland and Ireland. Farther afield the Rhine, the Seine and the Loire were ascended by the Viking fleets, whose warriors sacked most of the great cities from Paris in the north to Bordeaux and Toulouse in the south. When travelling in Morocco some years ago, I heard of a very early Viking raid on Arzilla, which was apparently the farthest point along the African coast which they harried. In the Mediterranean they sailed up the Rhone, and in Italy they plundered Pisa. By the middle of the ninth century the Vikings had established permanent camps at the mouths of the great rivers, from which they despatched powerful expeditions aiming not merely at plunder but at conquest.

To give familiar examples of their success, in the latter half of the ninth century King Alfred was engaged in a desperate struggle against the Danes, and he deserves immense credit for organizing the army with which he finally defeated the invaders. By the Treaty of Wedmore in 878 and by Guthrum's Fryth in 884, the boundaries of the Danelaw were laid down by a line drawn along the left bank of the Thames to London and thence north-west to the River Dee.

About 890, Othere of Halogaland [1] sailed round the North Cape and along the Lapland coast to the White Sea, which he discovered.

[1] Halogaland was a district of Norway situated between 65° and 66° N.

According to his account:

"He said that he was desirous to try, once upon a time, how far that country extended due north, or whether anyone lived to the north of the waste. He then went due north along the country, leaving all the way the waste land on the right, and the wide sea on the left. After three days he was as far north as the whale-hunters go at the farthest. Then he proceeded in his course due north, as far as he could sail within another three days; then the land there inclined due east, or the sea into the land he knew not which; but he knew that he waited there for a west wind or a little north, and sailed thence eastward along that land as far as he could sail in four days. The land then inclined due south, and he sailed along the coast due south, as far as he could sail in five days. There lay a great river up in that land."

This intrepid explorer described his voyage to the River Dwina, on which Archangel is now situated, to Alfred the Great, who embodied it as a geographical introduction in his Anglo-Saxon translation of the *General History* of Orosius, which has thus preserved for us this record of the daring Viking explorer.

On the other side of the Channel, by the treaty of Saint Clair-sur-Epte, Charles the Simple, in 911, was obliged to agree to the cession to Rollo, the chief of the "Northmen", of Rouen and of the lands stretching down to the mouth of the Seine. Rollo acknowledged himself the vassal of the French King : he also agreed to become a Christian, and his tomb is in Rouen Cathedral. A century and a half later, England was conquered by the "Northmen" of Normandy. We ourselves may thus claim to have much Norse blood flowing in our veins, and to it we mainly owe our love of exploration and adventure.

The Vikings, who attacked and settled in Western Europe, were mainly the inhabitants of Norway and Denmark, whereas the Swedes devoted their energies to Eastern Europe. In the ninth century they sailed up the Neva to Lake Ladoga and thence followed up the Volkhof to Lake Ilmen. There they built the fort of Novgorod, to serve as a mart for their trade with the Black Sea, exchanging slaves, furs, amber, honey and wax for weapons, metals and tissues. In 862 Rurik, the leader of these Varangians (or Franks) as they were called, established his rule over the surrounding tribes and laid the foundations of the Russian Empire. Three years later two other Varangian leaders marched on Kiev and founded a kingdom which was subsequently absorbed by Novgorod. Hardly were they established at Kiev when they descended the Dnieper in 865 and plundered the monasteries and palaces which lined the Sea of Marmora. They surprised the Byzantine authorities, who, in the absence of the army and fleet with the Emperor, were powerless to resist, and we are told that " they made a great slaughter of Christians ". However, a storm " wrecked the fleet of the Russian pagans so that but little of it escaped from disaster ". Undeterred by their losses, the Russians on four occasions during the tenth century attacked Miklagard or the " Great City ", but its walls were too strong, and peace treaties usually concluded these hostile operations. At the end of the tenth century the Russians were invited by the Emperor to attack the Bulgars. This they did with complete success, and decided to annex the entire country and to move their capital from Kiev to Pereyaslavetz on the Danube. The Emperor, realizing the peril of a strong power holding the Balkans, faced the emergency, and the danger was finally averted after much hard fighting.

The peace of 971, followed by the conversion of Russia to the Christianity of the Greek Church, terminated the era of hostilities between the Princes of Kiev and Byzantium, where their " barbaric yawp " had caused grave alarm.

Against their raiding propensities must be set the fact that the Vikings were great traders. We hear of them in the ninth century meeting the merchants of Baghdad at Rei (Rhages), close to modern Teheran, and again as bringing their wares to Baghdad itself. This commerce reached Europe through the Baltic, where Wisby in the island of Gottland served as an entrepôt for the distribution of Oriental products in Northern Europe. The discovery of vast hoards of Anglo-Saxon money in Gottland proves conclusively that our own ancestors purchased their spices at this mart.

The Vikings were born explorers, and when Harold Fairhair attacked the Norse colonies in the islands, whose inhabitants were guilty of raiding Norway, it was decided to colonize Iceland, which had been first discovered by Irish monks about 795 and by Norsemen in 870. In the course of a generation this great feat was accomplished, and the descendants of these colonists, who still inhabit the same lands that their forefathers marked off in this empty country, have recently celebrated the millennium of the establishment of a central moot for the whole island and of " a speaker to speak a single law ".

Greenland, the large continental island to the west, situated within a few days' sail of Iceland, was discovered later. In 982 Eric the Red spent three years exploring its south-west coast. Upon his return to Iceland, he gave such glowing accounts of the country, which to serve his purpose he termed Greenland, that he induced considerable numbers of his fellow-countrymen to colonize it. Ultimately two important centres were established, one of nearly 200 farms at " Osterbygd " and a second of half the size at " Vesterbygd " farther north. Both these districts were situated on the western coast, the eastern coast being apparently icebound. The hardy settlers in this Arctic climate found remains of a people similar to those met with in Vineland who were undoubtedly Eskimos. They penetrated along the coast to the far north, and a stone bearing a runic inscription has been discovered at 73° N. latitude.

Greenland was a stepping-stone to the Vikings' crowning achievement in exploration, the discovery of the continent of America, which was accomplished without the aid of the compass. According to the *Saga of Eric the Red* a certain Biarni Heriulfsson, while making a voyage from Iceland to Greenland, was driven out of his course to the south-west and sighted a new country. In spite of pressure from his crew he refused to explore it and sailed north-east to Greenland. Leif, the son of Eric, determined to follow up this information, and in 1002, setting out with thirty-five hardy Greenlanders, he skirted the forbidding coast of Labrador, which they named " The land of flat stone ". They next reached the beautiful forests of Newfoundland, which they appropriately called " Woodland ". Determined to continue their wonderful voyage, they finally reached a great river swarming with salmon, up which they sailed, and decided to winter on its banks. According to the *Saga*, " the amenities of the place were such, as it seemed to them, that no cattle need fodder there in winter. Day and night were more equally divided than in Greenland." [1] While exploring the new land they found grapes, and therefore called it Vineland. In the spring they loaded their ship with timber and grapes, which had presumably been dried, or may have been mountain cranberries. Thus laden they returned to Greenland after a most successful expedition. There has been much discussion as to which part of the coast of America should be identified with Vineland. A reference to an observation made by Leif on the shortest day and the general description of the climate tend to prove that his winter camp was in Maryland or Virginia.

[1] For this section *vide The Norse Discoverers of America*, by G. M. Cathorne-Hardy, 1921.

Leif's successful voyage caused much discussion, and his brother Thorvald decided to lead a second expedition to Vineland. They reached Leif's camp without difficulty, and in the spring they explored to the west and found " a fine wooded country, the trees coming down close to the sea. There were many islands." They saw no natives, but found a wooden barn. They again spent the winter at Leif's camp, and in the following spring explored to the east and north. On this expedition they saw three skin canoes and killed eight natives, while one escaped. They were soon attacked by hundreds of natives in their canoes. These were beaten off, but Thorvald was mortally wounded. There were other voyages, but the hostility of the natives ultimately drove the Norsemen from the country.

Fortunately the Saga-telling age, a remarkable period of intellectual activity, preserved the annals of these heroic voyages until they were enshrined in the *Saga* written by Ari the Learned, and this record enables us to pay homage to the superb achievements of the Vikings in the field of exploration.

From the Volga to the Atlantic Ocean and from Sicily to the Orkneys, every land in turn bowed before the warlike prowess of the stalwart Vikings, and every country which they conquered was ultimately strengthened by the infusion of vigorous northern blood.

CHAPTER VII

PILGRIMS AND CRUSADERS

" We are the Pilgrims, master; we shall go
    Always a little further: it may be
Beyond that last blue mountain barred with snow,
    Across that angry or that glimmering sea."
                JAMES ELROY FLECKER, " *Hassan* ".

" Must we then sheathe our still victorious sword;
    Turn back our forward step, which ever trod
O'er foemen's necks the onward path of glory;
    Unclasp the mail, which with a solemn vow,
In God's own house, we hung upon our shoulders;
    That vow, as unaccomplish'd as the promise
Which village nurses make to still their children,
    And after think no more of? "
                The Crusader: A Tragedy.

PILGRIMAGE is an ancient institution, and plays an important part in most religions, the fundamental conception being that the residence of the god is holy ground and that a visit thereto ensures spiritual and material benefits.

From very early times a pilgrimage to sacred Benares, situated on the holy Ganges, where the Hindu is purified and where of all places he would choose to die, has attracted and still attracts millions. Buddhism also drew its pilgrims from remote China, and one of these, Hsuan-tsang, as we have seen, added materially to our knowledge of Asia by his epoch-making travels.

In ancient Christian literature there is no special call to pilgrimage, but visits to the land which the feet of the Redeemer trod commenced in the second century. Perhaps the earliest reference to this subject is found in the writings of Origen, who lived early in the third century, and who states that at Bethlehem the cave in which Christ was born and the manger in which He was laid, were shown to visitors. At this period Bethlehem and the Mount of Olives were the places specially visited. The site of the Holy Sepulchre had been covered over with the debris of a mound erected by the Romans when they besieged Jerusalem, but Constantine had the ground cleared, and his mother Helena, who undertook a pilgrimage

PILGRIMS SETTING OUT FROM EUROPE (*above*); AND PAYING
TOLL ON LANDING IN PALESTINE (*below*)
(*From Harleian MSS. in British Museum*)

thither, not only built a church on the site, but is also credited
with the discovery of the True Cross and of its nails, which
were exhibited in her church. The earliest extant account
of a pilgrimage was written in 333 by an unknown author
who hailed from Bordeaux.

Of special interest to us is the pilgrimage of St. Willibald
the West Saxon, probably the first Englishman to visit the
Holy Land. He and his companions, early in the eighth
century, started from Hamble Mouth in Southampton Water,
with the original intention of proceeding no farther than
Rome. But having decided "to reach and gaze upon the
walls of that delectable and desirable city of Jerusalem", they
travelled to Naples, Syracuse, across Southern Greece and so
to Ephesus, whence they reached Cyprus, travelling most of
the way by land. From the port of Tortosa in Syria they
proceeded inland to Emesa, where they were arrested "as
strangers and unknown men", and were taken before the
Caliph, Yezid II. To his inquiry as to whence they came,
they replied: "From the western shore, where the sun sets,
and we know not of any land beyond—nothing but water."
The Caliph exclaimed "They have done no wrong; set them
free". St. Willibald died bishop of a Frankish see in 781,
and we owe this interesting account of his pilgrimage to his
biography written by a nun.

The great pilgrim route to Rome lay across the Alps by
what is now the Pass of St. Bernard, but was then called *Mons
Jovis* or Mount Joux, after a temple to Jupiter. Early in
the tenth century this important pass was seized by a band of
Saracens, who had established themselves at St. Tropez and
had penetrated to the Alps. Among their first victims were
French and English pilgrims, some of whom were killed.
Indeed, the pilgrims suffered great hardships in those early
days, and the percentage who never returned home must
have been very high. But to go on pilgrimage became a fixed
custom, as it remained until recently in Russia, and still is in
Persia and other Moslem countries. As Chaucer wrote:

> " And smale foules maken melodie
> That slepen alle night with open eye,
> So priketh hem nature in hir corages ;
> Than longen folk to gon on pilgrimages."

Pilgrimages to Palestine gradually increased until they were
numbered by thousands, and we are told that some 6,000
pilgrims were transported annually by the ships of the Knights

of St. John and of the Temple sailing from Marseilles, and that many more sailed from Italy. As their numbers increased, hospices were gradually erected for their exclusive use. The oldest one in the Alps was built in the Septimer Pass and dates from Carolingian times, while that on the Great St. Bernard is the best known. According to recent information its Canons are contemplating the foundation of a hospice on the frontier of Tibet, where, no doubt, they will render valuable services to exploration, as did their predecessors the Jesuits, frequently referred to in this work.

Pilgrims at first brought back little information, being absorbed in their visits to shrines and in the quest of a bone of a Saint or even a little dust from a tomb. In this connection the bones of the martyrs were exported from the catacombs at Rome and formed a staple article of commerce. We know also the importance that Venice attached to securing the bones of St. Mark from Alexandria. But as the years passed, views widened, and beautiful tissues, tiles, spices and other products of the East reached Europe, while her knowledge of the geography of Asia and of North Africa benefited in proportion. Such were the men and women pilgrims who in increasing numbers visited the Holy Sepulchre, until in 1010 the mad Fatimite ruler of Egypt, Hakim Biamrillah, destroyed the buildings of the Holy Sepulchre, thereby stirring Christendom to its depths. From that time the Crusades became inevitable, although not for many years did these armed pilgrimages, as they may be called, actually begin.

It is not sufficiently realized that Byzantium rendered invaluable service to the cause of civilization down the ages. Had Moawiyah captured the city in the seventh century, or Sulayman in the eighth, it is probable that the Arabs would have conquered the greater part of Europe at a time when her peoples were utterly unprepared for organized resistance.

The Crusades in the eleventh century marked a turning-point for benighted Europe. In 1016 the Pisans wrested Sardinia from the Moslems, and in 1060 the Norman conquest of Sicily, an amazing feat of arms, began. Later in that century, in 1072, Leon and Castille were united under Alfonso VI, who captured Toledo in 1085. When he died in 1108, the Christians, aided by Crusaders bound for the Holy Land, gradually gained the upper hand. So far as Byzantium was concerned, the position was much less favourable. For over three centuries the Moslems had made no progress against the Greek empire in Asia, but the appearance of the Seljuk Turks revitalized Islam. Togril Beg, the founder of the dynasty, was invested by the Caliph as ruler of the East and the West at Baghdad, and continuing his victorious career came into contact with the armies of Byzantium.

An interesting story is told of the *Nizam-ul-Mulk*, the celebrated Vizier of the Seljuks, which illustrates the extent of the empire and his power of organization. On the occasion of the Seljuk army crossing the Oxus, he paid the ferrymen by bills on Antioch, which were readily cashed.

Alp Arslan, the successor of Toghril, decisively defeated a numerically superior Byzantine army in 1071, at the battle of Manzikert. In this campaign we find mention of a body of Normans commanded by Ursel of Balliol, a kinsman of the Scottish King, who had indeed travelled far from his native heath. The spoils of the victors included most of the Byzantine provinces in Asia Minor, which in 1077 were formed into a separate state by their governor, Sulayman, a member of the ruling dynasty, who made Nicaea his capital. This branch of the Seljuks was known as the Seljuks of Rum.[1]

The position of Alexius the Emperor was pitiable. He appealed to the Pope for help to recover his lost dominions, and in 1095 Urban II addressed a great audience at Clermont, telling them how the cries of threatened Constantinople and oppressed Jerusalem were ringing in his ears. The Pope's knowledge of geography was somewhat vague, for he said that it would take two months to traverse the lands which "the accursed Persian race" had won from the Empire of Byzantium. The assembly was deeply moved, and to a mighty shout of "*Deus vult ! Deus vult !*" Urban launched the first Crusade. The appeal to mass enthusiasm was to redeem Jerusalem from the hands of the Saracens, who held the sacred soil that the Redeemer had trodden. The nobles were swayed by religious emotion, believing that death in action against the Paynims would gain them Heaven. They also no doubt hoped to carve out principalities or baronies for themselves, while thirst for honourable distinction on the field of battle was a very strong inducement among the knights.

The Venetians, Genoese, and men of other Italian states benefited enormously by the transport and victualling of the Crusaders, and generally supported the movement, although they were always equally ready to trade with the Saracens. From the point of view of the individual the movement was

---

[1] The Byzantine Empire was also known in the East as Rum, the word being a form of Rome.

the greatest manifestation of the pilgrim spirit. It was also of the highest value in teaching Europe geography, as in our own days was the Great War. Moreover, it strengthened the sea-power of Christendom. On the other hand the Crusaders, who never co-operated cordially with the Byzantine Emperors, in 1204 attacked and sacked Constantinople, the capital of the state they had sworn to save, while the powers of Europe never united to ensure the success of the sacred task to which they had solemnly pledged themselves.

The first Crusade was led by Duke Robert of Normandy and other experienced warriors. Indeed the Normans, recent converts to Christianity, constituted the steel head of the lance, just as the Seljuk Turks, recent converts to Islam, were their chief opponents in Asia Minor. The Crusaders assembled at Constantinople in 1097, and, crossing the Bosphorus, laid siege to Nicaea, which they captured. They decisively defeated Kilij Arslan, son of Sulayman, at Dorylaeum, and though he destroyed their supplies as far as possible, they marched across Asia Minor, suffering severe privations by the way. In October 1097 they besieged Antioch, which was captured after extraordinary vicissitudes of fortune. Two years later Jerusalem was stormed, its capture being followed by a deplorable massacre of its inhabitants, Moslems and Jews. As the result of this Crusade, Godfrey de Bouillon was elected " Defender of the Holy Sepulchre "—he refused the title of King—and held Jerusalem and Jaffa with less than 4,000 fighting men.

Three other Latin states were established ; Edessa, with its Armenian population, Antioch and Tripolis. In addition, various provinces of Asia Minor were recovered for the Byzantine Empire, mainly owing to the fact that the Seljuks were engaged in fighting among themselves after the death of Malik Shah in 1092, and that the Fatimids were weak at this period. The Crusaders were thus allowed to organize their conquests in peace, and a halo of glory surrounds the first Crusade, which constituted a sign that Christendom was awakening.

A generation later the situation had changed. The enemies of the Crusaders were the Seljuks of Asia Minor, already mentioned, the *Atabegs* of Mosul and the Fatimids of Egypt. In 1127 the Turk Zangi became *Atabeg* of Mosul, and in 1144 he captured Edessa. This disaster once more moved Europe and led to the second Crusade. The Emperor Conrad was first in the field, but his powerful army was cut to pieces ;

and the French under Louis VII of France fared little better. Consequently the second Crusade was a complete failure, but most fortunately the fall of Edessa was not followed up, as Zangi died shortly afterwards.

Nur-ud-Din his successor sent a force under his general Shirkuh to Egypt, and this ultimately resulted in the general's nephew Salar-ud-Din, the great Saladin, succeeding him as virtual ruler of Egypt. Upon the death of Nur-ud-Din Saladin made himself master of Syria, and concentrated his remarkable abilities on the overthrow of the Latin kingdom. In 1187, at the battle of Hattin, he decisively defeated Guy, King of Jerusalem, whose capital fell a few months later.

Again Europe was stirred, and the third Crusade was organized. Frederick Barbarossa was making a successful march across Asia Minor when he was drowned and his army melted away. Richard Cœur de Lion and Philip of France landed in Palestine in 1191 and captured Acre, after which success Philip, followed by his French knights, returned home. Cœur de Lion remained in Palestine and won deathless fame throughout Europe and the Moslem world, but lack of union and jealousies were too strong, while the sinews of war, gained from the spice trade, weighed down the scales on the side of the Moslems. Finally he was obliged to forgo the hope of reconquering Jerusalem for the Christians. Saladin, a worthy foeman of Cœur de Lion, granted the Crusaders liberal terms, leaving certain ports to them and guaranteeing free access to the Holy Sepulchre.

In the thirteenth century Egypt, which had become the centre of Moslem power, was the objective of more than one Crusade, culminating in that of St. Louis, who, after the capture of Damietta in 1249, was routed and taken prisoner by the Mamelukes of Egypt.

The Crusades practically ended with the expedition against Tunis, in which St. Louis died. But Prince Edward of England, afterwards King Edward I, led a small English force to Palestine. A few years after his departure from the Holy Land in 1272, the Latin states were finally overthrown.

It is a matter of extreme difficulty to estimate the exact results of the Crusades. There is, however, no question as to the immense advance in exploration to which they gave rise. Partly as the result of the far-reaching trade relations that were established, but still more owing to the missions which were an accompaniment of the Crusades, European knowledge of the Near East and of Egypt was much widened, not only by the voyages of tens of thousands of pilgrims and crusaders, but also by the books that were published, notably Jean de Joinville's *Life of St. Louis* and the history of William of Tyre. Of still greater importance, from the point of view of exploration, was the knowledge of Central Asia gained by the journey of John Plano de Carpini, who was despatched by Pope Innocent IV to the court of the *Kaan* or Great Khan at Karakoram in 1245 ; and William of Rubruquis, who was sent out by St. Louis in 1253, also visited the court of the *Kaan* at Karakoram. These journeys, whose great importance is evident, will be described in Chapter VIII.

As to the effect of the Crusades on the civilization of Europe, surely the fact that hundreds of thousands of men and thousands of women of all nations and of all classes were brought into contact with new people, saw new and wonderful things, encountered new ideas, and in some cases learnt an Oriental language or met with educated Saracens, can hardly be over-estimated. New plants, new fruits, such as lemons, apricots and melons, new manufactures, such as cotton, muslin, and damask came into use, and new words, such as cotton, satin, sofa, tariff, arsenal, admiral and magazine were introduced into Europe. Nor must we forget the great influence that the East exerted on European art, as in the case of the beautiful glass of Venice, the secret of which was learned in Tyre. The list is a long one ; for example, at Bokhara some twenty years ago I saw silver kettledrums on the horses of the mounted band of exactly the same pattern as those used in British Cavalry regiments. Even the hoods at Oxford and Cambridge are derived from the scarves of honour which the Caliphs awarded to learned men.

As to the question of sea-power, in which Europe ultimately found salvation from the Moslem menace, the Crusaders poured untold wealth into the states of Venice, Genoa and Pisa, which increased their fleets to meet the demand for the transport of pilgrims, armed and unarmed, and for the commerce fostered by the creation of the Latin states. Simultaneously there was improvement in sea-training, in ship-building and in the *portolani* or medieval sailing-charts, which led to the rediscovery of the Canary Islands in 1270 and to a Genoese expedition to the west coast of Africa some years later.

In London, the church of the Knights of the Temple, built in a circular form reminiscent of the church of the Holy Sepulchre, and consecrated in 1185 by the Patriarch of Jerusalem, constitutes a tangible link with the English Crusaders, whose armour-clad effigies carry us back to the days of Cœur de Lion.

" The Crusades ", writes Beazley, " are the central expression of Christian revival, and were entirely successful in kindling a spirit of patriotism and boundless enterprise, whereby our Western World finally attained to the discovery, conquest, colonization or trade-dominion of the best portions of the world."

CHAPTER VIII

MARCO POLO CROSSES ASIA

"I will go on the slightest errand now to the Antipodes that you can devise to send me on; I will fetch you a toothpicker now from the furthest inch of Asia; bring you the length of Prester John's foot; fetch you a hair off the great Cham's beard."

SHAKESPEARE, "*Much Ado about Nothing*," *Act III, Sc.* 1.

WE have now reached one of the greatest periods of exploration, but before dealing with it the stage must be set, and mention made of the forerunners of the illustrious Marco Polo.

Early in the thirteenth century a young Mongol chief fought his way to a position of supremacy, and, in 1206, assumed the title of Chengiz Khan. Campaign followed campaign in China, which was ever the main objective, but, in 1219, Chengiz decided to march west and conquered Central Asia, Persia and Russia. He died in 1227, but under the rule of his successor Ogotay the Mongols continued their conquests in Persia and raided Armenia and Syria. So far-reaching were these raids that, in 1244, they sacked Jerusalem and cut to pieces a force of Crusaders near Gaza. In Europe, under Batu, they advanced across Russia and devastated Poland and Hungary, while Germany lay at their mercy. Indeed, so widespread was the terror they inspired, that in 1238, to quote Matthew of Paris, "the people of Gottland and Friesland did not dare to visit Yarmouth for the herring fishery".

The death of Ogotay saved Central Europe, as the Mongols suddenly withdrew to attend the Diet for the election of his successor; but they riveted their hold on Russia for two centuries. In 1258, Hulaku Khan captured Baghdad, massacring its inhabitants and killing the Caliph. He dealt thereby a staggering blow to Moslem civilization, but the Mamelukes of Egypt defeated the Mongol invaders, and saved this important centre of Moslem culture. The western limits of the Mongol Empire in Asia were fixed by this defeat.

In Europe, upon the retirement of the invaders, the fears

that they had inspired began to give place to hopes that they might destroy the Moslems. There were also rumours as to the existence of Christian tribes among these savage horsemen, which were not without foundation.

In 1245, Innocent IV decided to despatch an embassy to the *Kaan*, to gain information as to the actual situation in Mongolia and to call on the ruler to adopt the Christian religion. John Plano de Carpini, a Franciscan monk, was selected for this dangerous task. Accompanied by Friar Benedict, a Pole, who was appointed to act as interpreter, he reached Batu's headquarters on the Volga. After some delay they started off on a post ride of 100 days, travelling day and night and suffering terribly from fatigue and hunger. However, their courage carried them through, and Carpini finally reached the Mongol camp near Karakoram at a time when a Diet was in session for the election of a successor to Ogotay.

Carpini gives an interesting account of the proclamation of Kuyuk at the Golden Orda. Two of Kuyuk's ministers were Christians, and so Carpini was well received by the *Kaan*, whom he describes as " very wise and politike, and passing serious and grave in all his demeanour ".[1] Carpini also considered that he was inclined to the Christian doctrine, but failed to win him as a convert. Letters to the Pope were given to the Franciscan, who, ignoring a suggestion that he should be accompanied by a Mongol envoy, set out on his long return journey. Carpini died shortly after his return to Europe, but the information he gave the Pope was of the greatest value, and proved that the Mongols were determined to wage war on Christendom. His descriptions of the countries he passed through and of the people he met are admirable.

We next come to the mission of William de Rubruquis, a Flemish monk, who was despatched by St. Louis to gain information as to the Christian tendencies of the Tartars. Like Carpini he was well treated, but suffered terribly from fatigue and hunger on the journey to Karakoram, where he found that Mangu was the *Kaan*. He was received kindly, and granted more than one audience, but Mangu, who was always half-drunk, never committed himself to an acknowledgment of his conversion to Christianity. Rubruquis met various Nestorian Christians, but, possibly from professional jealousy, could find nothing good to say of them. Perhaps the most important statement made by him related to : " Great Cathaya,

---

[1] *The Texts of John Plano de Carpini and William de Rubruquis*, edited by C. Raymond Beazley (Hakluyt Society, 1903).

the inhabitants whereof (as I suppose) were of old time called Seres." It is of interest to note that Roger Bacon not only " diligently read this book ", but talked with its author.

A third traveller of this period was Hayton I, King of Little Armenia, who had realized the power of the Mongols and had wisely submitted to them. In 1254 he proceeded to Karakoram to secure his position with Mangu. Hayton travelled by the famous Darband Pass on the west coast of the Caspian, and thence made for the Volga. He reached Karakoram by a route considerably to the north of that followed by the two Friars, and was received with honour by Mangu. On his return journey he passed through Otrar, Samarkand, Bokhara and Khorasan to Tabriz. Hayton related many wonderful things he had seen, and still more wonderful things he had heard.

Much credit is due to these three travellers, who visited the Mongol *Kaans* while they were still leading their nomad existence and give us a vivid picture of a life that was shortly to change to that of monarchs inhabiting magnificent palaces in China.

The story of the exploration of Asia by Nicolo Polo, his brother Maffeo, and Nicolo's son Marco, begins in 1260.[1] The vast empire of the Mongols acknowledged the supremacy of Kublai, who was elected *Kaan* in this very year, and removed the capital to Khan-baliq, the Cambaluc of Marco Polo, situated close to Peking, thereby founding a Chinese dynasty. In this year the two Polos were at Constantinople, and decided to cross the Greater Sea, as it was called, to Soldaia, situated to the west of Kaffa, where the family owned a house and had carried on business for two generations as jewellers. They decided to visit the court of Barka *Khan* at Sarai, the scene of Chaucer's *Cambynskan*, as he named Chengiz Khan.

> " At Sarra, in the Londe of Tartarie,
> There dwelt a Kyng that werriëd Russie,
> Thurgh which ther deyede many a doughty man,
> This nobil Kyng was cleped Cambynskan."

The Venetians were well received by Barka, to whom, in accordance with the custom of the country, they presented their entire stock of jewels. Barka accepted them, and " had twice their value given to the brothers ".

[1] I have consulted Yule's classic, *The Travels of Marco Polo*, as revised by Henri Cordier, 1903, and Professor Benedetto's remarkable *Marco Polo* (Broadway Travellers Series, 1931). The noble eulogy on the great Venetian explorer is by Yule, but other quotations are taken from Benedetto. I would thank Messrs. Murray for permission to quote from Yule's work.

The Polos had spent a year at Sarai when hostilities broke out with Hulaku, the captor of Baghdad, who is called Alau. In consequence of this, realizing that they could not retrace their steps owing to the disturbed state of the country, they determined to go eastwards " hoping to return by an indirect route ". Descending the Volga, which they called the Tigris, they travelled across the desert to Bokhara, described as " a very noble and large city ", as indeed it still was in the year before the Great War. The Polos remained at Bokhara for three years, seeking in vain to return home, when an envoy from Hulaku, bound for the court of the *Kaan*, appeared on the scene. Knowing that Kublai had never seen any " Latins ", he persuaded the two Venetians to accompany him to Cambaluc, where the *Kaan* received them most kindly. He was deeply interested in the information they gave him " concerning the Lord Pope and all the customs of the Latins ", and decided to send them back to Europe with letters to the Pope, in which he begged His Holiness to send him " some hundred wise men, learned in the law of Christ and conversant with the Seven Arts ", to preach to his people. He also " bade the two brothers bring him some oil from the lamp that burns near God's sepulchre in Jerusalem ". The Polos " toiled three years on the way " and finally, in 1269, reached Acre *via* the port of Ayas. There they found that the Pope had died, and on the advice of " a wise clerk who was Legate of the Church of Rome for the whole kingdom of Egypt " they returned to Venice, pending the election of a new Pontiff.

Two years later, " seeing that no new Pope had been chosen, they thought they ought not to delay any longer in returning to the *Kaan*. So they departed from Venice, taking with them the boy Marco, who was seventeen years of age. Before the party left the port of Ayas, the Legate had been elected Pope, and summoned them to return to Acre, where he furnished them with letters and " many splendid gifts " for the *Kaan*, while they had taken care to secure a flask of the sacred oil. The Pope also decided to send two preaching friars with the Polos, but unfortunately they feared to undertake the journey and turned back from Ayas. Had they been men of the stamp of Carpini or Rubruquis, they might well have converted Kublai and the Mongols to Christianity. No such opportunity as the invitation of the *Kaan* had ever been afforded, and the ignominious failure to take advantage of it is to be regretted.

Marco Polo begins his great work with an account of Lesser

Armenia, in which Ayas was situated. He next describes Greater Armenia, referring to Mount Ararat, and follows this up with a description of Georgia. He mentions the Caspian Sea, and states that the Euphrates, the Tigris and the Jon (the Jihon or Oxus) flow into it. He rounds off his account of this part of Asia with a short description of Baudas, as he calls Baghdad, and tells the story of the Caliph and Hulaku, an account which surely inspired Longfellow's " Kambalu ".

We are faced with the problem of deciding which route the Venetians followed, as, until they leave Yezd, no definite description of the way is given. Yule decided in favour of an itinerary which ran northwards through Arzinjan and then swung southwards to Mosul and Baghdad. Thence he led the Polos down the Tigris and the Shatt-al-Arab to Basra; from Basra to the island of Kisi (Keis), and so to Hormuz.

I am convinced that Yule was mistaken, as I do not believe that Marco visited Baghdad, nor that he descended the Tigris to the Persian Gulf.[1]

Marco almost certainly makes his survey of Persia from Tabriz, at which place he starts dealing with that country, but, with the typical medieval mind, he could not refrain from harking back to Baudas and telling his readers of a miracle there, returning afterwards to Tabriz and describing Persia from the geographical and commercial point of view.

Of Tabriz he writes that " the city is excellently situated, so that wares are brought thither from India, Baudas, Mosul and Cormus (Hormuz) and from many other regions besides. . . . One can also buy there precious stones, of which there is great abundance." After Tabriz, which is described as being in Iraq, the first city to be mentioned in Persia is Saveh, which, owing to the resemblance of its name to Sheba,[2] is stated to have been the home of the three Magi. He also visited the Cala Ataperistan, which signifies "the Fort of the Fireworshippers ", where he heard a legend of a miracle which obviously dated from the days of the ancient Zoroastrian religion.

There is no doubt that the Polos travelled along the main caravan route to Kazvin, which is mentioned as the first of the eight kingdoms into which Persia is divided, and thence

[1] The question is fully discussed in my *Ten Thousand Miles in Persia* and in the Cordier edition of Yule's great work. Sir Raymond Beazley, in *The Dawn of Modern Geography*, Vol. III, p. 49, accepts my views.

[2] Cp. Isaiah lx. 6; " The multitude of camels shall cover thee, the dromedaries of Midian and Ephah ; all they from Sheba shall come : they shall bring gold and incense."

to Sava and Kashan and so to Yezd, where reference is made
to the silk manufactures for which the city is still noted.

We then come to the first detailed description of the route,
which runs as follows : " When one leaves this region to
journey further, one travels for seven days over plains. . . .
There are many fine palm-groves, which one can ride through.
. . . There are also very fine wild asses. At the end of seven
days' journey one reaches a kingdom called Kirman." This
account furnishes a striking proof of the accuracy of Marco
Polo. There are two routes connecting Yezd and Kirman.
The eastern route lies throughout at an altitude of between
four and five thousand feet, where date palms could not grow.
On the western route, however, at Bafq, there are extensive
palm groves. There I have crossed a salt stream at the lower
altitude of 3,100 feet, and, looking northwards, seen a wide
salt expanse, the home of the *gur-i-khar* or wild ass.

At Kirman, Marco describes the embroideries for which
the city is still noted, in which connection the celebrated
shawls of Kashmir drew their models from the *shal* of Kirman.
At the time of the Venetians' first visit, the province was
ruled by an energetic lady named Turkan Khatun, and the
most noticeable building was the *Kuba-i-Sabz* or " Green
Dome ", erected by her family, which was still standing in
1895. It collapsed a year or two later.

The onward journey to the coast is again described as
riding for seven days over a plain in bitter cold when " one
reaches a very great mountain. After that begins a great
descent . . . after which one comes to a very vast plain, at
the beginning of which stands a city called Camadi ". In
tracing this section of the journey the first necessity is to
identify Camadi. In a *History of the Seljuks of Kirman*, the
Persian text of which was published some years ago, we read
that " Komadin was a suburb at the gate of Jiruft, a resort
of strangers from Turkey and Hind, and a meeting place of
travellers by sea and land." In 1894 I examined the site,
covered by thousands of kiln-burnt bricks, which the natives
are too indolent to utilize, contenting themselves with booths
made of boughs, or living as nomads in black tents. I also
made a small collection of seals and coins. In 1895, I undertook a journey to survey the unexplored district of Sardu,
which I discovered to be a very high-lying plateau terminating
in the Sarbizan pass. From this pass, situated at an elevation
of 9,000 feet, there is a very steep descent of some thirty
miles *via* Dilfard to the Jiruft Valley, in which lie the ruins

of Komadin, and this was undoubtedly the route followed by the Polos.

From Camadi the travellers descended the valley of the Halil Rud to the district of Reobar (Rudbar) where, as mentioned in Chapter II, Alexander the Great founded an Alexandria at Gulashkird. It was in this valley that Marco Polo crossed the route of his mighty predecessor. The onward journey to the coast lay down the Duzdi or " Robber " River, which I found, like Marco, to be " exceedingly bad and infested by robbers ". Indeed, we came on a caravan that had been looted on the previous day, and saw the cairn of stones which covered a camel-driver who had been killed.

The port of Hormuz was situated on the Minab River, the classical Anamis, where Nearchus beached his ships. Marco describes it as a great trade centre for " spices, precious stones, pearls, gold and silver cloths, elephants' teeth, and many other wares ".

Presumably the season for navigation was past, or else the Polos decided that " the very bad ships, which are not put together with iron, but sewn with twine ", were unsafe. In any case they turned their backs on Hormuz, returned to Kirman by a more westerly route, and then rode northwards to Cobinan or Kuhbanan, where " they make *tutia* (antimony) which is very good for the eyes ". In this connection may be quoted the Persian proverb : " The dust of a flock of sheep is *tutia* to the eyes of a hungry wolf."

The Polos had now reached the southern edge of the great desert of Persia, which constitutes its " dead heart ", and stretches for some 800 miles from the vicinity of Teheran to Baluchistan. Its width varies, and may average two to three hundred miles. It is the manifestation in an extreme form of the general aridity of Persia, itself surrounded by arid countries. To quote Marco's description : " One rides no less than eight days across a very arid desert, without fruits or trees." Of the water he says : " It is so bitter that no one could possibly drink it ; a single drop of it will purge a man violently." I believe myself to have been the first European to cross this desert in modern times by the same route as Marco Polo followed *via* Naiband and Duhuk,[1] and I can fully endorse his description. The trail is marked by dead animals and occasionally by corpses of travellers. Without a sign of bird or animal, it is indeed a land of death. The

[1] *Ten Thousand Miles in Persia*, p. 34 *et seq*. In the itinerary map Marco's route is shown as running through Tabas, but I do not accept this alignment.

Venetians fortunately escaped the " poison wind ", and also a storm that might have obliterated the track, and duly arrived at Tunocain—which signifies the two adjacent districts of Tun and Kain.

Marco at this point pauses to give an interesting account of the Assassins, his probable reason being that Hulaku had started his campaign for the extirpation of this sect at Tun some ten years previously.

From Tun the onward journey led north-east to Shiburghan —probably through ruined Herat—and thence to Balkh, the Bactra of Alexander and of Milton. This famous city had also been destroyed by the Mongols, who, on the pretence of counting its inhabitants, collected and then massacred them. Following up the valley of the Oxus in the footsteps of Hsuan-tsang, Marco gives an interesting account of Bala· shan (now Badakshan) and states that " the royal line descends from King Alexander . . . and their kings call themselves Zulcarnein ".[1] Marco refers to the Balas rubies which " are born in this country ", and, indeed, are still called after it. Better known is " the finest and best azure in the world ", the beautiful lapis lazuli, which was used by the goldsmiths of Ur in the fourth millennium B.C. The horses of Badakshan also are well bred and full of spirit.

The Polos spent a whole year in Badakshan, owing to Marco's illness, which he shook off only by visiting one of their mountains, " on the summit of which are broad plateaux, rich in grass and trees ". After Badakshan, he mentions Vocan or Wakhan, and proceeds : " One ascends so high that they say it is the highest place in the world. On reaching these heights, one finds a plain between the mountains, with a great lake, whence issues a very fine river. . . . There is an enormous number of wild sheep of very great size. Their horns reach a length of quite six spans. . . . To cross this plain one rides no less than twelve days. It is called Pamier."

Marco Polo was a true sportsman, as is proved time and again in his book, and when Wood, whose important journey is referred to in Chapter XXVIII, first brought specimens of these wonderful rams to England, the species was rightly named *Ovis Poli*.[2] For many years of my life, my chief ambition was to tread the Pamirs in the footsteps of Marco Polo and to shoot an *Ovis Poli*, and on no expedition that I have made does the golden haze of reminiscence lie more brightly than

---

[1] For Zulcarnein or Zulkarnain *vide* Chap. II, p. 14.
[2] The Royal Central Asian Society has recently adopted the *Ovis Poli* as its crest.

that on which I successfully stalked these mighty rams in the remote upland valleys of " The Roof of the World ".

To quote the stirring verse of Kipling :

"Do you know the world's white roof-tree—do you know that windy rift
　Where the baffling mountain-eddies chop and change ?
Do you know the long day's patience, belly-down on frozen drift,
　While the head of heads is feeding out of range ?
It is there that I am going, where the boulders and the snow lie,
　With a trusty nimble tracker that I know,
I have sworn an oath, to keep it on the horns of Ovis Poli,
　And the Red Gods call me out and I must go ! "

Marco reached the level plains with their large cultivated oases at Cascar or Kashgar, where he refers appreciatively to the splendid gardens and vineyards and fine farms. These must have offered a pleasing contrast to the Pamirs, where there is no cultivation, and where the Kirghiz consider a loaf of bread as a delicacy. He mentions the existence of a few Nestorian Christians. When I was residing at Kashgar, I tried to find out whether any custom that recalled Christianity was extant, and I was told that if a horse were not sold at a fair, the owner made the sign of the cross on its forehead to prevent its luck being spoilt.

From Kashgar the onward route lay through Yarkand, also a very fertile oasis, where Marco mentions the prevalence of goitre, still most distressing to-day. From Yarkand, crossing a bay of the desert which occupies the entire heart of the country, he reached Khotan. He makes no mention of the superb Kuen Lun range, which seems rather surprising. But when following in the footsteps of the illustrious Venetian, I realized that the atmosphere was seldom clear, and that it was only after a rare rainstorm that the snow-peaks appeared.

Khotan signifies the Kingdom of Jade, and still contains the pits dug in the dry river-bed, whence these valuable stones are " fished ". Marco, however, possibly by a lapse of memory, refers to jade in connection with Pem, which is believed to be Keryia, the next oasis to be reached by travellers bound for China. Then came Charchan, which still retains its name, and finally Lop, " which is a large city on the border of the Great Desert ". Sir Aurel Stein, our great authority on this part of Asia, who followed the route of Marco Polo across the Gobi, decided that at Charklik " he had indeed reached Lop ".[1]

----

[1] Vide *Ruins of Desert Cathay*, Vol. I, p. 336 *et seq.*

KUBLAI GIVES THE GOLDEN TABLET PAÏZAH TO THE BROTHERS POLO

(B.M. Royal Manuscript 19 ,D. I. ,fol. 59[b])

The Great Desert " where the width is least, is a month's journey. In all there are about twenty-eight places with water, and one must ride a day and a night to find water, which in three or four places is brackish and bitter, but elsewhere it is good." The Venetians reached the city of Sachin (Suhchan) in the province of Kansi, which they called Tangut, in safety, and Stein bears testimony to the remarkable accuracy of Marco's description. He surveyed the distance from " Lop ", across the Gobi, making it 380 miles, which is considered by traders as twenty-eight stages.[1]

The Venetians had now reached China proper, after having " toiled no less than three and a half years on the way, and the *Kaan* sent messengers to meet them at the distance of forty days' journey ". They heard that he was at his summer palace of Chandu, and upon their arrival, the three travellers paid their respects to Kublai and " presented the credentials and letters of the Pope, which pleased him exceedingly. They then handed over the holy oil, at which he rejoiced mightily, setting great store by it." Thus the Polos reached China, in the case of the two elder traversing the entire length of Asia for the third time, and, after an absence of some nine years, were warmly welcomed by the *Kaan*.

[1] *op. cit.*, p. 519.

CHAPTER IX

THE EXPLORATIONS OF MARCO POLO IN THE FAR EAST

"—I am become a name
For always roaming with a hungry heart.
Much have I seen and known; cities of men,
And manners, climates, councils, governments,
Myself not least, but honoured of them all."
                              TENNYSON, " Ulysses ".

MARCO POLO attracted Kublai's attention from the first, and set to work to learn " the customs, languages and manners of writing of the Tartars ".   He was consequently not only in close touch with the Court, but was employed on mission after mission by the *Kaan*, during which he explored far and wide, gaining more accurate information than any unofficial traveller could possibly have done.   At the same time he, generally speaking, took the Mongol point of view, and failed to study the Chinese as deeply as might have been expected.

Marco Polo's description of the palace of Chandu runs : " This palace on one side is bounded by the city wall, and from that point another wall runs out, enclosing a space of no less than sixteen miles, with numerous springs and rivers and meadows."   This account of Marco's was read by Coleridge, who fell asleep and dreamed :

"In Xanadu did Kubla Khan
    A stately pleasure-dome decree,
Where Alph, the sacred River, ran
Through caverns measureless to man
    Down to a sunless sea.
So twice five miles of fertile ground
With walls and towers were girdled round :
And there were gardens bright with sinuous rills
Where blossomed many an incense-bearing tree ;
And here were forests ancient as the hills,
    Enfolding sunny spots of greenery."

It was, however, by Marco's description of the winter palace at Cambaluc that the power and wealth of the *Kaan* were revealed to Europe.

"There is a great square wall with sides a mile long. In each corner stands a most beautiful and rich palace. . . . Further, in the middle of each side is another palace similar to those in the corners . . . and all eight palaces are full of war-equipment. Within this wall is another wall. Round it, also, are placed eight palaces, in which likewise war-harness is kept. In the middle of these circuits of walls rises the palace, the largest that was ever seen. It has no upper floor, but the basement is ten palms higher than the ground surrounding it, and the roof is surpassingly high. The inside walls are covered with gold and silver, and on them are painted beautiful pictures of ladies and knights and dragons and beasts and birds. The great hall is so vast that quite 6,000 men could banquet there. The beauty and size are so great that no one on earth could have built it better. The roof is varnished in vermilion, green, blue, yellow and all other colours, so that it glistens like crystal. Moreover, behind the palace there are great houses and halls where the treasures are kept and where his ladies and concubines live."

The palace opened on to a beautiful park well stocked with game.

At the feasts the guests were numbered by the thousand, and each pair of guests "had a golden cup with a handle, and with it he draws his drink from the large golden vessel, one of which is placed on the table for every two guests".

"On their New Year's Day, which comes in February, they all dress in white,[1] and all his subjects send the *Kaan* great gifts of gold, and silver and pearls and precious stones. . . . More than 100,000 splendid white horses are given to the *Kaan*. On that day his elephants, which amount to no less than 5,000, all covered with fine cloths, and each bearing two surpassingly beautiful coffers full of the Lord's plate, . . . and an immense number of camels, also covered with rich cloths, and loaded with the things necessary for this feast, file past the *Kaan*."

Marco gives a detailed account of the use of paper money by the Mongols, beginning with a description of the paper, which was manufactured from the "thin layer of the skin that lies between the bark and the trunk of the mulberry trees".[2] Paper money originated under the Tang dynasty, but the use of it was greatly extended by the Mongols. According to Marco, the *Kaan* bought up all the gold and jewels in the country with paper money, and the army was paid with it. He concludes: "All the princes in the world do not together possess the wealth of the *Kaan*." No wonder the Venetians gave Marco the sobriquet of *Il Milione*!

---

[1] White is the dominant colour in the rejoicings at the Persian New Year, but it is the colour of mourning in China.

[2] Similar paper is made to-day at Guma in Chinese Turkestan. Vide *Through Deserts and Oases of Central Asia*, p. 198.

Marco's first mission was to distant Carajan or Yunnan, to the south-west, and he was four months on the road. Some ten miles from Cambaluc, he crossed the San-Kan River, and described Pulisanghin with its beautiful marble bridge. Everywhere on the way to the city of Taiwanfu (T'ai-yuan) " one comes across many fine cities and towns, with much trade and industry, beautiful fields and splendid vineyards ".

The great River Caramoran—the Hwang-Ho or " Yellow River "—is " so wide that there is no bridge that can span it . . . Along the river there are numerous cities and towns, with many merchants and thriving trade."

Of Kenjanfu, the province of Shan-si, Marco writes : " They have great quantities of silk. Gold and silk cloths of all kinds are made there. They have all the necessaries of life in great abundance and very cheap."

The mountainous province of Cuncun (Han-chung) is next traversed, and Marco refers with keen interest to the wonderful sport—" lions, bears, lynxes, fallow-deer, roes, stags and many more ". After riding for twenty days " through mountains and valleys ", Marco reached level country in the province of Acbaluc Manji or the " White City on the border of Manji ". Again mountains are entered and traversed for another twenty days to the province of Sindufu or Cheng-tu-fu. The capital of the same name is situated on tributaries of the " Kiansui, which flows into the Ocean sea, at a distance of some eighty or a hundred days' journey. There is much shipping on it, such a number of ships as no one who has not seen them could ever credit. So big is the river, that you would rather think it a sea than a river." Here again we have a definite fixed point, for Cheng-tu is the capital of Ssu-chwan, and the great river is the celebrated Yang-tze-kiang, or Yangtze.

From fertile Ssu-chuan Marco continued his long journey, crossing a province of Tibet which he found devastated. " During all those twenty days' journey one finds no hostelries nor any supplies, except perhaps every three or four days." He refers to the coral necklaces " hung as a token of great joy round the necks of their idols and women ". When I travelled in the Pamirs, I was particularly struck by the number of coral necklaces that were worn, in view of the remoteness of the country from the sea.[1] Marco also mentions that they were worn by the women of Kashmir. Again, Marco describes the " very large mastiffs as big as

[1] *Through Deserts and Oases of Central Asia*, p. 118.

donkeys ". They are extremely fierce, and I recollect that
when travelling in Lesser Tibet some forty years ago, I waited
until the dogs were held before approaching an encampment.

Gaindu (Chien-chang), a region of Eastern Tibet, is next
described, with its great salt lake where salt loaves " as big
as a twopenny loaf " serve as currency with the *Kaan's* seal
imprinted on them. In Gaindu mention is made of the abundance of gold, especially from the River Brius or Chinsa-
Chiang, which aptly signifies the " River of Golden Sand ".

At last the wayworn explorer reached the province of
Carajan or Yunnan, " which is so large that it comprises no
less than seven kingdoms. One rides five days west to the
most important city called Yachi or Yunnan-fu. They have
a lake quite one hundred miles in circuit. On leaving Yachi
and travelling ten days westwards, one reaches the kingdom
of Carajan." Here Marco first hears of the crocodile, which
he describes as " a great snake having a very big head, and eyes
larger than a big loaf; their mouth is so big, that they can
swallow a man whole ". The farthest province of Yunnan
he termed Zardandan,[1] with its capital of Vochan or Yung-
chang-fu. " All the people ", he says, " have gold teeth;
that is to say, each tooth is covered with gold." He also
describes tattooing, and the strange custom of the *couvade*.

From Yunnan the tireless explorer rode downhill for two
and a half days, and reached " a province towards the south,
on the borders of India, called Mien (Burma). One travels
fifteen days through difficult country and great forests, where
there are elephants and unicorns in great numbers." He describes the capital, with its gold and silver towers, and the
conquest of the country by the Mongols.

We now leave Cathay and turn to Manji,[2] with its capital,
the famous city of Kinsai or Hang-chow, the " City of Heaven ".
To quote Marco :

> " On one side it has a beautifully clear fresh water lake; on the
> other side there is a very large river, which flows into every part of the
> city along a multitude of canals. There are ten principal squares,
> with sides half a mile long. In front of them is the main street, forty
> paces broad, running from one end of the city to the other; it is crossed
> by many bridges. All the aforesaid squares are surrounded by tall
> houses. Below these are shops. The citizens are idolators. They

[1] Yule considered that Persian was the colloquial language of foreigners at the Court
of the *Kaan*. To give instances from Marco Polo, Zardandan signifies " Gold-teeth "
in Persian, and Pulisanghin is probably *pul-i-sangi* or " stone bridge " in the same
language. On the other hand " Caramoran " and " Acbaluc " are Mongol words.
[2] This name as applied to Southern China originated in a nickname signifying
" Southern Ruffians ".

eat all kinds of flesh, including that of dogs. The majority always dress in silk, which is due to its great abundance. . . . They carry on their crafts and trade with great honesty. There are twelve guilds, one for each of the principal crafts, each guild possessing 12,000 workshops with not less than ten men in each shop."

The population was numbered by millions, and the revenue exceeded 20,000,000 golden ducats ; as Marco wrote, " it is the noblest and richest city in the world ". There is no doubt that the great explorer was fully justified in making this statement.

Continuing his survey southwards, Marco describes the city of Fu-Chow. One of the most important of Professor Benedetto's additions consists of an account of some of its inhabitants, whom, after making inquiries, the Polos took to be Christians. " They had three painted figures representing three apostles—three of the seventy who went about preaching." Pelliot, however, assures us that this was a community of Manichaeans, whose pessimistic religion, referred to in Chapter III, spread from Persia to the Pacific Ocean on the East and to the Atlantic on the West.

South of Fu-Chow lay the great port of Zaitun, identified with Chuan-Chow-fu north of Amoy. Here Marco describes the great ships which have sixty cabins and are divided up into " thirteen tanks or compartments ", by which arrangement many shipwrecks are avoided. These great ships " need 300 sailors ".

Marco Polo served the *Kaan* " no less than seventeen years, and during all that time never ceased going upon missions ". The Polos were anxious to return to Venice with their garnered wealth, but the *Kaan* was unwilling to part with them. However ambassadors appeared on the scene from Arghun, the *Ilkhan* of Persia, who asked for a " lady of the lineage of his wife Queen Bolgana, who had died ". The *Kaan* " received them honourably, and gave them a hospitable welcome. Then he summoned a lady called Cocachin, who was seventeen years old, and most beautiful and charming." They accordingly started off with the Princess, but found the land route impracticable owing to disturbances and returned to Cambaluc. There they met Marco, who had just completed a mission in India, and, probably at his suggestion, they begged the *Kaan* to send them back to Persia by sea and to allow the experienced Polos to accompany them.

The *Kaan* somewhat unwillingly complied with these requests, and prepared a squadron of fourteen ships to escort

the Princess to Persia. The voyage to Java took three months.
" This island is immensely rich. They have pepper, nutmegs,
spikenard, galingale, cubebs,[1] cloves : in a word all the precious
spices one can think of. The greater part of the spices sold in
the world come from this island." Continuing the voyage,
Marco Polo describes the islands as he passes, his Java the
Less being undoubtedly Sumatra, where Marco saw a rhino-
ceros, which he calls a unicorn. The flotilla was detained
five months in this island, where the crews were landed, and
constructed a strong fortress as a defence against the natives,
who were cannibals.

In due course the island called Seilan (Ceylon) was reached.
Marco refers with the enthusiasm of an expert to the most
beautiful ruby in the world, owned by the King ; it " is about
a palm long and quite as thick as a man's arm ".[2] He also
gives an interesting account of Sagamoni Borcan or " Sakya-
muni Buddha ". He refers to Adam's Peak, but states that
" the idolators say it is the sepulchre of Sagamoni Borcan ".

From Ceylon Marco visited " the great province of Maa-
bar ", which is now termed the Coromandel Coast. As a
jeweller he naturally refers in detail to the valuable pearl
fisheries. He also describes with enthusiasm the mass of
jewels worn by the King round his neck, arms, legs and on
his toes. After the pearls we hear of the diamonds at Mutfili
or Telingana and how they are procured.

"You must know that there are certain great, deep gullies, with
such precipitous sides that no one can go to the bottom of them. But
this is what the people do ; they take many pieces of raw and bleeding
flesh, and throw them into the gullies. The places into which the
flesh is thrown are full of diamonds, which get stuck to the flesh. Now
you must know that on these mountains there are many white eagles,
that feed on serpents. When they see the pieces of flesh at the bottom
of the gullies, they swoop down upon them, and carry them away.
Then the men, who have all the time been carefully watching whither
the eagles fly, as soon as they see them settled down and tearing the
flesh, hasten thither as fast as possible. The eagles fly away, and, in
their fear at seeing the men suddenly coming upon them, do not carry
the flesh away with them ; on reaching the spot where the flesh lies,
the men take it, and find plenty of diamonds stuck to it."

This industry also is described in the *Arabian Nights*.

In the Pepper Country Marco visited the famous port of
Coilum or Quilon, and refers to its brazil wood, its pepper
and its indigo. His description of the animal and bird life
merits quotation.

[1] Galingale is a species of ginger ; cubebs a variety of pepper.
[2] Sindbad the Sailor refers to this ruby in the passage quoted at the head of Chap. V.

"There are many strange animals, differing from those in any other part of the world. Thus, I assure you they have certain black lions, with not a spot or mark of any other colour on them. There are various kinds of parrots : some are white as snow, with vermilion beaks and legs ; others are vermilion and blue, and they are the prettiest things in the world to look at ; others again are green ; there are some very small ones, too, that are also exceedingly pretty. Their peacocks are much bigger and more beautiful than ours."

On continuing the voyage northwards, we are told of the province of Lar or Gujerat, where Marco was much impressed by the Brahmins, "who eat no meat, drink no wine and lead a very chaste life. They would kill no living creature." Again, "they have among them certain regulars known as Chughi or Yogis, who live from a hundred and fifty to two hundred years. They take quicksilver and sulphur, and mix them together, making a drink with them, and they say that it prolongs life. I would add that for nothing in the world would they kill a fly or a flea or a louse."

From Gujerat, we hear of Canbaet (Cambay) and Semenat or Somnat, with its "exceedingly cruel and fierce idolators", and so, coasting Kesmacoran (Kej-Makran), where Marco was following in the wake of Nearchus, he finally reaches the familiar harbour of Hormuz. Here the voyage ended, but at what a cost ! Without counting the sailors, out of 600 passengers, "all died except eighteen, and of Arghun's three envoys, only one survived". Fortunately the beautiful Coca-chin arrived in Persia safe and sound. Her intended husband Arghun had died in the meanwhile, but no doubt she much preferred to marry his son Ghazan, who was the greatest of the Ilkhan rulers of Persia. Marco tells us that "when the three envoys after the fulfilment of their mission bade the Princess farewell, she wept for sorrow at their departure".

In 1295, the wayworn Polos after an absence of twenty-five years reached Venice, where their reception may be compared to that accorded to their great prototype Ulysses.

Marco Polo has been criticized for not mentioning the use of tea as a beverage, and certainly the existence of the art of printing escaped his notice, although he describes the manufacture of paper money in some detail. As to the alleged overlooking of the Great Wall of China, his mention of the "place that in our country is known as Gog and Magog" tends to show that he was referring to it.[1]

In any case, these omissions are of very minor import-

---

[1] *Vide* Yule, Vol. I, p. 292, note.

MINIATURE IN THREE COMPARTMENTS

(a) The Emperor Baldwin and the Brothers Niccolo and Matteo Polo in Constantinople
(b) The Brothers Polo before the Legate Tebaldo de Vicenza
(c) The Brothers Polo set sail for the Black Sea

(*B.M. Royal Manuscript* 19, *D.I., fol.* 58(a))

ance. Exploration gained as never before in the history of Europe, and when I made a pilgrimage to the great explorer's house in the *Corte del Milione*, I felt that I was paying homage not merely to Venice's most illustrious citizen, but to the greatest of European explorers by land.

Marco Polo has been fortunate in finding a great biographer in Sir Henry Yule, and this chapter may fittingly be closed with a quotation from his noble eulogy :

" He was the first Traveller to trace a route across the whole longitude of Asia, naming and describing kingdom after kingdom which he had seen with his own eyes ; the Deserts of Persia, the flowering plateaux and wild gorges of Badakshan, the jade-bearing rivers of Khotan, the Mongolian steppes, cradle of the power that had so lately threatened to swallow up Christendom, the new and brilliant Court that had been established at Cambaluc : the first Traveller to reveal China in all its wealth and vastness, its mighty rivers, its huge cities, its rich manufactures, its swarming population, the inconceivably vast fleets that quickened its seas and its inland waters ; to tell us of the nations on its borders with all their eccentricities of manners and worship ; of Tibet with its sordid devotees ; of Burma with its golden pagodas and their tinkling crowns ; of Laos, of Siam, of Cochin China, of Japan, the Eastern Thule, with its rosy pearls and golden-roofed palaces ; the first to speak of that Museum of Beauty and Wonder, still so imperfectly ransacked, the Indian Archipelago, source of those aromatics then so highly prized and whose origin was so dark ; of Java the Pearl of Islands ; of Sumatra with its many kings, its strange costly products, and its cannibal races ; of the naked savages of Nicobar and Andaman ; of Ceylon, the Isle of Gems, with its Sacred Mountain and its Tomb of Adam ; of India the Great, not as a dream-land of Alexandrian fables, but as a country seen and partially explored, with its virtuous Brahmans, its obscene ascetics, its diamonds and the strange tales of their acquisition, its sea-beds of pearl, and its powerful sun ; the first in medieval times to give any distinct account of the secluded Christian Empire of Abyssinia, and the semi-Christian Island of Socotra ; to speak, though indeed dimly, of Zanzibar with its negroes and its ivory, and of the vast and distant Madagascar, bordering on the Dark Ocean of the South, with its Ruc and other monstrosities ; and, in a remotely opposite region, of Siberia and the Arctic Ocean, of dog-sledges, white bears, and reindeer-riding Tunguses."

CHAPTER X

IBN BATTUTA, THE GREATEST MOSLEM EXPLORER

"The Sultan sits cross-legged on a throne placed on a dais
carpeted in white. A hundred armour-bearers stand on the
right and a like number on the left, carrying shields, swords,
and bows. Fifty elephants are brought in, which are adorned
with silken cloths, and have their tusks shod with iron for
greater efficacy in killing criminals. These elephants are
trained to make obeisance to the Sultan, and when they do so,
the chamberlains cry in a loud voice *Bismillah*."
The Durbar of Muhammad ibn Tughlaq.

MARCO POLO opened the land-gates and the water-gates of
China to Christian travellers, among whom was John de
Monte Corvino, who died Archbishop of Peking. He was
followed by Friar Odoric, who wandered over Asia and
visited Lhasa. An explorer of quite a different kind, and
the greatest of all Moslem explorers, was Muhammad ibn
Abdulla, Ibn Battuta, an inhabitant of Tangier, who belonged
to a family of *Kazis* or Judges.

In 1325, when twenty years of age, he set out on his wonderful series of journeys, which lasted for some thirty years and
covered an even wider range than those of Marco Polo.
The original object of Ibn Battuta was to perform the pilgrimage to Mecca, and, in the first instance, he travelled by
land across Northern Africa to Alexandria, where he inspected
the famous lighthouse. He visited Damietta, and proceeded
thence to Cairo, which he enthusiastically describes as "mother
of cities and seat of Pharaoh the tyrant, mistress of broad
regions and fruitful lands, boundless in multitude of buildings,
peerless in beauty and splendour ".[1]

From Cairo Ibn Battuta "travelled into Upper Egypt
with the intention of crossing the Red Sea to Hejaz ". He
passed through Assiut and Luxor and traversed the desert to
the port of Aydhab, situated on the Red Sea opposite Jeddah.
Owing to disturbances no ships were sailing, and accordingly,

[1] Vide *Ibn Battuta*, by H. A. R. Gibb (Broadway Travellers Series), on which valuable
work I have mainly relied in this chapter, and from which my quotations are taken.
Sir Percy Cox has read this chapter and made valuable suggestions.

changing his plans, he returned to Egypt, determined to make the pilgrimage from Damascus.

Crossing the desert to Gaza, he visited Hebron, Bethlehem and Jerusalem, where he describes the celebrated Dome of the Rock. He also visited Acre, Tyre and Tiberias, and mentions the Sea of Galilee. He travelled through the states founded by the crusaders, visiting Tripoli, Kerak, once the great fortress of the Knights of St. John, and Antioch, and refers to the Syrian branch of the Assassins, " who are the arrows of the Sultan. By means of them he strikes those of his enemies who escape into other lands." Damascus, on which fair city Mohammed based his description of Paradise, " surpasses all other cities in beauty, and no description, however full, can do justice to its charms ".

Ibn Battuta was the first explorer of Arabia, and the vivid account which he gives of the pilgrimage to Mecca is of great importance. Starting from Damascus on September 1, 1326, and passing Kerak, the caravan reached Maan, the last town in Syria, and entered the desert of which it is said : " He who enters it is lost, and he who leaves it is born." Tabuk he describes as " the place to which the Prophet led an expedition ". A four days' halt was made at this station in view of the " terrible desert between Tabuk and Al-Ula ".

At Al-Hijr " in some hills of red rock, are the dwellings of Thamud. They are cut in the rock and have carved thresholds ". The story of the destruction of the tribe for disobedience is given in the Koran : " Whereupon a great earthquake overtook them with a noise of thunder, and in the morning they lay dead in their houses, flat upon their breasts." It was the examination of these tombs that first inspired Doughty to start on his wanderings in Arabia from this station, later known as Madain Salih. Doughty also visited Al-Ula or Al-Ala.

At Medina, Ibn Battuta prayed in the illustrious " garden ", situated between the tomb of the Prophet and the noble pulpit, and he reverently touched the remaining fragment of the palm-trunk against which Mohammed stood when he preached. In the onward journey a good description is given of the stages to Mecca, where Ibn Battuta duly performed the rites of the pilgrimage.

The journey of the great Moslem explorer from Medina across Arabia to Baghdad is of still greater importance. Leaving Mecca in November, he returned to Medina. From this city to Baghdad the pilgrim route, thanks to the generosity of Zubayda, wife of Harun-al-Rashid, was provided with reservoirs wherever there was water; and its stages are given by Hamdani, who calculates the distance between Medina and Faid at 234 English miles.

Four stages from Medina, the narrative continues, "we entered the land of Nejd, which is a level stretch of country extending as far as the eye can see, and we inhaled its fine scented air". Faid, the ancient capital of Nejd, situated some four stages to the south-east of Hail, is described as lying half-way between Mecca and Baghdad. From Faid onwards, the only difficulty was the defile known as the "Devil's Pass", beyond which was Waqîsa, with its water-tanks guarded by a castle. Upon entering Iraq, Ibn Battuta makes a reference to Kadesiya, "where the famous battle was fought against the Persians, in which God manifested the triumph of the religion of Islam". Later he gives an accurate description of the tomb of Ali at Najaf, with its silver threshold which is kissed by the devout pilgrim.

From Najaf the traveller set out for Basra, and thence to Ubulla, occupying the site of modern Basra, a place of palm groves and shady canals. From Basra he made an excursion into Central Persia, visiting picturesque Shushtar, with its dam constructed by Roman prisoners,[1] and so across the mountains to Isfahan and Shiraz. Of the latter city Ibn Battuta writes: "In the whole East there is no city that approaches Damascus in beauty of bazaars, orchards and rivers, but Shiraz." He then extols the Ruknabad River, which to-day is a very small rill. It must have shrunk to a minor measure since Hafiz sang:

> "Tell them, their Eden cannot show
> A stream so clear as Ruknabad."

Among the sanctuaries he mentions the grave of Sadi, whom he describes as the greatest poet of his time, and whose tomb I have myself visited more than once. Indeed I felt a deep affection for Shiraz, without going as far as Sadi, who wrote: "Even the stranger forgets his home, and becomes its willing thrall."

From Shiraz Ibn Battuta travelled to Kazerun, and returning to Mesopotamia, visited Kufa, which gave its name to Kufic writing, and was at one time the capital of the Caliphate. Baghdad had not recovered from its sack by Hulaku Khan, and mosques and colleges alike were in ruins. Of

[1] Vide *Ten Thousand Miles in Persia*, p. 253.

considerable interest was Ibn Battuta's meeting with Abu Said, the last of the Ilkhan rulers of Persia, in whose suite he travelled to Tabriz, where he struck Marco Polo's route. He then visited Samarra and Mosul. Thence he went to Nisibis, "an ancient town for the most part in ruins". This was the great frontier fortress of Rome, ceded to Persia after the disaster suffered by Julian in A.D. 363.[1]

Ibn Battuta returned to Mecca from Baghdad in 1327, and settled there for three years, partly no doubt with the intention of increasing his standing by studying under the leading doctors of the sacred law. In 1330 he again set off on his travels, and explored Yemen, the classical *Arabia Felix*, giving a good account of the three towns of Zabid, Taiz and Sanaa, and, in ignorance of the regular south-west monsoon, noticed that the rain only fell in the hot weather. From Yemen he proceeded to Aden, which "is surrounded by mountains and can be approached from one side only ; it has no crops, trees, or water, but has reservoirs in which rain-water is collected". The well-known port could hardly be better described.

From Aden, Ibn Battuta, following in the footsteps of Masudi, voyaged down the east coast of Africa, stopping at Zeila, "the town of the Berberah, who are a negro people. It is a city with a great bazaar, but it is the dirtiest town in the world." From Zeila fifteen days' sail brought the traveller to Magdashaw (Mogdishu), where he was well received, and noted that the *Shaykh*, who was of Berberah origin, knew Arabic. Ibn Battuta continued his voyage to Mombasa and Kilwa, and, at the latter port, was told of Sofala, "lying a fortnight's journey (south) from Kilwa", where gold dust could be bought.

From the African coast, Ibn Battuta touched at Dhufar, the Frankincense Land, and then reached Oman. Passing Sur, he landed and described the interior of the country, and then entered the Persian Gulf. He mentions Hormuz, situated on the coast, twice visited by Marco Polo ; and "nine miles from the shore is New Hormuz, which is an island. It is a large and fine city with busy markets." Hormuz is an extremely desolate island. The land is covered with salty efflorescence, while a bare, rugged range of volcanic origin crosses the island. There is no fresh water, and the city depends on tanks to catch the scanty rainfall and on water brought from the neighbouring island of Kishm. Yet Hormuz

[1] *Vide* Sykes, *History of Persia* (3rd ed.), Vol I, p. 422.

(or Ormus) became the emporium of the East, and of it Milton wrote :

> "High on a throne of royal state, which far
> Outshone the wealth of Ormus and of Ind,
> Or where the gorgeous East with richest hand
> Showers on her kings barbaric pearl and gold,
> Satan exalted sat."

From Hormuz Ibn Battuta made an excursion inland, visiting Lar and returning to the coast at Qays, the Kisi of Marco Polo. He then described the pearl fisheries and the Bahrein Islands, which I consider to be the only pleasant spot in the torrid Persian Gulf. Landing on the Hasa coast in 1332, the tireless voyager made a second journey across Arabia, of which he gives no description, merely mentioning Yamama, which, at that period, was the capital. But he evidently followed the pilgrim route which Philby explored some six centuries later. Ibn Battuta thus crossed Arabia in both directions by different routes.

His next journey led him to Anatolia. He landed at Alaya and thence coasted to Adaliya, the principal port of Anatolia, which was ruled by petty chiefs. He then made for Iconium where he visited the mausoleum of Jalal-ud-Din Rumi, the founder of the *Mevlevi* or "dancing dervishes", and the greatest of Islamic mystical poets. Continuing his wanderings he visited Ephesus, where he bought a Greek slave-girl for forty *dinars* or twenty guineas, and so to Smyrna, which he described as being "mostly in ruins".

At Brusa he gives a valuable account of the tribe of Osmanlis. "The Sultan of Brusa was Orkhan Beg, son of Othman Chuk. It was his father who captured Brusa from the Greeks; his son besieged Nicaea twelve years before he captured it, and it was there that I saw him." Continuing his journey Ibn Battuta visited Kastamuni, where British officers were imprisoned during the Great War, and from Sinope he crossed the Black Sea to Kaffa. An excellent description is given of a journey to Sarai and a visit to Constantinople, where he touches the lands described by the elder Polos.

The next journey of the indefatigable traveller led him to the fertile oasis of Khwarizm or Khiva, with its capital Urganj, "the largest, greatest, most beautiful and most important city of the Turks", which was destroyed by Chengiz. From Urganj, Ibn Battuta struck the route of the elder Polos at Bokhara, and visited Samarkand, destined before long to become the capital of Tamerlane.

From Samarkand he crossed the Oxus at Tirmiz, thereby entering the province of Khurasan, as it then was, and reached Balkh, which he describes as having been utterly ruined by Chengiz Khan. Thence he travelled to Herat, which had been rebuilt after its destruction, and continuing his journey reached Meshed, the burial-place of the *Imam* Riza and of the celebrated Harun-al-Rashid. He describes the beautiful tile-work, and the " great dome of elegant construction " which a Safavi monarch some two centuries later covered with gold plates. Nishapur too had been rebuilt on its present site, and its manufacture of silk and velvet is mentioned.

Ibn Battuta had determined to visit India, and accordingly he crossed the Hindu Kush or " Slayer of Indians ", whose name, he explains, originated from the number of slave-boys and slave-girls who died there from the cold. After the passage of the Hindu Kush, he reached Charikar, which is probably the site of Alexandria *ad Caucasum*, mentioned in Chapter II. He then visited Ghazna, " the town of the famous warrior-sultan Mahmud ibn Sabuktagin ", who is known in the East as the " idol-breaker ". He finally reached the Indus in September 1333 with the remark " Here ends the narrative of this journey. Praise be to Allah, Lord of the Worlds."

In no section of his journeys does Ibn Battuta show to greater advantage than in India. He was treated as a distinguished Moslem, and consequently was in a position to turn his residence of some eight years to good account. His object was to enter the service of Muhammad ibn Tughlaq, who welcomed men of position to his court and gave them posts of great importance.

At Multan he received an invitation to the Court at Delhi, a march of forty days. His keen eye noted the strict rules of caste as regards eating alone and being unobserved while eating. He also commented on the awful rite of *sati*, at which he assisted—and fainted. Again he referred to the practice of Indians drowning themselves in the sacred Ganges " to seek approach to *Kusay*,[1] *Kusay* being the name of God in their language ".

The distinguished traveller was warmly welcomed by the Sultan, whom he aptly describes as being " the fondest of making gifts and of shedding blood ". He was appointed a *kazi* and treated most generously. He was also made guardian of the Mausoleum of Sultan Qutb-ad-Din. Among the most

---

[1] *Kusay* is probably Krishna.

amazing acts of Muhammad Tughlaq was that of compelling the inhabitants of Delhi, whom he disliked, to leave that city and to proceed to Dawlatabad. To quote our author:

> "The majority complied with the order, but some of them hid in the houses. The Sultan ordered a search, and his slaves found two men in the streets, one a cripple and the other blind. He gave orders that the cripple should be flung from a mangonel and the blind man dragged from Delhi to Dawlatabad. He fell to pieces on the road, and all of him that reached Dawlatabad was his leg. It was in this state that we found Delhi on our arrival, empty and unpopulated."

Ibn Battuta resided at the court of this monster for nearly eight years. He remained in favour for a long time, but his curiosity, which prompted a visit to a *Shaykh* who was suspect, nearly caused his execution. However, by assuming the rôle of a hermit and giving away his property to the poor, he regained the royal favour, and was appointed an ambassador to the court of China.

The embassy started "accompanied by the Chinese ambassadors, fifteen in number" with an escort of a thousand cavalry, and some infantry. Not far from Delhi they engaged in a campaign against some rebels, during the course of which Ibn Battuta was captured, stripped, and only just escaped with his life. The ambassadors then resumed their journey, and mention is made of a "Sultan of Janbil who was killed after besieging Gwalior". This reference is to the Raja of Dholpur. The journey continued through Dhar, the chief city of Malwa, and so to Dawlatabad, which Muhammad, realizing its importance as a base for further conquests in Southern India, wished to make his capital. The sea was reached at Cambay, and at Gandhar the ambassadors embarked. They touched at the island of Sandabar, destined under the name of Goa to be the seat of the Portuguese dominion in the East, and in due course reached the land of Malabar, "which is the Pepper country". Ibn Battuta gives an excellent account of this coast. He finally landed at Calicut, where the embassy stayed for three months "awaiting the season of the voyage to China".

Disaster again befell the unfortunate Ibn Battuta, for, after the ships were laden, "the junk which carried the Sultan's presents and all on board were drowned. When those on the *Kakam* [1] saw what had happened to the junk, they spread their sails and went off, with all my goods and slave-boys and slave-girls on board, leaving me alone on the beach." After attempting in vain to rejoin his ship by land and then

[1] A smaller vessel on which Ibn Battuta had arranged to sail.

taking part in a successful attack on Sandabar, Ibn Battuta heard from two of his slaves who had returned to Calicut that "the ruler of Java the Less [Sumatra?] had taken my slave-girls, that my goods had been seized by various hands, and that my companions were scattered to China, Sumatra and Bengal". Thus was enacted a scene which constitutes an epitome of the dangers attending sea voyages in the Middle Ages, and might well be a chapter taken from the adventures of Sindbad the Sailor.

To this misfortune we owe the first account of the Maldive Islands, "which are one of the wonders of the world, and number about two thousand in all". Ibn Battuta was welcomed by the Queen, who appointed him *Kazi*, and he settled down, marrying the daughter of the Vizier and three other wives. "It is easy to get married in these islands", he remarks. The chief exports of the islands were coco-nuts, cowrie shells, and rope made from the fibre of the coco-nut. This rope is used for fastening the planks of ships, and Ibn Battuta points out that in view of the numerous reefs, this method gives a certain resilience and the ship does not fall to pieces.

For some time Ibn Battuta attempted to drive the primitive people to mosque by whipping the absentees. He also tried in vain to induce the women to wear clothes. Finally the Vizier grew jealous of his influence, and the restless traveller resumed his wanderings.

His next voyage brought him to Ceylon, where the "infidel Sultan" received him with much kindness and arranged for him to visit Adam's Peak. Passing through Kunakar, the capital, he reached the mountain, and scaled it by the aid of chains, which are still in existence. To quote his account, "The mountain of Sarandib (Ceylon) is one of the highest in the world. When we climbed it, we saw the clouds below us, shutting out our view of its base. On it there are many ever-green trees and flowers of various colours, including a red rose as big as the palm of a hand."

Leaving Ceylon for the Coromandel coast, Ibn Battuta's ship was wrecked, but he reached the shore in safety, and was welcomed by the Sultan, who was a Persian of Damghan and a relative of the wife the traveller had married at Delhi. He nearly died from fever, probably as the result of exposure, and, after his recovery, he embarked on a ship, was stripped by pirates of the jewels given him in Ceylon, and found himself back at Calicut, as poor as he had ever been. Nothing daunted, he again visited the Maldive Islands, where he was generously treated, but he decided not to remain, and set out on a voyage of forty-three days to Bengal, " a hell full of good things ". Landing at Chittagong, he made a journey across Assam to Sylhet, with the object of visiting " a notable saint, *Shaykh* Jalal ud-Din of Tabriz ". He was welcomed by the *Shaykh*, who presented him with a mantle of goats-hair, about which a wonderful story is told.

From Bengal, Ibn Battuta sailed for Java, a voyage of forty days. On landing he found that he had a friend at Court, whom he had met at Delhi. Consequently he was well received at the audience, where he saw with astonishment horses that danced before the Sultan. Arrangements were made for his onward journey to Mul-Java, which is identified with the Malay Peninsula, where the " infidel Sultan " entertained him. After a month's voyage, the " motionless sea " was reached, where the junks were towed by attendant vessels, aided by their own sweeps, and, after calling at a port which cannot be identified, the voyage to China was successfully accomplished.

Ibn Battuta was not in a position to add to the detailed account of China given by Marco Polo, and so we may follow him back to Fez, where he laid down the staff of travel.

*   *   *   *   *

Incredible as it might appear, there is an epilogue to this wonderful tale. Ibn Battuta had not visited Spain, but he determined to take part in the *Jihad* or Holy War, and from Ceuta, destined before very long to be captured by Prince Henry the Navigator, he crossed over to Gibraltar. Escaping Christian raiders, he visited Malaga, and then Granada, of which he writes : " Its environs have not their equal in any country in the world. Around it on every side are orchards, gardens, flowery meads, noble buildings and vineyards."

His last journey, certainly one of the most important from the point of view of exploration, was that to the Negro lands. Embarking at Gibraltar, he landed at Ceuta and travelled to Arzilla,[1] where he remained for some months. He then visited Sallee, the port from which sailed the dreaded rovers, and so to Marrakesh, which he describes as one of the most beautiful of cities. He makes special reference to the Mosque of the Kutubiyin, which was still standing some ten years ago, when I visited Morocco.

[1] These ports he termed Sabta, Asila and Sala.

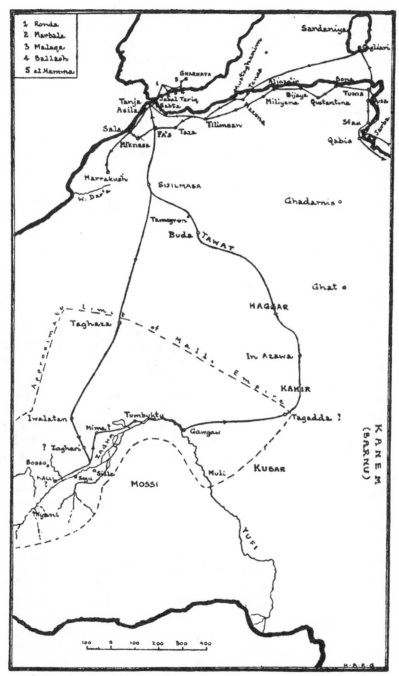

Legend:
1 Ronda
2 Marbala
3 Malaqa
4 Ballash
5 al Hamma

SKETCH MAP OF WEST AFRICA TO ILLUSTRATE IBN BATTUTA'S TRAVELS.

Ibn Battuta took leave of the Sultan at Fez, and, crossing the Atlas Range, reached Sijilmasa, in February 1352, a centre which has been succeeded by neighbouring Tafileh, over which the French have recently established their authority. There he bought "camels and a four months' supply of forage", and after twenty-five days reached Taghaza with its "houses and mosques built of blocks of salt". For ten days' journey from this dreary town there was a waterless tract of desert, till finally at Iwalatan the Sahara ended.

Before dealing with the traveller's further experiences, a brief reference to the Western Sudan at this period is called for. Asiatic influence reached the country through the conversion to Islam of large numbers of the pagan Sudanese, a process due to the Arab-Berber civilization. There is consequently a marked difference between the Africans of the Sudan, with their Asiatic blood, and the pure negroes of the west coast and of Central Africa.

Musa, the great ruler of Melle, captured Timbuktu in 1336, and built the great mosque of cut stone, employing a Spanish architect. Before his death he ruled over a wide empire, which included much of the Sahara. Ibn Battuta reached Malli or Melle under his successor at a time when Songhay was asserting its independence.

The latter state reached its zenith at the end of the fifteenth century, when it became the predominant state in the Sudan. Under Askia it stretched from the salt-mines of Taghaza in the Sahara to the range which defined the Guinea coast; eastwards it extended to Lake Chad, and westwards to the Atlantic Coast. Timbuktu was its capital, and a fleet with its headquarters at Kabara made the Niger safe for traders. The internal trade was centralized at Jenne, while foreign trade reached Timbuktu from Morocco, Tripoli and Egypt. Scholars and learned men from all over the Moslem world were welcomed at the Songhay Court. Its power lasted until the conquest of the Western Sudan by Morocco in 1595.

At Iwalatan the explorer had reached "the northernmost province of the negroes". He was not pleased with his reception, and disliked "their lack of manners and their contempt for the whites". Nor did he like the food; but he decided to make the journey to Malli, twenty-four stages farther south. On the way he noted the practice of storing water in the baobab trees, which still prevails. Of greater interest to him as a Moslem was a community of whites of the Ibadite sect, a remnant of the once powerful and Puritanical

Kharijites, a member of which assassinated the Caliph Ali. The Arabs of Oman mainly belong to this sect.

Finally, Ibn Battuta struck the Niger at Karsakhu.[1] He calls it the Nile, but lays down that it " flows from there down to Kabara and thence to Zagha. . . . Thence it descends to Timbuktu and Gawgaw. . . . It cannot be visited by any white man, because they would kill him before he got there."

Ibn Battuta presented himself at the Court of Sultan Sulayman at Malli, a state which is mentioned somewhat doubtfully by the Portuguese historian Azurara. He was disgusted at the hospitality-gift, which consisted of " three cakes of bread, a piece of beef fried in native oil, and a calabash of sour curds ", since he expected " rich robes of honour and money ".

The Arab explorer gives an interesting account of a reception.

> " The armour-bearers bring in magnificent arms—quivers of gold and silver, swords ornamented with gold and with golden scabbards, gold and silver lances, and crystal maces. The interpreter Dugha comes with his four wives and his slave-girls, who are about one hundred in number. They are wearing beautiful robes, and on their heads they have gold and silver fillets, with gold and silver balls attached. If anyone addresses the king and receives a reply from him, he uncovers his back and throws dust [2] over his head and back. Again witnesses of a statement confirm it by twanging their bowstrings."

Such was the wealth and civilization of the Malli Empire.

Ibn Battuta left Malli, after a stay of some eight months, in February 1353, and on reaching a channel of the Niger, was astonished at the huge hippopotami, " taking them to be elephants ". At Timbuktu, he makes no reference to the mosque, which was obviously inferior to those he had recently seen in Spain and Morocco, but he remarks that " most of the inhabitants are of the Massufa tribe ". From Timbuktu " I sailed down the Nile [Niger] on a small boat, hollowed out of a single piece of wood ".

Gao was the farthest point to which Ibn Battuta penetrated on the Niger. There he prepared to recross the desert to Tagadda, the largest town in the Tuareg country, where he waxes lyrical about the women, describing them as " the most

---

[1] Karsakhu is the " market of Kara " on the left bank of the Niger, and Gawgaw (now Gao) is to-day an important aviation centre. Idrisi's description of the Nil-al-Sudan flowing westwards to the Atlantic is given in Chapter V.

[2] In Persia a petitioner used to say : " This is the petition of the dust of the foot," etc. The intention in both cases is to emphasize humility.

perfect in beauty and the most shapely in figure, of a pure white colour and very stout ".

At Tagadda, Ibn Battuta received a message from the Sultan of Morocco ordering him " to proceed to his sublime capital ". He started off " with a large caravan which included 600 women slaves ", and travelling by Air, Haggar and Sijilmasa, finally arrived at the royal city of Fez, " where I kissed the hand of the Commander of the Faithful, and, after long journeying, settled down under the wing of his bounty ".

Here we may leave Ibn Battuta, whose claim to fame rests not only on his journeys in Arabia and the Western Sudan, of which he was the first explorer, but on travels to almost every part of the known world. On reading his narrative, the salient characteristic we discover is its accuracy in dealing with places and with historical personages and events. There is the charm of the *Arabian Nights* in his adventures, and throughout he is frankness itself as to his motives, and seldom exaggerates. It is remarkable how his work completes that of Marco Polo. The illustrious Venetian supplied Europe with a wonderful account of China, but was less at home in Moslem lands, whereas the descriptions given by Ibn Battuta of Moslem centres from Canton to Timbuktu are unsurpassed.

CHAPTER XI

BARTHOLOMEW DIAZ CIRCUMNAVIGATES AFRICA

" Let things be—not seem.
I counsel rather—do, and nowise dream !
Earth's young significance is all to learn :
The dead Greek lore lies buried in the urn
Where who seeks fire finds ashes."

ROBERT BROWNING.

HITHERTO in this work we have been dealing with the ancient or medieval world. Suddenly, a few years before the close of the fifteenth century, by the practically simultaneous discovery of the ocean route to India and of the immense New World that lay beyond the Atlantic Ocean to the west, Europe burst the shackles of the Middle Ages, and, mainly through her development of sea-power, gradually evolved the might, wealth and civilization of the present day. To set the stage for these amazing events, which ultimately put an end to the deadly fear of Moslem ascendency in Europe, we must refer briefly to the position of affairs in the world as then known.

The period of Mongol supremacy had lasted but a century, and Tamerlane, who shattered it, so far as Central Asia and Persia were concerned, at the end of the fourteenth century, was succeeded by a dynasty of Princes whose rule included only those countries. Consequently there was no longer any direct communication with China by land. Indeed, it cannot be too clearly realized that, at this period, the trade-routes of Asia, Africa and the sea-routes of the Indian Ocean were almost without exception in Moslem hands.

Politically, the advance of the Osmanli Turks constituted a terrible menace to Europe. In 1354 they crossed the Dardanelles and seized Gallipoli, and seven years later they occupied Adrianople. In 1379 they defeated a coalition of the Slav Princes at Kossovo and annexed Bulgaria, Serbia and Wallachia ; and at the battle of Nicopolis, fought in 1396, the chivalry of Europe broke and fled, utterly outmatched by the Janissaries. The defeat of Bayazid by Tamerlane in 1402 saved Constantinople for half a century, but, in 1453, the great barrier-city of European civilization, left to its fate by the short-sighted Christian powers, was captured, and Turkey continued her westward advance, which threatened the very existence of European civilization.

The bitter rivalry between the Italian states exhausted their resources, and opened the way for the Turks. Venice finally crushed Genoa, while Florence and Genoa had previously broken the strength of Pisa. It is interesting to reflect that had the Italian states been able to combine as effectually as did the members of the Hansa League, the Turks would never have penetrated to the walls of Vienna.

While the Turks were advancing in Eastern Europe from strength to strength, albeit not to final victory, in the Iberian peninsula the Moslems were slowly but surely being driven out. Before the end of the thirteenth century the western seaboard, down to Cape St. Vincent, had been conquered by the Counts of Portugal, while the Kings of Castile had expelled the Moors from Andalusia and occupied Seville. Portugal was fortunate in the possession of a coast-line some 300 miles in length, containing many deep and sheltered harbours. On the other hand, Castile and Leon lay between her and the markets of Central Europe. Consequently she had every inducement to seek her fortune at sea.

The organizer of the marvellous naval development of Portugal was Prince Henry the Navigator, whose mother was a daughter of John of Gaunt. In 1415 he initiated a crusade against the Moors of North Africa and captured the port of Ceuta. He then set to work to train the hardy fishermen into skilled navigators and seamen. He was equally determined to build ships suitable for long ocean voyages, and before his death the fishing vessel had developed into a decked ship of 200 tons with three or four masts. Meanwhile, the best navigators and cartographers had been brought from Italy and Sicily to train his pilots in ocean voyaging, and improvements were effected in the compass. Finally, Europe was ransacked for books, among them the work of Marco Polo.

The original design of the Prince, who was the greatest man of his age, was to outflank the Moors by sea, to join forces with Prester John, who was now identified with the Prince of Ethiopia, and thus crush the Moslems. As time passed, Prince Henry aimed rather at the development of commerce, whereby he could strengthen Portugal in her crusades against the Moslems, whose cruisers were often met with at sea. He was the first statesman to realize that oceans

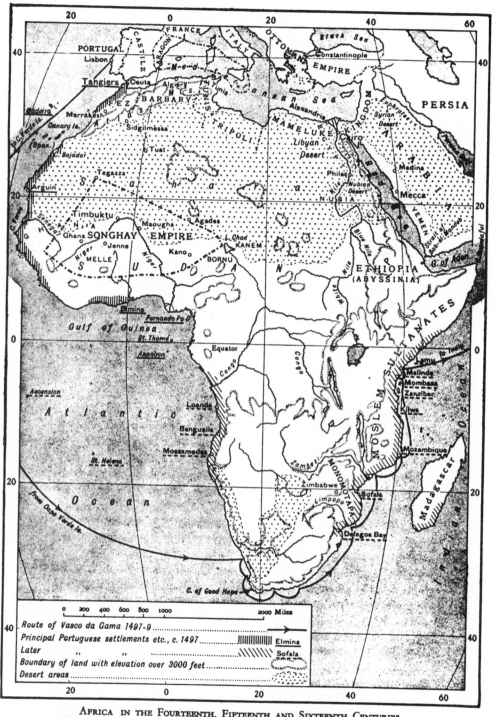

AFRICA IN THE FOURTEENTH, FIFTEENTH AND SIXTEENTH CENTURIES.
(Reproduced from " *The Universal History of The World*," edited by J. A. Hammerton, by courtesy of the publishers, The Educational Book Co. Ltd.)

were not barriers, but rather great highways for commerce, and that sea-power would win dominion.

It is interesting to ascertain what maps and information were available to the Portuguese explorers. In Chapter V reference is made to Idrisi's map, and a chapter has also been devoted to Ibn Battuta's journeys. Again, in 1413, the planisphere of Mecia de Viladestes shows the caravan routes from Egypt, which converged on Timbuktu. Generally speaking, there was better information available about the interior than about the west coast of Africa. There was, however, as the Laurentian Portolano in 1351 proves, a strong belief that Africa could be circumnavigated, but there was little if any definite knowledge concerning the western coast south of the equator. As regards the east coast, Idrisi and other Moslem travellers knew of the ports of Zeila, Mombasa, Kilwa and Sofala, on which were based petty states founded by Arabs in the eighth century A.D., while Persians ruled at Malindi.

In 1487, the year after Diaz sailed, King John sent Covilham "to discover and learn where Prete Janni dwelt, and whether his territories reached unto the sea; and where the pepper and cinnamon grew. . . . They were further charged to find out whether it were possible to sail round the southern end of Africa to India and to gather information about sailing in the Indian Ocean." Covilham visited India, and then took ship to Sofala. Returning to Cairo, he sent home a report in which he stated that "the ships which sailed down the coast of Guinea might be sure of reaching the termination of the continent, . . . and that when they should arrive in the eastern ocean, they should inquire for Sofala". He then visited Abyssinia, where his abilities were so highly appreciated that he was permanently detained as a highly honoured guest. It is, of course, uncertain whether the Portuguese had all the above information at their disposal. Probably they had not.

It is difficult for us to realize to what an extent superstition barred the path of exploration at this period. To quote the contemporary historian Azurara:[1] "Said the mariners, this much is clear, that beyond this Cape of Bojador there is no race of men nor place of inhabitants: nor is the land less sandy than the deserts of Libya, where there is no water, no tree, no green herb—and the sea so shallow that a whole

---

[1] Vide *The Discovery and Conquest of Guinea*, by Gomes Eannes de Azurara, translated by C. R. Beazley and E. Prestage (Hakluyt Society), 1896.

league from land it is only a fathom deep, while the currents are so terrible that no ship, having once passed the Cape, will ever be able to return." We may add to this the belief of Ptolemy that the torrid zone was uninhabitable and impassable.

Year after year Prince Henry despatched expeditions, whose leaders feared to sail southwards; but he never relaxed his efforts, and in 1434, after twelve years of exploration, the spell was broken by one of his squires and the fateful Cape Bojador was rounded with the utmost ease. During these years the island groups of Madeira and the Azores were re-discovered and colonized by Portugal, while Spain occupied the Canaries.

It must be borne in mind that in its northern section the west coast of Africa was, and is, most uninviting, the Sahara, arid, waterless and treeless, coming down to the ocean. Consequently explorers were repelled and were generally anxious to return home lest worse befall.

Azurara gives a valuable account of the experiences of John Fernandez, who volunteered to stay in the desert country. He described it as " peopled by shepherd folk in greater or smaller numbers, according as they find pasturage; and there are no trees in it save small ones. . . . And all the water is from wells." One of his most interesting remarks runs: " It is said that in the land of the Negroes there is another kingdom called Melli, but this is not certain." From this remark it would seem that the work of Ibn Battuta, who visited Malli, as told in the previous chapter, was unknown to the Portuguese historian.

Hitherto in these expeditions no natives of the country had been seen. Prince Henry was most anxious to secure captives, to convert them to Christianity and to utilize their services as intermediaries and interpreters. This was effected without much difficulty, and started a lucrative slave-trade, which encouraged the merchant class to support these ventures. The Portuguese captains pushed farther south mainly because the Moors became aware of these slaving raids, and it was therefore desirable to strike areas where they could surprise the wretched inhabitants. In 1446 they rounded Cape Verde, beyond which lay the Land of the Negroes or Guinea.[1] Here, even though unable to land owing to the rough sea, " it was clear from the smell that came off the land how good must

[1] The word is probably derived from Ghana, the name of the oldest known state in the Western Sudan, which, from various capitals, including Malli, during the Middle Ages ruled from the Atlantic to the great bend of the Niger. The English guinea was made from gold imported from this country in the reign of Charles II.

be the fruits of that country, for it was so delicious that from the point they reached, though they were on the sea, it seemed to them that they stood in some gracious fruit-garden ordained for the sole end of their delight ".

Among the leading explorers of the period was Cadomosto, a Venetian. Entering the Portuguese service in 1455, he visited Madeira, and at Cape Branco began a study of the country, its inhabitants and its resources, charting the coast as he proceeded. He discovered the Cape Verde islands and reached the Gambia, where he opened trade with the natives. Altogether his report gives a better account of the geography, trade routes and people than does that of Azurara, whose history records nothing later than the events of 1448.

Prince Henry the Navigator died in 1460, by which year his captains had explored the western coast of Africa to a point beyond the River Gambia, and had become the best trained and most experienced navigators in Europe. To him is due the credit not only for the discovery of the ocean route to India, which he foretold, but also for that of America. He was also the creator of modern colonization.

The work of exploration was continued after the death of its originator, and in 1461 the Portuguese advanced 600 miles along " the southern coast of Guinea ", passing a mountain which was named Sierra Leone or " Mount Lion ", and reaching the point where the fort of Elmina was constructed a few years later.

In 1469, King Alfonso leased the West African trade for five years to Fernan Gomez, who by his contract was bound to send out annual expeditions to continue the exploration of the coast at the rate of 100 leagues a year from Sierra Leone. In 1470, the island of St. Thomas, situated on the equator, was discovered, and in 1471 Fernando Po reached the island which bears his name. Bitter disappointment was now felt that the coast of Africa trended to the south, thus lengthening the hoped-for direct approach to the spice islands of Asia.

After the accession of John II in 1481, the fort of St. George of the Mine, generally termed Elmina, was constructed in 1482, and became the mart for the rich goldfields situated behind the Gold Coast.

In 1484 Diego Cam was instructed to push on to the south. He reached the mouth of the Congo, up which he sailed for some distance. He brought back four natives, whom he took out with him on a second voyage, during which he penetrated still farther south to the vicinity of Walvis Bay. To his credit must be placed the exploration of over 1,400 miles of the coast of Africa : a notable feat, paving the way for final success.

In 1486, Bartholomew Diaz set out in the belief " that ships which sailed down the coast of Guinea might be sure to reach the end of the land by persisting in a southward direction ". At Angra Pequeña he set up a pillar, a fragment of which I inspected at Cape Town. He then began to be affected by adverse currents, and putting well out to sea, sailed south before the wind into the Atlantic for thirteen days. He next shaped an easterly course, but not sighting land, he changed his direction to the north and landed at Mossel Bay, on February 3, 1488. Following up the coast, he reached the Great Fish River. There, realizing that he had fulfilled his mission to circumnavigate Africa, Diaz decided to return, and reached Lisbon in December 1488. By this splendid achievement the labours of Prince Henry the Navigator and his school of sea-captains were crowned with success. The ocean route to India had been proved practicable, a temperate zone to the south of the Tropics had been found, and it only remained to take advantage of these discoveries, which rank among the greatest feats of exploration.

Before describing the epoch-making voyage of Vasco da Gama and the remarkable feats of his successors, I propose to give an account of the important journeys of Ludovico di Varthema of Bologna,[1] whose knowledge of the Eastern countries was of the greatest value to the Portuguese. A soldier by profession and a born traveller, he starts his narrative with Egypt, which he considered to be too well known, and therefore he crosses into Syria. At Damascus he spent some months " in order to learn the Moorish language ", and he describes the castle which was built by a Florentine Mameluke of the Sultan, who sculptured on it the arms of Florence.

At Damascus Varthema, in the spring of 1503, through the friendship of the Mameluke officer in command, was enlisted into that body, which escorted the pilgrim caravan to Mecca. After describing attacks by the Arabs on the huge pilgrim caravan, he gives an interesting account of the Jews of Khaibar, who were conquered by the Prophet Mohammed.[2]

---

[1] For this section I have consulted *Ludovico di Varthema*, edited by Sir R. Temple, Argonaut Press, 1928.

[2] Sykes, *History of Persia*, Vol. I, p. 518. Opposite p. 534 (2nd ed.) is a coloured reproduction of a miniature painting depicting Ali slaying Marhab, the champion of Khaibar.

According to our traveller, " If they can get a Moor into their hands they skin him alive." Varthema gives an accurate account of Mecca and of the ceremonies, which he was the first European to describe. He also notes that the Portuguese had already prevented the usual supply of spices from reaching the Mecca market.

When the pilgrimage was ended, Varthema, deserting from the Mamelukes, made his way to Jeddah, and, sailing down the Red Sea, reached Aden in March 1504. At this port he was thrown into prison on the charge of being a Christian spy, and since the Portuguese had captured some of their ships, the sailors who had escaped thirsted for his blood. He was brought before the Sultan for sentence, but ultimately, winning the affection of the Sultan's wife, Varthema was released from prison.

He then travelled to Yemen, and visited Sana, " situated on the top of a very large mountain and extremely strong ". He also described Taiz, with its rose water and " all kinds of elegancies ". Returning to Aden, everywhere following in the footsteps of Ibn Battuta, whose descriptions he most ably supplements, Zeila is visited and described as a mart for gold, ivory and Abyssinian slaves. His ship sailed thence to Diu, calling at Gogo in Kathiawar. Varthema crosses the Indian Ocean to Dhufar in the frankincense country, from which port Bertram Thomas, four centuries later, started on his successful attempt to cross the sinister *Rub'-al-Khali*. Coasting eastwards, Maskat is merely noticed, and the " noble city of Hormuz " was reached in the spring of 1504, or three years before its capture by Albuquerque.

From Hormuz Varthema made a journey into Persia in the summer of 1504, and " travelling for twelve days I found a city called Eri ". This section of Varthema's journey has caused considerable discussion, but Eri certainly cannot be the celebrated city of Herat. During my first journey in Persia, I visited a rich oasis named Herat-i-Khara,[1] situated some five or six stages to the north-east of Shiraz, which was evidently the Eri of Varthema. From it he made for Shiraz, following the Eufra, which " I believe is the Euphrates, on account of its great size "—an amazing statement. Actually it is the Kur, which in its lower reaches is termed the Band-i-Amir, from a dam[2] constructed by an Amir in the tenth century. This word inspired Moore to write—

[1] *Ten Thousand Miles in Persia*, p. 78.
[2] For an illustration of this fine dam *vide* Sykes, *History of Persia* (2nd ed.), Vol. II, p. 24

"There is a bower of roses by Bendemeer's stream,
And the nightingale sings round it all the day long."

At Shiraz, Varthema met a wealthy merchant, *Khoja* Junair, whose acquaintance he had made at Mecca. He not only offered him his niece in marriage, but accompanied him on his voyages to India and the Far East. In the autumn the friends sailed to India, and Varthema gives a good description of its ports, which were also described by Marco Polo and Ibn Battuta. From Goa he travelled inland to Bijapur, which, using the name of the province, he terms Deccan. "The King of the said city lives in great pride and pomp. A great number of his servants wear on the insteps of their shoes rubies and diamonds."

Landing again farther south at Cannanore, Varthema visited Vijayanagar, the last Hindu empire in India, which "appears to me to be a second paradise. The King is a great friend of the Christians, especially of the King of Portugal." In his description of Calicut he mentions that if the "untouchables", to give them their modern name, fail to give notice of their polluting presence, the Brahmins or Nairs may kill them.

In discussing the "manner of navigation" at this point Varthema explains that "they make their vessels, such as are open, each of 300 or 400 butts", thus proving that, as in the case of our "tonnage" measurement of capacity was based on the number of "tons" or "casks" that could be carried. *Khoja* Junair "could not sell his merchandise because Calicut was ruined by the King of Portugal", and so the travellers continued their voyage in January 1595 to Quilon, Ceylon and the Coromandel Coast. They then crossed the Bay of Bengal to Tenasserim. Again the name of the country is used for the town, and a list is given of the domestic and game animals and birds.

Bengal was the next country to be visited. It struck Varthema as "abounding more in grain, sugar, ginger and cotton than any country in the world". There they met some Nestorian Christians, inhabitants of Siam, who joined forces with them, and the party sailed to Pegu. The King, who was visited at his camp fifteen days inland, gave *Khoja* Junair rubies in exchange for his coral, and Varthema described the enormous quantities of jewels worn by the monarch, "whose ears hang down half a palm, through the great weight of the many jewels he wears". He also noted the "canes which were really as thick as a barrel", this being a reference to the giant bamboo.

From Pegu the travellers sailed to Malacca, where they arrived in the spring of 1505. Varthema mentions an "extremely great strait . . . and opposite there is a very large island, which is called Sumatra". This is a reference to the Straits of Singapore, and the earliest mention of Sumatra under that name, Marco Polo and Ibn Battuta calling it Java the Less. Varthema testifies to the enormous trade of Malacca, which four years later was visited by Sequeira. Owing to the lack of security at Malacca, the travellers proceeded to Sumatra, where Varthema revelled in its wonderful perfumes.

From the point of view of exploration Varthema's account of his voyage to Banda and the Moluccas is of the greatest importance, for he was the first European to reach these famous Spice Islands. He was unfavourably impressed by Banda, "which is very ugly and gloomy. . . . Nothing grows here but nutmegs and some fruits." Of the nutmeg he gives a good account, but the people he describes as being "like beasts without understanding". From Banda the travellers sailed on for twelve days to Monoch (Moluccas). "Here the cloves grow. The tree of the clove is exactly like the box tree."

It is curious that Varthema failed to realize the importance of his discoveries. Indeed throughout he apparently made no effort to profit by his wonderful opportunities of amassing wealth. Sir Richard Temple considers that the small island at which Varthema studied the clove trees was Ternate, and, as we shall see, it was at Ternate that Drake secured a cargo of cloves.

The untiring travellers had now reached the eastern limit of their wonderful voyages. Sailing westwards on the return journey, and approaching Java, we find a most remarkable passage: "The captain of the ship showed us four or five stars, among which there was one which he said was opposite to our north star. . . . He also told us that on the other side of Java, towards the south, there are some other races, who navigate by the said four or five stars opposite to ours." The reference is to the Southern Cross, and the extraordinary importance of a statement showing acquaintance with navigation in seas still farther south is manifest.

Upon his return to Calicut in the summer of 1505, Varthema determined to join the Portuguese at Cannanore. This he effected with some difficulty, and was able to give information of the greatest value about the fleet that was being assembled at Calicut to attack the Portuguese. Varthema gives a vivid description of the sea-fight off Cannanore. Subsequently he was appointed factor by the Viceroy, and held this post until the autumn of 1507. The great traveller was now anxious to return home, and having been knighted by the Viceroy—Tristan d'Acunha was his sponsor—he sailed to Europe with the Portuguese fleet, and arrived safely at Lisbon in the autumn of 1508.

Doubt has been thrown on the reliability of Varthema's accounts, but for me he is a great explorer possessing the true traveller's spirit and endowed with excellent powers of observation and criticism. The value of the information he was able to give the Portuguese must have been priceless.

CHAPTER XII

VASCO DA GAMA SAILS TO INDIA

" To their triumphant arms, the Chersonese
In golden treasures rich, distant Cathay,
And all the farthest Islands of the East,
And all the seas, to them shall homage pay."
CAMOENS, " *The Lusiad* ".

VASCO DA GAMA won deathless fame by making the first ocean voyage to India. It was the culmination of nearly a century of persistent effort by Portuguese navigators, and represented a great epoch in exploration.

The famous Captain was born in 1460 at the small fishing town of Sines, set in a waste of barren dunes, which impelled its inhabitants to reap the harvest of the sea. Well equipped as a scientific navigator, and an experienced mariner, he was thirty-six years of age, unmarried, ambitious, and capable when appointed to command this important expedition. He was fortunate in having two ships, each of 120 tons, specially constructed for the voyage by Bartholomew Diaz, whose experience must have been invaluable, and the squadron was completed by a *caravel* of fifty tons and a store ship of 200 tons. The expedition consisted of about 170 officers and men.[1]

On July 8, 1497, the explorers started on their momentous voyage and were favoured by good weather as far as the Canaries. Then came a dense fog, during which the various ships lost touch with one another, but regained it at the Cape Verde Islands. Instead of painfully creeping along the coast, as his predecessors had done, Da Gama boldly shaped a course across the Atlantic to the Cape of Good Hope. The direct distance to be covered was nearly 4,000 miles, but his course, which involved spending more than three months out of sight of land, was considerably longer, and constitutes one of the greatest achievements hitherto recorded in the annals of maritime exploration. Passing well to the west of Ascension and St. Helena, Da Gama finally sailed due

[1] See *Vasco da Gama*, by K. G. Jayne, and *Vasco da Gama's First Voyage*, by E. G. Ravenstein (Hakluyt Society), 1898. The latter work includes a translation of a *roteiro* or journal, kept by an unknown writer.

east to avoid missing Cape Agulhas, and sighted land, which he followed down to a bay, named by him Santa Helena.

Upon landing, he made the acquaintance of some Hottentots, whose food consisted of the flesh of seals, whales and gazelles, together with the roots of herbs. At first relations were friendly, but, possibly owing to a misunderstanding, assegais were thrown, one of which slightly wounded the Captain-Major. Continuing the voyage, he rounded the Cape of Good Hope, not without some difficulty, and, like Diaz, landed at Mossel Bay, to which Da Gama gave another name. There "we remained for thirteen days. We broke up our store-ship and transferred her contents to other ships." The natives possessed fine oxen and sheep, but were none too friendly, and the pillar which the Portuguese erected was demolished under their eyes as they sailed away.

Upon resuming the voyage, the distances are given with remarkable accuracy, and Vasco da Gama sailed past the Rio de Infante or Great Fish River, the last discovery made by Diaz. But, owing to the strong Agulhas current, the explorer was carried back to Santa Cruz, an island in Algoa Bay. Fortunately a strong wind astern overcame these currents, to the intense relief of all.

Vasco da Gama had some 800 miles of unknown coast to explore before reaching the Moslem ports, where he hoped to engage pilots. By Christmas Day he had discovered seventy leagues of coast, to which he gave the name of Natal. Farther north, he landed near the mouth of the Limpopo, where the Portuguese were hospitably received by the Bantu tribesmen, who were armed with "long bows and arrows and spears with iron blades". Copper appeared to be plentiful, for which reason Vasco da Gama named the Limpopo the "River of Copper". The Bantu country he called the "Land of the Good People".

Sailing steadily northwards, and passing Sofala on January 22, Da Gama entered the Kiliman River, where he gained touch with Moslem civilization in the person of a young man "who had come from a distant country, and had already seen big ships like ours". The first Moslem port Vasco da Gama entered was Mozambique, where he found four Arab vessels "laden with gold, silver, cloves, pepper, ginger, and silver rings, as also with quantities of pearls, jewels, and rubies. We were told moreover that Prester John resided far in the interior, and could be reached only on the back of camels." The Sultan visited the Portuguese ships, but treated with contempt the presents they offered, and asked for scarlet cloth, of which they had none.

It is to be noted that when the Portuguese appeared in Eastern waters, the carrying trade in the Indian Ocean and the Malay Archipelago was in the hands of the Arabs. They were not only carriers, but in India and Iraq they were merchants, as the *Arabian Nights* prove. They had founded petty states along the east coast of Africa, but in India, although their influence was considerable, they did not attempt conquest.

At first the relations of the Portuguese with the Sultan and his people were friendly, since it was believed that the newcomers were Moslems. Da Gama set sail from Mozambique, but, owing to the state of the wind, he was obliged to return to the port. The Portuguese proceeded to the watering-place on the mainland where hostility was shown them. Accordingly they bombarded the palisades which had been erected, and later captured some vessels and took some prisoners.

On March 29, having secured two Arab pilots who were accustomed to the use of the compass, the quadrant and charts, they sailed for Mombasa, where an attempt was made to capture the ships by a midnight surprise. As at Mozambique, the knowledge that the Portuguese were Christians created intense hostility, which was fully reciprocated. However, vigilance frustrated all treacherous attempts, and the fresh fruit restored the health of the sailors, who were suffering from scurvy.

From Mombasa it was only a day's sail to Malindi, where they were received in a most friendly manner by the King, who belonged to a Persian family. A Hindu pilot was provided, to the great satisfaction of the Portuguese, who one and all throughout this expedition believed that the Hindus were Christians. The town of Malindi was compared with Alcochete, a town situated on the Tagus above Lisbon: "Its houses are lofty and well whitewashed, and have many windows; on the land side are palm-groves, and all around it maize and vegetables are cultivated."

Da Gama left Malindi on April 24, bound for Calicut. "After having seen no land for twenty-three days, we sighted lofty mountains, and having al _his time sailed before the wind, we could not have made less than 600 leagues." On May 20, 1498, the squadron anchored two leagues from Calicut, and thus the great feat of exploration was accomplished.

Vasco da Gama visited the *Samuri*. Stopping on the

way to the palace, " they took us to a large church. Many saints were painted on the walls of the church, wearing crowns. They were painted variously, with teeth protruding an inch from the mouth, and four or five arms." Yet the Portuguese still persisted in the fond belief that they were among Christians !

The *Samuri* was inclined to be friendly at first, but, partly owing to Da Gama being unprovided with suitable gifts and partly owing to Moslem intrigues, the situation finally became strained, and it was with some difficulty that the Captain-Major was able to return on board. Finally, after seizing some " six persons of quality " to serve as hostages, the Portuguese who had been arrested on shore were sent back.

Da Gama then set sail on the return voyage. Three months were spent in reaching Africa, during which period thirty men died from scurvy, making a total of sixty men or one-third of the whole number who had died from this dire scourge. When they sighted land they found that they were off Magadoxo—the Magdashaw of Ibn Battuta—and on January 7, 1499, they reached friendly Malindi. Owing to his terrible losses in personnel Da Gama was obliged to burn the *St. Raphael*, but, once the east coast of Africa was struck, the homeward journey was prosperous and a direct course was taken from the Cape of Good Hope to the Cape Verde Islands. Finally, after an ocean voyage of two years, during which 24,000 nautical miles had been sailed, the great expedition reached Lisbon in July 1499.

The Portuguese lost no time in following up this wonderful achievement, and in March 1500 a powerful fleet of thirteen ships sailed under the command of Pedro Alvares Cabral. Keeping farther to the west than Da Gama, on April 22 he struck the coast of Brazil, which had been discovered by Amerigo Vespucci, as described in the following chapter. Upon his arrival in India, Cabral founded a factory at Calicut. The Moslems, however, stormed it and killed the Portuguese, whereupon Cabral bombarded Calicut. He then established a factory at the neighbouring port of Cochin, whose ruler was an enemy of the *Samuri*. Loading his fleet with pepper, and leaving a squadron to cruise along the east coast of Africa, Cabral reached Lisbon in the summer of 1501, with the most valuable cargo that had ever enriched Portugal.

In 1505, Francisco d'Almeida sailed in command of a powerful fleet to take up the important post of first Viceroy of India. He realized that the Portuguese position rested on sea-power and was opposed to annexation of territory. He would certainly have approved of Bacon's maxim "that he that commands the sea is at great liberty, and may take as much and as little of war as he will". Almeida's policy aimed at securing the whole of the carrying trade for Portugal by ousting the Moslems from the Indian Ocean.

His ability to pursue this ambitious policy was challenged in 1506 by a powerful fleet composed of Arab Moslems and Hindus, which had been assembled by the *Samuri* at Calicut. News of the impending attack was brought by Varthema, who had escaped from Calicut disguised as a Moor, and upon receiving it the Portuguese, under Lorenzo, Almeida's heroic son, attacked and utterly defeated the Indians, inflicting crushing casualties. Egypt had next to be reckoned with, and in 1508 her fleet surprised a small Portuguese squadron off Chaul, killing Lorenzo, and then took up a position in the island port of Diu. In 1509 the Portuguese attacked. The fight between the two forces raged with fury, but finally Almeida could rejoice over "the good vengeance Our Lord has been pleased, of his mercy, to grant us".

In 1509 a squadron reached India under Diego Lopes de Sequeira with orders to reconnoitre Malacca. It was joined by Magellan, and passing Ceylon, steered for Sumatra. The Portuguese were the first European navigators in these seas, which Marco Polo and Varthema had described, and Sequeira, after concluding a treaty with a local chief in the northern part of Sumatra, proceeded to Malacca, which he reached in September 1509. This port was crowded with shipping from Arabia, Persia, Gujerat, Bengal, Burma, Java, China and the Philippine Islands, and the volume of its trade amazed the Portuguese. Their arrival at first caused a panic, but apparently friendly relations were established and the Portuguese arranged to load their ships with spices. The Malay ruler, however, determined to kill them, and the plot nearly succeeded, but Sequeira was warned just in time and sailed away, leaving some of his men prisoners.

Almeida was succeeded by the great Albuquerque in 1509. A man of vast ambitions, he determined to occupy Goa as a naval base and to make it a Portuguese town. He also understood that, to cut the Moslem arteries of commerce, he must hold both Aden and Hormuz. Finally he realized that Malacca was the key to the commerce of the Far East.

Albuquerque wisely made the seizure of Goa his first objective, and in this he succeeded, after a severe reverse, in

1510. In the following year he captured Malacca, thus securing the key to the Eastern Gate of the Indian Ocean and the control of the Spice Islands. After the fall of Malacca, a Portuguese squadron cruised in the Malay Archipelago. No account of this memorable voyage has been preserved, but it included the chief islands and reached the important clove centre of Amboina.

Trade rapidly followed the flag. The Portuguese landed in China in 1514, and within a generation there was an important colony established in that country. In 1542, commercial relations were opened up with Japan. Embassies were also despatched to Siam, where the Portuguese settled in considerable numbers, and to Burma. Upon his return to India in triumph, Albuquerque found that Goa was once more being besieged. Again there was desperate fighting, but Albuquerque gained the victory, and definitely secured Goa for Portugal.

In 1513 Albuquerque set sail for Aden, which was a strong natural position and strongly fortified. He decided on an attack by escalade. Everything, however, went wrong. The water was so shallow that the soldiers were obliged to wade ashore, wetting their powder, and the ladders were too short. The Portuguese, in spite of heroic efforts, were repulsed with heavy losses in men and in prestige. A cruise was then made to Kamaran Island in the Red Sea, where the lack of food and the heat added to the losses sustained at Aden.

Some years earlier, in 1507, Albuquerque had sailed from Socotra with a squadron of seven ships to attack Hormuz. He followed the Oman coast, sacking the ports and mutilating his prisoners of both sexes in order to inspire fear. At Hormuz he attacked the ships which he found in the harbour, but no resistence was offered, their cowardly crews swimming to the shore. The boy-King submitted, and agreed to pay tribute. At this juncture the representative of Shah Ismail appeared on the coast and demanded the tribute due to Persia. Albuquerque provided the boy-King with cannon-balls, matchlocks and grenades, bidding him to send these and to say that this was the currency in which tribute would be paid. He then set to work to build a fort, but the disloyalty of his captains forced him to retire from the scene—for a while. In 1515 he returned as Viceroy with a powerful fleet. He met with no opposition, and erected the splendid fort which at a recent date was practically intact, while numerous cannon lying about bore mute witness to the stormy past.[1]

Albuquerque had failed before Aden, and in 1538 a Turkish fleet consisting of sixty-six ships with 20,000 troops sailed from Egypt [2] to India and besieged the Portuguese garrison in Diu fort. By dint of heavy bombardments and repeated assaults, the fortress was nearly taken, when the Turks, who had quarrelled with the Sultan of Gujerat, suddenly sailed back to the Red Sea, leaving the Portuguese in undisputed possession of the Indian Ocean, and never reappeared on the scene.

It now remains to sum up the results of the explorations of the Portuguese in Eastern waters. During the Middle Ages spices, perfumes and incense, on which Europe depended for her luxuries and, in the case of incense, for her religious ceremonies, reached her through Moslem countries, the two arteries of commerce being the Red Sea and the Persian Gulf. The duties levied on this trade were enormous. In practice, the Sultan of Cairo took one-third of the value of every cargo that entered Egypt. In addition customs were charged on the importers, and in the *Roteiro* we learn that the customs paid by the Venetians and Genoese alone were estimated at £300,000—a huge sum in those days. As a result of the Portuguese operations we read that, in 1504, the Venetian merchants could purchase no spices at Alexandria or Beirut. The arteries of commerce up the Red Sea and the Persian Gulf had been effectually cut.

The Portuguese had indeed fulfilled the hope of Henry the Navigator, far more completely than that great man had dared to expect, and had justified the paean of triumph quoted in the motto to this chapter. Of even greater importance was the shifting of sea-power and world domination from the Mediterranean, that great nursery of maritime development, to the states bordering on the Atlantic. This process was completed by the discoveries of Columbus.

[1] *Vide* Sykes, *History of Persia* (2nd ed.), Vol II, p. 186, for an illustration of the fort.
[2] Selim the Grim had annexed Syria and Egypt in 1517.

Text within image: PRINCE HENRY OF PORTUGALL · HONI SOIT QVI MAL Y PENSE · CEUTA

PRINCE HENRY THE NAVIGATOR AS A KNIGHT OF THE GARTER
(From an old engraving in the British Museum)

CHAPTER XIII

CHRISTOPHER COLUMBUS DISCOVERS THE NEW WORLD

"I wrote this to you from which you will learn how in thirty-three days I passed from the Canary Islands to the Indies. And there I found very many islands filled with people innumerable, and of them all I have taken possession."

Letter of Columbus.

THE discovery of the New World by Christopher Columbus was undoubtedly the greatest event in the history of exploration. There have been many conflicting accounts as to the hero of the enterprise, but it is now generally accepted that he was born in 1451 at Genoa, where his family were weavers.[1] Owing to his humble birth he had little or no education in his youth, and was illiterate, as indeed was to be expected. The fact that he used Castilian even when writing to Italians proves that he had learned to write after leaving his country.

At first Columbus worked as a weaver, but in 1475 he made his first voyage to Chios, at that time a possession of Genoa, and resided there for some time. In 1476 he took part in a Genoese trading voyage to Lisbon, England and Scotland. In 1477 he settled at Lisbon, where he married the daughter of a deceased sea-captain who had served Prince Henry the Navigator, and had been appointed Hereditary Captain of Porto Santo, Madeira's little neighbour. He spent some time at this island and at Madeira, and acquired literacy and some smattering of the science of the period. He also claimed to have been present when Diaz gave an account of his wonderful voyage to the King of Portugal.

His scientific views were those of the Middle Ages. Chief among his few books was the *Imago Mundi* by Cardinal Pierre d'Ailly, written about 1410. To quote one passage: "Aristotle says that the sea is little between the farthest bound of Spain from the East and the nearest of India from the West.

[1] I have consulted *The Great Age of Discovery*, edited by A. P. Newton, 1932, *Histoire critique de la grande entreprise de Christophe Colomb*, by Henri Vignaud, 1911, *Letters of Christopher Columbus*, by R. H. Major, 1870, and *Select Documents illustrating the Four Voyages of Columbus*, by Cecil Jane (Hakluyt Society), 1933.

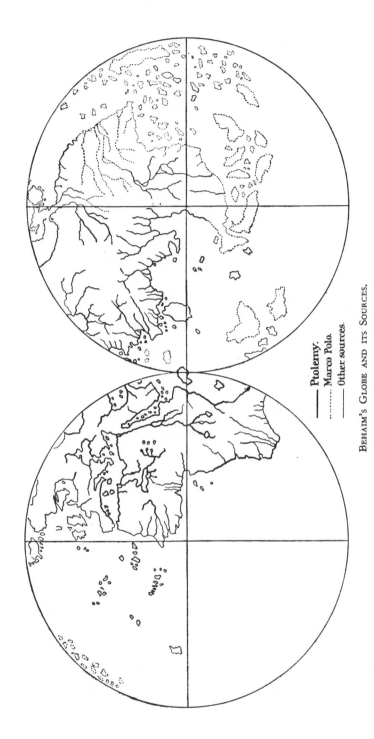

Ptolemy.
Marco Polo.
Other sources.

BEHAIM'S GLOBE AND ITS SOURCES.

Moreover, Seneca says that this sea is navigable in a few days if the wind be favourable." There are other passages in the work expressing similar views, and Columbus not only studied, but annotated this standard work of the time. His copy has fortunately been preserved, as also has his "Marco Polo", which was similarly annotated. These views, based almost entirely on conjecture, are naturally shown on the maps of the period. On the famous globe of Behaim, which appeared in 1492, owing to the enormous extension given by Ptolemy to Asia, the space intervening between Spain and China is shown at 130° of longitude, whereas it is actually 230°. When we realize that Japan was reported by Marco Polo to be situated 1,500 miles east of China, it may be realized how utterly inaccurate were the premises on which the explorers of the period worked.

Columbus had made more than one voyage, and had discussed exploration with the captains and sailors, and "with wise people, as well clergy as laity ".[1] Moreover, there is no reason to doubt that there was truth in the reports of " a piece of wood artificially worked " picked up 450 leagues west of Cape St. Vincent, and of " very large canes " found on the shore of Porto Santo, and other indications of unknown lands in the Atlantic mentioned by Las Casas.[2]

Brooding over these matters, Columbus gradually decided that his mission in life was to sail westward across the Atlantic to discover new and fertile islands and to reach the Indies. His strength of purpose was not due to any special knowledge of navigation. He was not a seaman but a very intelligent trader who had made voyages. Rather he considered that he had a divine mission to discover lands whose inhabitants should be converted to the true faith. It was this belief which impressed his hearers, who were ready to see the hand of God in the most ordinary affairs of life.

Columbus, in the first instance, attempted to interest John II of Portugal in his project, but that monarch's Council reported unfavourably on it. He consequently proceeded to Spain in 1484 and joined his brother, who was a map-maker and in touch with explorers. In 1486, he presented himself before Queen Isabella at Cordoba, who referred the question to a Royal Commission which decided against his scheme. Isabella did not throw over Columbus, but, in view of the fact that Spain was devoting all its resources to completing

[1] *Ferdinand Columbus*, pp. 506–7.
[2] *Historia de las Indias*, Lib. I, Cap. XIII.

the expulsion of the Moors, she decided that the moment was not opportune for undertaking new commitments. Columbus retired to the monastery of La Rabida, where the Prior was his friend and supporter, and where one of the monks was a cosmographer. While staying there he met Martin Alonso Pinzon, a leading navigator of the neighbouring port of Palos, who had decided to undertake an expedition to the island of Chipangu or Japan, and had been seeking information on the subject at Rome.

Columbus again tried to interest Portugal in his enterprise, but without success, nor would Henry VII of England take it up; but upon the capture of Granada in January 1492, which marked the final defeat of the Moors, Isabella sent for Columbus and informedhim that she had decided to support his project.

On August 3, 1492, Columbus sailed from the port of Palos on his memorable voyage. His flag was hoisted on the *Santa Maria*, a decked vessel of 100 tons, and two *caravels* of fifty and forty tons respectively were commanded by Martin Pinzon and his brother. The question arises of the exact objective of Columbus. Did he believe that he would find Chipangu or Japan,[1] which was inaccurately described by Marco Polo as being situated 1,500 miles east from China? Martin Pinzon undoubtedly enlisted men for a voyage to Chipangu, and, accepting the views expressed in the *Imago Mundi*, Columbus apparently sailed in the belief that he would find Chipangu and, later, strike the east coast of Asia. He also vaguely hoped to discover and annex unknown lands and islands.

From Palos he shaped his course for the Canaries in fine weather, the only cause of anxiety being that the rudder of the *caravel Pinta* became unshipped, " possibly by contrivance of its owners ".[2] On August 9 the Canaries were sighted, and Gomera was reached on September 2, with the *Pinta* repaired. " Having taken in water, wood and meat ", the voyage was resumed on September 6. The weather remained favourable, " like April in Andalusia ", with the north-east trade winds wafting the squadron steadily to the west. Entering the Sargasso Sea " they saw much very fine grass and herbs

---

[1] In view of the importance attached to Chipangu, I quote from the account given from hearsay by Marco Polo : " You must know that the Lord of this island has a very large palace, all covered with fine gold. Just as we roof our houses and churches with lead, so this palace is all roofed over with fine gold. . . . And all the other parts of the palace, namely the halls and the windows, are similarly adorned with gold."

[2] *The Journal of Christopher Columbus*, by Sir C. Markham (Hakluyt Society), 1893.

from rocks which came from the west ". The sight of this weed-covered sea must have strengthened the belief of the explorers in the proximity of land. Numerous birds were also sighted flying westward. On October 7, acting on the advice of Martin Pinzon, who was probably influenced by the flight of the birds, Columbus changed his direction from west to west-south-west.

The mutinous behaviour of the sailors, who were afraid they would never see Spain again, threatened the success of the enterprise, but, by lessening the actual length of the run in the log and by temporizing, Columbus was able to continue the voyage. On October 11, thirty-three days after leaving the Canaries, he sighted land. Columbus had not reached the Indies, as he believed, but had discovered a New World.

On the morning of October 12, 1492, Columbus landed in state on the small island of Guanahani, one of the Bahamas, which he solemnly annexed to Spain and named San Salvador. On continuing the voyage, a week was spent among the islands of the Bahama Archipelago, and on October 28 the important island of Cuba was reached, which Columbus at first " thought it must be the mainland, the province of Catayo (Cathay) ". An expedition penetrated inland, during the course of which tobacco was discovered. Columbus then sailed on to the modern Haiti, which he told his officers was Chipangu, but which he named Española, while Cuba was pronounced to be part of the continent of Asia. His description of Española runs :

> " In it there are many harbours on the coast of the seas, and many rivers, good and large. Its islands are high, and there are very lofty mountains. All are most beautiful, of a thousand shapes, and all are accessible and filled with trees of a thousand kinds and tall, and they seem to touch the sky. And some were flowering and some bearing fruit. And the nightingale was singing, and other birds of a thousand kinds. There are six or eight kinds of palm, which are a wonder to behold on account of their beautiful variety."

Of the inhabitants he wrote :

> " The people all go naked, men and women. They have no iron or steel or weapons, nor are they fitted to use them, not because they are not well built men, but because they are marvellously timorous. They are so guileless and generous with all they possess, that no one would believe it who has not seen it.
> " There was one large town in *Española* of which especially I took possession, situated in a locality well adapted for the working of the gold mines, and for all kinds of commerce, either with the mainland

on this side, or with that beyond which is the land of the Great Khan. To this city I gave the name of *Villa de Navidad* and fortified it." [1]

Columbus started homeward in January 1493. He reached the Azores after a prosperous voyage of thirty-four days. He was warmly welcomed in Spain by Ferdinand and Isabella, who received him in full court, when he exhibited the natives, together with the unknown birds, beasts and vegetable products of the Indies.

In his second voyage Columbus shaped a more southerly course, and on a Sunday struck an island which he appropriately named Dominica. Many other islands were discovered on the way to Española, where he found that *Villa de Navidad* had been attacked by natives from another island and the garrison massacred. He founded a second town which he named Isabella. In his third journey Columbus added to his wonderful discoveries. He shaped a course to the Cape Verde Islands, and struck land at Trinidad. He reported "houses and people on the spot, and the country round was very beautiful, and as fresh and green as the gardens of Valencia in the month of March". He also reported that the meeting of the waters of the Orinoco with the sea produced " a sound as of breakers on the rocks ".

From Trinidad, when he noted the great volume of fresh water pouring into the sea from the Orinoco, and the high mountains that he sighted to the west, he was convinced that he had found a land of infinite extent. He reached " a country called Paria, one of the most lovely countries in the world. The inhabitants came· to the ship in their canoes, many of them wearing pieces of gold on their breasts, and some with bracelets of pearls on their arms ". But he destroyed the importance of this discovery by the fantastic interpretation he put upon it. He returned to Europe discredited and in chains in 1500, and although kindly treated by Queen Isabella, his credit at court was never regained.

In his fourth voyage, Columbus steered south from Jamaica. He landed upon the coast of Veragua, where he believed that he was only nineteen days' sail from the mouth of the Ganges, but he could find no strait through which to reach the Spice Islands. In his report he claimed to have " reached the province of Mangi, which is contiguous to that of Cathay ". He

---

[1] There are differences of opinion as to whether Cuba was finally believed to be an island by Columbus or whether he considered it to form part of the continent of Asia. Again, which island did Columbus " officially " hold to be Chipangu ? Actually he was utterly bewildered, and the one thing he failed to grasp was that he had discovered a new world.

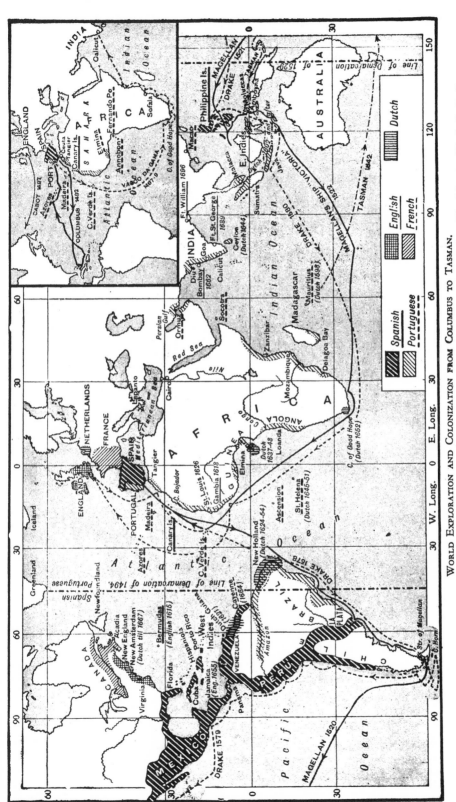

WORLD EXPLORATION AND COLONIZATION FROM COLUMBUS TO TASMAN.

(Reproduced from "The Universal History of The World", edited by I. A. Hammerton, by courtesy of the publishers, The Educational Book Co. Ltd.)

returned to Spain in 1504, a worn-out and disappointed man, and died two years later.

To secure the discoveries of Columbus, Queen Isabella applied to the Pope to delimit the Spanish sphere. Alexander VI thereupon issued a bull in 1493 laying down a line a hundred leagues west of the Azores, beyond which the ocean, and all lands that had been or might be discovered, were reserved for Castile. John II protested, and, by the Treaty of Tordesillas, negotiated in 1494, Spain and Portugal accepted a line drawn 370 leagues west of the Cape Verde Islands [1] as the line of demarcation, and thus divided the world outside Europe, threatening severe penalties to all intruders. In 1529, after the voyage of Magellan, by the Treaty of Saragossa, the line of demarcation in the Pacific was fixed as the continuation round the globe of the line drawn in the Atlantic. This monstrous treaty, which gave the monopoly of the East and West to Portugal and Spain respectively, was challenged by England and other European Powers as soon as they were in a position to do so. Incidentally, as we shall see, it was the main cause of the exploration of the North-East and North-West Passages.

Until quite recently the great achievements of the Florentine Amerigo Vespucci, who gave his name to the New World, have been obscured [2] by the uncertainty that prevails about them. According to his own account in his *Letters*, he sailed from Cadiz in May 1497 "towards the Great Gulf of the Ocean Sea". Apparently this voyage of discovery included the coast of Honduras and the Gulf of Mexico. In any case, he returned safely to Spain in the autumn of the following year with a cargo of 222 slaves. In his second voyage Vespucci struck Brazil. He then sailed north-west to the mouth of the Amazon, which he explored for some distance.

In his third voyage, he set sail from Lisbon in 1501, and explored the east coast of South America from latitude 5° to latitude 50°. In January 1502, a wide opening was discovered, and named Rio de Janeiro. Heawood considers that the names given to points on the coast of Brazil are derived from Saints' days which fell during Vespucci's presence in these waters, and this fact incidentally strengthens our belief in the genuineness of the exploration. He certainly prepared the

[1] *Vide* "The World Map before and after Magellan's Voyage", by E. Heawood, *Geographical Journal*, Vol. LVII, 1921.
[2] Vide *Amerigo Vespucci*, by A. Magnaghi, 1924. This work is judicially summarized in "A New View of the Vespucci Problem", by E. Heawood, in the *Geographical Journal*, Vol. LXVI, p. 339; also in *The Great Age of Discovery*, by A. P. Newton, 1932.

KING FERDINAND DESPATCHES SHIPS TO DISCOVER NEW ISLANDS

(*From a woodcut in the First Account of the Voyage of Columbus, by Guiliano Dati, 1493*)

way for Magellan, who refers to Vespucci as his predecessor. This exploration was undertaken in the service of Portugal, but Vespucci subsequently returned to the service of the King of Spain, and his influence on Spanish exploration and cartography alike were paramount. It is a great pity that no detailed account of these important voyages has come down to us.

So far no mention has been made of English participation in the field of ocean exploration. There had been commercial relations with Portugal and Spain for many centuries before Columbus sailed across the Atlantic. Bristol was the centre for this trade, whereas London and Southampton dealt chiefly with Venice and Genoa. Bristol also traded with Iceland from the fifteenth century, exporting cloth, wool and salt, and bringing back fish and " occasionally consignments of volcanic brymston ".[1] Owing to this intercourse, it is probable that the expeditions of the Norsemen to North America were known in Bristol. In 1480, John Jay of Bristol despatched a ship to discover the island of Brazil, which was believed to be situated not very far from the west coast of Ireland. The venture was of course a failure, and indeed, cruising to find a non-existent island prevented English explorers from sailing across the Atlantic. At the same time voyages to Iceland and elsewhere trained English seamen, and John Cabot was destined to be their successful leader in the field of exploration. Of Cabot little is known for certain until, in 1476, he was granted the privilege of Venetian citizenship. While living in Venice he was engaged in the eastern trade, and on one occasion he crossed the Isthmus of Suez and reached Mecca, which at that time was an important centre of the spice trade. He was a merchant rather than a seaman, but was a skilled navigator with a sound knowledge of geography.

Cabot came to England at some unknown date between 1484 and 1490 and settled at Bristol. There he interested the merchants in his scheme for crossing the Atlantic and discovering new lands, with the result that Henry VII was approached, and, after negotiations, a patent was issued in March 1496 by the terms of which Cabot was to sail under the English flag " to all parts, regions and coasts of the eastern, western, and northern sea ", and to make discoveries in parts of the world hitherto unknown to Christians and occupy them

[1] My chief authority for Cabot is *The Voyages of the Cabots*, by James A. Williamson, Argonaut Press, 1929.

in the King's name. This patent, which undoubtedly infringed the Treaty of Tordesillas, constitutes a proof that Henry VII did not intend to allow Spain and Portugal to divide the Atlantic and the new lands that it washed between themselves. He proposed to have a share, but, to avoid throwing down the gauntlet to Spain, this discovery must be of " heathen islands or countries hitherto unknown to Christians ". It must also be made in the latitude of England, that being the area Henry VII intended to stake out for his country.

Cabot sailed on his great voyage of exploration on May 2, 1497. The best account of it is given in a letter, from which I quote.[1]

> " He started from Bristol, a port on the west of this kingdom, passed Ireland, which is still further west, and then bore to the north. . . . After having wandered for some time, he at length arrived at the mainland, and after taking certain tokens he returned. . . . They assert that the sea there is swarming with fish, which can be taken not only with the net, but in baskets let down with a stone. I have heard this Messer Zoane Caboto state so much."

It appears that the outward voyage took fifty-four days, and there is no certainty as to the point where Cabot touched the New World; but Williamson considers that he struck Cape Breton. He was certain that he 'had reached the mainland of Asia, but being steeped in the account given of China and Japan by Marco Polo, he considered that he had landed to the north of these civilized countries. He hoisted the flags of England and of St. Mark of Venice, and then sailed along the coast to observe its south-westerly trend for some 300 leagues. He saw no inhabitants, but had proof of their existence, picking up some snares set for game and similar trifles. Before sailing for home, two islands were sighted, but supplies were running short, and no delay was permissible on what was intended to be a reconnaissance. All went well on the homeward journey, and the explorers reached Bristol on August 6. John Cabot immediately proceeded with the Bristol merchants to London, where he was well received by Henry VII.

A second expedition was immediately organized, consisting of five ships, which sailed in May 1498. Cabot's purpose was to follow the coast southwards to the spice regions adjoining Chipangu. One of his ships was damaged, but the others

---

[1] This delightful letter was written by a certain de Soncino to the Duke of Milan on December 18, 1497.

reached the New World safely. Cabot then sailed southwards, surveying the coast as he went. Williamson in dealing with the extent of Cabot's exploration on these two voyages
refers to the map of Juan de la Cosa which was drawn in
1500. He shows that, in the 1497 voyage, Cabot missed Newfoundland in the outward passage and struck land near Cape
Breton. Sailing along the coast of Nova Scotia, he crossed
the Bay of Fundy to Maine, a point which, in view of the
width of the bay, might well be termed *Cavo Descubierto* or
" Cape Discovered ". On the homeward voyage, Newfoundland was sighted, but not explored.

In the 1498 voyage Cape Cod was passed, and this area
is shown as " sea discovered by the English " on Juan's map.
The explorers probably reached the mouth of the Delaware
River. One delightful point to note is that Cabot shows the
coast running approximately east and west in the latitude of
England instead of from north-east to south-west, the reason
for this being that he was determined to remain within the
limits of the patent as regards latitude. Juan de la Cosa,
who accepted the " political " survey of Cabot, also deliberately falsified his own map to show San Salvador in the latitude of Palos, the starting-point of Columbus.

To sum up, Cabot had made great discoveries, but he had
not started a profitable trade. Instead of ships laden with
spices, as was hoped, he returned without having sold his
cargo or brought home anything of the slightest commercial
value. Consequently the adventure was temporarily abandoned. The Spaniards were hostile to it, and Henry VII
wished to remain on good terms with Spain. Nothing can
however obscure the importance of Cabot's exploration, which
opened up lands of the greatest value, and discovered the cod
fisheries. Nor can it be forgotten that Newfoundland was
the first English colony.

Sebastian Cabot followed in his father's footsteps as an
explorer. Peter Martyr, the famous letter-writer, gives an
account of his Arctic voyage of 1508-9 in which " he found
numerous masses of floating ice in the middle of the month
of July. Daylight lasted nearly twenty-four hours." He also
made an expedition to the La Plata Valley, which ended in
failure. An English family, descended from a certain John
Strickland, believes that the founder of their family accompanied Sebastian Cabot to South America and introduced the
turkey; which was a domesticated bird in Mexico, into England. This belief is supported by the fact that "a turkey-

cock in its pride" appears in the coat of arms granted to him in 1550,[1] while the Sheldon tapestries of this period show the turkey as a subsidiary ornament.

Christopher Columbus remains for all time the central figure in the discovery of the New World. The fact that the geographical information on which he relied was inaccurate in no way lessens the credit that is his due, and he fully merits his epitaph:

> " *A Castilla y a Leon*
> *Nuevo mundo dió Colon.*"

Much credit is also due to Amerigo Vespucci, to John Cabot and to Magellan. The wonderful achievements of these explorers, combined with the splendid work of Diaz and Da Gama, who discovered the ocean route to India, inaugurated the modern world, and dwarf all other events in history.

---

[1] It is interesting to note that the name of "turkey" was first applied in England to the guinea-fowl. The French word *dinde* is the more correct, as showing that the bird was, like the potato, maize and tobacco, a gift of the New World.

CHAPTER XIV

THE CONQUISTADORS

*" When the great Montezuma examined the helmet which
Cortes had sent him and that which was on the god Huichilo-
bos, he felt convinced that we belonged to the race which, as his
forefathers had foretold, would come to rule over that land."*
" The Discovery and Conquest of Mexico ",
by BERNAL DIAZ DEL CASTILLO.

THE first phase of exploration in the New World was continued in the second by the search for a western route to
the Spice Islands, which resulted in the exploration of the
eastern and, later, of the western coast-line of America, and
in the circumnavigation of the world by Magellan.

Among the most important discoveries of this wonderful
period was that of Vasco Nuñez de Balboa, who, in 1513,
crossed the Isthmus of Panama, and sighting a new ocean,
rushed into its waters in full armour. Naming it the South
Sea, he took possession of it and the countries bordering on
it in the name of the King of Castile. This discovery, which
gave a great stimulus to the quest of the Spice Islands, led
to the foundation of Panama in 1519, and this town became
the base for further explorations, while the adjoining town
of Balboa commemorates the heroic *Conquistador*.

In 1517, an expedition which was based on Cuba discovered Yucatan.[1] " From the ships we could see a large
town, and as we had never seen such a large town in the
Island of Cuba . . . nor in Hispaniola, we named it the
Great Cairo. . . . The Indians were clothed in cotton shirts
made like jackets, and covered their persons with a narrow
cloth, and they seemed to us a people superior to the Cubans."
They were certainly warlike, and attacked the Spaniards when-
ever they landed, inflicting severe losses on them. Finally,
the expedition returned to Cuba to report the discovery. A
second exploring party, which also met with a hostile reception, brought news of the existence of Mexico and of its gold.
The Governor of Cuba determined to send a powerful

[1] For this section I have consulted Bernal Diaz del Castillo's *Discovery and Conquest
of Mexico*, translated by A. P. Maudslay (Broadway Travellers).

squadron to explore this land of golden promise, and appointed Hernan Cortes, " who held a grant of Indians " in Cuba, to command it. In February 1519 the expedition, which consisted of eleven ships with 100 sailors and 500 soldiers, sailed from Cuba. Like their predecessors, the Spaniards met with a most hostile reception in Yucatan, but thanks mainly to the small force of horsemen—the Indians believed that they were attacked by Centaurs—they defeated their opponents, albeit not without suffering losses. Cortes founded Vera Cruz to serve as his base, and was welcomed by representatives of Montezuma, the Aztec monarch who, inspired by the prophecy which serves as the motto to this chapter, sent rich gifts to the Spaniards.[1] He had heard of the previous expeditions and had received a pictorial report of the bearded white men, which had caused him deep anxiety, and accounts for the tortuous but vacillating policy he pursued.

The Aztecs, who ruled from Mexico City situated in a lake some 200 miles from the coast, were a dominant tribe which, like the Dorians in Greece, had gained the hegemony over a more civilized race by warlike prowess and administrative capacity. Their religion was based on human sacrifice, the victims usually being prisoners of war whose hearts were offered to the idols. As in other parts of the world, the custom of sacrificing the human representative of the god to ensure fertility was observed.[2] This blood tax represented thousands of victims, and Aztec policy encouraged revolt, so as to secure prisoners, while they fought to capture prisoners for sacrifice rather than to kill, a custom which saved Cortes and the Spaniards from disaster.[3] Cortes was favoured not only by this fortunate prophecy and by the Aztec unwillingness to kill. He soon discovered the hatred with which the dominant race was regarded, and made allies, by whose assistance he finally conquered Mexico.

His march to the interior began from Cempoala, where an influential *cacique* declared for the Spaniards and served them loyally. The route ran between high mountains, rising to a pass of some 10,000 feet, followed by a descent to the upland plains of Tlaxcala, which were situated at about 7,000 feet. This march occupied a fortnight, and the reception of

[1] The masks presented on this occasion are among the treasures of the British Museum.
[2] Vide *The Golden Bough*, by Sir James Frazer, p. 587. On p. 488 there is an interesting account of the sacramental eating of bread as the body of the god in Mexico.
[3] In Persia a reward was given for each head that was brought in, a custom which lowered the military value of a Persian army by preventing an effective pursuit.

the Spaniards by the Tlaxcalans was at first very hostile. They threatened " to kill those whom you call Teules (gods), and to eat their flesh, and we will see whether they are as valiant as you announce ". The Tlaxcalans displayed extraordinary valour, but on being defeated they wisely decided to make peace and became the devoted adherents of the Spaniards.

Cortes was welcomed at their chief town, Tlaxcala, where he received ambassadors from Montezuma, who sent him more

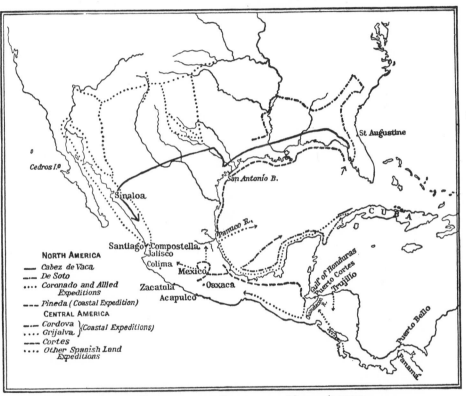

SPANISH EXPLORATION IN CENTRAL AND NORTH AMERICA.

rich gifts and promised to pay tribute on condition that the Spaniards stayed their advance. Encouraged by these unmistakable signs of weakness, Cortes marched on, and from Tlaxcala he made for Cholula, where, through the treachery of Montezuma, the Spaniards were attacked. However, warned by his allies, Cortes surprised his assailants and inflicted severe losses on the townspeople, who readily submitted, while the Mexican troops who lay in ambush outside the town, upon hearing of the failure of the plot, hastily retired.

From Cholula, Cortes despatched a party of volunteers to climb the volcano near Huexotzingo, which was in eruption at the period. None of them had ever seen a volcano, but, undeterred by stones and ashes and "great tongues of flame", the explorers climbed to the lip of the crater and enjoyed a wonderful view of "the great city of Mexico, and the whole of the lake, and all the towns which were built in it". They also acquired much prestige from the feat.

Cortes steadily advanced, and, to quote Diaz: "When we saw so many cities and villages built in the water and other great towns on dry land, we were amazed, and said that it was like the enchantments they tell us of in the legend of Amadis. And some of our soldiers even asked whether the things were not a dream." But the historian soon realized the facts: "Gazing on such wonderful sights, in front of us stood the great city of Mexico, and we—we did not even number 400 soldiers!" The capture of Montezuma, his death, the temporary withdrawal of the Spaniards from Mexico City, known as the *Noche Triste*, and their final success, fall outside the scope of this work, but may be read in the glowing pages of Diaz.

Mexico City fell in August 1521, and Cortes despatched troops in every direction to explore the country and to found towns at important centres. Northwards the victors reached the Pacific coast, founding the port of Zacatula, and penetrated into California and Texas. Southwards Alvarado explored Guatemala, while another expedition explored Honduras. Indeed, within three years the Conquistadors marched armed forces from Panama to beyond the northern boundary of Mexico, a distance of perhaps two thousand miles.

Among the greatest explorers of what was later to become the United States of America was Cabeza de Vaca.[1] He joined an expedition under Pamfilo de Narvaez, who had been granted the right to conquer and colonize the country between Mexico and Florida. De Narvaez landed in Tampa Bay on the west coast of Florida in April 1528 and, instead of exploring the coast, decided to leave his ships and to march northwards. From the first the question of supplies was acute, while the natives were generally hostile. The party reached the "town" of Apalache, which consisted of forty huts in the vicinity of Apalache Bay. There De Narvaez, who had entirely lost touch with his squadron, decided to construct some boats, and in

[1] For this section I have consulted *Spanish Explorers in the Southern United States*, by F. W. Hodge and T. H. Lewis, 1925.

these, without a single navigator to guide them, they embarked. During this unfortunate voyage " we took fresh water from the sea, the stream entering it in freshet ", this reference being the first mention of the waters of the mighty Mississippi.

As might have been anticipated, the expedition ended in disaster, from drowning, starvation, wounds and slavery. Finally De Vaca and three survivors, after years of privations, and entirely naked, made their way westwards to the Colorado River. The intrepid explorer won veneration as a healer, and thus obtained food and was enabled to pass safely through the country. Throughout, he gave a remarkable description of the various tribes, and wrote : " I believe these people see and hear better, and have keener senses, than any others in the world. They are great in hunger, thirst and cold, as if they were made for the endurance of these more than any other men, by habit and nature." He also described in some detail the vegetable products and the animals, including the bison. Finally, in 1536, after having traversed the continent for the first time, he reached Mexico.

Another most important expedition was that of Francisco Vazquez de Coronado, who in 1540, relying on the accounts of De Vaca and of an imaginative friar, marched north from Mexico parallel to the coast, but keeping a certain distance inland. His first objective was the seven cities of Cibola, represented by the friar as containing houses of many storeys and infinite wealth. Upon arrival, to the fury of the Spaniards, " it was a little crowded village looking as if it had been crumpled up all together and containing about 200 warriors ". A party, headed by Coronado, reached Quivira, believed to be the area where the Arkansas and Kansas Rivers approach one another in the centre of America, Kansas City being considered to be situated in the heart of the continent.

During this journey they " came to some settlements of people who lived like Arabs and who are called Querechos (Eastern Apaches). They lived on the bison, killing them as required for food and for their skins, and following them in their migrations." Another party reached the Grand Canyon, where " they spent three days looking for a passage down to the river, which looked from above as if the water was six feet across, although the Indians said it was half a league wide ". I visited the Grand Canyon some years ago, scrambling down a mule track for perhaps 3,000 feet, and spent two days on the banks of the Colorado River, which was about 100 yards wide so far as I can remember. This great chasm particularly interested me, since I had seen similar formations in Persia, albeit on a much smaller scale. Indeed, Arizona resembles the Persian plateau in its altitude of 5,000 feet, its lack of rainfall, its steppe vegetation, its serrated ranges and the domed adobe huts of the Indians. To complete the comparison, the scanty population of Spanish descent uses Spanish saddles and bridles, which came to Spain through its Moslem conquerors from Persia. The Grand Canyon at dawn exhibits nature in her most austere mood, and impressed me deeply.

> " What makes the lingering Night so cling to thee ?
> Thou vast, profound, primeval hiding-place
> Of ancient secrets,—grey and ghostly gulf
> Cleft in the green of this high forest-land,
> And crowded in the dark with giant forms !
> Art thou a grave, a prison, or a shrine ? " [1]

Like Cabot, Coronado was considered to have failed, since he found no gold or other valuable products. But, as the successor of De Vaca, and of De Soto, who discovered the Mississippi, he explored the vast plains of the interior of North America and, like the illustrious navigator, he certainly deserves a niche in the temple of Fame.

We next come to the exploration of the west coast of America and the conquest of Peru by the celebrated *Conquistador* Francisco Pizarro. He sailed from Panama in 1524, " and for three years they suffered great hardships from hunger and cold. The greater part of the crews died of hunger. . . . All was swamp and inundated country, without inhabitants." [2] With indomitable courage Pizarro at length crossed the equator and reached a country whose inhabitants lived in villages and towns. Their products included bananas, maize, sweet potatoes, pineapples and coconuts, while golden ornaments were worn. The llama was seen for the first time by the explorers, who had reached the province of Quito, which formed the northern division of the empire of Peru.

At this period the Incas of Peru were the predominant power in South America. They were mountaineers who had entered the country from the south and, settling at Cuzco, had gradually conquered the country as far as Quito in the north. The inhabitants of the coastal regions, who possessed

---

[1] From a poem by Henry Van Dyke.
[2] *Reports on the Discovery of Peru*, by Clements Markham, Hakluyt Society, 1872
This work includes reports by Francisco de Xeres from which the quotations are taken.

a higher civilization, had resisted, but, as their cultivation depended on irrigation water drawn from the mountains, and the Incas had seized the sources, they unwillingly submitted. The Incas possessed no script, their only form of record consisting in knotted cords, called *Quippu*, which served for accounts.

The monarch was looked upon as the son of the tribal god, the Sun, and the entire administration was centred in his person. When Pizarro appeared on the scene the ruling god had just died, and a pretender, Atahualpa by name, had seized the throne after desperate fighting in the spring of 1532. This was an amazing piece of good fortune for Pizarro, who landed in Peru at an especially opportune time.

After this reconnaissance, during which he had sailed nine degrees of latitude farther south than any of his predecessors, Pizarro returned to Spain, where " he was granted the government and command of that land ".

In 1531 he set out on his famous expedition with " 180 men, with thirty-seven horses, in three ships ", and landed at Tumbez in May 1532. In the first instance, he decided to reconnoitre the country, and founding a town to serve as his base, named it San Miguel. Meanwhile, he heard of the civil war and of its result. He also ascertained that Atahualpa was encamped at Cajamarca, distant some twelve stages on the far side of the Andes.

Resolved to dare all things, in the autumn Pizarro, at the head of 160 men, of whom sixty were cavalry, marched inland towards the camp of the Inca monarch. At many stages he found royal buildings furnished with supplies, while the population was friendly. On the way he received gifts from Atahualpa, who welcomed him to his country and invited him to his camp.

Leaving the fertile area, Pizarro crossed the sandy desert of Sechura in three stages to Motupe. Here he rested the tiny force for three days, and Xeres noted that " each month they sacrifice their own children ". The crossing of the Andes, which was " so steep that, in places, they had to ascend by steps " was a severe test alike to man and horse. The cold was bitter after the warmth of the plains, and position after position could have been held against them by a mere handful of men. However, there were no signs of hostility, and the little force finally reached the fertile valley of Cajamarca, where Atahualpa was encamped with an army 50,000 strong. Pizarro, basing his policy on that of Cortes, decided to seize Atahualpa, which he did by treachery. The execution of the unfortunate Inca followed, Peru fell like a ripe pear, and Pizarro occupied the capital, Cuzco, with its fine buildings and swarming population. Generally speaking, there was much less resistance than at Mexico, albeit the prize was richer, and before long Peru was occupied from Cuzco to Quito. Lima was founded in 1535, and became the capital.

The first expedition into Chile was led by Diego de Almagro. In 1535, with 600 Spaniards and 15,000 Indians, most of whom he lost in the snows of winter, he occupied the northern part of the country, but, in the absence of gold, no permanent conquest was attempted. Later Valdivia,[1] with a very small force, invaded Chile, and founded Santiago in 1541. Realizing that the country was suitable for farmers, he gradually occupied the fertile lands and penetrated to the site of the present town of Valdivia, which was founded in 1552. In no part of America was the resistance offered so determined as was that of the Araucanians, but under Mendoza the Spaniards penetrated farther south, and, in 1577, discovered the archipelago of Chiloe. It is interesting to note that not until the nineteenth century were the warlike Indians of Southern Chile finally subdued.

In the space at my disposal I cannot describe the many expeditions that were made up the Magdalena River and elsewhere in that area to find a rumoured El Dorado. Nor can I do more than mention the expedition of Pizarro's brother Gonzalo which led to the discovery of the Amazon by Orellana,[2] who followed the river down to its mouth.

These conquests, which were permanent, were among the most amazing ever made. Alexander and Caesar conquered with powerful armies, whereas the Spaniards were merely a handful of cavalry and infantry, though supported, it is true, by artillery and firearms, which represented a superior armament, while their horses inspired terror both in Mexico and in Peru.

Well might Xeres write :

" For when, either in ancient or modern times, have such great exploits been achieved by so few against so many, over so many climes, across so many seas, to subdue the unseen and unknown ? Whose deeds can be compared with those of Spain ? "

---

[1] Vide *Pedro de Valdivia, Conqueror of Chile*, by R. B. Cunninghame Graham, 1926
[2] In *Expeditions into the Valley of the Amazons*, edited by Sir Clements Markham (Hakluyt Society, 1st Series, Vol. XXII), Franciso de Orellana gives an account of the Warlike Indian women who suggested to him the name he gave to the great river.

HERNAN CORTÉS

(*From an oil painting in the Municipal Palace, Mexico*)

CHAPTER XV

MAGELLAN AND THE CIRCUMNAVIGATION OF THE WORLD

" He was more constant than ever anyone else in the greatest
of adversity. He endured hunger better than all the others,
and more accurately than any man in the world did he under-
stand sea charts and navigation."

PIGAFETTA's *Eulogy of Magellan.*

THE great age of exploration with which we are dealing
enshrines three outstanding names : Christopher Columbus,
Vasco da Gama and Magellan. The last of the illustrious
trio completed the epoch by the circumnavigation of the
globe, discovering the straits that are called by his name, crossing
the Pacific Ocean, which he so named from the absence of
storms, and reaching the Spice Islands of Asia, which were
still the main objective of all explorers.

Ferdinand Magellan was born about 1480 at Sabrosa,
situated in the extreme north of Portugal. He belonged to
a noble family, and after serving at Court as a page, he enlisted
in 1505 as a volunteer in the great armada of Francisco
d'Almeida, and was wounded in the two fierce naval engage-
ments described in Chapter XII. He also served in Sequeira's
reconnaissance of Malacca in 1509, in Albuquerque's capture
of the city in 1511, and in the cruise to Java and Amboina.[1]
He had certainly distinguished himself during the seven years
of his service in the East, and upon his return to Portugal,
this was recognized by an increase in his official stipend and
by his promotion to the rank of *Fidalgo escudeiro.*

In 1513 Magellan took part in a campaign in Morocco,
in which he was again wounded. Upon his return to Lisbon,
he was charged with irregularities in connection with the
distribution of the booty, and was coldly received by Dom
Manuel, who evinced his displeasure. Realizing that there
was no future for him in Portugal, and deeply hurt by the
injustice of the King, Magellan publicly repudiated his nation-

---

[1] In this section I have consulted *The Life of Ferdinand Magellan,* by F. H. H. Guille
mard, 1870, and *Magellan's Voyage around the World,* by Antonio Pigafetta, translated by
J. J. A. Robertson, 1906.

ality and entered the service of Charles V. With his excellent record of wide exploration, which had included the Spice Islands, a native of which he was able to exhibit, as well as a slave-girl from Sumatra, Magellan was taken seriously at the Spanish Court. His plan was to sail southwards along the coast of South America, beyond the point explored by Amerigo Vespucci, and he asserted his firm belief in the existence of a passage from the Atlantic to the South Sea, which would open a westerly route to the Spice Islands.

Charles V, after due consideration, gave orders for the expedition, and, in spite of strong remonstrances from Portugal, a squadron of five ships was prepared and on September 20, 1519, set sail from San Lucar. It is uncertain whether Magellan possessed any definite information as to the existence of a cape or strait which would enable him to round South America. To a certain extent he must have been influenced by the classical belief in symmetry, which, as mentioned in Chapter I, made Herodotus trace the course of the Nile to correspond with that of the Danube. Apart from this, he certainly possessed some vague information as to the existence of a strait, and Pigafetta writes : " Had we not discovered that Strait, the Captain-General had determined to go as far as seventy-five degrees toward the Antarctic Pole." In any case he was a lion-hearted explorer, determined to sail by way of South America to the Spice Islands.

From San Lucar Magellan shaped a south-westerly course, touching at Teneriffe and passing between Cape Verde and its islands. He struck bad weather on the equator, but continuing the voyage the coast of South America was sighted at Santo Augustino and was followed to Port St. Julian, situated in latitude 49° 20′ S., which was reached on March 31, 1520. In this sheltered harbour, which had been discovered by Vespucci, it was decided to winter, and the long period of inaction in a cold climate on reduced rations, combined with fears for their own safety, led to a plot, headed by some of the chief officers, which aimed at the assassination of Magellan and his supporters and the abandonment of the enterprise. Truth is stranger than fiction, and the amazing courage and subtle resourcefulness displayed by the leader in dealing with an apparently hopeless situation, crushed the mutiny.

Towards the end of April a reconnaissance led to the discovery of a river abounding in fish, which was named the Santa Cruz. The reconnoitring ship was wrecked in a heavy storm, but the crew escaped. The winter had set in, and

although the country appeared to be uninhabited, one morning a giant appeared on the beach, dressed in skins, with boots
of the same material, which originated the name of Patagon
or " large clumsy foot ". According to Pigafetta " he was
so tall that we reached only to his waist, and was well pro-
portioned ". In August the expedition sailed south to the
Santa Cruz River, where two months were spent in cutting
wood and drying fish, as the stores were running out.

In mid-October the voyage was resumed, and on October
21, 1520, a notable date in the history of exploration, the
Straits destined to be named after Magellan were discovered
in latitude 52° S., or only some two degrees beyond the limit
reached by Vespucci. " Then ", to quote Pigafetta, " all
together thanking God and the Virgin Mary, we went to
seek the strait further on." At a point where " we found
two openings " a reconnaissance was made, and " the men
returned within three days, and reported that they had seen
the cape and the open sea. The Captain-General wept for
joy."

The Straits are only some 300 miles in length, but took
over a month to negotiate. When this had been safely
accomplished, Magellan found himself in the vast ocean,
which he termed the Pacific, with only three ships, the *San
Antonio* having deserted.

Supplies had run short, but Magellan after his splendid
discovery scorned all thoughts of turning back, and the
voyage was resumed. Sailing north within sight of land for
some days, he shaped a north-westerly course, and thereby
missed islands at which supplies and water could have been
obtained had he kept more to the south. The sufferings of
the explorers were terrible. Pigafetta writes : " We ate powder
of biscuits swarming with worms. We drank yellow water
that had been putrid for many days. Rats were sold for one-
half ducado apiece." For ninety-eight days they sailed over
this vast ocean, and, at last, sighted the Ladrone Islands,
where the natives stole Magellan's skiff and thus earned their
unenviable designation.

Refreshed by fruit and vegetables the sailors resumed
their voyage, and, seven days later, the Philippine or St.
Lazarus Islands, as Magellan named them, were reached.
Here their reception was most friendly. At the small island
of Limassana, Magellan's slave, Enrique of Malacca, was
able to act as interpreter, and thus paved the way for real
intercourse. Rejoicing in the fertility of this wonderful un-

explored archipelago, Magellan entered the port of Sebú, where a formal treaty was concluded with the King.

Magellan had circumnavigated South America and had reached the Philippine Islands, as they were renamed a generation later. He had won through to the neighbourhood of the Spice Islands, and it now remained to return to Spain and receive the reward that he so richly deserved. But the gods thought otherwise, and he was killed in a skirmish with natives on the neighbouring island of Mactan on April 27, 1521.

Under Sebastian del Cano the survivors of the expedition, which had been further weakened by an act of treachery at Sebu, shaped a course to Brunei, the chief port of Borneo, which "is entirely built in salt water and contains 25,000 fires". The Sultan received them hospitably, but, after a while, there was reason to suspect treachery, so they set sail north-east to find an islet where they were able to beach the ships, which were caulked and generally repaired. Continuing the voyage, the Moluccas were reached, and the two remaining ships anchored close to the shore of Tidor, ruled by a Moslem, who welcomed the Spaniards, and supplied them with cloves.

Reduced to one serviceable ship, the *Victoria*, the Spaniards sailed from Tidor in December 1522. They touched at Timor and shaped a course across the Indian Ocean for the Cape of Good Hope. They feared to visit Mozambique, and touching at the Cape Verde Islands, where some of their sailors were made prisoners by the Portuguese, three years almost to a day after their departure from Spain, the survivors finally reached Seville. They had sailed round the world.

Magellan will remain for all time a heroic explorer who was worthy of his great achievement. He was not only the greatest navigator of his age, and a man of indomitable courage and resource, but his unselfishness and wide outlook were equally remarkable. The geographical results of this wonderful voyage corrected the error of Ptolemy as to the size of Asia which appears on Behaim's famous globe of 1492, and revealed the Pacific Ocean in its true magnitude. Belief in this great geographer's second error of a great southern continent was rather strengthened by Magellan's report that Tierra del Fuego was part of such a continent, whereas it actually consists of several islands.[1]

[1] Vide "The World Map before and after Magellan's Voyage," by E. Heawood, *Journal R.G.S.*, Vol. LVII, p. 431, 1921.

MAGELLAN PASSING THROUGH THE STRAITS

(*From de Bry*)

The Philippine Islands were conquered in 1564 by a Spanish squadron which sailed from Navidad, a Mexican port. This inaugurated an annual despatch of ships during the season of the north-east winds. The pioneer of the passage of the Pacific from east to west was Andres de Urdaneta,[1] who accomplished this difficult feat by sailing as far north as latitude 42°. The return voyage from the Philippines to New Spain now became a matter of routine, but was always considered to be dangerous. During this period New Guinea and other islands were discovered, but there was little attempt to undertake new exploration, the energies of Spain and Portugal being devoted to colonization and commerce in their rich possessions.

In 1578 the monopoly of the Pacific Ocean was rudely broken by the appearance on the scene of Francis Drake. That great English navigator set out on his memorable voyage from Plymouth in November 1577 with a squadron of five ships and a personnel of 164 officers and men.[2] Following the west coast of Africa, where he made prizes of Spanish and Portuguese vessels, from the Cape Verde Islands he sailed across the Atlantic to Brazil, which was sighted in latitude 33° S. He anchored in the River Plate, the appointed rendezvous, and continuing southwards reached sinister Port St. Julian, where, like Magellan, he dealt successfully with an attempt at mutiny. The passage of the Straits of Magellan was difficult, but on September 6, 1578, Drake reached the Pacific Ocean, on which he was the first Englishman to sail a ship. Unlike Magellan he was met by very bad weather, and, to quote from Hakluyt's work, " wee were driven by a great storme from the entring into the South Sea to the Southward of the Streight in 57 degrees and a terce : in which height we came to an anker among the Islands ". This was in effect an important discovery, as the storm had taken the English explorers beyond Cape Horn, to the north of which they had found safety among the islands. Drake's claim to have been to " the southernmost knowne land in the world " is fully justified, and his discovery actually proved that Tierra del Fuego did not form part of the mythical southern continent of Ptolemy, but consisted of islands.

Drake sailed northwards, searching in vain for his lost ships—Winter had deserted and sailed home—" full sore

---

[1] Vide *The Philippine Islands, etc.*, by Antonio de Morga, Hakluyt Society, 1st series, Vol. XXXIX, pp. 355-6.
[2] For this section *vide* Hakluyt's *Principal Navigations*, Vol. XI, p. 191 *et seq.*

against the mariners minds ". He found that the coast ran
north-east and eastwards, and not north-west, " as the generall
Maps have it ". At Valparaiso he came into contact with the
Spaniards, and made a valuable prize of a ship from which
he replenished his stores. His successful cruise along the
coast of South and North America lies outside the scope of
this work, but he " sayled on the backside of America to 43
degrees Northerly latitude ", where the " faire and good
Baye " which he discovered has been identified with the
Bay of San Francisco. It is one of the most beautiful harbours
I have visited. Drake " calling this countrey Nova Albion
. . . set up a monument of our being there, as also of her
Majesties right and title to the same ". So far as Drake
could ascertain, the Spaniards had not penetrated so far
north.

The voyage across the Pacific, thanks to the ample supply
of stores taken from the Spaniards, and the favouring winds,
was successfully accomplished, and the English adventurers
anchored at Ternate in the Moluccas, where they were received
in the most friendly manner, and where Drake made a treaty
which was looked upon as of considerable value by the
ministers of the Queen. Continuing the voyage " we ranne
suddenly upon a rocke, where we stuck fast from 8 of the
clocke at night, til 4 of the clocke in the afternoon of the
next day ". Fortunately the wind changed, and " the happy
gale drove our ship off the rocke into the sea againe ". At
Java Drake was equally well received, and having shipped a
rich cargo of spices, he shaped his course for the Cape of
Good Hope, which he " passed by the 18 of June " and, on
November 3, 1580, he reached Plymouth. His voyage, like
that of his great predecessor, had taken three years, but, more
fortunate than Magellan, Drake lived to accomplish his task
and to receive the rewards bestowed upon him by his grateful
sovereign.

CHAPTER XVI

EXPLORERS IN NORTHERN LATITUDES DURING THE SIXTEENTH AND SEVENTEENTH CENTURIES

> "Learned men and painefull travellers have affirmed with one consent and voice, that America was an Island : and that there lyeth a great Sea between it, Cathaia and Grondland, by the which any man of our countrey, that will give the attempt, may with small danger passe to Cathaia, the Moluccae and India."
>
> *Discourse of Sir Humphrey Gilbert.*

It is not generally realized that the early exploration of the Arctic regions, which was mainly undertaken by English navigators, was due to the desire to reach Cathay and the Spice Islands. It was hoped to sell broad-cloth, the chief manufacture at that period, to the Chinese and to purchase spices with the proceeds.[1] The eastern and western routes by the Cape of Good Hope and the Straits of Magellan were monopolized by the Portuguese and Spaniards respectively, albeit this monopoly was being challenged, as we have already seen. But, should a northern route to the Moluccas be discovered, it would avoid the risk of death, capture or imprisonment, if not of becoming the victim of an *auto da fé*, and, so far as Cathay was concerned, it would be a much shorter route.

In the first instance a search was made for a North-East passage to Cathay by the merchant adventurers of the Muscovy Company, on whose behalf Sebastian Cabot drew up the instructions for the first voyage, which enjoined that " You use all wayes and meanes possible to learne how men may passe from Russia either by land or by sea to Cathaia ". Its leaders were Sir Hugh Willoughby and Richard Chancelor, who sailed in command of three ships from Deptford in 1553. Before striking the coast of Norway, Willoughby disappeared in a great storm, and both he and his crew died of cold in the bay of Arzina, on the coast of Lapland. The third ship was also lost, but Chancelor had better fortune, for " he held on his course towards that unknown part of the world, and

---

[1] I have to thank Mr. J. M. Wordie for valuable suggestions in this chapter.

sailed so farre, that he came at last to the place where he found
no night at all, and it pleased God to bring them into a certaine
great Bay ".[1]   This was the White Sea, and the voyage led to
the discovery of Russia by the English.   On landing, Chancelor
was well received, and proceeded to Moscow, " a troublesome
journey, wherein he had the use of certaine sleds ".   The
Grand Duke Ivan entertained the Englishman most hospitably,
and thus was inaugurated a valuable trade with Russia, regarding which country Chancelor collected much valuable information, the earliest to be received in England.   It was speedily
utilized, and in 1555 Chancelor returned to Russia, and secured
from Ivan a monopoly of trade in the White Sea for the
Muscovy Company.

From the standpoint of Arctic exploration, Stephen
Burrough led a more successful expedition, which sailed in
April 1556.   He was off the North Cape a month later, and,
meeting some friendly Russian fishermen, he accompanied
them across the Cronian Sea, as Pliny called it, to the Kola
River.   In July he " went in over the dangerous barre of
Pechora ",[2] and sailed as far east as the island of Vaigaich,
where he found Samoyeds who " for their catriages have no
beasts to serve them, but Deer only ".

We learn from Purchas [3] that Antony Marsh, a Chief
Factor of the Muscovy Company, not only gained detailed
information about the Ob, but despatched some members of
his Russian staff, who reached it by land in 1584.   He refers
to an English vessel which had reached Ob, where it had
been shipwrecked and its crew murdered by the natives.
This was the eastern limit of the English.

The Dutch, who had watched the voyages of the English
explorers with deep interest, now began to take part in expeditions to the Arctic.   The object of Jan van Linschoten's
expedition, consisting of four ships, two of which were
commanded by William Barents, was " to saile into the North
seas, to discover the kingdoms of Cathaia and China ".[4]
Starting in June 1594, Novaya Zemlya was reached a month
later.   Barents sailed up its west coast, in spite of much
difficulty owing to the ice, and reached its north part, which
is called after its discoverer.

A second voyage in 1595 was not so successful, but in

---

[1] Hakluyt's *Voyages*, Vol. II, p. 248 *et passim*.
[2] The Petsora of Milton's passage quoted below.
[3] *Pilgrimes*, Vol. III, pp. 804–6.
[4] Vide *The Three Voyages of William Barents*, by Lieut. Koolemans Beynen (Hakluyt
Society), 1876.

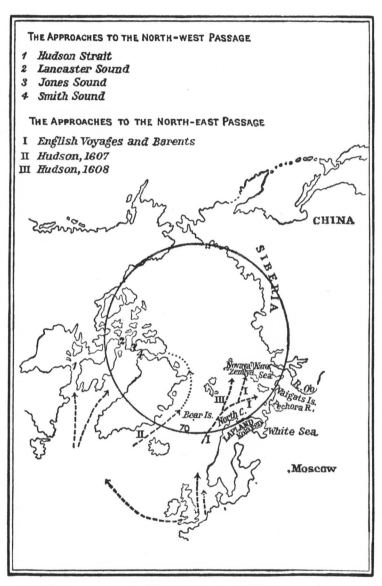

THE APPROACHES TO THE NORTH-WEST PASSAGE

1 Hudson Strait
2 Lancaster Sound
3 Jones Sound
4 Smith Sound

THE APPROACHES TO THE NORTH-EAST PASSAGE

I English Voyages and Barents
II Hudson, 1607
III Hudson, 1608

CHINA

SIBERIA

Novaya Zemlya

Kara Sea

R. Ob

Vaigats Is.

Pechora R.

Bear Is.

North C.

LAPLAND

Kola Pen.

White Sea

70

.Moscow

THE APPROACHES TO THE NORTH-EAST AND THE NORTH-WEST PASSAGES.

the following year a third expedition was made under Heems-kerck with Barents as pilot and was notable for the discovery of North-West Spitsbergen. Later the explorers attempted to sail round Novaya Zemlya, but were unable to do so. The unfortunate crew were forced to winter in great misery —the first time an Arctic winter had been faced. The heroic Barents, who died during the homeward voyage, certainly ranks among the great Arctic explorers.

In 1607, Henry Hudson[1] sailed from England in an attempt to reach Japan by the North Pole. In this expedition he explored the east coast of Greenland, but bore away to Spits-bergen when a very high latitude was reached. He found his way barred by ice, and returned to England. It is interesting to note that in the map of Ortelius published in 1570, and indeed in other maps of the period, a clear passage is shown running due east across the northern coast of Asia. Actually the strenuous efforts made by the brave and experienced navigators barely succeeded in traversing one quarter of the enormous distance which separated North Cape from Bering Strait. To quote Milton:

> "As when two polar winds, blowing adverse
> Upon the Cronian sea, together drive
> Mountains of ice, that stop the imagin'd way,
> Beyond Petsora eastward, to the rich
> Cathaian coast."

The search for a north-east passage had failed, but attempts continued to the north-west. Sir Humphrey Gilbert wrote a learned work " to prove a Passage by the North-west to Cathaia and the East Indies ". His thesis was that America was undoubtedly the lost Atlantis of the classical geographers, and while relying on " Plato, Aristotle and other phyloso-phers ", he argued that symmetry demanded a strait in the north of America to balance the Straits of Magellan in the south. Martin Frobisher, who was undoubtedly encouraged by such views as these, led an expedition to find a north-west passage in 1576. Rounding the south of Greenland (which he thought was the fictitious Frisland), he found what he hoped was the sought-for strait ; but it was merely a bay, which is called after the explorer. He described the Eskimos as " like Tartars, with long blacke haire, broad faces, and flatte noses, and tawnie in colour, wearing Seale skinnes. . . . The women are marked in the face with blewe streekes down the cheekes,

---

[1] Vide *Henry Hudson the Navigator*, by G. M. Asher (Hakluyt Society), Vol. XXVI, 1860.

and round about the eyes."[1] His experience of these
" salvages " was not happy, as they carried off five of his
men who were never seen again. He, in return, kidnapped
a male Eskimo to show in England.

After Frobisher came John Davis, who, in 1585, sailed
along the western shores of Greenland, naming it the Land
of Desolation, and crossing Davis Strait discovered the vast
Cumberland Sound which he believed would prove to be
the elusive Strait. In a third voyage, undertaken in 1587,
Davis reached latitude 72° 41' N. on the west coast of Greenland.

We now return to Hudson, who started on his fourth and
last voyage in 1610. From Greenland he entered the Strait
which had been accidentally discovered by Frobisher on a
third voyage which he had made in search of gold. Following it up in the hope that it would lead to the passage, the
ill-fated Hudson reached the vast bay which, like the Strait,
was destined to be called after him. The last entry of Hudson
runs : " The third day we put through the narrow passage.
. . . After wee had sailed ten leagues, the land fell away to
the southward, and the other iles, and land left us to the
westward. Then I observed and found the ship at noone
in 61 degrees, 20 minutes, and a sea to the westward." Hudson explored the east side of the vast bay, the ship " being
haled aground " on November 1, and, ten days later, it was
frozen in. The following summer the crew mutinied, and
Hudson with his son, Philip Staffe the carpenter, and the
sick men were forced into the shallop and were never heard
of again. It is satisfactory to read in the report of the not
altogether blameless Abacuk Prickett, that the leaders of the
mutiny all came to a miserable end.[2]

We next come to William Baffin, who was one of the
greatest of the splendid line of English navigators and explorers. The discovery of Hudson Bay had naturally excited
high hopes, but further examination by Baffin proved that
the quest must be continued farther north.

Under Bylot as Captain he explored Hudson Strait in
1615. In the following year they sailed again much farther
north than any of their predecessors up the coast of Greenland, naming the various peninsulas, and discovering Smith
Sound and then Jones Sound and Lancaster Sound to the
west, all three leading out of Baffin Bay as it is fittingly called.
Baffin came to the conclusion that he had failed in his quest,

---

[1] *Vide* Hakluyt's *Voyages*, Vol. VII, p. 209.   [2] *Op. cit.*, p. 98 *et seq.*

whereas he had in reality marked out the route which, followed by his successors, led to final achievement, though not until two centuries later.

William Baffin ended his splendid career in the Persian Gulf. He had surveyed its coast, for which he received a gratuity from the East India Company, and in 1622 he took part in the attack by the English on the fort of Kishm, held by the Portuguese. To quote *Purchas his Pilgrimes*, " Master Baffin went on shoare with his Geometricall Instruments, for the taking the height and distance of the castle wall ; but as he was about the same, he received a small shot from the Castle into his belly, wherewith he gave three leapes, by report, and died immediately." [1] I have visited Kishm fort, where I was shown the Portuguese guns and cannon-balls.

The search for the North-West Passage was unsuccessful at this period, but as in the case of the earlier quest it yielded invaluable results to the successors of these great navigators, while the training in navigation in the Arctic was of inestimable value to the seamen.

Hitherto in this chapter we have dealt with sea voyages. We must now turn to the discovery of Canada by Jacques Cartier,[2] who, like other explorers, was searching for a new route to the Spice Islands. The cod fisheries discovered by Cabot were regularly visited by French, Spanish, Portuguese and English vessels. The French fishing fleet sailed from Saint-Malo, where its departure and return are still the chief subjects of interest in that picturesque port.

No attempt at serious exploration had been attempted since the voyages of Cabot until Cartier appeared on the scene off Cape Bonavista, Newfoundland, which is situated in the same latitude as Saint-Malo, in 1534. Coasting New-foundland he sailed through the Belle Isle Strait, and examined the coast of Labrador, the sterile appearance of which caused him to write that " I am rather inclined to believe that this is the land God gave to Cain ".[3] The inhabitants he described as " wild and savage folk clothed with furs and painted with tan colours ".

Sailing along the west coast of Newfoundland, he crossed Cabot Strait to the fertile Magdalen Islands, " the best land we have seen ; for two acres of it are worth more than the whole of Newfoundland ". He admired Prince Edward

[1] *Some Years' Travels*, etc., p. 106.
[2] *The Voyages of Jacques Cartier*, by H. P. Biggar, 1924.
[3] Cp. Genesis iv. 12 : " When thou tillest the ground, it shall not henceforth yield unto thee her strength."

Island, but could not land owing to the absence of a good harbour, and after reaching the mainland of Canada he crossed the mouth of the St. Lawrence to Anticosti Island. He attempted to explore the great river, but the "tides ran so strong that the vessels only lost way", and so it was decided to return to Saint-Malo.

In the following year Cartier started exploration at the point where he had left off, and after examining the northern shore for the hoped-for strait, he ascended the Hochelaga, as he called what is now the St. Lawrence. Friendly relations with the Indians were established through the agency of two natives, who had been taken to France and well treated, and, in spite of the strong current, good progress was made as far as Stadacona, the Indian village in the Charles River, of which he writes: "The region is as fine land as it is possible to see, being very fertile and covered with magnificent trees."

Continuing up the river with a bark and two long-boats, the grapes and the wonderful bird life delighted Cartier, who reached Hochelaga in the long-boats, to be received with dances and other signs of joy, the women bringing their babies to be touched by the strangers. He found Hochelaga to be a village of fifty large houses circular in shape and defended by a wooden palisade. Climbing an adjacent mountain, which he named Mount Royal, the French explorers enjoyed a marvellous view, ranging over plains with mountain ranges to the north and south, while following up the course of the great river they sighted "the most violent rapid it is possible to see". Thus was discovered the celebrated Lachine rapid.

Cartier had been remarkably successful. Not only had he discovered the fertile lower valley of the St. Lawrence and gained much valuable information as to the reaches above Hochelaga, which country was shortly destined to be colonized by France, but his discovery of the Strait of Cabot and of other islands bordering on the Gulf of St. Lawrence justify the high honour in which his name is held as an explorer.

CHAPTER XVII

EXPLORATION IN SOUTHERN ASIA DURING THE SIXTEENTH AND SEVENTEENTH CENTURIES

" As when the Tartar from his Russian foe,
By Astracan, over the snowy plains,
Retires, or Bactrian Sophi, from the horns
Of Turkish crescent, leaves all waste beyond
The realm of Aladule, in his retreat
To Tauris or Casbeen."

MILTON.

THE sixteenth century was dominated by Spain and Portugal. Before dealing with the successful efforts of the Dutch and English to challenge their world hegemony, we turn to the Near East, where, a few years before the opening of the sixteenth century, the Ak Kuyunlu, or " White Sheep " dynasty, had built up a kingdom which included the western provinces of Persia and the eastern provinces of Asia Minor. Uzun Hasan had supported the claims of the Prince of Karamania (as Cilicia was then called) against the Turks, and had been defeated. Realizing that he could not hope for success without the co-operation of a naval power, he despatched an ambassador to Venice, whose reception is the subject of a magnificent painting by Caliari Veronese which is to be seen in that city. Diplomatic intercourse was thus established, and Venice, which was attempting with scant success to secure united action by Christendom, despatched ambassadors to the Court of Hasan.

In 1471 Josafa Barbaro,[1] charged with this mission, landed on the coast of Asia Minor and made for Tabriz. Like Xenophon, who suffered from the attacks of the Carduchi, Barbaro, when he entered the Taurus Mountains, was attacked by their descendants the Kurds, whom he terms the Corbi, " exceeding crewell, and not so much thievishe as openly given to roberie . . . Having in my companie an Ambassador of the said Assambei (Hasan Beg), we were assaulted by the Corbi,

---

[1] *Travels of Venetians in Persia* (Hakluyt Society), 1873. The translation of the travels of Josafa Barbaro was made by William Thomas in the reign of Edward VI.

who slew the said Ambassador, and having hurte me and the rest, they tooke our sompters and all that they founde."

Josafa Barbaro, who reached Tabriz in rags, was well received by Hasan, and gives an interesting account of the court, the jewels and the "most beautiful carpetts". He accompanied Hasan to Isfahan, Kashan amd Kum. Thence he proceeded in the footsteps of Marco Polo to Yezd, which was at that period a flourishing city "with very great suburbes . . . they all arr wevers and makers of divers kindes of sylkes". Barbaro's descriptions of the tombs of the Achaemenian monarchs and of the Sasanian bas-reliefs near Persepolis are a masterpiece of quaint phraseology and misconception : "There is a mightie stone of one piece, on the which arr many ymages of men graven as great as gyaunts, and above all the rest of one ymage like unto that we resemble to God the Father in a circle. . . . A little further there is a great ymage on horsbacke, seemyng to be of a boysterouse man ; who they saie was Sampson ; about the which arr many other ymages apparailed of the frenche facon, with longe heares."[1] "Sampson" was Shapur, the captor of the Roman Emperor Valerian, who, with chains on his hands, appeals to the victor for mercy.

The rise of the Safavi dynasty in Persia as the successors of the "White Sheep" at the beginning of the sixteenth century was an event of great importance in world history. It reconstituted Persia as an independent and intensely nationalistic kingdom which, for religious and political reasons, was invariably hostile to Turkey. Consequently, as Busbecq, the ambassador of the Emperor, pointed out, Persia helped materially to save Europe from Turkish domination.

The founder of the dynasty was Shah Ismail, under whose successor, Tahmasp, Jenkinson travelled in Persia.

In the last chapter we have seen that the fruitless struggle to find a North-East passage resulted in the creation of a valuable trade with Russia. It was also hoped to reach Cathay by land. Anthony Jenkinson, who was Chief Factor of the Muscovy Company, and had accompanied Richard Chancelor, reappeared on the scene in Russia in 1557. He was well received by Ivan the Terrible, who had taken Kazan from the Tartars in 1552, and had followed up this important success by the capture of Astrakhan two years later, thus making the Volga a Russian river. In the spring of 1558, furnished with letters from the Tsar, Jenkinson started on a journey into

---

[1] For the description of these rock tombs with the figure of Ahura Mazda *vide* Sykes, *History of Persia*, Vol. I, p. 182.

Central Asia towards Cathay. He first made for Nijni Novgorod, the seat of the annual fair. He then travelled with the Governor-elect of Astrakhan, who had " 500 great boates under his conduct ". He described Kazan as " a fayre towne with a strong castle. Being in the hands of the Tartarres, it did more vexe the Russes in their warres, than any other nation." Continuing his exploration, Jenkinson refers to the nomad tribes who, living on meat and milk, mock at Christians for eating bread, " saying we live by eating the toppe of a weede, and drinke a drinke made of the same ". Lower down the river, reference is made to the sturgeon fishing, and in due course Jenkinson reached Astrakhan, where he described the trade as " so small and beggarley, that it is not worth while the making mention ". From Astrakhan he sailed along the east coast of the Caspian, passing the mouth of the Ural River and landing at Mangishlak, he hired camels, and crossed the desert for twenty days. " We found no water, but such as we drewe out of olde deepe wells, being very brackish and salt." He describes Urganj, which had been destroyed by Chengiz, and adds " there are many wilde horses, which the *Tartars* doe many times kill with their haukes ".

From Urganj, Jenkinson followed up the Ardocke, as he calls the Amu Darya or Oxus. He was attacked by a " prince banished from his Countrey ", and " had it not been for 4 hand gunnes, we had been overcome and destroyed ".

He finally reached Bokhara, of which he writes : " There are many houses, temples and monuments of stone, sumptuously builded, and gilt, and specially bathstones so artificially built that the like thereof is not in the worlde." This is clearly a reference to the beautiful tiles, which I have admired at Bokhara and Samarkand.

In the spring of 1559, Jenkinson returned to the Caspian and sailed back to Astrakhan. True Englishman that he was, he writes : " During the time of our navigation, wee sette uppe the redde crosse of St. George in our flagges." It is worthy of note that, during the Great War, the white ensign was flown on the Caspian Sea, where the British Navy gained fresh laurels. In the autumn, Jenkinson returned to Moscow and presented Ivan with a " white Cowes taile of Cathay " —actually a yak's tail. He also handed over various ambassadors from Central Asia " with all the *Russe* slaves ". His expedition had been crowned with success.

In April 1562 he sailed down the Volga with the object of opening up trade with Persia. From Astrakhan, weathering a severe storm in the Caspian, he reached Derbent, where he refers to the famous fort, " now under the power of the Sophie [1] of Persia ", which is one of the strongest castles I have seen. Upon landing at a port farther south, Jenkinson was most hospitably received by Abdulla Khan, King of Shirwan, whom he found in his summer camp ; and he was provided with an escort to the Persian Court at Kazvin, which city is referred to as Casbeen in the motto to this chapter.

Starting from Shamakhi, Jenkinson makes one of the earliest references to Baku, and traversing " a fruitful countrey, inhabited with pasturing people ", he reached Ardebil. There he visited the tomb of Ismail, who " lieth buried in a faire Meskit (mosque) with a sumptuous sepulchre ".

Jenkinson duly reached Kazvin, and gives a vivid account of his reception by Shah Tahmasp : " I delivered the Queenes majesties letters with my present, which he accepting, demanded of me what countrey of Franks I was : unto whom I answered that I was of the famous Citie of London and was sent for to treate of friendship, and free passage of our merchants and people." The question of religion was inevitably brought up by the fanatical Shah, who, learning that the Englishman was a Christian, replied : " We have no neede to have friendship with the unbeleevers, and so willed mee to depart." Indeed, it might have gone hard with Jenkinson, since the Shah was inclined to send his head as a suitable gift to the Sultan of Turkey, with whom peace had just been concluded. But Abdulla Khan of Shirwan wrote that " if he used me evill, there would few strangers resort into his countrey ".

Jenkinson finally returned to Moscow with raw silk and dye-stuffs for the Muscovy Company, and with precious stones and silk brocades for the Tsar. The brave attempt to trade across Russia to Persia was continued, but anarchy, storms and pirates brought it to an end in 1581. Jenkinson, the first Englishman to descend the Volga, to navigate the Caspian and to visit Bokhara, was one of the great Elizabethans, whose journeys enlarged the outlook of his fellow-countrymen. Milton was certainly indebted to him in connection with the lines already quoted, while Marlowe as certainly refers to him in *Tamburlaine the Great* :

> " And Christian merchants, that with Russian stems
> Plow up huge furrowes in the Caspian Sea,
> Shall vaile to us, as Lords of al the Lake."

Among the celebrated English travellers in Persia were

[1] The term Sophie is a corruption of Safavi, the name of the dynasty.

the Sherley brothers, who, accompanied by a large staff, reached Kazvin in 1598. Upon the return of Shah Abbas, the greatest of the Safavi monarchs, from a successful campaign against the Uzbegs, they presented themselves as English knights, who had heard of his fame, and desired to enter his service. With the assistance of their gun-founder, the Sherleys created a regular army for Shah Abbas, who had hitherto depended entirely on tribal cavalry, which could not defeat the highly trained Turkish army. Sir Anthony Sherley was despatched as Persian Ambassador to the Courts of Europe, where he had a chequered career, but Sir Robert Sherley remained in Persia, and had the pleasure of leading the charge in which the new Persian army defeated the Turks. He, in his turn, was despatched as an ambassador to the Courts of Europe, and is probably alluded to in *Twelfth Night*, where Fabian says, " I will not give my part of this sport for a pension of thousands to be paid from the Sophy."

The seventeenth century was one of extreme importance in world history. At the beginning of the period Spain and Portugal, entrenched behind the Treaty of Tordesillas, had built up great empires and a lucrative commerce, albeit not without straining to the utmost the populations and resources of these two states. The inability of England and Holland to challenge this monstrous agreement in the sixteenth century is proved by the painful and fruitless search for a passage to the Spice Islands and Cathay across the ice-bound Arctic. As the years passed, England became more powerful at sea and developed fast-sailing handy ships, mounting heavy guns which fired at comparatively long ranges. When the inevitable clash occurred, in 1588, the " Invincible Armada " was outmatched, and, by its defeat, the ultimate freedom of the ocean highways was assured.

Portugal and Spain at this period furnished excellent illustrations of the French proverb *Qui trop embrasse mal étreint*. Moreover, the splendid Portuguese and Spanish navigators of the fifteenth and sixteenth centuries had few successors in the seventeenth. Their amazing efforts had apparently exhausted the two countries, which gradually retired into the background.

The protagonists in the quest for power and commerce in Eastern waters were the Dutch and the English, and the causes that led to their commercial activities are of exceptional interest. As mentioned in Chapter XII, Antwerp had been the chief centre of the spice trade in Northern Europe, but after its fall in 1585, Amsterdam took its place. At this period the Dutch were forbidden to trade with Lisbon by Philip II, under whom, from 1580 to 1640, Portugal was united to Spain. Faced with ruin to their trade, the Dutch, in 1595, profiting by the defeat of the Armada, boldly despatched a fleet which reached Java and returned safely. After this pioneer venture, large fleets sailed annually to Eastern waters, and by the formation of the United Company, to which sovereign powers were delegated, a powerful instrument of conquest and colonization was created. Among the promoters of these expeditions was Linschoten, whose *Itinerario* was a veritable gazetteer of information on the Portuguese Empire.

The Dutch attacked the Portuguese wherever they met them. In the Moluccas they ultimately succeeded in driving them out, though the Portuguese, supported by the Spanish, fought desperately. In the course of a single generation the Dutch, who captured Malacca in 1641, had expelled the Portuguese from Ceylon and from the southernmost parts of India, while they had firmly established themselves in the Malay Archipelago, which became, and still remains, the seat of their power.

We now come to the appearance of the English in the East. Having failed to discover a passage across the Arctic, after negotiations had been carried through in Constantinople for " capitulations " similar to those enjoyed by other nations, Queen Elizabeth issued letters patent for the establishment of the Levant Company, in 1581.

At this period adventurers bound for India usually travelled by land and, from Aleppo, took a route across the desert to a point on the Euphrates near ancient Babylon or followed the Great Desert Route to Basra. In 1580 John Newbery was the first Englishman to make this journey. He reached Hormuz, where he studied the commercial prospects for some weeks. He then crossed to Gombroon (Bandar Abbas) and turning homewards was again the first Englishman to traverse Persia, visiting Shiraz, Isfahan and Tabriz. He thence travelled to Constantinople and reached England *via* Poland and Dantzig.

In 1583, Newbery headed an important expedition under the recently created Turkey Company, and sailed from London in the *Tiger*.[1] From Aleppo, where two members of the party established themselves, Newbery, Fitch and two other merchants continued the journey to Hormuz. On this occasion

---

[1] Did not the First Witch in *Macbeth* say, " Her husband's to Aleppo gone, master of the Tiger " ? Shakespeare evidently thought that Aleppo was a port !

the Portuguese Governor arrested them and sent them to Goa as prisoners. Managing to make their escape they reached Agra, where Newbery probably presented the Queen's letter to Akbar. He then decided to return home and apparently died on the way. Much credit is due to this great English pioneer. We consequently rely on Fitch who, if he has usurped some of the credit due to Newbery, was also a great explorer.[1]

Fitch's description of Agra and Fatehpur Sikhri runs as follows. " Agra and Fatepur are two very great cities, either of them much greater than London and very populous. Hither is the great resort of the merchants from Persia and out of India, and very much merchandise of silke and cloth, and of precious stones, both rubies, diamants, and pearles." Reaching Kuch Behar, he writes : " I went from Bengala into the country of Couche. The King is a Gentile ; His country is great and lieth not far from Cauchin China. They poison all the waters if any war be." From Serrepore on the Ganges, the intrepid Englishman sailed for Pegu in November 1586. Crossing the bar of the Irrawaddy, " we came to Cosmin (Bassein) which is a very prettie towne. The people be very tall and well disposed ; the women white, round faced, with little eies. The houses are high built, set upon great high postes, and they go up to them for fear of the tygers. The countrey is very fruitful. Here are very great figs, oranges, cocoes, and other fruits." Among the King's elephants, " he hath foure white elephants, which are very strange and rare ". This King in his title is called the " King of the White Elephants ". Among the curious customs which Fitch carefully noted was that " they have their teeth blacked, both men and women ; for they say a dogge hath his teeth white, therefore they will black theirs ".

From Pegu Fitch sailed to Malacca, " where the Portugals have a castle which standeth nere the sea ", and bore testimony to the extent of its commerce. In 1588, on his return voyage, he sailed back to Bengal, whence Ceylon, " a brave island, very fruitful and faire ", was visited. Here again at Colombo " the Portugals have their fort, with an hundred thousand men, and many elephants ". From Ceylon " we passed by Coulam (Quilon), which is a fort of the Portugals ; from whence cometh great store of pepper ". Continuing his journey homewards, he more or less followed his outward route. Fitch reached England in 1591, " having been eight yeeres out of my native countrey ". The information he gave was of the

England's Quest of Eastern Trade, by Sir William Foster, 1933.

SHAPUR AND THE CAPTIVE VALERIAN

(*From Sarre and Herzfeld's Iranische Felsreliefs*)

greatest value to the East India Company when it was constituted, and we cannot but admire the courage and initiative displayed by this sturdy English merchant-explorer.

Our ancestors were anxious to reach the Spice Islands, but one or two pioneer voyages had been unsuccessful and the Dutch outstripped them in the race. Indeed the English, who were slowly preparing to imitate their rivals, were undoubtedly influenced by the commercial policy of the Dutch who, in 1599, raised the price of pepper from three shillings to six and eight shillings per pound. The merchants of London had already petitioned Queen Elizabeth, who, on December 31, 1600, granted a charter to the East India Company, as it was ultimately named.[1]

In 1601, James Lancaster, who had led an unsuccessful expedition a decade earlier, sailed in command of four " tall ships ", with John Davis of Arctic fame, who had already served as Chief Pilot in a Dutch expedition. After touching at Table Bay and at a port on the coast of Madagascar, the sunken reefs of the Chagos Islands were successfully avoided and the Nicobar Islands reached. A good cargo of pepper was secured at Bantam, where agents were stationed, as also at the Moluccas, and, in the autumn of 1603, the squadron reached England with a rich cargo, which included 1,000,000 pounds of pepper. In the second voyage, commanded by Henry Middleton, the Moluccas were reached, but the unfriendliness of the Dutch, who captured the Portuguese forts at Amboina and Tidor, created serious difficulties.

In 1607 William Hawkins commanded a ship in which he sailed to Surat and travelled inland to the Court of the Emperor Jahangir. He was well received by the Great Moghul, but Portuguese influence was too strong, and he was obliged to leave. He gained, however, much valuable information about the trade of the country and the Court.

In 1614 the Portuguese attacked the English, who were anchored in a harbour situated to the north of the mouth of the Tapti River, known as Swally Hole. In spite of their great superiority of force, the Portuguese were repulsed ; and by 1619, thanks to the personality and activities of Sir Thomas Roe, the first envoy to be accredited to the Moghul Court, factories were established at Surat, Agra, Ahmadabad and Broach.

[1] For this section I have consulted *Letters Received by the East India Company*, edited by Sir William Foster ; *A History of Geographical Discovery in the Seventeenth and Eighteenth Centuries*, by E. Heawood, 1913 ; and *The Cambridge History of India*, Vol. V, 1929.

The factors at first sold their broadcloth to the Moghul courtiers, but could not find a regular market for it in Eastern waters. At this juncture Richard Steele, who had travelled by the desert route from Aleppo to the Euphrates and thence to the Persian Gulf, arrived in India. He reported that, in Persia, they might feel sure " of the vent of much cloth, in regard their country is cold ". Steele also added that silk could be purchased fifty per cent. cheaper than at Aleppo. With admirable initiative, representatives of the Company were despatched to Isfahan to secure the necessary *farman*, and in 1616 a trial cargo was landed at Jask. The Portuguese attacked the English ships off Jask in 1620,[1] but were decisively beaten, and two years later the English, in alliance with Persia, captured the fort at Hormuz. This was the first great feat of arms of the English in Eastern waters.

John Jourdain was among the important travellers of this period. Sailing in 1608, he gave the earliest account of the Seychelles, where I first realized the overpowering beauty of the tropics. He also travelled to Sana, and was thus the first English explorer of Yemen. To his credit also must be placed the discovery of " Swally Hole ". After travelling to the Spice Islands to purchase pepper and cloves, Jourdain was killed by the Dutch. His *Journal*[2] is full of interesting information about the struggle for the spice trade.

Finally, Pietro della Valle deserves mention among these travellers. Starting from Venice in 1614 with the intention of visiting the holy places of the East, he travelled by Damascus to Aleppo and Baghdad, thence proceeding to the Court of the Shah. He gives an interesting description of the ruins of Persepolis, which he was the first modern traveller to identify, and reaching the Persian Gulf by Shiraz and Lar, he travelled extensively in India.[3]

Shortly after the capture of Hormuz, Sir Thomas Herbert[4] entered Persia from the south. Landing at Bandar Abbas, Herbert travelled to Shiraz by way of Lar. Shiraz delighted him, as it had Ibn Battuta before him, and, upon leaving it, he wrote a charming charistery or " Song of Thanksgiving " in praise of the city of Sadi and Hafiz. Continuing his journey,

---

[1] For an account of the struggle with the Portuguese in the Persian Gulf *vide* Sykes, *History of Persia*, Chap. LXIV.
[2] *John Jourdain's Journal of a Voyage to the East Indies, 1608–17*, edited by Sir William Foster (Hakluyt Society), 2nd series, Vols. I and II.
[3] Vide *The Travels of Pietro della Valle to India*, ed. by E. Gray (Hakluyt Society), Vols. LXXXIV and LXXXV.
[4] *Travels in Persia*, by Sir Thomas Herbert, edited by Sir William Foster (Broadway Travellers).

Herbert gives an excellent description of the palaces and parks of Isfahan, one of which he compares to Fontainebleau. The *Maydan* or Royal Square he describes as, " as spacious and aromatic a market as any in the universe, resembling our Exchange, or the Place-Royal, but six times larger ". It served as the polo ground, and the stone goal-posts still survive intact. From Isfahan the Mission travelled north to Ashraf, situated on the Caspian Sea, where Shah Abbas received the Ambassador.

Herbert is generally interesting, as, for example, when he writes : " Choava-berry (coffee) is much drunk, though it please neither the eye nor the taste, being black as soot and somewhat bitter, or rather relished like black crusts ", " and again when he sums up the Persians : " They are generally well-limbed and straight ; the zone they live in makes them tawny ; the wine cheerful ; opium salacious. The women paint ; the men love arms ; all affect poetry."

In the latter half of the seventeenth century, we have the instructive works of Tavernier and of Bernier. Of even greater value was Chardin, who learned to read and to speak Persian and who made a really serious study of the country between 1665 and 1677.[1] Chardin, who left Paris in 1671 on his second journey to Persia, gives a vivid description of the dangerous state of affairs in Constantinople, owing to the French Ambassador being on bad terms with the Grand Vizier. He landed in Mingrelia where " the Gentlemen of the Country have full power over the Lives and Estates of their Tenants, with whom they do what they please. They seize upon 'em, whether Wife or Children ; they sell 'em, or dispose of 'em otherwise as they think fit."

Chardin gives an admirable description of Georgia, at that time tributary to Persia, where he was hospitably received by the Prince, and assisted at gargantuan banquets. He reached Isfahan in safety and, while his chief business was to extract payment from the Shah for his jewels, he wrote by far the best description of Persia that has come down to us from the seventeenth century. In his company we may attend the solemn audiences granted to foreign Envoys, and the sumptuous banquets, where the value of the gold plate was duly apprized. Elsewhere we are taken behind the scenes and realize the desperate intrigues and the cruelty of the drunken Shah. In addition we have chapters on the geography, climate, soil and customs,

[1] Vide *The Travels of Sir John Chardin into Persia and the East Indies*, 1686, Argonaut Press, 1927.

which no student can afford to neglect. Among many delight-ful passages we select the following: "There is such an exquisite Beauty in the Air of *Persia*, that I can neither forget it myself, nor forbear mentioning it to everybody. One would swear that the Heavens were more sublimely elevated, and tinctur'd with quite another colour there, than they are in our thick and dreary *European* climates."

Chardin returned to France after his adventurous travels, but, on the revocation of the Edict of Nantes, he settled in England. He was knighted by Charles II, and, on his death, a tablet was erected to his memory in Westminster Abbey bearing the inscription *Sibi nomen fecit eundo*.

In no part of this work has it been found harder to refrain from quoting at length from the vivid narratives of these great travellers, whose heroic achievements added lustre to the period, and the charm of whose writings has seldom, if ever, been surpassed.

CHAPTER XVIII

THE PENETRATION OF CHINA AND TIBET IN THE SEVENTEENTH AND EIGHTEENTH CENTURIES

"You must know that as the Kingdom of Tibet is very mountainous, the water draining off the mountains forms rivers, especially there is one which flowing from West to East traverses the centre of Third Tibet, and then, turning to the South-East, at last this principal river flows into the Ganges."

Desideri on the Tsangpo or Brahmaputra.

IN Chapter X, brief reference was made to John de Monte Corvino, the first Archbishop of Peking, and to Friar Odoric. On the fall of the short-lived Mongol dynasty, in 1370, intercourse with China ceased until the ships of the Portuguese appeared in her ports. Albuquerque, at the capture of Malacca in 1511, established good relations with the Chinese captains of some trading junks, and in 1514 [1] a Portuguese ship was despatched to Canton to open commercial relations with the Celestial Empire. Landing was not permitted, but the Portuguese sold their spices at a good profit.

Shortly afterwards a mission was despatched, but, before it was received at Peking, the Portuguese had made themselves detested by kidnapping Chinese children for slaves and by other misdeeds. The Emperor, enraged at the insolence of these " outer barbarians ", sentenced twenty-three Portuguese to be executed at Canton in 1523, while the envoy died in prison. As a sequel to these events China was closed to European traders. In 1552, St. Francis Xavier landed at Chang-chuen-shan off the coast of Kwang-tung, which served as a port for the Europeans, who were not admitted to the mainland. He fell sick and died shortly afterwards.

At the beginning of the seventeenth century a new and happier era was opened by the arrival at the Chinese Court in 1598 of Matteo Ricci, a Jesuit.[2] At first the Emperor was inclined to expel him, but his pleasing personality and know-

[1] *Letters from Portuguese Captives in Canton*, by Donald Ferguson, 1902.
[2] *Early Jesuit Travellers in Central Asia*, by C. Wessels, S.J., 1924.

ledge of astronomy gradually won him universal esteem, and in 1601 he was able to establish himself at Peking. He set to work to explore China and published a European map with Chinese names which has come down to us. Thanks to the influence of Ricci, the Jesuits began a survey of the whole country. At first they surveyed the plain south of Peking, but in 1708 their operations were extended to the Great Wall and ultimately included part of Manchuria, during which the Amur was crossed. Year by year the survey spread over the eastern provinces, beginning with Shantung, until gradually it came to include the greater part of China. Nor were they defeated by Tibet, which was partially surveyed by two Lamas, who were trained by the Jesuits. The results of these valuable explorations were published in Paris together with maps by D'Anville, in 1735.

The deep interest taken in exploration by Ricci in China, was shared by the Fathers in India. Reports reached them of the existence of large numbers of Christians in Cathay, and it was decided to despatch a mission to seek them out, and to ascertain definitely whether or no Cathay was China.

Bento de Goes, a lay Jesuit, was selected for the expedition, of which Philip II of Spain approved. Still more valuable was the support of the Emperor Akbar, who furnished Goes, for whom he had both liking and respect, with valuable letters of recommendation and with gold. Goes travelled *via* Peshawar to Kabul, hearing on the way tales about the Kafirs, who wore black clothes and drank wine, this being the earliest mention of these pagan Aryans of the remote valleys of the Hindu Kush.

The explorer crossed that mountain barrier not without difficulty, and reached Talikhan. He then followed in Marco Polo's footsteps up the Oxus Valley to Badakshan, and crossing the Pamirs, where " both men and beasts felt oppressed beyond endurance and gasped for breath ", he reached the Sarikol Valley.[1] He nearly lost his life on the Chichiklik Pass from the cold, but reached the fertile oasis of Yarkand safely.

Goes was detained for a year at Yarkand pending the organization of the annual caravan to Cathay. He took advantage of the delay to visit Khotan, and writes : " There is no article of traffic more valuable than lumps of a certain transparent kind of marble, which we, from poverty of lan-

[1] For the Aryans of Sarikol vide *Through Deserts and Oases of Central Asia*, p. 148 *et seq.* For Khotan, see *op. cit.*, p. 209.

guage, usually term jasper. These marbles are called by the Chinese Jusce." This is an accurate description of *Jusce*, more exactly *Yu-shih* or Jade Stone ; and Khotan is more correctly termed *Yu-tien* or " Jade Country ".

Leaving Yarkand in November 1604, Goes travelled by way of Turfan. He then crossed the Gobi to the " Jade Gate " of the Great Wall. At Suchow, where the explorer arrived at the end of 1605, he fell ill, and after receiving the visit of an emissary from Ricci, he died in April 1607. Perhaps it was just as well. He had indeed discovered that Cathay was China, but Ricci had already proved this to be the case. In 1931, the grave of this intrepid explorer was discovered and photographed by Miss Mildred Cable, an intrepid member of the China Inland Mission.[1]

In 1624, Antonio de Andrade, who was at Delhi, heard of an exceptional opportunity of following the quest for lost Christian communities in Tibet, owing to the organization of a Hindu pilgrimage to distant Badrinath. He and a brother Jesuit joined the caravan disguised as Hindus, and were the first Europeans to cross the Himalayas from India and to reach one of the principal sources of the Ganges, situated underneath mighty Kamet, rising to 25,447 feet, which was scaled by Smythe in 1931.

From Badrinath the explorers crossed the Mana Pass, at an altitude of 18,300 feet, and arrived safely at Tsaparang, the capital of Guge, situated in the valley of the Upper Sutlej. Andrade found that there were no Christians to be rescued, but considering Tsaparang to be a fruitful field, he decided to found a mission. The King was most favourable to the Jesuits, but this naturally created intense jealousy among the Lamas, whose chief was the King's brother. The result was a rebellion, supported by the King of Ladakh, who seized the friendly monarch and broke up the mission.

Nearly a century later, Ippolito de Desideri[2] was fired with the determination to reopen the Jesuit mission in Tibet. Starting from Delhi in 1714, with another Father named Freyre, he travelled to Kashmir by the Pir Panjal route and noted the caravanserais at each stage. Some of them are indeed delightful pleasaunces built by the Moghul Emperors overlooking the Chenab. From Srinagar, Desideri travelled eastwards to Ladakh, and he gives an excellent account of a *jubla* bridge which will appeal to all travellers in that country.

[1] *Journal of the Royal Central Asian Society*, Vol. XX, Part II, April 1933.
[2] *The Travels of Ippolito Desideri*, edited by Filippo de Filippi (Broadway Travellers), 1932.

"From one mountain to the other two thick ropes of willow are stretched nearly four feet apart, to which are attached hanging loops of smaller ropes of willow about one foot and a half distant from one another. One must stretch out one's arms and hold fast to the thicker ropes while putting one foot after the other into the hanging loops to reach the opposite side. With every step the bridge sways from right to left, and from left to right. Besides this, one is so high above the river and the bridge is so open on all sides, that the rush of water beneath dazzles the eyes and makes one dizzy."

I myself recollect that my Indian servant howled with fear at his first experience of one of these bridges, which he finally crossed on his knees with two Tibetans to help him along. Nor did I enjoy my own first crossing of a *juhla* bridge. Desideri also feelingly described his escape from an avalanche, while he suffered more than once from painful snow-blindness.

The King of Leh treated the Fathers most kindly, so much so that Desideri was tempted to stay there. But Freyre, accustomed to the climate of India and worn out with fatigue, determined to abandon the enterprise. He did not, however, wish to return by Kashmir, with its difficult passes. Accordingly he made inquiries and ascertained the existence of a still greater Tibet, with its capital at Lhasa. His decision to return to India by Lhasa led to the important exploration of Southern Tibet.

On August 17, 1715, Desideri continued his great journey. His route lay close to the Panggong lake, which was the farthest point reached by me in 1890. On September 7, the explorers arrived at Tashigong, a strong fortified post on the frontier between Ladakh, which is called Second Tibet, and Third Tibet.[1] The onward journey lay across "a vast, sterile and terrible desert, to cross which takes about three months". A body of Tartar and Tibetan troops, who were garrisoning neighbouring Gartok, were returning to Lhasa, under the command of the widow of their chief, and fortunately this Tibetan lady "esteemed it a great honour to be able to assist two Lamas from a distant land". The missionaries started from Gartok in mid-October, and "arrived at the highest point reached during the whole journey in this desert. Close by is a mountain of excessive height . . . most horrible, barren, steep, and bitterly cold." This mountain was Kailas Parbat, which rises to 22,000 feet, while the pass which separates the Indus from the Tsangpo system was crossed at an altitude of 16,000 feet on November 9.

---

[1] Desideri called Baltistan "First" or "Lesser Tibet", while Ladakh he named "Second" or "Grand Tibet". To-day Ladakh is termed "Lesser Tibet".

By January 4, 1716, the explorers had safely crossed the desert and reached Saka Dzong, " a big place and well fortified as beseems a frontier town ". The ordeal had been terribly severe, and, during one march, Freyre, who had stayed behind with his worn-out horse, was nearly frozen to death. Indeed the description given by Desideri of the total lack of supplies on the way, the scarcity of dried dung, which constitutes the only fuel, and the unwholesome water, has been fully corroborated by modern travellers. The onward journey lay through Sakya, Shigatse and Gyantse, and, on March 18, 1716, Desideri entered Lhasa, " one year and a half since our departure from Delhi ".

Desideri was not the first European to reach Lhasa. Odoric and later Grueber had crossed Tibet from China and had passed through the sacred city. Moreover, it was the centre of a recently established Capuchin Mission, although the representatives of that order had temporarily abandoned it. But Desideri lived in Tibet for five years, and was the first European to study the literature, the religion, the geography, the customs, the flora and fauna of that country.

This chapter may be concluded with Desideri's account of polyandry, of which he writes :

> " The bridegroom knows when the wedding is to be, but not the bride, who tries to escape, cries, screams, kicks, tears her hair, but is dragged to the door of her future abode. On the threshold stands the bridegroom with the professor of magic, who recites spells for the success of the marriage, and the defeat of all evil spirits. He then gives a small piece of butter to the bridegroom, who smears it on the head and hair of the bride. . . . He performs this rite not only for himself, but for all his brothers big or little, men or boys, and she is recognized and regards herself as the legitimate wife of them all."

Such is marriage in this fantastic land.

CHAPTER XIX

THE DISCOVERY OF SIBERIA AND JAPAN

" Now the Sable is a beast full marvellous and prolific,
and it is found nowhere else in the world but in Northern
Siberia . . . a merry little beast it is, and a beautiful ; and its
beauty comes to it with the snow, just as with the snow it
disappears.   And this is the beast that the ancient Greeks and
the Romans called the Golden Fleece."

SPATHARY (BADDELEY).

In no part of Asia has there been so rapid an advance in exploration as that made by Russia in Siberia, an advance which ultimately solved problems which had defeated Arctic explorers,
and opened up for colonization a country which compares in
its extent and natural resources with the Dominion of Canada.[1]

In Chapter XVII Jenkinson made a reference to the
conquest of the valley of the Volga by Ivan the Terrible.
This marked the turning-point in the relations of Russia with
Asia, and it was from this base that Russia advanced into
Siberia.   In 1558 the Tsar granted a charter to the Stroganov
family, which had built up a lucrative trade in furs.   It included
a large grant of land on the Kama Valley, which led up into
the Ural Mountains.[2]   Stroganov founded several settlements
and enlisted Yermak, chief of a band of robbers, who in 1579,
at the head of some 5,000 men, attacked the principal Tartar
chief, Kuchum Khan, and defeated him on the banks of the
Irtish.   He then occupied Sibir, laid his conquest at the feet
of the Tsar, and was subsequently killed by the Khan in a
night attack.   Yermak will remain for all time among the
greatest heroes of Russia, and his amazing career is summed
up by Baddeley in the verse :

" Death-doomed, by wrath of dread Ivan,
Yermak makes eastward, boat and man,
Down Asian rivers—nor in vain—
Conquers a realm, is pardoned, slain."

---

[1] Among my authorities are *Russia, Mongolia, China*, by John F. Baddeley, 1919.
Mr. Baddeley has read this chapter and made valuable suggestions.

[2] At the point where the railway crosses the Ural Mountains, I found to my surprise
that they were a mass of rolling hills, and in no sense constituted a barrier, as I had
been taught when I was young.

The advance eastwards, in which the fur-traders and Cossacks played the leading part, was amazingly rapid. As in the case of Canada, the magnificent river system helped the pioneers, since although the great rivers, with the solitary exception of the Amur, flowed north, their tributaries flowed at right angles and almost touched one another at various points. Moreover, the native tribes were comparatively weak and offered little resistance.

Tobolsk was founded close to Sibir in 1587 and became the capital of a province which extended to the Ob. Tomsk was founded in 1604 in the upper valley of the Ob, and the explorers crossing by portage to the Yenisei, followed it down for hundreds of miles, and founded Turukhansk close to the Arctic Circle, at the junction of the Lower Tunguska with the Yenisei. They then went up this great tributary due east and struck a feeder of the Lena, down which, in 1632, they sailed to the Arctic Ocean.

An advance farther south struck the Upper Yenisei, where Yeniseisk was founded in 1619. Proceeding up the valley, the Angara River was reached, where the Buriats offered some resistance, but the Russians pressed on and discovered Lake Baikal. Skirting the east side of the lake, the upper valley of the Lena was reached, where Yakutsk was founded, in 1632, in territory owned by the Yakuts, who were driven north by the merciless Russian pioneers. From Yakutsk the explorers pushed on to the east, and, crossing the range which bounds the Lena Basin, founded Okhotsk in 1638. In some fifty years, these fearless pioneers had crossed Northern Asia to the Pacific Ocean.

Farther north, the Kolyma River was discovered, and this extraordinary epoch of exploration was crowned by Deshnev, who sailed from the Kolyma River round the extreme north-east point of Asia, which is called Cape Deshnev. He thus discovered the Strait dividing Asia from America, belief in which had hitherto been based merely on conjecture.

In 1643 a Cossack, Poyarkof by name, led an expedition from Yakutsk eastwards over the divide, and, descending tributary streams, finally discovered the Amur; after a voyage of three months he reached its mouth.

At the end of the seventeenth century Russian Cossacks explored Kamchatka. A fort was constructed on its river, and the country subjugated by barbarous methods, but it was not until 1716 that its west coast was explored.

Among the leading travellers of this period was a Moldavian

who is known as Spathary. In 1678 he set out for China as Russian Ambassador, and gives a clear account of his journey through Tomsk, Yeniseisk, and thence up the Angara to Lake Baikal. "Nowhere", he writes, "is Baikal so narrow as opposite the mouth of the Angara, where there is no harbourage—nothing but cliffs and rocks; in a word, it is very terrible, for all around are lofty snow-covered mountains, impenetrable forests and rocky precipices." Continuing the journey Selenghinsk, situated on the Mongolian frontier, was reached in October, and Nerchinsk in December; the Chinese frontier was crossed shortly afterwards. From Tobolsk to Selenghinsk, with the exception of a single portage of some twenty miles from the Ob to the Yenisei, Spathary had travelled entirely by water. From Selenghinsk onwards he journeyed by land. No traveller of the period gives such a good description of the country, its inhabitants and its products. However, Spathary was unable to negotiate a treaty with the Chinese, and Russia, after suffering defeat at the hands of the Chinese, agreed to evacuate the valley of the Amur in 1689.

It is interesting to note that the return embassy despatched by China was accompanied by a Jesuit, Gerbillon, who visited Nerchinsk, where the agreement referred to above was signed. In a subsequent journey he reached the junction of the Orkhon with the Tula, and gained valuable information about the Altai. He thus explored the country lying between China and Siberia, and ranks high among the explorers of Asia.

Peter the Great took a deep interest in exploration, and is reported to have said : " I have been thinking over the finding of a passage to China through the Arctic. On the map before me, there is indicated such a passage bearing the name of Anian.[1] There must be some reason for that. Now that the country is in no danger, we should strive to win for her glory along the lines of the Arts and Sciences." Bering, a Dane by birth, was selected for this important task. His instructions were to build boats and " to sail along the shore of Kamchatka which runs to the north and which (since its limits are unknown) seems to be a part of the American coast, and to determine where it joins with America ".

In 1728, Bering sailed to Cape Deshnev, or East Cape as Cook named it, and as the land ended at that point, he turned back, having carried out his instructions, and sailed through the Strait which is called after him. He would probably have

---

[1] For the supposed Strait of Anian, *vide* Heawood's *Geographical Discovery in the Seventeenth and Eighteenth Centuries*, p. 121.

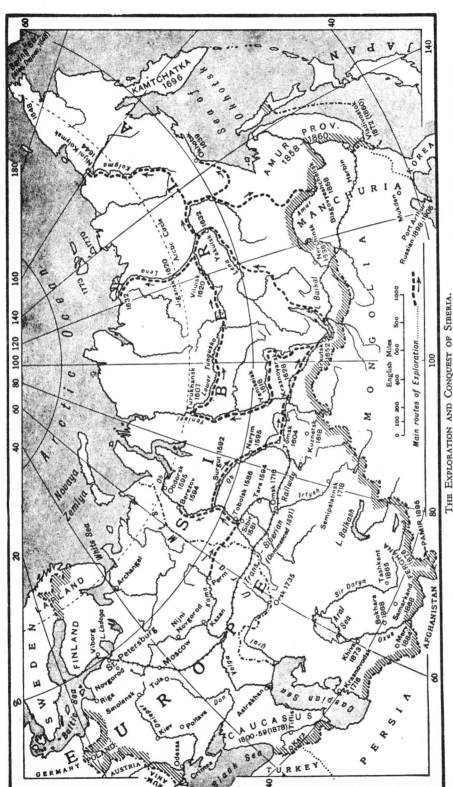

THE EXPLORATION AND CONQUEST OF SIBERIA.

(Reproduced from "The Universal History of the World", edited by J. A. Hammerton, by courtesy of the publishers, The Educational Book Co. Ltd.)

sighted the American shore on this expedition, but for the thick weather. At more than one point, natives who had heard of the Russians boarded the ship. They stated that they went to the Kolyma River " on deer and never by sea ", and Bering was blamed for not extending explorations to this river. In his second journey, undertaken in 1741, " a chain of high, rugged and snow-covered mountains loomed in view in latitude 58° 28' ". Thus the coast of North America was discovered in this high latitude, and the width of the Strait definitely laid down. The return voyage followed the coast of Alaska for some distance. Intercourse was opened with the natives, and Steller the naturalist made a collection of plants. He also made valuable reports on the animal life and the inhabitants. Bering, who had been ill with scurvy and had lost control over his command, died and was buried in Bering Island. By these two voyages the chief problem of the Northern Pacific was solved.

At the beginning of the nineteenth century, Russia renewed her activities in the north of Siberia. In 1828, Erman systematically examined the country between the north of the Ural Mountains and the mouth of the Ob. But the most important expeditions were those of Middendorf, who, leaving Turukhansk in 1843, descended the frozen Yenisei and crossed the tundra to the Khatanga basin. He finally made for the Taimir Peninsula and reached the sea in August. Suffering cruelly from lack of supplies, he managed to bring back a valuable report on these practically unexplored lands.

In 1854, Muraviev led an expedition down the Amur and reopened it to Russian explorers, geologists and naturalists, among whom may be mentioned Radde. In 1864, Prince Kropotkin led an expedition across Manchuria from the Argun to the Sungari; and in 1876, he crossed the Tian Shan from Farghana to Kashgar.

Japan was known to Marco Polo as Chipangu, but was not visited by the great Venetian explorer. It was first discovered in 1542 by Portuguese adventurers in a ship which was carried in a storm past the ports of China to unknown islands. The inhabitants put off in boats to trade with the strangers, and informed them that the islands were called Nippon. In 1546, Ferdinand Mendez Pinto, author of the fascinating *Peregrination*, landed at " the isle of Tanixumas, which is the first land of Japan ". He was received most hospitably, and the adventurer won the favour of the governor by the gift of an arquebus, the first to be seen in Japan. Some years later Pinto travelled with St. Francis Xavier, who preached in Japan from 1549 to 1551, and mentioned the presence of Portuguese vessels at Hirado.

We now come to the arrival in Japan of William Adams. In 1598, the first Dutch expedition to the Pacific reached the Straits of Magellan and was dispersed by storms. One ship, under its English pilot William Adams, crossed the Pacific and reached Japan. Here Adams, whose knowledge of shipbuilding and navigation was valued, became an influential personage, and was able to foster European trade with the kingdom of the Mikado. He married a Japanese wife and never returned to England.

In the eighth voyage of the East India Company, John Saris sailed in 1611 to the Moluccas, and continued his voyage to Hirado, where he was received by Adams. Saris, after establishing a factory, left Hirado for the capital with William Adams and ten other Englishmen. He was rowed through islands which " were well inhabited and divers proper townes built upon them. All along the coast, and so up to Osaka, we found women divers. These women would catch fish by diving, and that in eight fathome depth. We found Osaka a very great Towne, as great as London within the walls, with many faire timber bridges of a great height ". The castle was " marvellous large and strong, with very deepe trenches about it, and many draw-bridges, with gates plated with iron ".

From Osaka Saris travelled by land in a " Pallankin " to the capital Surunga (Sumpa). He was received with much courtesy by the Emperor, to whom he " delivered the King of England's letter and his present ". The Emperor agreed to most of the demands of Saris—indeed, owing no doubt to the influence of Adams, he displayed remarkable reasonableness in his dealings with the English captain.

Saris decided to pay his respects to the young king at Yezo, which city he described as " much greater than Surunga, farre fairer building ; the ridge-tiles and corner-tiles richly gilded, and the posts of their doors gilded and varnished ". Here we have a reminiscence of Marco Polo's account of Japan, which is given in Chapter XIII. His reception was again most courteous, and he returned to Surunga, where a Spanish Ambassador had arrived to demand permission to round up all Spaniards and Portuguese. The reason was " the great want of men they had to defend the Molucca Islands from the Dutch, who then made great preparations for the absolute conquest thereof ". This demand was refused, the

Emperor replying that " his country was a free country ". Saris was handed the reply of the Emperor to King James, which was couched in most friendly language, and the capable Englishman had every reason to be satisfied with his success as a diplomatist. The description of Japan in feudal times given by Saris is noteworthy, while his notes on currents and the monsoons, and his correction of the charts added materially to the knowledge of navigation in Eastern Seas.

In spite of European nations having opened up commercial relations with Japan, much uncertainty prevailed as to the geography of the country. In 1738 Martin Spangberg, a colleague of Bering, and Lieutenant Walton made a preliminary reconnaissance of the Kurile Islands, and in the following year, having been separated in the gale, they both reached Japan. Spangberg, on the return voyage, met the hairy Ainus, but the problem of Yezo was not yet solved.

One of the successors of Captain Cook was Captain François de la Perouse, a French officer, who in 1787 passed through the strait separating Japan from Korea. Later in the voyage, sailing northwards from Manchuria, the island of Sakhalin was sighted. On continuing his voyage, La Perouse was stopped by a submarine bank at the narrowest part of the channel. Accordingly he turned southwards and discovered the strait between Sakhalin and Yezo, which bears his name. Gallant La Perouse then sailed away into the Pacific, where his ships struck a reef and all hands were lost.

Captain Broughton, who had served under Vancouver, sighted Japan in 1796, near the strait which separated Yezo from the main island. By this discovery, supplementing that of La Perouse, the main geographical problems connected with Japan were solved.

THE LANDING OF CAPTAIN COOK IN BOTANY BAY

(From the painting of E. Phillips Fox, by permission of the High Commissioner for Australia)

CHAPTER XX

CAPTAIN COOK EXPLORES THE PACIFIC OCEAN

" We mean to travel to the antarctic pole,
Conquering the people underneath our feet,
And be renowned as never emperors were."
MARLOWE, *Tamburlaine the Great.*

" I flatter myself that a final end has been put to the searching after a southern continent, which has at times ingrossed the attention of some of the maritime powers for near two centuries past, and has been a favourite theme among the geographers of all ages.
" That there may be a continent or large tract of land, near the Pole, I will not deny; on the contrary, I am of the opinion that there is; and it is probable that we have seen a part of it."
CAPTAIN JAMES COOK.

THE question of the existence of *Terra Australis* or the Southern Continent has already been alluded to more than once in this work. It was strengthened by the belief of Magellan that Tierra del Fuego formed part of it, whereas the voyage of Drake actually proved the fallacy of the theory. Yet geographers were reluctant to abandon Ptolemy's views, which in this respect were based on mere conjecture and the belief in symmetry which he inherited from the Greeks. There was also a theory that a southern continent was needed to counterbalance Europe and Asia.

The seventeenth century opened with the discovery of Australia, due to Dutch enterprise.[1] New Guinea was already known, but little more, when, in 1605, the *Duifken* or *Little Dove*, commanded by Willem Janszoon of Amsterdam, sailed from Bantam "for the discovery of the land called Nova Guinea which, it is said, affordeth great store of gold". Janszoon struck New Guinea in latitude 5° S. and followed its irregular coast-line, rounding Prince Frederick Henry Island, to Torres Strait. Thence, steering south, he struck the east coast of the vast Gulf of Carpentaria and sailed as far as 13° 45′ S. Owing to the islands which filled the Strait,

---

[1] For the question of an earlier discovery the reader is referred to the admirable article *Was Australia Discovered in the Sixteenth Century?* by E. Heawood, *Geographical Journal*, Vol. XIV, No. 4, October 1899. I have also used his *History of Geographical Discovery in the Seventeenth and Eighteenth Centuries.*

the Dutch explorer, to whom the credit for the discovery of Australia is due, believed that the land he was coasting formed part of New Guinea. To quote from the report of the voyage : " They found this extensive country for the greatest part desert, but in some places inhabited by wild, cruel, black savages, by whom some of the crew were murdered . . . and by want of provisions and other necessaries, they were obliged to leave the discovery unfinished." The *Duifken* returned to Banda before June 15, 1606, and this important discovery was made about March of that year, or six months before the discovery of Torres. This was indeed an *annus mirabilis*.

To turn to a rival expedition, in 1605, nearly a century after the epoch-making voyage of Magellan, Quiros [1] sailed from Callao on a voyage of discovery. He shaped a W.S.W. course for some distance, passing to the north of Easter Island. He then, partly owing to the strong south-easterly gales, steered W.N.W. and discovered various islands. Information given by natives induced him to turn southwards, and on May day 1606 he reached the mountainous groups of the New Hebrides, as Cook later called them. Here, like Columbus at Cuba, he thought he had reached the mainland. In his case he believed it to be the *Terra Australis*. He took possession of his discovery for the King of Spain and named it Australia del Espiritu Santo.

Quiros then returned to America, and, proceeding to Spain, declared " that there are two large portions of the earth severed from this of Europe, Africa and Asia. The first is America, which Christopher Colon discovered ; and the second and last of the world is that I have seen and solicit to people and completely discover."

Quiros was, however, mistaken, and the important discovery of Torres Strait was made by Diego de Prado, who was in command of the exploring vessel, whereas Luis Vaez Torres, whose name alone is remembered, apparently sailed under his orders.[2]

The explorers started on this venture at the end of June 1606, and approached Torres Strait by its eastern entrance. They sailed along the south coast of New Guinea, miraculously escaping its many lurking dangers in the shape of coral reefs and strong currents, until shoals compelled them to steer to the south-west. Large islands were noted, and possibly

[1] Vide *The Voyages of Pedro Fernandez de Quiros*, edited by Sir Clements Markham (Hakluyt Society), 2nd series, Vols. XIV and XV.
[2] *New Light on the Discovery of Australia*, by Henry Stevens (Hakluyt Society), 1930.

Cape York peninsula was sighted. The explorers sailed along the entire length of the southern coast of New Guinea, and traversing the island-studded sea, ended their important voyage, which had proved the insularity of New Guinea, at Manila in May 1607.

We next come to the important discoveries of Abel Tasman. His instructions, which proved that the existence of Torres Strait was unknown to the Dutch, were to explore the South Indian Ocean as far south as 54°, and to discover a short passage to Chile " to snatch rich booty from the Castilian ".[1] Sailing from Batavia in 1642, he made for Mauritius, and thence shaped a southerly course, which upon reaching 40° he changed to south-east. On November 4, he discovered the island of Tasmania. Stormy weather made landing difficul, but the island was seen to be high-lying and covered with dense forests, while signs of natives were apparent, although none were actually seen.

Tasman, after surveying the east coast for some distance, resumed the voyage in an easterly direction, and on December 13 land was again sighted, really the west coast of the South Island of New Zealand, a second great discovery. Sailing northwards, Tasman surveyed the coast and reached a point at which " the land fell off so abruptly that we did not doubt this was the furthest extremity ". Actually it was the northernmost point of the South Island, which Cook, in 1770, named Cape Farewell.

Tasman tried hard to find a strait, but tide and weather were against him, and after losing some men in a skirmish with the warlike Maoris, he sailed along the west coast of North Island. When he had rounded its northern cape, he considered that he had discovered the passage to Chile, and determined to sail back to Batavia. He again crossed the trackless ocean, aiming for the Solomon Islands but, keeping far to the east of a direct line, he discovered the Tonga and then the Fiji Islands. Finally the north coast of Guinea was struck, and Tasman ended his momentous voyage at Batavia.

Tasman stands high among the great explorers. He had sailed thousands of miles through the unknown ocean in latitudes never before reached in this area, and had discovered Tasmania and New Zealand. He had sailed round Australia, and thus proved that it had no connection with *Terra Australis*, but he believed that New Zealand formed part of it. To quote his views : " It (New Zealand) seems to be a very

---

[1] For this section I have consulted *The Discovery of Australia*, by G. A. Wood, 1922.

fine country, and we trust this is the mainland coast of the unknown south-land."

The treatment Tasman received may be guessed from the report of the Governor-General to the effect that " he had found no treasures or matter of great profit ". Cabot was similarly treated, but the names of both these explorers are inscribed in letters of gold on the roll of fame.

We have now reached the epoch of the great discoveries made by Captain James Cook. The son of a Yorkshire labourer, he early took to the sea, where his promotion was rapid, and he was offered the position of Master of a coal ship. He decided, however, to volunteer for the Royal Navy, and in 1758 he sailed to Canada and took part in the operations which culminated in the capture of Louisberg and Quebec. He rapidly won distinction as a surveyor of the St. Lawrence, and later of the coasts of Labrador and Newfoundland, and in 1768 he was selected by the Royal Society to observe a transit of Venus. He was also commissioned to discover the elusive Southern Continent.

The *Endeavour*, a roomy bark of 368 tons, sailed from England in the summer of 1768, with Joseph Banks, the great botanist, as a member of the expedition. Cook took the route round Cape Horn, and sailed in latitude 38° through the area which the Southern Continent was believed to occupy. The transit of Venus was observed in cloudless weather at Tahiti, where the expedition remained from April to July 1769. Cook's instructions were to sail from the Society Islands, as he named the group, due south to latitude 40°, and there to ascertain the truth of the conjectured existence of the Southern Continent in that area.

Having proved the fallacy of the theorists, Cook sailed north into a better climate, and then west to New Zealand, which he struck half-way up the east coast of the North Island. He sailed into a bay which he termed Poverty Bay. Maoris appeared in canoes, but his attempt to capture them was resisted with great courage, and some of them were killed to save the lives of the crew. Cook at first sailed south, but later decided to return and survey the coast to the north. Rounding Cape Maria van Diemen and the Three Kings' Islands, he proved the truth of Tasman's claim that that navigator had discovered a sea-route to Chile.

Sailing down the west coast, Cook with British thoroughness charted its features until he reached " a very broad and deep bay which, on the southern side, seemed to form several

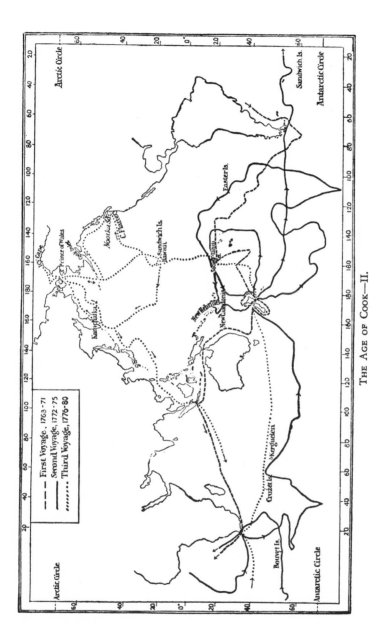

First Voyage, 1763-71
Second Voyage, 1772-75
Third Voyage, 1776-80

Arctic Circle

Antarctic Circle

Arctic Circle

Antarctic Circle

Sandwich Is.

Easter Is.

Owhyhee

Sandwich Is.

Hawaii

New Hebrides

New Caledonia

C. Prince of Wales

Montka Sd.

C. Fincio

E. Cape

Kamtschatka I.

Crozet Is.

Kerguelen

Bouvet Is.

THE AGE OF COOK—II.

175

bays ". Here he decided to careen the *Endeavour* among natives who were friendly. Tasman, who had entered this great bay from the same side, had suspected, but not discovered, the strait dividing the two islands, but the great English navigator, on February 7, 1770, in spite of the tide, " which roared like a mill-stream ", sailed through Cook's Strait, and coasted North Island until he had completed his survey.

The east coast of South Island was charted with equal care, and on rounding it, " much to the regret of us continent-mongers ", as Banks wrote, it was proved to be an island. Thus was dispelled the myth of a southern continent in this part of the Pacific Ocean. Coasting northwards along " a beautiful and fertile country " the survey of the coast of the two islands was completed.

Cook considered New Zealand to be suitable for coloni-zation, and wrote : " So far as I have been able to judge of the genius of these people, it does not appear to me at all difficult for strangers to form a settlement ; they seem to be too much divided among themselves to unite in opposition."

Cook had spent some six months in his valuable survey of New Zealand, and on April 1, 1770, he sailed west and struck Australia, or New Holland as it was then called, on April 19, at Point Hicks " because Mr. Hicks, first lieutenant, was the first who discovered it ". This historical nomen-clature has been unfortunately changed to Cape Everard. To be exact, Point Hicks forms part of Cape Everard, both being marked on the maps of Victoria. He followed up the surf-bound coast for some days, and then made the discovery of Botany Bay.

" On the 29th April at daylight ", he writes, " we discovered a Bay which appeared to be tolerably well sheltered from all winds, into which I resolved to go with the ship." As the *Endeavour* sailed into the inlet, natives were seen on both headlands. The *Endeavour* anchored off the south shore, close to a hamlet of six or eight huts, where the inhabitants cooked their fish without taking any apparent notice of the ship. However " as soon as we approached the rocks, two of the men came down, each armed with a lance about ten feet long . . . resolved to dispute our landing to their utmost ". Finally, after a fruitless parley, muskets, loaded with small. shot, were fired and the two brave natives fled. The invaders went to the " houses " and distributed beads and ribbons to the children. In this dramatic manner the historical landing of Captain Cook in Australia was effected.

Resuming the voyage, Cook passed but did not enter Port Jackson, which, eighteen years later, Commodore Phillip explored for three days and then selected Sydney Cove for the site of the first English settlement, owing to its possession of " the best spring of water " and good anchorage close to the shore.

On continuing the exploration of the coast, the land was noted as sandy—indeed worse than at Botany Bay. Cook sailed so close to the land that he knew nothing about the Great Barrier Reef, which approaches the coast in this part.

He sighted the first coral reef, and, although carefully feeling his way, the *Endeavour* was suddenly spiked. To quote Banks : " We were called up with the alarming news of the ship being fast upon a rock. . . . We were upon sunken coral rocks, the most dreadful of all on account of their sharp points and grinding quality." The situation appeared to be desperate, but after strenuous heaving, the *Endeavour* was floated and hauled into deep water. On beaching her, it was shown that the rock had broken off and plugged the ship.

While the repairs were being made " an animal as large as a greyhound, of a mouse colour, and very swift ", was observed " which went only upon two legs, making vast bounds, just as the jerboa does ". Thus the kangaroo, the representative animal of Australia, bounded on to the scene. Upon leaving Endeavour River, Cook was in constant danger. He risked sailing through the passage in the Barrier Reef, now called after him, but only to face outside the greater peril of being thrown back upon it by the violence of the trade wind. But he sailed back through it, and after weeks of anxious navigation, traversed Torres Strait, of whose existence he had heard. Accordingly he wrote : " I claim no other merit than the clearing up of a doubtful point." The dangers to the navigator of Torres Strait were very serious, and Cook was thankful when " a swell from the south-west left me no room to doubt that we had now an open sea to the westward ".

Before quitting Australia, Cook named its north point Cape York, and, confident that the eastern coast had never been visited by any European, he took possession of it in the name of King George " by the name of New Wales ".

From Australia Cook made for Timor in the Moluccas, where the Dutch possessed a strong fort. He then sailed along the south coast of Java and passed through the Straits of Sunda to Batavia. Here the great navigator makes the important statement that either his determination of longitude was inaccurate or the Straits were wrongly shown in the published charts. Actually the error of three degrees of longitude was his, and this explains how utterly unreliable were the longitudes taken by his predecessors. Their latitudes, on the other hand, were fairly accurate from comparatively early days.

The *Endeavour* was repaired at Batavia, but the unhealthy climate levied a heavy toll in death and sickness. " The unwholesome air of Batavia ", Cook wrote, " is the death of more Europeans than any other place upon the globe of the same extent." The *Endeavour* sailed from this death-trap in December 1770, and calling at Cape Town, the great voyage of exploration ended on July 13, 1771, when Cook anchored in the Downs. The wonderful collection of plants made by Banks added lustre to his splendid achievement.

Cook had proved that the Southern Continent did not exist where Ptolemy had placed it, and that New Zealand did not form part of it. In 1772, in command of two ships, he sailed to complete the proof that it did not exist at all. The instructions given to the great navigator were to proceed to the Cape of Good Hope and thence sail to seek for undiscovered lands in the great unknown area to the south. No land was sighted in this area, but the Antarctic Circle, situated in 66° 32′ S., was crossed for the first time in the history of mankind on January 17, 1773 ; and it was proved that the ocean covered the land that had been supposed to exist in this quarter of the globe. " The southern frigid zone foreseen by Aristotle," says Mill, " reasoned on by the Greek philosophers, who declared it existent but inaccessible, denied and stigmatized as heretical by the medieval Church, never hitherto deliberately sought for, had at last been entered by the *Resolution*, with only one iceberg in sight." [1]

After accomplishing this feat, Cook decided to make for New Zealand, from whose islands both ships cruised eastwards nearly half-way across the Pacific, disproving the existence of the *Terra Incognita* in that vast area. After a visit to Tahiti for refreshment, Cook again returned to New Zealand. Yet again, sailing without his consort, on January 30, 1774, Cook reached his southern limit at 71° 10′ S.

" At four o'clock in the morning ", he writes, " we perceived the clouds, on the horizon to the south, to be of an unusual brightness,

---

[1] *The Siege of the South Pole*, by H. R. Mill, 1905, p. 71.

which we knew announced our approach to field ice. Soon after it was seen from the topmasthead, and at eight o'clock we were close to its edge. It extended east and west far beyond the reach of our sight. Ninety-seven ice hills were distinctly seen within the field, besides those outside—many of them very large, and looking like a ridge of mountains rising one above another till they were lost in the clouds. . . . Since, therefore, we could not proceed one inch farther to the south, no other reason need be assigned for my tacking and standing back to the north."

Cook broke down with a " bilious colic " after this trying experience on a diet of over-salted meat and rotten ship's biscuits, and made for Easter Island, where the statues and terraces delighted the explorers.

After again spending a month at Tahiti, the refreshed navigators visited Australia del Espritu Santo, and reduced the discovery of Quiros to a small, unhealthy archipelago. When the *Resolution* shaped a course for home, the existence of a vast temperate continent in the Pacific had been completely exploded, but Cook had expressed his belief in the existence of an Antarctic Continent.

Calling at the Cape of Good Hope, Cook anchored at Spithead on July 30, 1775, thus concluding another voyage of discovery, the greatest since that of Magellan.

The last voyage of Cook had for its main objective the discovery of a passage from the Pacific into the Atlantic. At the same time he was instructed to annex lands not already discovered by other powers. The *Resolution* and *Adventure* sailed from Plymouth in July 1776 and examined Kerguelen, recently discovered by the French. Cook reached New Zealand in February 1777, and then, sailing north, rediscovered the Sandwich Islands. Striking the coast of North America, the great navigator sailed steadily northwards, and, after overhauling his ships at Nootka Sound on the west coast of Vancouver Island, he examined the coast of Alaska in the vain search for a strait leading into Hudson Bay. Coasting northwards he named the most western cape of the American continent Prince of Wales Cape. He then sailed across to the coast of Asia, where he landed to study the natives and named the most easterly point of that vast continent East Cape. Returning to the American continent, the great explorer sailed north-east along the American coast. On reaching latitude 70° 29′ N. and longitude 161° 42′ W., his way was blocked by ice, and he gave the appropriate name of Icy Cape to his " Farthest North ".

Cook paid much attention to soundings, and discovered

that the sea at Bering Sea was shallow, and exercised no influence on the currents, as might have been supposed.

Returning to the continent of Asia once again, he coasted along it for some days to latitude 65° 56′ N. and longitude 179° 11′ W., where he named the nearest promontory Cape North.

Sailing towards the Pacific Ocean, Cook named a bay on the American coast Norton Sound. Landing a party, he collected spruce for making beer, and berries, while two Russians were discovered, who furnished valuable information. For half a century Cook's Icy Cape marked the bound beyond which no navigator sailed.

Sailing southwards for the last time, Cook discovered Hawaii. There pilfering by the natives led to a fight, in which the explorer was killed.

Thus died Captain James Cook, the greatest explorer of his age and the greatest of British navigators, who had accomplished a task worthy of his genius in solving the problem of the Pacific. The inscription on the base of his statue in London runs :

" Circumnavigator of the Globe—Explorer of the Pacific Ocean— He laid the foundations of the British Empire in Australia and New Zealand—He charted the shores of Newfoundland and traversed the Ocean Gates of Canada both East and West."

CHAPTER XXI

THE PENETRATION OF AMERICA DURING THE SEVENTEENTH AND EIGHTEENTH CENTURIES

" Alexander Mackenzie, from Canada, by land, the twenty-
second of July, one thousand seven hundred and ninety-
three."
The Inscription of Alexander Mackenzie on the Pacific Coast.

FRANCE played an insignificant part in the struggle for the
trade of India and the Spice Islands at the beginning of the
seventeenth century, but French explorers, continuing the
important discoveries of Cartier, took the lead in the exploration of North America[1] and founded Quebec; Montreal was
founded later by Maisonneuve.

Chief among them was Samuel de Champlain, who had
travelled to the West Indies and Mexico before he made a
preliminary voyage up the St. Lawrence in 1603. He returned
in 1608, and founded Quebec, and later Montreal. In the
spring of 1609 he joined an Indian war-party of Hurons, and
travelling southwards up the Richelieu River, discovered the
lake which is called after him. In 1613 he continued his
voyages, and explored the Ottawa, the chief northern tributary
of the St. Lawrence.

In 1615 Champlain made his most important journey.
Following up the course of the Ottawa and its tributary the
Mattawa, he crossed the divide to Lake Nipissing, and reached
the wide Georgian Bay in Lake Huron. He then made for
Lake Ontario, and accompanied the Hurons in an attack on
the stronghold of the Iroquois, situated to the south near Lake
Oneida. This expedition, in which Champlain was wounded,
was unsuccessful, and the great Frenchman returned to
Quebec where, though he made no further discoveries himself,
he encouraged others to follow up the trails he had blazed.

Montreal and Quebec were captured by an English squadron
in 1628, but, upon the declaration of peace, Canada was restored
to France in 1632, and the Jesuits were placed in sole religious

[1] Cf. *The History of Geographical Discovery in the Seventeenth and Eighteenth Centuries*,
by E. Heawood; *A History of Geographical Discovery and Exploration*, by J. N. L. Baker;
The Life of Champlain, by R. Flenley, 1924.

charge of both settlers and Indians. They acquitted themselves nobly of this onerous task, which, as one of the Fathers wrote, was a long and slow martyrdom.[1]

Among the chief successors of Champlain was Jean Nicollet, who in 1634 was commissioned by him to find a passage to the South Sea. Nicollet, from Lake Huron, reached Lake Michigan. He then followed up the Fox River to the portage, crossing to the Wisconsin, and reached the watershed separating the St. Lawrence from the Mississippi, which latter river was called "The Great Water" by the Indians. Misled by the information he had acquired, Nicollet reported that the Pacific was not far distant, and that he had discovered a new route to China.

The greatest of the later explorers of this important period was La Salle, who in more than one expedition navigated Lake Ontario and reached the Niagara Falls.

In 1672 Joliet and Marquette—the latter of whom had been in charge of a mission at the entrance to Lake Michigan —started on a voyage of exploration to discover the Mississippi. The explorers ascended the Fox, and, crossing the watershed, launched their canoes on the Wisconsin, down which they navigated to the mighty Mississippi. Floating down its broad stream, they reached the great prairies with their herds of buffalo, and terminated their important voyage at the junction of the Arkansas River, having proved that the Mississippi must reach the Gulf of Mexico, and not the Pacific. They also met Indians who had guns, hatchets, hoes, knives, etc., purchased from European traders.

This discovery was followed up by La Salle, who in 1681 navigated the Mississippi, being generally welcomed by the Indians. Upon reaching the delta, the explorers separated and descended the three main channels. On the shores of the Gulf of Mexico La Salle took formal possession of the valley of the Mississippi for France under the name of Louisiana. La Salle thus solved the problem of the great river, whose waters had been noted by De Narvaez a century and a half earlier. This feat ended a wonderful period of discovery in which French officials, monks and trappers had, in the face of great difficulties, explored the interior of North America with its remarkable group of great lakes.

We now come to the appearance of the English in the area that subsequently became the United States of America. The English in North America drove out and almost exterminated

[1] Cf. *The Jesuit Relations*, 1610–1791, ed. by Edna Kenton.

THE FALLS OF NIAGARA

(From Hennipin's New Discovery)

the warlike Indians, who delayed their advance into the interior for many years. They intermarried with them but little, whereas the Spaniards, generally speaking, settled as an aristocracy among vast populations of submissive Indians with whom they intermarried freely. The English, moreover, usually settled in a climate suitable for a northern race to lead a life similar to that of Europe, whereas the Spaniards relied almost entirely on slave labour in tropical or semi-tropical climates.

The attempts of Sir Walter Raleigh to found the colony of Virginia in 1585 and 1587 had failed, but in 1607 a permanent settlement was made by the London Company at Jamestown on the banks of the muddy James River. Among the leading pioneers was John Smith, who, penetrating into the interior, was taken prisoner by Indians and was only saved by the influence of the Chief's daughter, Pocahontas, who became such a romantic figure to later generations.

In 1614 Smith examined the shores between Cape Cod and Penobscot Bay, and published a map of the country to which he first gave the name of New England. In 1620 the Pilgrim Fathers reached the coast of Massachusetts and founded the colony of New Plymouth. Twelve years later Lord Baltimore founded a settlement on the shores of the Potomac in the country north of Virginia, which he named Maryland.

Indeed, from New Brunswick on the north to Florida in the south, English colonies were founded. From these colonies explorers penetrated short distances into the interior, but it took them more than a century to cross the Alleghanies. Once that barrier was conquered, the continent was crossed to the Pacific in eighty years. As a result of this slow advance, the French, who were already established in the interior of Canada, completely shut in the English and Dutch colonies, whose energies at that period were almost entirely devoted to establishing themselves. In 1645, after suffering from an Indian outbreak, forts were built to guard the settlers, which, like Richmond, became towns, but for more than a century little was undertaken in the way of serious exploration. In 1769 Daniel Boone of North Carolina led a party across the mountains to the beautiful blue-grass valley of Kentucky, swarming with buffaloes and other game, which was gradually occupied, albeit not without setbacks owing to the hostility of the Indians.

The Dutch had appeared on the scene early in the seventeenth century. In 1609 Henry Hudson, of Arctic fame, in the service of the Dutch East India Company, sailed up the river called by his name, ascending it for 150 miles and entering into relations with the Mohawk Indians on its banks. In 1614 the Dutch constructed a fort on Manhattan Island, and in 1622 founded New Amsterdam, which subsequently became New York. They also founded towns on the banks of the Hudson and Delaware Rivers. The English realized the danger involved in the separation of their colonies into two areas and, in 1664, they occupied New Amsterdam and changed its name to New York.

The Spaniards at this period, partly owing to the activity displayed by rival European powers, were sending out expeditions from Mexico. By 1565 they had reached Monterey to the south of San Francisco. In 1604 Onate followed down the Colorado River to its mouth. It was believed at this period that Lower California was an island, and this error persisted until a survey of the coast made early in the eighteenth century proved it to be a peninsula. As in Canada, the missionaries proved themselves intrepid explorers, and their work among the Indians was most successful. Indeed California to-day owes much of its old-world charm to the buildings erected by the Friars, albeit recent earthquakes have wrought havoc among them ; while their self-sacrificing labours are enshrined in *Ramona*, the classic of California.

In Chapter XVI an account is given of explorations in the Arctic and of the discovery of Hudson Bay in 1610. Sixty years later the Hudson Bay Company received its charter, which was intended to promote discovery and trade in " Furs, Minerals, and other considerable Commodities ". For a long time little was done in the way of exploration, except that it was proved that no strait opened out from Hudson's Bay to the Pacific, a fact of considerable negative importance. But in 1754 Anthony Hendry led an expedition into the interior to the Saskatchewan River, where he found a French fort. However, he was permitted to continue his journey into North Saskatchewan, where he met the Blackfoot Indians. Crossing the Red Deer River, he spent the winter in the vicinity of 114° W., exploring the country in various directions in the modern state of Alberta.

Of far greater importance was the journey of Samuel Hearne, who set out in 1769 to find an exit from Hudson Bay on the west, and to examine the country for copper-mines that the Indians had reported. Failing not once but twice, this determined Englishman in December 1770 reached the Coppermine River which he followed to its mouth. On his return journey he discovered the Great Slave Lake. Incidentally, the negative results of this great journey were most valuable, as proving that there was no possibility of finding the North-West Passage through Hudson Bay.

The greatest British explorer of these northern lands was the fur-trader, Alexander Mackenzie,[1] who in 1789 determined to discover whether the waters of the Great Slave Lake reached

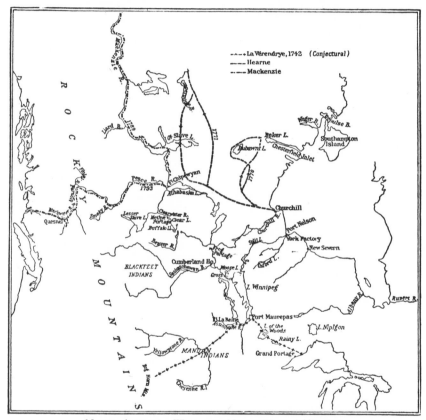

NORTH AMERICA—WEST AND NORTH-WEST, 1668–1800.

the Arctic or the Pacific Ocean. His starting-point was Fort Chipewyan, situated on Lake Athabasca, which had been founded in the previous year. From this base a strong party, which included several Canadians and Indians, entered the Slave River, and effecting portages where necessary, reached the Great Slave Lake. Ice made the crossing very difficult, but the outlet from the lake was found, and Mackenzie River,

[1] Vide *Voyages*, by Alexander Mackenzie, 1801.

as it was rightly named, was followed in a north-westerly direction. Supplies ran very low, but Mackenzie induced his companions to persevere, and on July 12 the expedition reached the Arctic Ocean, after following the river for 1,000 miles.

A second and still more important journey was made in 1792. Starting again from Fort Chipewyan, Mackenzie pushed south-west up the Peace River and constructed a fort, in which he spent the winter. In May 1793, continuing his voyage up the Peace River, he crossed the Rocky Mountains, making a portage through the bush on the mountain-side to avoid the deep canyon, which cuts through the main divide.

He writes :

> " At the break of day we entered on the extraordinary journey, which was to occupy the remaining part of it. The men began, without delay, to cut a road up the mountain, and as the trees were of but small growth, I ordered them to fell those which they found convenient, in such a manner that they might fall parallel with the road. The baggage was now brought from the waterside to our encampment. This was likewise from the steep shelving of the rocks, a very perilous undertaking, as one false step would have instantly been followed by falling headlong into the water. When this important object was attained, the whole party proceeded with no small degree of apprehension to fetch the canoe ; and, as soon as we had recovered from our fatigue, we advanced with it up the mountain."

Thanks to his guides, he followed the west-north-west branch at a point where the river forked, and reached the Fraser River, down which he floated for some distance. Indians, however, warned him of difficulties in navigation in its lower reaches. Mackenzie consequently left the Fraser River, and, crossing a divide, reached a tribe of friendly Indians dwelling on the Bella Coola River. Using their canoes, the river was followed to its mouth, and Mackenzie reached the Pacific Ocean.

He found a bay some two miles wide, and, paddling along the shore in stormy weather, landed in a small cove, but could not take observations owing to the continuously cloudy sky. On the following day he continued his voyage and landed at the Cape which Vancouver had recently visited and named Cape Menzies.[1] He was now faced with hostility owing to the Indians having been fired at by Vancouver's men, but taking up a strong natural position on a commanding rock, he waited until he had completed his observations, and then,

---

[1] Captain Bishop informed me that Mackenzie, writing his book some years later, had made a mistake, and that " Mackenzie's Rock " is at Point Edward. *Vide* " Sir Alexander Mackenzie's Rock " in Canadian Historical Sites Series, by Captain R. P. Bishop.

ALEXANDER MACKENZIE, ESQ.

(*From his Voyages . . . through the Continent of North America*

mixing some vermilion, he painted the inscription quoted at the beginning of this chapter, and started on the return journey.

Mackenzie was the first European to cross the continent of North America at its greatest width, in spite of the most serious physical obstacles and constant liability to attack by the Indians. Reading his modest account, one admires the courage, tact and patience he displayed in his dealings with his own followers, and with the Indians, hostile or friendly, with whom he was brought into contact. In view of his splendid achievements in exploration Alexander Mackenzie may be considered worthy of the highest place among the great explorers of North America.

This brief survey of the chief explorers of North America may fittingly be concluded by an account of the discoveries of Captain George Vancouver. The finding of lands abounding in fur-bearing animals brought ships of many nations to the north-west coast of America. The Spaniards were especially active, and despatched expeditions to examine the coast near Nootka Sound and the Strait of Juan de Fuca, which was reported to lead to the Atlantic. They seized the British post at Nootka Sound, whereupon Great Britain insisted on restoration and indemnity. In the event, Spain yielded, and Vancouver was despatched to effect a settlement of the dispute with Spain and to examine the coast for the " Strait " which still loomed large in the mind of Europe.

Vancouver, who had accompanied Captain Cook on his third voyage, started from Falmouth in command of two ships in the spring of 1791, and sailing by the Cape of Good Hope, struck the south-west coast of Australia, which he carefully surveyed for some 300 miles. He reached the coast of America a year after leaving England and spent three seasons in surveying it from 39° 30′ N. northwards. The Strait of Juan de Fuca, with its complicated system of channels and inlets, was surveyed with a thoroughness unexampled in voyages of discovery, and Vancouver was finally able to report : " I trust that the survey will remove any doubt and set aside every opinion of a North-West Passage." Vancouver also surveyed the Strait separating the island called after him from the mainland and, although his work received little notice at the time, his name is now honoured as that of a great surveyor and a worthy successor of Captain Cook.

*   *   *   *   *

Exploration in South America, compared with the great

discoveries of the *Conquistadors*, struck a minor note during the period under review. The struggle for the valley of the Amazon was the most important event, as it led to considerable activity on the part of the Portuguese, while the Spaniards also took a hand in the game.

In 1616, alarmed by the creation of Dutch and French settlements on or near the delta of the Amazon, the Portuguese despatched an expedition from Pernambuco and founded Para. In 1637 Pedro Teixeira led an expedition up the great river. He moved very slowly in order to survey the river and to note important branches, which were, in many cases, rivers of considerable size. As a result the voyage to Quito took ten months. There orders were received from Lima —Portugal did not recover her independence until 1640— that Teixeira should follow the same route back to Lima to perfect his survey. On the return voyage, the Portuguese leader solemnly took possession of a certain site in the name of King Philip IV, and set up a delimitation mark between the Spanish and Portuguese areas. This Act of Possession caused much bad feeling between the Spanish and Portuguese, owing, in part, to the ignorance that was displayed as to the exact locality of the boundary memorial. Indeed the question was not finally settled until 1771.

The great explorer of the upper reaches of the Amazon was Samuel Fritz,[1] a Jesuit of Bohemian origin, who converted the Omaguas and other Indian tribes to Christianity, and spent nearly forty years among them. He also made journeys to Para in one direction and to Quito and Lima in the other, these important explorations being embodied in a map which was published in 1691, and was of considerable geographical value. The Omaguas he describes as " wear their forehead flattened and level, like the palm of your hand, and of this they are exceedingly proud ; the women especially, to such an extent that they jeer at the women of other tribes by saying that they have their head round like the skull of a savage from the forest ". The Father's account of his illness during the flood is most moving :

" As I was staying in this village, already almost wholly inundated, in a shelter on a roof made of the bark of trees, I fell sick of most violent attacks of fever. . . . In the daytime I felt somewhat easier, but spent the nights in unutterable burnings, as the river, though it was but a

---

[1] Vide *The Travels of Father Samuel Fritz*, edited by the Rev. Dr. George Edmundson (Hakluyt Society), 1922.

hand-breadth from the bed, was out of reach of my mouth, and in sleeplessness caused not only by my infirmities, but also from the grunting of the crocodiles that all night long were roving round the village, beasts of terrible deformity."

Fritz was worshipped as a Saint by the Indians, and was a splendid type of the Jesuit missionary explorer, whose services to discovery have been so remarkable in every continent.

CHAPTER XXII

AMERICA: THE FINAL PHASE

" We had to pass where no human should venture. Steps are formed like a ladder by poles hanging to one another and crossed at certain distances with twigs, the whole suspended from the top to the foot of immense precipices, and fastened at both extremities to trees and stones."

SIMON FRASER.

" South America is full of amazing romances, of unknown rivers, lakes, and mountains, of unknown races, of riches still untouched, almost beyond imagination. Almost without exception the savages are hostile ; they are very numerous and they use poisoned arrows. For years, civilized and savage have shot one another at sight."

COLONEL P. H. FAWCETT.

"Brazil is like the book of Genesis. In the begining there was forest. On succeeding days, gamblers who dreamed in millions said, ' Let there be cocoa, rubber, coffee, cattle.' The red earth responded with a prodigality that shook the scheme of creation."

ROSITA FORBES.

THE successors of Mackenzie were men of great determination and courage, and Canada was such a vast country that there was plenty of scope for their journeys of exploration, which, like those of Mackenzie, were mainly based on the desire to open up new areas to the fur trade. Among the stories which thrilled me as a boy was the descent of the terrible canyons of the Fraser River by its explorer, which stands out, among other feats of the period, for the indomitable courage that was displayed alike by the British leader and the hardy *Voyageurs*.[1]

Simon Fraser joined the North-West Company as a youth of sixteen in 1792, and for several years travelled in various parts of the West. In 1805 he founded a post on McLeod Lake, and in the following year, accompanied by John Stuart, he explored the headwaters of the Fraser River, discovering various rivers, lakes and streams which united to form the great waterway. In 1807 he founded Fort George at the

[1] Vide *The Search for the Western Sea*, by L. T. Burpie, 1908.

190

point where the Nechako joined the Fraser River, and from this post he started on his great adventure, believing that he was exploring the Columbia River.

Almost immediately dangerous rapids were met with. To quote Burpie,[1] "the channel was contracted to forty or fifty yards, and through this narrow gorge the immense body of water rushes turbulently, its foam-crowned waves dashing hither and thither against the rocky walls ". Five picked men manned a light canoe, but " only for a moment could they control her. Over the first cascade she rode in safety. Then the men lost all power. Drawn into an eddy she was whirled about like a reed . . . surging round for a time, she flew out into the current, and finally she was forced against a low, projecting rock and the men sprang out." It was necessary, if the baggage was to be saved, to haul everything up the perpendicular bank. Steps were cut with daggers, and, with infinite risk and toil, the canoe and the baggage were hauled up the cliff. The natives advised him that the river lower down was mpracticable for navigation, but Fraser was determined to carry out his instructions to the letter. At the next rapids, he took the desperate expedient of letting empty canoes float down them, and this was accomplished without loss. But carrying packs weighing some ninety pounds was terribly exhausting, while moccasins wore out in a day.

The crux of the voyage was a canyon where no portage was possible, and so the very serious risk of shooting the rapids with fully loaded canoes was run, and safely accomplished. Finally, Fraser perforce left his canoes, and, each man shouldering a heavy pack, started off on foot. Fortunately another section was navigable by canoes, which Fraser was able to hire, albeit there were dangerous eddies. At last he reached the section which was served by the tide. Here the party met with hostility, as the sea-coast Indians were enemies of the river Indians. The intrepid Scotsman finally came in sight of a bay of the sea where the party halted, having accomplished their mission. They had run out of provisions, and in view of Indian hostility, Fraser reluctantly decided to take advantage of the flowing tide and returned upstream. He took his latitude at 49° N. and, as the mouth of the Columbia was known to be about 46° N., he realized that he had descended an unknown river, which was useless for navigation. But, as an explorer, he deserves the credit that he won by his important discovery. By a most curious

[1] L. J. Burpie, 1908.

191

coincidence Thompson at this very time "was paddling up the true Columbia without knowing it".

David Thompson, who was a greater explorer than Fraser, began his surveys in 1790 by exploring the Saskatchewan River to its source. He was, at that period, in the service of the Hudson Bay Company, but, to quote Burpie, joining the North-West Company seven years later, he began a remarkable series of journeys which were of the greatest importance. In 1807 Thompson set out to explore west of the Rockies, and, to quote Burpie, " One gains an idea of the magnitude of the rivers that drain this great western country when it is remembered that within a few miles of the point where Thompson now stood, in the heart of the Rocky Mountains, he had followed one and the same river for a distance of 1,199 miles." Thompson descended the Blaebery River, and was the first European to reach the Upper Columbia. But his greatest feat was the discovery of the Athabaska Pass, which for many years constituted the main route to Columbia. To quote Burpie once more :

" Provisions were scarce and the men ready to desert at any moment On January 1, 1811, the thermometer registered 24° below zero, and the travelling was so bad that the dogs could not move the sleds. . . . On they went, spurred to their utmost by the untiring Thompson. Finally they crossed the pass, but the snow getting deeper and softer as they descended the pass, the dogs could no longer haul the loads, and Thompson abandoned everything except what was absolutely essential."

Before dealing with the great explorers of the United States of America, a brief reference must be made to Louisiana, where New Orleans was founded in 1717. After its exploitation in the notorious Mississippi Bubble, a considerable number of Frenchmen had remained in the country, and suitable wives were procured for colonists by the Ursuline nuns, who invented the picturesque yet practical expedient of *les filles à la cassette*.[1]

Napoleon, at one time, had decided to restore and enlarge New France, and taking back the eastern portion of Louisiana, which had been ceded to Spain in 1762, he prepared to despatch a powerful army and fleet to enforce his policy. The United States viewed this movement with apprehension, but suddenly Napoleon realized that he dared not engage his strength so far from Europe, and sold the whole of Louisiana to the United States for 15,000,000 dollars.

The scene was thus set for exploration, and, in 1804, Lewis

[1] *History of the Expedition of Captains Lewis and Clark*, by J. K. Hosmer, 1902. The nuns collected money with which they were able to provide outfits and dowries for the selected girls.

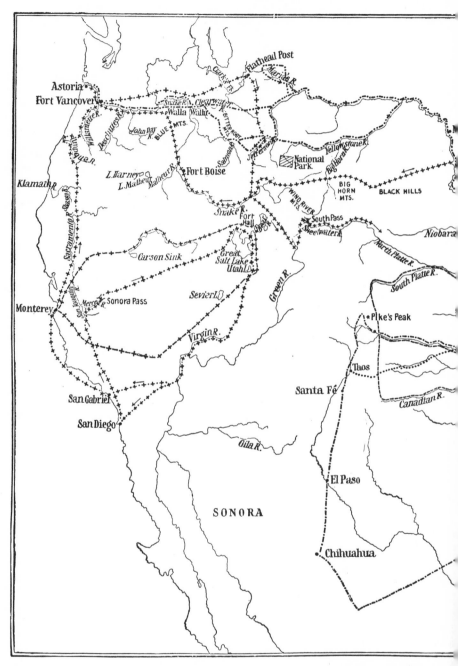

THE UNITED STA'
(From J. N. L. Baker's *History of Geographical Discovery*

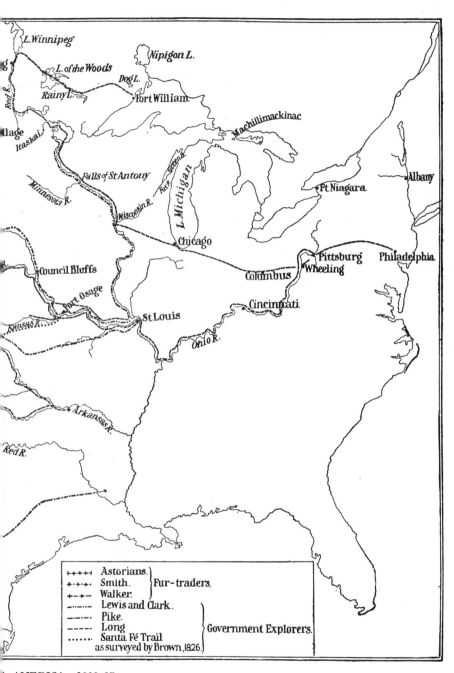

L.Winnipeg

Nipigon L.

L. of the Woods

Dog L.

Rainy L.

Red R.

Fort William

Machillimackinac

llage

Itaska L.

Falls of St Antony

L. Michigan

Fort Niagara

Albany

Minnesota R.

Wisconsin R.

Fox R. Green B.

Chicago

Pittsburg

Philadelphia

Council Bluffs

Columbus

Wheeling

Fort Osage

Cincinnati

Kansas R.

St Louis

Ohio R.

Arkansas R.

Red R.

Astorians.
Smith.   } Fur-traders.
Walker.
Lewis and Clark.
Pike.
Long   } Government Explorers.
Santa Fé Trail
as surveyed by Brown, 1826.

AMERICA, 1800–37

loration, by permission of Messrs. George G. Harrap & Co.)

and Clark started from St. Louis, situated on the Mississippi just below its junction with the Missouri, to discover the unknown interior. Their instructions included the exploration of the Missouri with the object of finding the best trade route across the Rockies to the Pacific, using the Columbia or another river for the purpose. The party, composed of some forty men, used a decked boat which could be rowed or sailed, with a defensible position amidships, on which a swivel gun was mounted. During the summer all went well, the Indians proving friendly, and the expedition went into winter quarters some 1,600 miles up the Missouri among the Mandan Indians, who were subsequently exterminated by smallpox. So far the pioneers were in fairly well-known country, and, during the winter, they were visited by agents of the North-West and Hudson Bay Companies.

In the spring of 1805, the voyage up the Missouri was resumed in canoes, and the explorers, traversing unknown lands full of game, discovered the source of the Missouri River. As the author puts it : "from the foot of one of the lowest of these mountains, which rises with a gentle ascent of about half a mile, issues the remotest water of the Missouri". Thanks to a slave-woman accompanying the expedition, who belonged to the Shoshonee Indians, horses were supplied by her tribesmen, and the passage of the Rockies was effected without great difficulty, though colts had to be killed owing to scarcity of game. Descending the Columbia River in canoes, there were difficulties owing to falls and rapids, which were overcome by portages, and the Pacific Ocean was reached in November 1805. Thus a great feat was accomplished.

On the return journey the explorers separated at the Missouri, Clark following the Yellowstone River to its junction with the Missouri, and in September 1806 the expedition reached St. Louis, after accomplishing a journey of over 7,000 miles. This expedition had not only blazed a trail to the west and opened up much new country for the fur-traders, but it was mainly on these discoveries that the United States based its claims to the territories now known as the states of Oregon and Washington.

The last great explorer in North America was Fremont, who from 1838 explored and surveyed vast tracts of the interior. He began by exploring a large area between the Missouri and the Mississippi. In 1842 he led an expedition up the Kansas and Great Platte Rivers to the South Pass, where the trade route to Oregon crossed the Rockies; and Fremont Peak in the Wind River Mountains still bears his name. On this expedition he gives a vivid account of a buffalo hunt : [1]

"A grand herd of Buffalo, some seven or eight hundred in number, came crowding up from the river, where they had been to drink. A crowd of bulls, as usual, brought up the rear, and every now and then some of them faced about as if more than half inclined to stand and fight... In a few moments the route was universal, and we were going over the ground like a hurricane. My horse was a trained hunter, and, with his eyes flashing, and the foam flying from his mouth, sprang on after the cow like a tiger. In a few moments he brought me alongside of her, and, rising in the stirrups, I fired at the distance of a yard, and she fell headlong."

To turn to his description of the country we read :

"It seemed as if, from the vast expanse of uninteresting prairie we had passed over, Nature had collected all her beauties together in one chosen place. We were overlooking a deep valley, which was entirely occupied by three lakes, and from the brink the surrounding ridges rose precipitously 500 and 1,000 feet, covered with the dark green of the balsam pine, relieved on the border of the lake with the light foliage of the aspen. The surprise manifested by our guides when these impossible obstacles suddenly barred our progress, proved that they were among the hidden treasures of the place, unknown even to the wandering trappers."

In 1843 Fremont led another expedition, which, starting from Kansas City, aimed at the discovery of a new route across the Rockies, but failed to find it. During this journey Fremont explored the Great Salt Lake : "To travellers so long shut up among mountain ranges, a sudden view over the expanse of silent waters had in it something sublime." However, the reality of the bare rocky island which they visited "dissipated our dream of fertile islands, and I called this Disappointment Island".

The main objective of the expedition was to explore the country between the Columbia Valley and California. Fremont accordingly crossed the Rockies and travelled from the Snake River to the Columbia. In November the expedition started to traverse the unexplored country south of the Columbia. The passage of the Sierras was accomplished with extreme difficulty, but, even so, Fremont found time to describe the sunrise : "Immediately above the eastern mountains was repeated a cloud-formed mass of purple ranges, bordered with bright yellow gold; the peaks shot up into a narrow line of crimson cloud, above which the air was filled with a greenish orange; and over all was the singular

[1] Vide *John Charles Fremont*, by C. W. Upham, 1856.

194

EL CAPITAN, CALIFORNIA

(From the collection of Reunion of British Official Missions to the United States)

beauty of the blue sky." Finally, the stout-hearted explorers reached the Sacramento River.

Fremont in his report pointed out the extreme importance of the Columbia River :

> " It is the only river which traverses the whole breadth of the country, breaking through all the ranges, and entering the sea. Drawing its waters from a section of ten degrees latitude in the Rocky Mountains, which are collected into one stream by three main forks, this great river thence proceeds by a single channel to the sea, while its three forks lead each to a pass in the mountains, which opens the way into the interior of the continent."

Fremont made other discoveries, but the old order was changing, and, a decade later, great trans-continental railway surveys began, while the surveys of the Corps of Topographical Engineers to which Fremont was gazetted, took the place of the earlier explorers. Fremont continued his explorations for many a year and had many adventures. He was the last great explorer of North America.

* * * * *

In the exploration of South America, so far as the nineteenth century is concerned, the leading figure was Humboldt. Landing in Venezuela in 1799, he travelled up the valley of the Orinoco for a distance of some 1,700 miles, and proved the connection of that river with the Amazon. After a visit to Cuba, the explorer returned to South America, and ascending the Magdalena River, traversed the Andes to Quito. He then explored the Andes as far as Peru, and examined the sources of the Amazon. He finally returned to Europe in 1804.

Humboldt's work [1] shows a deep insight into every subject which he touches. Take his first impressions of the tropics :

> " If the traveller feel strongly the beauty of picturesque scenery, he can scarcely define the various emotions which crowd upon his mind ; he can scarcely distinguish what most excites his admiration, the deep silence of those solitudes, the individual beauty and contrast of forms, or the vigour and freshness of vegetable life which characterize the climate of the tropics. It might be said that the earth, overloaded with plants, does not allow them enough space to unfold themselves. The trunks of the trees are everywhere concealed under a carpet of thick verdure ; and if we carefully transplanted the orchidae, the pipers and the pothos, which a single fig-tree nourishes, we should cover a vast extent of ground."

Or take his description of the celebrated " Cavern of the *Guacharo* " :

[1] *Travels to the Equinoctial Regions of the New Continent*, by Alexander von Humboldt, 1822.

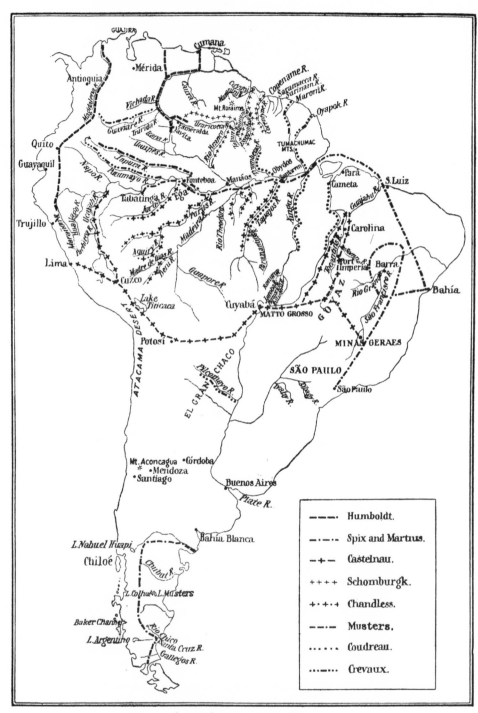

SOUTH AMERICA AFTER 1800.

196

" We came suddenly before the immense opening of the grotto. The aspect of this spot is majestic even to the eye of a traveller accustomed to the picturesque scenes of the higher Alps. . . . The vegetation continues and does not disappear till, advancing into the interior, we reached thirty or forty paces from the entrance, and we went on about 430 feet, without being obliged to light our torches. Where the light begins to fail, we heard from afar the hoarse sounds of the nocturnal birds. The guacharo is of the size of our fowls, and has the mouth of the goatsuckers and procnias, and the port of those vultures, the crooked beak of which is surrounded with stiff silky hairs."

Nothing escapes the vigilance of this wonderful explorer in any field of science, whether he describes the natives, or waxes eloquent on volcanoes, or refers to experiments on electric eels.

Humboldt, apart from being an explorer, was a very great scientist, and the founder of modern physical geography and meteorology. It is difficult to estimate the effect of this great figure on the progress of mankind. Dr. Johnson in the epitaph he composed for Oliver Goldsmith used the expression *nihil tetigit quod non ornavit*. To Alexander von Humboldt it also applies with at least equal appropriateness.

During the third decade of the nineteenth century, King and Fitzroy surveyed the east coast of South America, south of the Plate River to Chiloe on the Pacific coast. In 1831 Fitzroy returned to South America in command of the *Beagle*, with Charles Darwin on board. This truly great English scientist made a special study of Patagonia, and, like Humboldt, by his researches has greatly influenced the progress of mankind.

Another notable British explorer was Schomburgk, who in 1835 commenced a series of important journeys in British Guiana and the adjoining countries. In many cases he followed in the footsteps of the *Conquistadors*, while his explorations linked up Guiana with the Orinoco Valley. Among other explorers of this period was Castelnau who, in command of a French expedition, reached Brazil in 1843. After exploring in the interior of this enormous country, he marched west, skirted the Gran Chaco, crossed Bolivia, and, passing through Cuzco, the ancient capital of the Incas, reached the Pacific at Lima.

To turn to Patagonia, Musters,[1] in 1869, landed at the Chilean settlement of Punta Arenas in Magellan's Strait and arranged to accompany an officer and some soldiers, whose mission was to recapture convicts who had fled north to

[1] " A Year in Patagonia ", by Lieutenant Musters, *J.R.G.S.*, Vol. XXXIV, p. 205.

Santa Cruz. Of the Patagonians he wrote: "They were all fine-looking men, more than one standing over six feet, and one being at least six feet four inches." To-day these measurements would not be as remarkable as they were sixty years ago. Settling down at Santa Cruz until climatic conditions were favourable, Musters made friends with the Indians whom he accompanied on their hunting expeditions. On the second part of his expedition, Musters travelled north with a tribe of Indians, who lived by hunting the guanacos and ostriches, which were abundant. During the march an Indian was killed, and, to quote the explorer: "On the death of an Indian, his horses and dogs are killed; his arms, mantles and all his property gathered together and burnt. The body, enveloped in a shroud or mantle, is buried in a sitting posture with the face to the east."

Musters, whose name is commemorated by Lake Musters, finally reached the Rio Negro, having explored some 700 miles in Patagonia. His successor was Moreno, whose journeys made him the leading authority on the Argentine, filling in the blanks of these vast areas. In 1902 he served on the Argentine-Chili Boundary Commission under Holdich, and to him we mainly owe the scientific survey of the Argentine.

Among the greatest explorers of the huge Amazon basin in modern times is Hamilton Rice. Beginning his series of expeditions in 1907, he systemmatically explored tributary after tributary in the north-west of the basin. To quote one of his most interesting experiences: "The Casiquiare canal, which links the Orinoco and Amazon systems by a natural waterway, is the only example of its kind in the world. . . . The integrity of the canal as a connection between two rivers of separate systems, without its capture by one of them, may be likened to any material system in a state of neutral equilibrium, a condition where as much work is resisted as is performed by the applied and internal forces."[1] Later in this expedition the American explorer penetrated to the upper reaches of the Orinoco, until the hostility of the Indians compelled him to return downstream.

In 1925 another expedition was undertaken to explore Brazilian Guiana.[2] Altogether Hamilton Rice has made five expeditions, and has not only surveyed, and added much to our scientific knowledge, but has gained a remarkable insight into, and knowledge of, the Indians. He has made considerable use of seaplanes for surveying, while his wireless

[1] *G.J.*, Vol. LVIII, p. 323. [2] *G.J.*, Vol. LXXI, pp. 113-43, 209-23, 345-56.

messages reached England in one direction and New Zealand in another. Hamilton Rice is the foremost scientific explorer of South America, and there is every reason to hope that he will win fresh laurels before his race is run.

In the southern basin of the Amazon the unexplored area was equally vast. Many of the great tributaries were explored by Rondon, who year after year has not only surveyed, but has made friends with the Indians. In 1913 Theodore Roosevelt undertook an expedition which, starting from Asuncion, followed up the Paraguay River, where he noted that the *piranha* fish—only eighteen inches in length—" are the most ferocious fish in the world. . . . They will rend and devour alive any wounded man or beast; for blood in the water excites them to madness." [1]

On the Brazilian frontier Roosevelt was met by Rondon, who had lost one of his toes by the bite of a *piranha* and had been severely bitten in the thighs and hands. Under his guidance, continuing up the Paraguay River, the old Portuguese fort of Coimba, now garrisoned by Brazilian troops, was reached.

Crossing the Matto Grosso, the expedition reached the scene of Rondon's exploration, of which Roosevelt wrote that it " was as remarkable as, and in its results even more important than, any similar work undertaken elsewhere on the globe at or about the same time ". From Tapirapoan, on the river of that name, the expedition started northwards across the Plan Alto or " Highland Wilderness " of Brazil. The route lay through a land inhabited by Nhambiqueras, natives of the most primitive type. Both sexes were naked, and " the men had holes pierced through the septum of the nose and through the upper lip, and wore a straw through each hole ". One wonders what the origin of this custom could have been. Thanks to Rondon's remarkable influence on these natives, the explorers were well received, and on February 27, 1914, they reached the banks of the River of Doubt, as they termed this unknown stream.

Using seven dugouts, they started downstream, and Roosevelt writes : " The lofty and matted forest rose like a green wall on either hand. The trees were stately and beautiful. The looped and twisted vines hung from them like great ropes. Now and then fragrant scents were blown to us from flowers on the banks." The rapids took their toll of life and necessitated exhausting portages, some of considerable length.

[1] *Through the Brazilian Wilderness*, by Theodore Roosevelt, 1914, p. 40.

But at last, on April 15, the explorers of the Rio Roosevelt, as it was named, reached a hut inhabited by rubber-gatherers, who called the river Castanho, and, towards the end of April, worn out with illness and fatigue, they entered the mighty Amazon. To quote Roosevelt again : " We had put upon the map a river some 1,500 kilometres in length, of which the upper course was not merely utterly unknown to, but unguessed at, by anybody."

The last great explorer in Brazil was Fawcett. In 1902 there was a revolution in the Acre area of Bolivia, with the result that some 70,000 square kilometres were ceded to Brazil in return for a money payment and access to the navigable waters of the Paraguay River. Fawcett was invited to act as Chief Bolivian Commissioner, and in 1906 he undertook the ascent of the Alto Acre and the descent of the Abuna. To quote : " Parrots, dense forest, and half a mile of coffee-coloured river cutting a sinuous course in red lacustrine deposit is the tale of months—never the sign of a hill—weeks of laborious dragging of heavy canoes over sharp sandstone rocks—constant vigilance, heavy rains and not too much food —a story of much small incident and very hard work." [1]

After completing this survey to the satisfaction of both countries, Fawcett was commissioned to undertake similar work on the eastern frontier, for Bolivia, like Switzerland, has no seaboard. He accordingly proceeded to Corumba, where the frontier was to be rearranged to give Bolivia access to navigable waters. There was also a dispute in connection with the River Verde.

The exploration of this river called for exceptional courage and tenacity. Unable to drag the boats up the rapids, they were sunk and supplies were abandoned. " For nearly three weeks we lived upon occasional palm tops ; we were eaten up by insects ; were drenched by a succession of violent storms with a southerly wind, bitterly cold for wet and blanketless people." Through this " green hell ", as it has been aptly termed by a recent traveller, the heroic explorers emerged into open country near the source of the river. Upon the return journey conditions were even worse, and five of the six persons died in Matto Grosso, which is noted for its deadly climate. In a later expedition, Fawcett explored the Heath River, where the Guarayos Indians were hostile. At

---

[*] The passage at the head of this chapter is quoted from *G.J.*, Vol. XXXIII, p. 181. This quotation is taken from *G.J.*, Vol. XXXV, p. 523. For the special maps dealing with these Boundary Commissions, vide *G.J.*, Vol. XXXV, opposite p. 620.

their first meeting they fired steadily at the party, but Fawcett, by the display of extreme forbearance and equal courage, at last made friends with them. In 1913 Fawcett penetrated among cannibal tribes, who were absolutely naked savages ignorant of metal.

In 1925 Fawcett started off on his last journey from Cuyaba in Matto Grosso, whence he disappeared into the vast territory of the Xingu. He hoped to discover a civilized race which had lost contact with the outer world. He was last heard of near Bakari, situated some distance to the north of Cuyaba, in May 1925. A search, involving considerable hardship and danger, was made by Dyott, an experienced explorer in South America. Starting on this quest in 1928, he not only traced the route, but found relics of the great explorer, including an air-tight case, and his final summing up runs: "that Colonel Fawcett and his companions perished at the hands of hostile tribes seems to me and to all my party beyond dispute ".[1] Thus perished a splendid pioneer whose name is inscribed for all time in the list of the great explorers of South America.

[1] " The Search for Colonel Fawcett ", G. M. Dyott, *G.J.*, Vol. LXXIV, p. 583.

CHAPTER XXIII

THE EXPLORATION OF AUSTRALASIA

" They are rhymes rudely strung with intent
   Less of sounds than of words,
In lands where bright blossoms are scentless,
   And songless bright birds ;
Where, with fire and fierce drought on her tresses,
Insatiable Summer oppresses
Sere woodlands and sad wildernesses,
   And faint flocks and herds.
     .   .   .   .   .
In the Spring when the wattle gold trembles
   'Twixt shadow and shine,
When each dew-laden air-draught resembles
   A long draught of wine ;
When the skyline's blue burnish'd resistance
Makes deeper the dreamiest distance,
Some song in all hearts hath existence—
   Such songs have been mine."

Adam Lindsay Gordon.

In Chapter XX, an account is given of the discovery of Australia by Janszoon, and of the exploration of its eastern coast by Captain Cook. Many problems remained for their successors. The coast west of the point at which Cook's survey commenced was unknown. It was also quite uncertain whether Tasmania was an island or a peninsula, and finally there was a belief that the vast continent might be divided by a strait running up to the Gulf of Carpentaria.

In 1795 Flinders and Bass, either together or separately, explored the coast west of Cook's survey and reached Bass Strait, called after its discoverer. In 1798 they sailed together through the strait and circumnavigated Tasmania. In 1801–2 Flinders explored the coast of what is now South Australia, and disproved the theory that the continent was divided by a strait. Flinders, on a visit to England, secured the powerful support of Banks and returned to Australia in command of a ship on which John Franklin sailed as a midshipman. The unknown southern coast was charted by Flinders in the *Investigator*, by Grant and Murray in a sixty-ton boat, the *Lady Nelson*, and by the French explorer Baudin in *Le Géogra-*

SUNSET ON THE MURRAY
(*From Sturt's Central Australia*)

phe. Flinders, however, was the greatest of these explorers, and in 1803 completed his task by the circumnavigation of Australia. He was a worthy successor of Captain Cook.

As in the United States of America, so in Australia, penetration was barred by a range of mountains. The coastal area was explored easily enough, but the Blue Mountains, with their precipitous ravines, sorely hindered access to the interior. It was not until 1813 that Blaxland, impelled to seek fresh pastures by a severe drought, pushed inland and crossed the Blue Mountains. He discovered a well-watered country in which Bathurst was founded in 1815.[1]

The great explorer of Eastern Australia was Sturt. He first explored to the north-west, in 1828, and wrote: " We suddenly found ourselves on the banks of a noble river. . . . The channel was from seventy to eighty yards broad, and enclosed an unbroken sheet of water, evidently very deep and literally covered with pelicans and other wild fowl." But " the water was so salt as to be unfit to drink ". Sturt, owing mainly to lack of fresh water, decided to explore no further on this occasion, and " as we mounted our horses, I named the river the ' Darling ' as a lasting memorial of the respect I bear the Governor ".

In November 1829, Sturt started to explore to the south-west, providing himself on this occasion with a boat. Reaching the Murrumbidgee, he launched his boat on its waters on January 7, 1830, and after a week's voyage, the junction of the Murray was reached. " Hopkinson called out that we were approaching a junction, and in less than a minute afterwards, we were hurried into a broad and noble river. We had got on the high road, as it were, either to the south coast, or to some important outlet ; and the appearance of the river itself was such as to justify our most sanguine expectations."

The natives had so far given no serious trouble, but while sailing down the Murray—

" we observed a vast concourse of natives, and, on a nearer approach, we not only heard their war-song, if it might be so called, but remarked that they were painted and armed, as they generally are prior to their engaging in deadly conflict. . . . As I did not wish a conflict with these people, we passed quietly down the stream in mid-channel. The natives ran along the bank of the river, endeavouring to secure an aim at us ; but, unable to throw with certainty, in consequence of the onward motion of the boat, they flung themselves into the most extravagant attitudes and worked themselves into a state of frenzy by loud and vehement shouting.

[1] *Australian Discovery*, Vol. II, by E. Scott, 1929.

" It was with considerable apprehension that I observed the river to be shoaling fast, more especially as a huge sand-bank projected nearly a third-way across the channel. To this sand-bank they ran with tumultuous uproar, and covered it over in a dense mass. . . . As we neared the sand-bank, I stood up and made signs to the natives to desist, but without success. I took up my gun, therefore, and cocking it, had already brought it down to a level. A few seconds more would have closed the life of the nearest savage. But at that very moment, when my hand was on the trigger, and my eye was along the barrel, my purpose was checked by M'Leay, who called to me that another party of blacks had made their appearance upon the left bank. Turning round, I observed four men at the top of their speed. The foremost of them threw himself from a considerable height into the water, and in an incredibly short space of time, stood in front of the savage, against whom my aim had been directed. Seizing him by the throat he pushed him backwards, and forcing all who were in the water upon the bank, he trod its margin with a vehemence and an agitation that were exceedingly striking."

Finally—

" curiosity took the place of anger. Thus, in less than a quarter of an hour from the moment when it appeared that all human intervention was at an end, and we were on the point of commencing a bloody fray that would have blasted the success of the expedition, we were peacefully surrounded by the hundreds who had so lately threatened us with destruction."

I have quoted this dramatic episode in full, as it brings out the splendid qualities of Sturt, of which Australians may well feel proud.

On January 23 the entrance of the Darling was passed, and on February 9 the explorers reached " a beautiful lake, which appeared to be a fitting reservoir for the noble stream that had led us to it ". The lake was unfortunately so shallow as to be useless for navigation, and the explorers finally reached the seashore on foot. They had discovered the great river-system of South-Eastern Australia.

After Sturt came Mitchell, who, travelling during the fourth decade of the nineteenth century, completed the work of his predecessors. Of the Loddon, a tributary of the Murray, he wrote : " The turf, the woods, and the banks of the little stream which murmured through the vale, had so much the appearance of a well-kept park, that I felt loath to injure its surface by the passage of our cart-wheels." And again : "We had at length discovered a country ready for the immediate reception of civilized man ; and destined perhaps to become eventually a portion of a great empire."

We now come to the expeditions into the interior, which

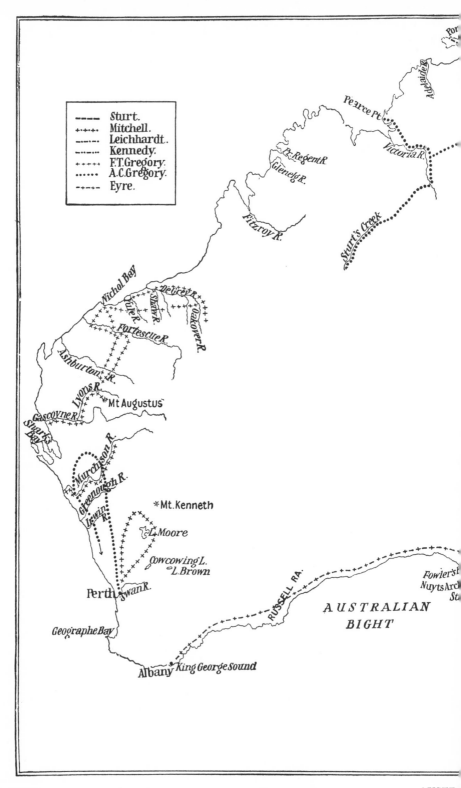

Sturt.
Mitchell.
Leichhardt.
Kennedy.
F.T.Gregory.
A.C.Gregory.
Eyre.

Por

Adelaide

Pearce Pt

Victoria R.

Pt.Regent R.

Glenelg R.

Sturt's Creek

Fitzroy R.

Nichol Bay

De Grey R.

Yule R.

Shaw R.

Oakover R.

Fortescue R.

Ashburton R.

Lyons R.

Mt Augustus

Gascoyne R.

Sharks Bay

Murchison R.

Greenough R.

Irwin R.

*Mt. Kenneth

L.Moore

Cowcowing L.

L.Brown

RUSSELL RA.

Fowler's

Nuyts Arc

St

AUSTRALIAN
BIGHT

Perth

Swan R.

Geographe Bay

Albany King George Sound

quills, stopt up with cotton; and the washers are fond of displaying a number of these quills in their hair." The whole of the hill country of Manding was auriferous. Here, then, was one of the sources of the gold of the Ethiopians mentioned by Herodotus.

With the arrival of the dry season, the caravan of slaves was organized and the great explorer set out on the last stage of 500 miles. He gives a vivid description of the dangers from wild beasts and robbers.

Park, who was distinctly a humane man, noted that three-quarters of the negroes were "in a state of hopeless and hereditary slavery, with this aggravation, that their children are born to no other inheritance". He also noted that the unfortunate slaves, male or female, were flogged when exhausted, and then either killed or left to be devoured by wild beasts. Moreover he bears testimony to their kindness: "During a wearisome peregrination of more than 500 miles, exposed to the burning rays of a tropical sun, these poor slaves, amidst their own infinitely greater sufferings, would bring water to quench my thirst, and at night collect branches and leaves to prepare me a bed in the wilderness." He probably realized that slavery was wrong, but felt that it was useless to fight against the established order of things. It must also be recollected that Bryan Edwards, the secretary of the African Association, was hostile to the total abolition of slavery. Yet Park's moving description of this inhuman traffic appealed deeply to the conscience of thousands. As Wilberforce wrote: "It pleads, trumpet-tongued, against that diabolical system of wickedness and cruelty." [1]

Park finally reached the Gambia, where he was welcomed as one risen from the dead. He had accomplished a great feat in reaching the Niger, but he had not been able to follow its course to its mouth, or, according to Major Rennell's theory, to an inland swamp. Park himself considered that it became the Congo in its lower reaches.

In 1805, Park left England at the head of a badly organized expedition to complete his task. He reached the Niger with but a handful of his party left, all of whom were dying or sick. Undeterred, he started on his voyage down the Niger, and met his death in the Bussa Rapids below.[2] His heroic

---

[1] *Life of Wilberforce*, by his sons, Vol. II, p. 346.
[2] Mr. H. S. W. Edwardes has given me the following valuable note: "Park landed at Bussa and evidently got on well with the people there, as he gave the headman a large silver medal on leaving. As one approaches the rapids coming down-stream, the river is seen to divide. The broad middle channel goes straight on and seems to

achievements, effected in spite of almost insuperable obstacles, entitle him to rank as one of the greatest explorers of Africa.

In the years that followed, other explorers failed in the quest, but in 1823 Denham,[1] thanks partly to a large escort furnished by the Pasha of Tripoli, crossed the Sahara as the leader of a British Government expedition, and on one happy day " The great Lake Tchad, glowing with the golden rays of the sun in its strength, appeared to be within a mile of the spot on which we stood."

To return to the Niger, in 1825 Clapperton landed at Lagos at the head of an expedition with Bornu as his objective.[2] The west coast fully merited its sinister title of the " White Man's Grave ", for hardly had the journey to the interior been begun when three English members of the mission died, leaving Clapperton and Richard Lander to continue the task. Everywhere treated with much friendliness, Clapperton reached Katunga in January 1826. Thence he proceeded to Bussa, an important town on the Niger, where he ascertained the details of Park's death.

From Bussa he proceeded to Kano. Clapperton left Lander at this city while he himself proceeded to Sokoto, where Lander finally rejoined him. Owing to the hostilities that were in progress with Bornu, Clapperton was unable to proceed thither, and he finally died at Sokoto, one more heroic explorer to be sacrificed to Africa. Lander, whose personality, tact and knowledge of the people were remarkable, returned to ' Bussa, whence, after many adventures, he reached the coast and found safety from Portuguese slave-traders, who attempted his life through the native rulers, on board a British ship.

In 1830 Richard Lander undertook a second expedition to discover the lower course and the mouth of the Niger. He and his brother John[3] returned to Bussa, where they were warmly welcomed by the King and his subjects. The question of descending the Niger was discussed, and the King said: " I will go down and ask the black water whether it will be safe for the white men to embark on it." Fortunately the response was favourable.

be quiet water, but it is barred by impassable rocks before rejoining the main channel. Park, without a pilot, would almost certainly have chosen the quiet looking middle channel straight ahead. He may have been wrecked where the canoe is shown in the photograph, or he may have gone over the cataract a couple of hundred yards ahead."

[1] *Narrative and Discoveries in Northern and Central Africa*, 1826.
[2] *Captain Clapperton's Last Expedition*, by Richard Lander, 1830.
[3] *The Niger*, by Richard and John Lander, 1833.

Upon reaching the state of the *Kaja Aga*—presumably a corruption of the Arabic *Khwaja Aga*—the explorer was robbed of one-half of his property by orders of the King. However, the position of affairs was improved by the appearance of a nephew of the Mandingo King of Kasson, under whose protection Park reached the Senegal, " a beautiful but shallow river, moving slowly over a bed of sand and gravel ". The passage of the river was safely effected, and his rapacious protector was rewarded with seven bars of amber. The King of Kasson proved to be friendly, and Park was able to replenish his store of gold by drawing on a merchant who had dealings with Dr. Laidley.

Continuing his journey, Park was well received by the King of Kaarta, but owing to the existence of a state of war with neighbouring Bambarra, he perforce marched north to Ladamar, " a Moorish Kingdom ". There his real troubles began. He was robbed of his property and made prisoner by Ali, the Moorish chief, who was encamped on the borders of the Sahara. Escaping with much difficulty and without his interpreter or slave, neither of whom he saw again, the intrepid Park continued his journey and entered the Fulah kingdom of Bambarra. At last, on July 20, 1796, he reached the Niger, and wrote the historical words which serve as the motto to this chapter. He was not permitted to cross the river to Sego, but was able to follow down the Niger a short distance and to cross it.

" Worn by sickness, exhausted with hunger and fatigue, half naked and without any article of value," Park wisely decided to return to the Gambia, but determined to travel by a different route. Accordingly he followed up the Niger to a point where its headwaters were not far distant from the valley of the Senegal, and here the explorer was stripped bare by Fulah bandits, but upon reaching the district of Manding in a state of complete destitution, the Governor recovered his horse and clothes. Yet Park would never have reached the English posts on the Gambia, had it not been for the remarkable kindness of a slave-dealer of Kamalia in Manding, who made him his guest for some months, during which he nearly died from fever.

However, upon recovering his health, he made good use of his opportunities, and observed the gold washing which " is practised in the height of the dry season, by digging a deep pit, like a draw-well, near some hill which has previously been discovered to contain gold. The gold dust is kept in

The French established themselves on the Senegal River, as the English had done on the Gambia, and the traders of both powers aimed at reaching the commercial centre of Timbuktu. The Dutch lost their dominant position early in the eighteenth century, and as the result of almost continuous fighting, Great Britain emerged the victor in the Napoleonic Wars of 1815.

It will be seen from the above epitome that Africa had not been penetrated at this period, and that Swift summed up the situation correctly in the verse:

> " Geographers in Afric maps
> Make savage pictures fill their gaps,
> And o'er inhabitable downs
> Place elephants in place of towns."

In 1788 the African Association was founded to promote exploration and the advancement of British interests. The first problem to be solved was that of the mysterious Niger, as neither its source nor its mouth was known, nor even the direction in which it flowed. Four explorers had died from sickness or been murdered, when Mungo Park,[1] a surgeon, who had made a voyage to Sumatra, offered his services for the adventure, undeterred by the fate of his predecessors.

Upon his arrival in the River Gambia, in 1795, he spent some months with a Dr. Laidley, studying the Mandingo language and the customs of the various races, who came to trade with the English. In December 1795, he set out on his great adventure, travelling with slave-traders for the first few stages. He was well received by the King of Woolli, whose subjects were Mandingoes, the majority of them being pagans with a Moslem minority. The King cheerfully remarked that he must expect quite a different treatment farther east in kingdoms " where the people had never seen a white man, and would certainly destroy me ".

From Woolli, Park crossed into Bondou, which was inhabited by Fulahs, who show marked traces of Semitic blood, and he notes that the ruling class and most of the people were Moslems. In this state he created great interest among the wives of the King, " who rallied me with a good deal of gaiety upon the whiteness of my skin, and the prominency of my nose ". At Bondou he was obliged to give the King his best coat, but was provided with " five drachms of gold " for the onward journey.

[1] *Travels in the Interior Districts of Africa*, by Mungo Park, 1799 ; and *The Journal of a Mission to the Interior of Africa*, 1815.

account of the country and people as far as Timbuktu and Gogo ; in the chapter dealing with that explorer, some account is given of the great empire of the Western Sudan. Like Herodotus, he believed that the Niger constituted the upper reaches of the Nile. Leo Africanus, who flourished early in the sixteenth century, was frankly puzzled about the Niger. He wrote : " These two rivers of Senegal and Gambia are not certainly known, whether they be the maine rivers of themselves, or branches and mouthes of the Niger." [1]

When the era of ocean exploration arrived, the Portuguese navigators and their successors devoted their chief energies to the profitable trade of India and the Spice Islands, and, generally speaking, regarded the stations they founded along the west coast of Africa as ports of call and refreshment or as centres for the collection of " black ivory ", which constituted the chief export from this unfortunate continent. On the east coast they occupied the ports founded by the Arabs and Persians. There were, of course, exceptions to this rule. Henry the Navigator, as mentioned in Chapter XI, was anxious to form an alliance with the Prince of Ethiopia, and the world-map of the Venetian Fra Mauro, constructed in the middle of the fifteenth century, shows a remarkable knowledge of that country, based mainly on native information. Later, in 1613, the Jesuit explorer Paez discovered the source of the Blue Nile, and other Jesuits explored the Galla country.

Portugal, as we have seen, had won the mastery of the Eastern Seas in 1538, but before that date she had secured a dominating position along the western and eastern coasts of Africa, which was strengthened by the Treaty of Tordesillas into a monopoly.

In 1553 the first English ships sailed to the west coast of Morocco—much to the anger of the Portuguese—and in the following year John Lok bartered cloth for Guinea pepper, elephants' tusks and gold, and made a good profit, in spite of Portuguese hostility. The Dutch, entering the field in 1595, swept away the Portuguese monopoly, and in their turn attempted to establish a similar system. At this period slaves, destined mainly to work in the sugar plantations of the New World, became the chief export, which they long remained.

---

[1] *The History and Description of Africa,* edited by R. Brown (Hakluyt Society), 1st series, Vols. XCII–XCIV. I have to thank Sir William Gowers for kindly reading this and the following three chapters and for making valuable suggestions.

CHAPTER XXIV

THE PROBLEM OF THE NIGER

"Looking forwards, I saw with infinite pleasure the great
object of my mission ; the long sought for, majestic Niger,
glittering to the morning sun, as broad as the Thames at Westminster, *and flowing slowly to the eastward.*"

MUNGO PARK.

THE neglect of Africa as a field for exploration by Europeans
until comparatively recent years is remarkable and requires
explanation. Egyptian civilization, which ranks among the
greatest of the ancient world, was developed in North-East
Africa, and yet, at the beginning of the nineteenth century,
we knew less about that continent than about Australia or
New Zealand.

The Egyptians undertook voyages to Palestine, and also
down the Red Sea, while their influence extended towards
Ethiopia. But the valley of the White Nile was blocked by
the *sadd*, and they had no knowledge of what lay beyond,
while to the west the Sahara constituted a very serious barrier
to intercourse. Nor must it be forgotten that ancient Egypt
was chiefly concerned with her powerful neighbours in Asia,
who conquered her time and again, whereas the barbarous
tribes on her western frontier caused her relatively little
concern.

In previous chapters some account has been given of
Africa as it was known to Herodotus and Ptolemy. The most
important event, after the Roman annexations in the north,
was the Moslem invasion. Beginning with the conquest of
Egypt by Amr in 640, the Moslems rapidly overran North
Africa, and by 711 the entire northern coast was in their
hands. Wave after wave poured into the conquered lands,
which gradually included the Sudan, where Kordofan, Darfur,
Wadai and Kano became Moslem cities, while more caravan
routes were established across the Sahara. It is of interest to
note that, as we see in the celebrated map of Idrisi, the cities
of the Central Sudan were known to the Arab geographers.

In the fourteenth century came the important journeys of
Ibn Battuta, who voyaged down the Niger, and gave a detailed

The main peak of the great central range, Mount Carstenz, which rises to nearly 16,000 feet, was climbed by Wollaston in 1913. The work of exploration in this great island has in recent years been carried on mainly by administrative officers, and the entire country is now fairly well known.

in the backs of their heads." [1] New Zealand is eminently a happy land, and it is significant that in his last chapter, Pember Reeves quotes the words :

"No hungry generations tread thee down."

New Guinea was known to the Spanish explorers, who discovered it in the middle of the sixteenth century. As mentioned in Chapter XX, Janszoon's objective was Nova Guinea, while De Prado explored its southern coast and discovered the Strait called after Torres. Yet it was not until the middle of the nineteenth century that its coast was charted. Moresby's survey in 1873 was especially important. Not only did he definitely settle the shape of the island, but he fixed peaks in the high ranges of the interior. His name is recorded in Port Moresby, which is the centre of the British Administration.

Inland exploration began about the same period. It was stimulated in 1884, when Germany annexed a part of New Guinea. The Kaiserin Augusta River was almost immediately discovered, and ascended for some 400 miles, while in 1896 the Bismarck Mountains were reached from Astrolabe Bay. Later boundary commissions, dividing the island between the British, the Germans and the Dutch, added greatly to the area surveyed.

Most important explorations were undertaken in the British area by MacGregor. In 1889 he navigated the Fly River for 600 miles to the point where it reached the German boundary. In 1896 he crossed the island from the Mambura River on the east coast. He reported that the Peak of Mount Scratchley rose to 12,850 feet. As a result of these explorations, it was proved that a very high range ran right across the island from east to west.

In 1910, Captain Rawling explored in Dutch New Guinea and reached the Nassau Mountains from the south coast. The difficulties of exploration were very great. "Every march ", he wrote, " included at least one great river, sometimes fordable and sometimes impassable, not counting the endless small streams between, each of which meant a wetting breast-high. During the first year twelve per cent. of the total force died, while eighty-three per cent. were invalided out of the country." [2]

[1] *The Long White Cloud*, by W. Pember Reeves, p. 80.
[2] *Explorations in Dutch New Guinea*, by Captain C. B. Rawling, *G. J.*, Vol. XXXVIII, p. 243.

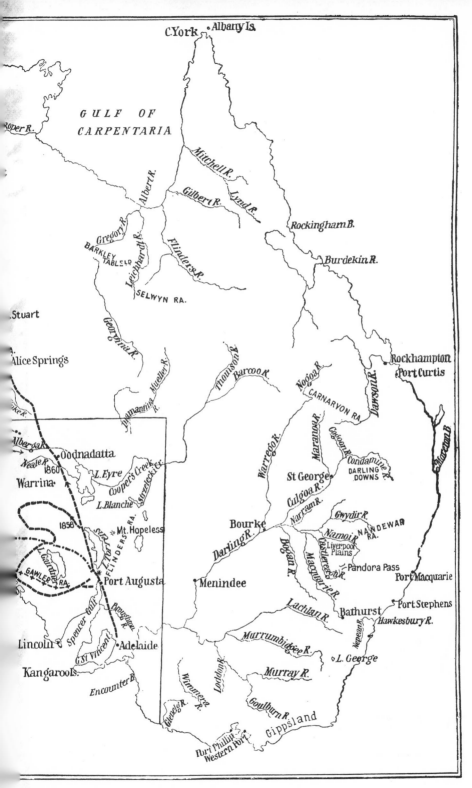

GULF OF CARPENTARIA

Roper R.

Mitchell R.

Albert R.

Gilbert R.

Lynd R.

Gregory R.

BARKLEY TABLE LD

Leichhardt R.

Flinders R.

SELWYN RA.

Rockingham B.

Burdekin R.

.Stuart

Georgina R.

Alice Springs

Diamantina

Mueller R.

Thomson R.

Barcoo R.

Nogoa R.

CARNARVON RA.

Dawson R.

Rockhampton
Port Curtis

Alberga R.

Neale R.

1860

Oodnadatta

L. Eyre

Cooper's Creek

Strzelecki Cr.

Warrego R.

Maranoa R.

St George

Cogoon R.

Condamine R.

DARLING DOWNS

Fitzroy R.

Warrina

L. Blanche

STURT'S STONY DESERT RA.

1858

*Mt. Hopeless

Bourke

Culgoa R.

Narran R.

Gwydir R.

NANDEWAR RA.

Namoi R.

Liverpool Plains

Castlereagh R.

Pandora Pass

Port Macquarie

GAWLER RA.

FLINDERS RA.

Port Augusta

Darling R.

Bogan R.

Macquarie R.

Port Stephens

Gardiner

Menindee

Lachlan R.

Bathurst

Hawkesbury R.

Lincoln

Spencer Gulf

Broughton

G. St Vincent

Adelaide

Murrumbidgee R.

Nepean R.

L. George

Kangaroo Is.

Murray R.

Encounter B.

Wimmera R.

Loddon R.

Goulburn R.

Gippsland

Glenelg R.

Port Phillip
Western Port

1858–75

...oration, by permission of Messrs. George G. Harrap & Co.)

had traversed a waterless area of 135 miles. Amazing to relate, the sheep had survived, after being six days without water.

Obtaining water by tapping roots and by collecting the dew, the party struggled on, and the animals, who had gone thirsty for a week, were again watered. These cruel hardships led to the murder of Baxter by two of the natives, who made off with most of the supplies. Followed for some distance by the two murderers, Eyre pressed on. He was at the end of his resources when he sighted a French whaler, whose captain treated him with generous hospitality and supplied him with stores for the onward journey. Finally, Eyre reached Albany, and by accomplishing this journey, connected the explorers of Central with those of Western Australia. He had proved by bitter experience that no river from the interior discharged into the Great Bight.

The early explorers were succeeded by others too numerous to mention. Pioneers in search of minerals or of fresh pastures gradually traversed and opened up the country. There was, however, a big gap, which was filled by John Forrest, who in 1874, travelling up the Murchison River, made his way across country eastwards, and finally struck the Overland Telegraph Line which had been constructed from Adelaide to Port Darwin in 1872. With the use of the camel, and later of the motor-car and the aeroplane, not only have remote districts in Australia been explored and settled, but, thanks to the telephone and other modern inventions, these pioneers can keep in touch with every part of the world.

New Zealand, as mentioned in Chapter XX, was discovered by Tasman in 1642. He first named it Staten Land, believing that it formed part of the great Southern Continent, and so was connected with the Staten Land near Cape Horn. Afterwards he altered the name to New Zealand, from a province in Holland to which it bears no resemblance.

New Zealand, as we know, was rediscovered by Captain Cook, who charted both islands with wonderful accuracy. Crozet, a French navigator, writes : "I found his survey to possess an exactness and minuteness which astonished me beyond all expression." [1] The captains of whalers discovered various islands, but no exploration of the interior was undertaken at this period.

The first explorer to penetrate inland was Samuel Marsden, who, while serving as chaplain to the New South Wales colony,

[1] Quoted in *Some Account of the Earliest Explorations in New Zealand*, by T. M. Hocken, 1891.

made journey after journey in New Zealand. In 1814 he landed at North Cape, and explored almost as far south as the River Thames. For twelve axes, he purchased 200 acres of land at Rangihihoura. This purchase was conveyed to the Church Missionary Society by a deed of sale. As the vendor could not write, the chief's *moko* or face-tattoo was copied on the deed. Here Marsden founded his first missionary settlement.[1] Altogether he travelled some 600 miles in the interior by canoe and on foot.

In 1839, under the auspices of the New Zealand Company, a pioneer expedition reached the islands and selected Port Nicholson as the site for a colony, which has now developed into the city of Wellington. Among the earliest explorers of this period was Bidwell, who discovered the hot springs and Lakes Rotoaira and Taupo. But his fame chiefly rests on his daring ascent of the volcano of Tongariro. "The crater", he writes, "was the most terrific abyss I ever looked into or imagined." Upon descending, after accomplishing this feat, he was attacked by the Chief of Taupo for having dared to pollute the sacred mountain. However, a gift of tobacco appeased the furious Maori.

The company, which was well organized, soon sent out surveyors, who gradually explored far and wide in North Island. In South Island progress was far less rapid, but the situation was changed by the gold rush to Otago, which brought many settlers. In Southland there are snow-clad peaks exceeding 12,000 feet in height, with glaciers and lakes which rival Switzerland. Generally speaking, New Zealand is happy in its rich pastures and its splendid climate, in which Europeans thrive even better than in Europe. It is also blessed by the fine qualities of the Maoris, who, Polynesians by descent, improved in physique and warlike qualities in New Zealand. They were keen fishermen and agriculturalists, and " Let us die for the land ! " was the appeal of their chiefs when fighting the English invaders. They owned no flocks or fowls. Their great benefactor was Captain Cook, who gave them seed potatoes and the seeds of cabbages and turnips. He also turned pigs and fowls loose. The descendants of the pigs, termed " Cookers ", still flourish, and are hunted by the settlers. The views of the Maoris on Captain Cook · were fortunately preserved. They run : " The people at Mercury Bay knew at once that the English were goblins, because a boat's crew pulled ashore rowing with their backs to the land. Only goblins have eyes

[1] *The Long White Cloud*, by W. Pember Reeves, p. 100.

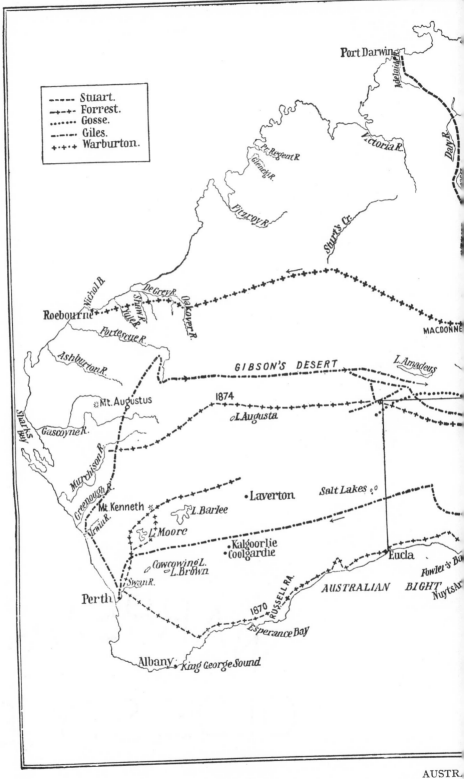

Legend:
- ------ Stuart.
- -+-+- Forrest.
- .... Gosse.
- -.-.- Giles.
- +-+-+ Warburton.

Port Darwin

Adelaide R.

Day R.

Victoria R.

Pr. Regent R.

Glenelg R.

Fitzroy R.

Sturt's Cr.

Nichol B.

De Grey R.

Shaw R.

Yule R.

Oakover R.

Roebourne

Fortescue R.

MACDONNE

Ashburton R.

GIBSON'S DESERT

L. Amadeus

Sharks Bay

Mt. Augustus

1874

L. Augusta

Gascoyne R.

Murchison R.

Greenough R.

Mt. Kenneth

L. Barlee

Laverton

Salt Lakes

Irwin R.

L. Moore

Kalgoorlie

Coolgardie

Cowcowing L.

L. Brown

Eucla

Fowler's B.

Swan R.

AUSTRALIAN   BIGHT

Nuyts Ar

Perth

RUSSELL RA.

1870

Esperance Bay

Albany

King George Sound

AUSTR.

(From J. N. L. Baker's *History of Geographical Discovery a*

relief expeditions added materially to geographical knowledge in Australia.

After these explorers followed Stuart, who, starting from Adelaide, passed to the west of Lake Eyre, and, reaching the centre of Australia, with true courtesy named a conspicuous peak Central Mount Sturt. He was attacked by natives, whom he repelled, but, considering his party too small to cope with their hostility, and as his supplies were running short, he wisely decided to return to his base. In 1861 Stuart made a second attempt, and penetrated farther north, but was foiled by the thick scrub. In 1862, however, he found a way through the scrub and " came upon a broad valley of black alluvial soil, covered with long grass ; from this I can hear the wash of the sea. Thring, who rode in advance of me, called out ' The Sea ! ' which so took them by surprise, that he had to repeat the call before they fully understood what was meant." Stuart's explorations were of the greatest value. Not only did he prove that, given a knowledge of bushcraft supplemented by careful preparations, travel across Australia was not a dangerous enterprise, but he discovered rich lands " suitable for the growth of any and every thing ".

Australia, as already stated, was discovered by the Dutch, who, although they decided that it was not worth occupation, charted the western coast, which they explored as far south as Cape Leeuwin.[1] The British, as was only natural, neglected Western Australia at first, and it was due to rumours of French activity that King George Sound was occupied in 1826, while some five years later the Swan River was explored, Perth being founded on its banks in 1829. Grey, in a series of expeditions, explored the coastal area from Sharks' Bay to Perth, his last journey resulting in the discovery of ten rivers, while he penetrated inland as far as the Darling.

Eyre, who explored from his sheep-run, situated 150 miles north of Adelaide, sighted Lake Torrens, which, misled by patches of ground covered with water, he reported as constituting a wide lake barring all advance northwards. Foiled in this direction, in February 1841 he set out from Fowler's Bay,[2] with John Baxter and three natives, determined to reach Albany by a direct route round the shores of the Great Australian Bight. He travelled with pack-horses, and soon suffered from lack of water, but " on the fifth day of our sufferings, we were again blessed with abundance of water ". The party

[1] Baker, *op. cit.*, p. 153.
[2] Admiral Fowler, who charted this part of the coast, is thus commemorated.

ultimately led to the crossing of the continent. In 1844 Sturt, starting from Adelaide, followed up the Murray and Darling Rivers, completing the exploration of the latter. He then marched almost due north into the " Dead Heart " of Australia, which he named the Great Stony Desert. In January 1845 the explorers discovered a lagoon and some pasture. There, owing to lack of water between them and the Darling some 200 miles away, " we were ", to quote Sturt, " locked up in this desolate and heated region as effectually as if we were ice-bound at the Pole ". In 1846 the worn-out members of the expedition reached Adelaide.

The next great explorer was Leichhardt, who in 1844 started from Moreton Bay with the Gulf of Carpentaria as his objective. This, the first journey of exploration through tropical Australia, took fifteen months to accomplish, and the intrepid explorer finally reached the coast half dead from hunger and almost naked. In 1848, Leichhardt started on an attempt to cross Australia from Moreton Bay to the Swan River, but he was lost, nor has any trace of him been found. Search expeditions were sent out and much exploration was accomplished by various parties.

In 1860, Burke and Wills set out from Melbourne to cross the continent from south to north. This expedition was supplied with camels specially brought from India and was well equipped in every respect. The plan was to establish a depot at Menindee on the Darling and, from that advanced base, to cross the continent to the Gulf of Carpentaria. After forming the depot, Burke marched northwards to Cooper's Creek, to which point, finding good grazing and water, he ordered the depot to be moved. After waiting some time in vain for the arrival of the rear party, Burke started off with Wills and two other Englishmen with supplies carried on six camels. Burke and Wills went ahead of the slow-moving camels, and reached the tidal estuary of Flinders River, thus accomplishing their task.

On the return journey one of the explorers died, and the others reached Cooper's Creek only to find that the man in charge had just left. Their best plan would presumably have been to make for Menindee, but Burke insisted on taking a direct route to Adelaide, and the two leaders perished from hunger and thirst. King, who survived, was kindly treated by the natives, with whom he lived until a rescue party arrived. Thus ended in tragedy the first journey across Australia from south to north. At the same time both the explorers and the

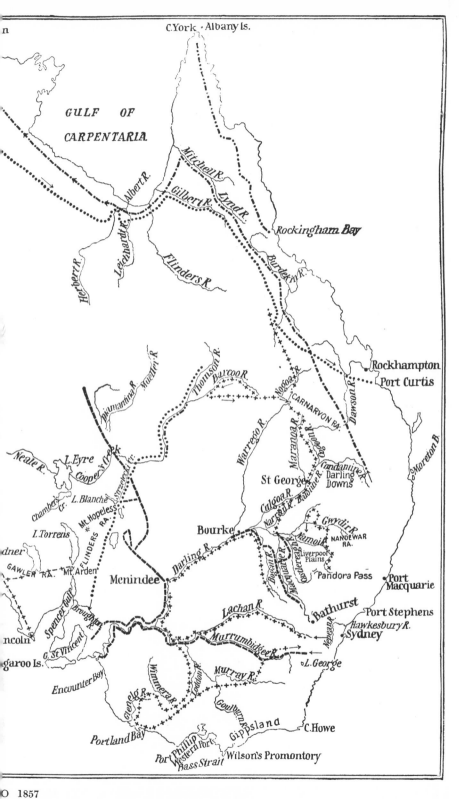

ration, by permission of Messrs. George G. Harrap & Co.)

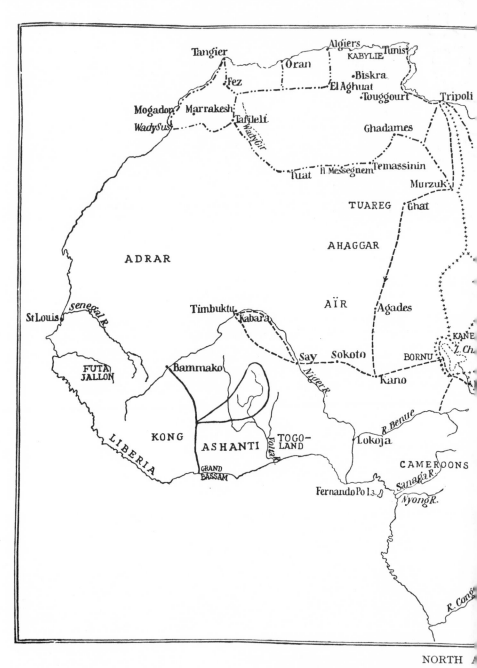

NORTH A

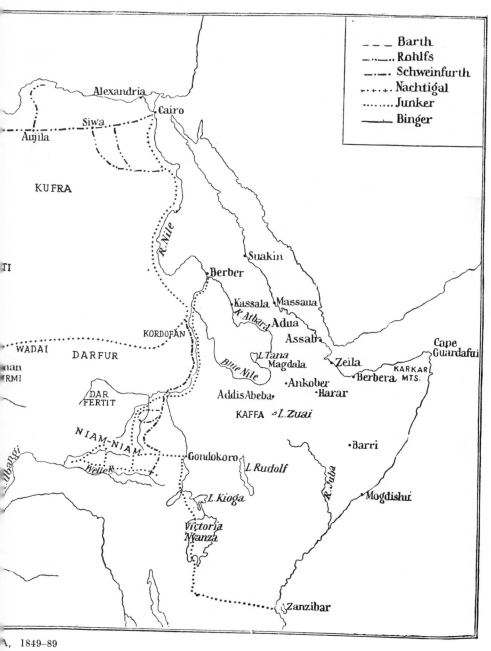

The explorers had to wait a long time until the King's messenger had informed the Kings along the course of the Niger to Rabba of the proposed expedition and gained their good will. At last the messenger returned, and a start was made at the end of September. From the first stopping-place of Liaba—

> " we ran down the stream very pleasantly for twelve or fourteen miles, the Niger, during the whole of this distance, rolling grandly along— a noble river, neither obstructed by islands, nor deformed with rocks and stones. Its width varied from one to three miles.
> " The market of Rabba is very celebrated, and considered by traders as one of the largest and best in the whole country. . . . The price of a strong healthy lad is about 40,000 cowries (£8), a girl fetches as much as 50,000, and perhaps more, if she be at all interesting."

At Egga, where " we were struck with the immense number of large bulky canoes which lay off it ", they were hospitably received, and excited intense curiosity. Lower down, the population, fearing a hostile attack, prepared to fight them. But the two Englishmen laid down their arms, and advancing unarmed prevented bloodshed. Indeed, the Chief hailed them as " Children of Heaven " who had dropped from the skies.

At Damuggoo, the explorers met traders who were in touch with the coast, and were most kindly treated, but lower down, off Kiree, they were attacked, robbed and made prisoners. They were taken to the King of Eboe, in whose state much of the palm oil exported to Europe was produced. There, after much palaver, a ransom was demanded, and the explorers were handed over to King Boy of the Brass River, who, in return for a bill of goods to the value of twenty slaves with the value of fifteen slaves for himself, agreed to hand over the two brothers to a British brig that was anchored off his town. Under his guidance the Landers penetrated the forest-clad delta to the mouth of the Nun branch of the great river. Thus the problem of the Niger was at last solved. Lander was awarded the first Royal Premium by the Royal Geographical Society, which had started its splendid career of service to exploration in the very year that he had accomplished his great feat.

In 1850, the British Government despatched a second expedition to the Sudan under Richardson, with whom was associated Barth,[1] who had studied Arabic. Starting from Tripoli, the expedition travelled to Murzuk in Fezzan. From this centre it followed a route to Ghat and Agades, being in

---

[1] *Travels and Discoveries in North and Central Africa*, by H. Barth, 1859.

constant danger from the turbulent tribesmen. From Agades, Richardson proceeded direct to Kuka, where he died, while Barth visited Kano and then proceeded to Kuka.

Barth was able to examine Lake Chad. He then penetrated southwards, traversing unknown country until he reached the Benue, that mighty tributary of the Niger, at a point where it was joined by the Faro. With the true explorer's spirit he wrote : " The Benue flowed in a broad and majestic course through an entirely open country. . . . I looked long and silently upon the stream ; it was one of the happiest moments of my life." Throughout this journey high ranges were sighted, mainly to the east, while the explorer waxed eloquent on the beauty of the scenery. Camels were apparently almost unknown in Adamawa, for we read : " A great many women managed to pass under the bellies of these tall creatures, in the hope of obtaining their blessing, as they thought them sacred animals." On reaching Yola, the capital of Adamawa, the Governor was found to be unfriendly, partly because Barth came with recommendations from hostile Bornu, and he was obliged to return to Kuka.

Nothing daunted, he explored Baghirmi, and then travelled to Timbuktu, where he was in constant danger of attacks by fanatics. Barth reached England in 1855, after exploring this large area of the Central Sudan, with a rich harvest not only of geographical, geological and ethnographical data, but also valuable commercial information regarding the country he had made known to Europe. He deserves a high place among the explorers of Africa.

In continuation of Barth's explorations, in 1869 Nachtigal started from Tripoli for Murzuk. From this oasis he explored the unknown Tibesti area to the south-east. Later he visited Kanem, to the north of Lake Chad, and Baghirmi. But his most important journey was the successful penetration of Wadai, where previous explorers had been murdered, and thence to Darfur and Kordofan. He was thus able to connect the area explored by Barth with the Nile Valley.

In North-East Africa we have the journey of the Englishman Browne, who, in 1792, was probably the first European explorer to visit the Siwa Oasis since Alexander the Great. He made a still more important journey in 1793, penetrating into the Sudan as far as Darfur, and travelling by the caravan route from Asyut. Owing to intrigues, and fanatical hostility to Christians, Browne was detained at Darfur for a period of three years, during which he suffered alike in health and

THE RAPIDS BELOW BUSSA

(*Through the courtesy of H. S. W. Edwardes, Esq.*)

in pocket. Finally he was able to depart, and embodied much valuable information in a work which remained the authority on the subject for many years.[1]

In the middle of the nineteenth century Rohlfs, travelling in disguise, visited Tafilelt, which has recently been occupied by the French, and then Tuat. Later he travelled to Bornu, and, striking the Benue, sailed down it to the Niger. In 1869 he travelled from Tripoli to Siwa, and some years later took part in an expedition to the Libyan Desert and revisited Siwa. His last expedition was a journey from Tripoli to the Kufra oasis, where he was imprisoned, but escaped with the loss of his camp and records.

The period under review constitutes a great age of exploration, especially signalized by the solution of the problem of the Niger. Elsewhere other heroic explorers, many of whom were murdered or died from sickness, blazed trails along which their successors were destined to make further discoveries until Darkest Africa was opened up to civilization.

[1] *Travels in Africa, Egypt and Syria*, by W. G. Browne, 1806.

CHAPTER XXV

LIVINGSTONE, THE GREATEST EXPLORER OF AFRICA

"Most geographers are aware that before the discovery of Lake Ngami, and the well-watered country in which the Makololo dwell, the idea prevailed that a large part of the interior of Africa consisted of sandy deserts, into which rivers ran and were lost. During my journey in 1852–6 from sea to sea, across the south inter-tropical part of the continent, it was found to be a well-watered country occupied by a considerable population; and one of the most wonderful waterfalls in the world was brought to light."

DAVID LIVINGSTONE.

IN 1841, David Livingstone, destined to rank as the greatest of African explorers, landed in Algoa Bay.[1] By way of setting to his epoch-making discoveries, I propose to refer briefly to the opening-up of South Africa. This country, discovered by the Portuguese, began to be settled by the Dutch in the middle of the seventeenth century, farms being established to supply ships with provisions, but little attempt at exploration was made during those early years. In 1752, a well-equipped expedition left Cape Town, passing Mossel Bay, keeping close to the coast, and examining Algoa Bay. The explorers crossed the Great Fish River, the Bantu country was entered, and intercourse was opened with those warlike tribesmen. In the centre of the country the Karroo, which closely resembles the sinister Lut, the great central desert of Persia,[2] constituted a formidable barrier, but it was crossed by Paterson in 1778, who struck the Orange River in its lower course. This, the most important river of South Africa, had already been crossed by Coetsee, an elephant-hunter, in 1760.

The fame of Livingstone has somewhat eclipsed the memory of other travellers, but the survey of the greater part of the Orange River by Robert Moffat in 1856 constituted a valuable piece of exploration. In Bechuanaland and the Kalahari Desert, Anderson, between 1864 and 1880, added considerably

---

[1] *Missionary Travels and Researches in South Africa*, 1857.
[2] Persian fat-tailed sheep have been imported, and, under the name of "persies", thrive on the scanty grazing of the Karroo. Camels also have been imported.

to geographical knowledge of those districts and of their inhabitants, while gallant Selous travelled for twenty years, from 1872 to 1892, in the Zambezi; towards the end of this period he explored Mashonaland. He was a worthy successor of Oswell, both men being " mighty hunters before the Lord ".

From Algoa Bay Livingstone trekked across Cape Colony

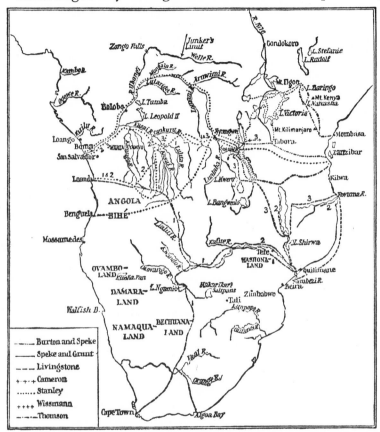

CENTRAL AND SOUTH AFRICA, 1849–89.
The routes of Speke and Grant to Tabora and of Stanley to Lake Victoria are not shown. They are practically identical with that of Burton and Speke.

to Kuruman in Bechuanaland, the headquarters of Robert Moffat and " the farthest inland station of the London Missionary Society ". Almost immediately he began to explore northwards, cutting himself off from all European society for six months in order to learn the language and the customs of the tribesmen.

Livingstone possessed a great gift for friendship and for grasping the point of view of the African. As a proof of his influence, Sechele, Chief of the Bechuanas, said to him, " Do you imagine these people will ever believe by your merely talking to them ? If you like I will call my headmen, and with our whips we will soon make them all believe together."

Livingstone's missionary labours among the Bechuanas at Koboleng, where he had settled, were sorely hampered by Boers, who were established in the Magaliesberg Range, and attacked the surrounding tribes to secure slaves and cattle. On one of these raids during his absence, " my house, which had stood perfectly secure for years under the protection of the natives, was plundered, my stock of medicines was smashed ; and all our furniture and clothing carried off and sold at public auction to pay the expenses of the foray ". However, Livingstone was not daunted : " The Boers resolved to shut up the interior, and I determined to open the country ; and we shall see who has been the most successful in resolution—they or I."

For eight years Livingstone was maturing his plan for crossing the Kalahari Desert, and establishing relations with the people of Lake Ngami. In 1849, accompanied by Oswell, he started off on his first great journey. Thanks to his relations with the tribes and his tact in dealing with the Bushmen, the desert was crossed without any untoward incident, and on August 1, 1849, " for the first time, this fine-looking sheet of water was beheld by Europeans . . . It is shallow, and on the West there is a space devoid of trees. . . . This is another proof of desiccation." Sad to relate, this desiccation is still increasing.

In 1851, Livingstone pushed 200 miles farther north and made the acquaintance of Sebituane, Chief of the Makololo, a great conqueror, who had defeated the Matabele Chief, Mosilikatse. The latter attacked Sebituane twice, but on each occasion was defeated.

Thanks to the establishment of good relations with the Makololo, in June 1851 the explorers were rewarded by the discovery of the Zambezi in the centre of the continent, where its existence was unknown. At this period Livingstone decided that the hostility of the Boers had made further missionary work among the unfortunate Bechuanas out of the question. He thereupon escorted his family to Cape Town *en route* for England, and trekked north again, determined to devote his life to exploration.

Upon returning to the country of the Makololo, the great explorer was well received by Sekeletu, son of the deceased Sebituane, in what was considered royal style. In November

1853, he decided to travel across unknown Africa to Loanda to open up a trade-route to the Atlantic. With a strong party of the Makololo, he followed up the Liambai, as the upper reaches of the Zambezi are named, both words signifying " River ".

In February 1854 the expedition crossed the watershed into the basin of the Congo. As the Atlantic coast was approached, each petty chief attempted to blackmail the weak party, which " had only five guns ", while supplies were only forthcoming in return for value received—and Livingstone was ill provided. He suffered terribly from fever, but pressed on through the tropical forests, and at last reached the province of Angola and the port of Loanda, where the Makololo, upon seeing the sea, observed, " we marched along with our father, believing what the ancients had always told us was true, that the world has no end, but all at once the world said, ' I am finished ; there is no more of me ! ' " Of a house they remarked : " It is not a hut ; it is a mountain with several caves in it ! "

Livingstone was treated kindly by the Portuguese authorities, by the solitary resident Englishman, who nursed him through a long illness, and also by officers of the British cruisers who appeared in the port. When he was sufficiently rested, he started on what was to be a great trans-continental journey to the Indian Ocean. After many trying experiences, the expedition reached Linyanti in triumph, after an absence of two years, and Livingstone writes : " We were looked upon as men risen from the dead, for the most skilful of their diviners had pronounced us dead long ago." Sekeletu and his tribesmen fully realized that a trade route to the Atlantic had been opened for them by the intrepid white " Father ", and their trust in him was now unbounded.

After a rest, Livingstone organized a new expedition to follow down the Zambezi to its mouth, with a view to opening up a trade route to the Indian Ocean. Arranging with Sekeletu for a supply of tusks with which to purchase a sugar mill and many other things for the chief, the party started, travelling partly by water. Livingstone reached the wonderful " Smoke Sounding " Falls, and described them as seen from above.

" Creeping with awe to the verge, I peered down into a large rent which had been made from bank to bank of the broad Zambezi, and saw that a stream of a thousand yards broad leaped down a hundred feet, and then became suddenly compressed into a space of fifteen or twenty yards. In looking down into the fissure, one sees nothing but a dense white cloud. From this cloud rushed up a great jet of vapour exactly like steam, and it mounted 200 or 300 feet high; there condensing, it changed its hue to that of dark smoke, and came back in a constant shower which wetted us to the skin. It had never been seen before by European eyes; but scenes so lovely must have been gazed upon by angels in their flight."

Livingstone named these beautiful falls after the great Queen Victoria.

For some distance the explorer left the Zambezi and travelled north-east across the Batoka plateau, through beautiful country in which elephants and other big game abounded. Gradually as they neared the coast the " oppressive steaminess in the atmosphere " made itself felt, while tsetse-flies, the greatest bar to progress, made it necessary for the oxen to travel by night. The natives were hostile to the Portuguese, but had heard good accounts of the English. They were travelling through the kingdom of Monomotapa, or " Supreme Chief ", whose empire was described by Leo Africanus in the 16th century as " the fourth general part of the lower Ethiopia ". He adds that " their principal cities are Zimbas and Benamataza, the first whereof is one and twenty and the second fifteene daies journey from Sofala ". The first name is surely reminiscent of Zimbabwe; and Livingstone mentions a chief as Katolosa (Monomotapa), thus proving that the title still remained, albeit the empire, which was in existence when the Portuguese first appeared on the scene, had lost its importance. Yet Katolosa was strong enough to prevent direct intercourse between the Portuguese and the populations of the interior. Livingstone refers to the gold mines of the country, which were not in a flourishing condition.

The Portuguese were expecting the explorer, as a native had arrived at Tete who had said, alluding to the sextant and artificial horizon, " that 'the Son of God' had arrived and that he was able to take the sun down from the heavens and place it under his arm ". Livingstone finally reached Quilimane, having accomplished his greatest feat of exploration with miserable resources at his disposal. He had written a new chapter in the history of Africa by opening up an immense region for trade and for anti-slavery action. Apart from traversing so much unknown country, " The peculiar form of continent was ascertained to be an elevated plateau, somewhat depressed in the centre, and with fissures in the sides by which the rivers escaped to the sea." This alone was an epoch-making discovery.

In 1856, Livingstone returned to the Zambezi as British

Consul, with instructions to continue his fruitful explorations, to open up the country for trade, and to put down slavery. His chief assistant was Dr. (afterwards Sir John) Kirk. His first task was to discover the real mouth of the Zambezi, which had been concealed in order to deceive the British cruisers. Livingstone soon found it, when it was carefully surveyed, a considerable service to the commerce of the world. He then pushed inland in his unsatisfactory paddle steamer, and, at Tete, found his faithful Makololo. In January 1859, Livingstone [1] with Kirk made his first expedition up the Shiré. The Manganja were at first hostile, but the great explorer soon established friendly relations with them, being much aided by their knowledge that the British were suppressing the slave traffic. Lake Shirwa, " a considerable bit of water ", with " exceedingly lofty mountains near the eastern shore ", was discovered after a very trying journey over rough country. As Kirk pithily expressed it : " The heat now is like Hell—you cannot hold on at any time by the rocks." Yet the explorers had discovered the healthy Shiré uplands, which Kirk describes as a fertile district with highlands, " a healthy position for Europeans ".

In the early autumn of 1859, a still more important expedition was undertaken to find the great lake, information of which had reached Livingstone. They found the women of the Manganja disfigured by the horrible lip-ring but, on Kirk remonstrating with a chief, the reply was, " Woman no lipring! Why, they would be men, no longer women!" Farther up the Shiré, owing to the accursed slave trade, the appearance of the explorers created a panic or marked hostility. Information was refused or grudgingly given, but on September 16, 1859, Lake Nyasa [2] was discovered. In the absence of a boat, no immediate attempt was made to survey this important body of water, but Livingstone pointed out that, by placing a trading steamer on the lake and purchasing the ivory, the slave trade would receive a heavy blow, " for it is only by the ivory earned by the slaves that the latter do not eat up all the profits of a trip . . . water-carriage exists by the Shiré and Zambezi all the way to England, with the single exception of a porterage of about thirty-five miles past the Murchison Cataracts ". Nyasaland constituted the great discovery of Livingstone's second expedition. It led in due

---

[1] *The Zambesi*, by David and Charles Livingstone ; *Kirk on the Zambesi*, by R. Coupland, 1928.
[2] Nyasa and Nyanza both signify a lake.

course to the establishment of missionaries, followed by traders, and culminated in the creation of the Nyasaland Protectorate. Nyasaland was truly the bequest of Livingstone to Great Britain.

In 1866, Livingstone started on his last journey. His base was Zanzibar, where the Sultan supplied him with letters of recommendation to the Arab Chiefs, which proved to be of considerable value. He followed up the Rovuma River, which he had already examined, to the Yao country, passing ghastly proofs of the slave trade in the shape of abandoned victims, dying or dead. He reached Lake Nyasa without any special difficulty, and, marching round the southern end of the lake, crossed the Shiré River to the settlement of Mponda, a powerful chief, who had become a Moslem. His rascally servants became alarmed at rumours of Mazitu or Zulu raiders, and were mostly dismissed, but, thanks to the excellent relations the great explorer knew so well how to establish, he was passed from chief to chief. Crossing a range with an altitude of 4,000 feet, and moving steadily northwards, Livingstone finally reached Tanganyika in April 1867. During this journey his health had begun to give way seriously, and the loss of his medicine-chest constituted a serious blow. Here he met " Tippo-Tib ", a noted slave-raider of the Upper Congo, who became a friend of Stanley and other explorers. From Tanganyika, after resting for three months, Livingstone travelled to Lake Mweru, where again his health broke down. But nothing daunted he marched south to find Lake Bangweolo, which he discovered on June 11, 1868.

Livingstone then returned to Lake Tanganyika and crossed it to Ujiji, where he found that the goods despatched for him from Zanzibar had almost all been stolen on the way. Recrossing the lake, Livingstone explored the Lualaba River in 1871. He then returned to Ujiji, where he met Stanley, who had been despatched by the proprietor of the *New York Herald* to seek the lost explorer. Together they examined the northern end of Lake Tanganyika and proved that the river at that point flowed into it and thus could not be a source of the Nile. Livingstone refused to return to England until he had solved the problem of the Nile, and once more, with a well-equipped party supplied by Stanley, he marched to Lake Bangweolo, hoping to discover the sources of the Nile in this area. There on April 30, 1873, the great explorer died.

It is difficult to sum up the achievements of Livingstone

adequately. As an explorer he revolutionized the map of Africa, and opened an epoch for which the whole world is in his debt. Equally great were his services to humanity. He took up the abolition of slavery as the successor of Wilberforce and Buxton, and became the first instrument of its execution inland. Finally, his utter fearlessness, his complete devotion to the highest ideals and his amazing insight into the native mind mark him out for all time as a model to explorers and an inspiration to mankind.

CHAPTER XXVI

THE PROBLEM OF THE NILE

"I saw that old Father Nile without any doubt rises in the
Victoria Nyanza, and, as I had foretold, that lake is the great
source of the river."

SPEKE.

THE problem of the Nile has exercised mankind down
the ages. In Chapter IV I have referred to the belief of
Ptolemy that its sources were to be found in twin lakes, which
were fed by the Mountains of the Moon. I added that, in
all probability, this information was gained from merchants
trading with the ports on the east coast of Africa. Reference
has also been made to the mission to Abyssinia of Covilham
in 1487. He was succeeded by military expeditions and by
missionaries, one of whom, Pedro Paez, discovered the source
of the Blue Nile in 1613.

The long line of British explorers in North Africa starts
with James Bruce,[1] who, in 1768, sailed up the Nile to Assuan.
He crossed the desert to the Red Sea at Massawa and sailed
round those torrid waters, visiting Tor, Jedda and the Bab-al-
Mandeb. Bruce then returned to Massawa, from which port
he made for the Ethiopian capital. With some slight knowledge of medicine, he gained the favour of the Queen-mother,
and, after surmounting many difficulties due to the disturbed
state of the country, he reached the source of the Blue Nile.
Following down its course to the White Nile, Bruce nearly
perished from thirst in the Nubian Desert between Berber and
Korosko. He took observations throughout his journeys,
and published a record of his adventures.

The invasion of Egypt by Napoleon in 1798 stimulated
French activity in the valley of the Nile. Not only was the
Rosetta Stone discovered, but geographical information was
eagerly collected and published in the *Atlas d'Égypte*. After
the defeat of the French and the subsequent evacuation of
Egypt by the British, under the strong rule of Muhammad Ali,
the Sudan was conquered as far south as Kordofan. At this
period, moreover, definite progress in the exploration of the

[1] *Travels to Discover the Source of the Nile in 1768.*

228

White Nile was made, one expedition penetrating through the *sadd* area as far as 4° 42′ N. But the Nile problem was not to be solved as yet.

In the fourth decade of the nineteenth century, two German missionaries, who were established at Mombasa by the Church Missionary Society, heard accounts from the Arab caravan leaders of vast lakes and great mountains, whose highest peaks were covered with a substance resembling salt in appearance. They penetrated some way into the interior, where Rebmann, in 1848, sighted the snowy peak of Kilimanjaro from afar, and Krapf, a year later, saw in the distance snow-clad Mount Kenya. Their discoveries were discredited, but they had blazed the trail for greater explorers.

In 1854 Richard Burton, who had already made his famous journey to Mecca in disguise, was stationed at Aden, which had been annexed by the British in 1839. In the following year he accomplished an adventurous journey to Harrar.[1] Starting from Zeila, he marched through a country infested with brigands and at last " About two miles distant on the crest of a hill, stood the city—a long sombre line, strikingly contrasting with the white-washed towns of the East." Upon his reception by the Amir, Burton handed him a letter written by himself, which purported to have been sent by the Governor of Aden, and expressed his good wishes to the Amir. Burton's remarkable knowledge of the Koran and of Arabic customs carried him most successfully through a ten days' visit in this fanatical city, and he reached Berbera after accomplishing a dangerous but valuable piece of exploration.

In 1856, Burton, accompanied by Speke, who had been his companion in a later but unsuccessful expedition into Somaliland, reached Zanzibar, having been commissioned " to penetrate inland from Kilwa or some other place on the east coast of Africa, and to make the best of your way to the reputed Lake Nyasa ".[2] Furnished with letters from the Sultan of Zanzibar, the expedition started off from Bagamayo in August 1857, to follow the caravan route to Lake Tanganyika,[3] at the head of a number of unwilling carriers. The maritime region extended for about a hundred miles, and upon reaching the mountain area which succeeded it, we read : " By resting after every few yards, and by clinging to our supporters, we reached, after about six hours, the summit of the Pass

---

[1] *First Footsteps in Africa*, by Richard F. Burton, 1856.
[2] *J.R.G.S.*, Vol. XXIX, p. 5.
[3] *The Lake Regions of Central Africa*, by Richard F. Burton, 1860.

Terrible. . . . My companion could hardly return an answer ; he had advanced mechanically and almost in a state of coma."

In the district of Ugogo, situated some 3,000 feet above sea-level, the general health improved, but the explorers were subjected to exorbitant taxes by the chiefs, and Burton remarks : " The African traveller's fitness for the task of exploration depends more upon his faculty of chafing under delays and kicking against the pricks, than upon his power of displaying the patience of a Griselda or a Job." Traversing the table-land of Ugogo, a hundred miles in width, the harassed explorers entered Unyamwezi, the " Land of the Moon ". Thanks to the Sultan of Zanzibar's letters, they were most hospitably received by the Arab merchants, whose centre was at Tabora, distant some 600 miles from the coast. In addition to the help afforded in the way of supplies and transport, they were given definite information as to the existence of three great lakes, with their approximate distances. It was from this information that Burton knew the number of stages to Tanganyika, while it was by relying on Arab reports that Speke discovered Victoria Nyanza. Livingstone had no such reliable informants until his last journey.

A long halt was made at Tabora, the onward march was then resumed, and on February 13, 1858, Burton was able to write : " Nothing, in sooth, could be more picturesque than this first view of the Tanganyika Lake, as it lay in the lap of the mountains, basking in the gorgeous tropical sunshine. . . . In front stretch the waters, an expanse of the lightest and the softest blue, in breadth varying from thirty to thirty-five miles, and sprinkled by the crisp east wind with tiny crescents of snowy foam." Burton and Speke, in spite of serious illness, had discovered mysterious Tanganyika, at a distance of some 900 miles from Bagamayo. They soon made a cruise on the lake, but were unable to visit the river at its northern end, or to ascertain whether it flowed into, or out of, the lake.

After spending a month on this voyage, the explorers, who had run short of calico, returned to Tabora, Burton making the apt remark that " baggage is life " in these countries. Here Burton, who was broken down in health, agreed to Speke attempting to discover what was known as the Ukerewe Lake. Accordingly, in July 1858, Speke started off on one of the most important journeys undertaken in Africa. Everything favoured him, and on August 3, having travelled 218 miles in twenty-four days—

"the pale-blue waters of the Nyanza burst suddenly upon my gaze. It was early morning. The distant sea-line of the north horizon was defined in the calm atmosphere, between the north and west points of the compass, but even this did not afford me any idea of the breadth of the lake, as an archipelago of islands, each consisting of a single hill, rising to a height of 200 or 300 feet above the water, intersected the line of vision to the left, while, on the right, the western horn of the Ukerewe Island cut off any further view of the distant water to the eastward of north." [1]

Speke had promised to return to Burton within a fixed period, and was consequently unable, on this occasion, to explore the lake, which he christened Victoria Nyanza.

Upon returning to England, his epoch-making discovery was received with great enthusiasm by the Royal Geographical Society, whose President, Sir Roderick Murchison, arranged for him to lead a second expedition, with Grant as his companion, to confirm and amplify his discovery and to ascertain the connection of the Lake with the Nile system.

Starting from Zanzibar in October 1860, Speke suffered, as in his former journey, from troubles with porters and from theft. When he reached Tabora he wrote : " My losses were one Hottentot dead and five returned ; one free man went back and one flogged and turned off ; ninety-eight of the original porters deserted ; twelve mules and three donkeys dead. Besides which more than half my property had been stolen."

Speke's onward journey was delayed by the eternal difficulty of securing porters ; while to the north-west of his route Suwarora, chief of the country of Usui, was a notable robber, and fleeced the explorer outrageously. Speke's troubles were almost overwhelming, but at last he reached Karagwe, a district situated to the west of Victoria Nyanza. There Rumanika, a chief of Hamitic (Galla) descent, welcomed the traveller with true hospitality, and for the first time he really enjoyed some repose in delightful surroundings, while the big game shooting was superb.

In this district Speke discovered the Kagera River, and, as Sir William Gowers pointed out in a letter to me—

"it is evidence of Speke's great accuracy and thorough grasp of the topography of the region that he fixed on this river as the true source of the Nile. It has been left for the present century to confirm this by the discovery that not only does the Kagera River bring down into Lake Victoria a larger volume of water than any other tributary, but also its headwaters rise only about twenty miles from Lake Tanganyika."

---

[1] *What led to the Discovery of the Source of the Nile,* by J. H. Speke, 1864 ; *The Discovery of the Source of the Nile,* by the same author, 1863. The above quotation is taken from the first-named work.

Continuing to march northwards, Speke was the first European to enter Uganda in January 1862, and wrote: " The temperature was perfect. The whole land was a picture of quiescent beauty, with a boundless sea in the background." Upon reaching the court of Mutesa, Speke found a monarch occupying a palace built of palm trunks, with a hierarchy of officials. He soon found favour with Mutesa and his mother, who admired his beard and were amazed at his prowess in killing rhinoceroses and in shooting birds on the wing. They also appreciated the valuable presents with which the Government of Bombay had supplied him.

After paying a long visit to Mutesa, during which he witnessed acts of cruelty and realized the utter lack of purpose of the tyrant, the explorers resumed their march to the north, and on July 28, 1862, Speke, who had struck the left bank of the Nile, reached the famous " stones ", which he named the Ripon Falls after the President of the Royal Geographical Society. " It was a sight ", he wrote, " that attracted one to it for hours—the roar of the waters, the thousands of passenger-fish leaping at the falls with all their might . . . hippopotami and crocodiles lying sleepily in the water, and cattle driven down to drink at the margin of the lake . . . made as interesting a picture as one could wish to see." But of still greater importance was the fact that " the expedition had performed its functions " and the memorable words, which constitute the motto to this chapter, were evidently written with a full and thankful heart. It remains to add that the Victoria Nyanza is the second most extensive lake in the world, being exceeded only by Lake Superior.

Descending the Nile for some distance, the explorers marched to the capital of Unyoro overland. There, owing to his justifiable hostility to the Baganda, Kamurasi the king detained Speke and Grant for two months. During this period they heard of the existence of another great lake to the west, but were not permitted to visit it. At last they were able to depart, and striking the Nile they travelled partly by canoe to the Karuma Falls. Finally, on February 15, 1863, they reached Gondokoro, where they were greeted by Samuel Baker, after having accomplished feats of exploration that will never be forgotten.

Another great explorer of this wonderful period was Samuel Baker, a great hunter and a born adventurer. In 1861 he landed in Egypt and spent some time exploring and hunting in the upper reaches of the Atbara. Accompanied everywhere by his devoted wife, Baker reached Khartum in 1862, and decided to ascend the Nile in search of Speke and Grant. Upon meeting them, he was at first disappointed that his expedition had been organized in vain. Speke, however, informed him of the existence of another great lake to the west of Unyoro, and Baker determined to take up the quest.[1]

His troubles were manifold, as the Arab slave-dealers were most hostile and caused a mutiny among his rascally followers. Baker's personality, however, triumphed. The King of Unyoro was at first unwilling to allow him to proceed, and fleeced him unmercifully, but when Baker threatened to shoot him, he realized that he had gone too far and despatched the explorers with an escort, whom the Englishman dubbed " The Devil's Own ", and speedily dismissed. The heroic Mrs. Baker had nearly died from sunstroke, and he was worn out when on March 14, 1867, he discovered the Albert Nyanza.

Striking it on the south-east coast, Baker writes : " Far as the eye could reach to the south-west and west, the boundless sheet of water lay like a mirror. On all sides where land was visible, the lake was completely shut in by mountains." The explorers secured canoes and coasted the lake to its north-east corner, where it is entered by the Victorian Nile which almost immediately passes on again. Ascending the Victoria Nile, or the Bahr-el-Jebel as it is called by the Arabs, they discovered the Murchison Falls " where the river drops in one leap 120 feet into a deep basin, the edge of which literally swarms with crocodiles ". Leaving the canoe, the explorers marched upstream towards Karuma Falls. They suffered terribly owing to Unyoro intrigues, but finally reached Khartum in May 1865. Here we take leave of a born leader of men, who had accomplished a great feat in connection with the problem of the Nile.

The last of the great explorers in Africa was Stanley. He returned to that continent in 1874, and, reaching the Victoria Nyanza in the following year, he sailed round it.

" From January 17, 1875, to April 7, 1876, we had been engaged in tracing the extreme southern sources of the Nile from the marshy plains and cultivated uplands, where they are born, down to the mighty reservoir called the Victoria Nyanza. We had circumnavigated the entire expanse, penetrated to every bay, inlet and creek ; . . . we had

---

[1] *Sir Samuel Baker*, by T. D. Murray and A. Silva White, 1895.

travelled hundreds of miles to and fro on foot along the northern coast of the Victorian Sea and finally had explored with a large force the strange countries lying between the two lakes Muta Nzige (i.e. Edward) and the Victoria. . . . I have not ventured beyond the limits assigned to me, viz. the exploration of the southern sources of the Nile, and the solution of the problem left unsolved by Speke and Grant. Is the Victoria Nyanza one lake, or does it consist of five lakes, as reported by Livingstone, Burton and others? This problem has been satisfactorily solved, and Speke has now the full glory of having discovered the largest inland sea on the continent of Africa, also its principal affluent, as well as the outlet." [1]

After his survey of the Victoria Nyanza, and his important discovery of Lake Edward, Stanley turned his attention to Lake Tanganyika, which he surveyed with equal thoroughness, but he decided—wrongly, as was subsequently proved—that the Lukuga was not the regular outlet of the lake. He then followed the Congo down its course and forced his way through the country, where Livingstone had turned back owing to the hostility of the Arabs. In August 1877 he arrived safely at Boma, having accomplished one of the great journeys in Africa which happily supplemented the explorations of Speke and Livingstone.

Stanley undertook yet another great journey in connection with the relief of Emin Pasha, a German official of the Egyptian Government, who was Governor of the Upper Nile provinces. The fall of Khartum in 1885 resulted in Emin being cut off, and Stanley, who had been founding the Belgian Congo, was commissioned to undertake his relief. This was his most arduous journey, since the Congo forests were almost as far-reaching as those of the Amazon and the population was frequently hostile.

The most important discovery made by Stanley was that of Ptolemy's " Mountains of the Moon ", locally known as Ruwenzori. Curiously enough Speke had been told of them by the Arabs and had passed not far from them during his journey to Uganda. Stanley again, after surveying Victoria Nyanza and visiting Mutesa in Uganda, had accompanied an expedition to the base of the great range, and yet failed to realize their importance. In his last journey he wrote:

" My eyes were directed by a boy to a mountain said to be covered with salt, and I saw a peculiar-shaped cloud of a most beautiful silver colour, which assumed the proportions and appearance of a vast mountain covered with snow. Following its form downward, . . . I became

---

[1] *Through the Dark Continent* (8th ed.), 1890, pp. 306–7.

CAPTAIN JOHN HANNING SPEKE
(*By J. Watney Wilson, by permission of the Royal Geographical Society*)

first conscious that what I gazed upon was not the image or semblance of a vast mountain, but the solid substance of a real one, with its summit covered with snow. It now dawned upon me that this must be the Ruwenzori." [1]

As Stanley comments, it was remarkable that neither Baker nor Emin Pasha had discovered it long ago.

Stanley's other important discoveries included tracing the Semliki River to the Edward Lake, which he had discovered on his former journey and now explored.

By these two great journeys Stanley completed the proofs that the White Nile has two separate sources of supply. The principal one is Victoria Nyanza, whose catchment area he explored, while the other comprises the Lakes Edward and Albert, connected by the Semliki River, which derive their main supply from the heavy tropical rainfall, but also from the snowfields of Ruwenzori. It remains to add that by these discoveries Ptolemy was, at long last, justified.

Looking back on the splendid achievements of Livingstone, Burton, Speke, Baker and Stanley, there seems to be little doubt that the solution of the Nile problem produced a band of explorers whose greatness has seldom, if ever, been surpassed. Their achievements added lustre to the great Victorian Age.

[1] *In Darkest Africa*, by H. M. Stanley, 1890, p. 405.

CHAPTER XXVII

AFRICA—THE LAST PHASE

" The sand-dunes hide many wells
That brim with waters unfailing.
You come to their margins like bracelets
Wrought of gold and rare gems in far countries."
The Beduin's Song to his Camel.

DURING the last fifty or sixty years no discoveries have been made in Africa comparable with the solution of the problems connected with the Niger or the Nile. Yet many important journeys have been made, and this chapter records the completion of the exploration of Africa, so far as any wide tracts of land are concerned.

Among the notable successors of Mungo Park, Livingstone, Speke and Stanley was Joseph Thomson.[1] Originally appointed geologist to an expedition despatched by the Royal Geographical Society in 1878, he succeeded to the leadership upon the death of Keith Johnston. The object in view was to explore the country between Dar-es-Salaam and Lake Nyasa and to open up the most practicable route into the interior. Thomson, who possessed remarkable tact in dealing with the natives, penetrated to Lake Nyasa, and then explored the country to the north, discovering Lake Rukwa. He next marched up the west coast of Lake Tanganyika, and examining the Lukuga outlet, reported that it had " a swift resistless current " and proved that the waters of the lake fed the Congo. Unable to reach that river owing to the marked hostility of the natives, Thomson returned to the coast *via* Tabora, after accomplishing a difficult task with complete success.

In 1885 Thomson was entrusted by the Royal Geographical Society with the still more difficult task of opening up a direct route from Mombasa to Uganda. Traveller after traveller had made the attempt, but the warlike Masai had hitherto proved to be an insuperable obstacle. Upon leaving the coast, 200 miles of desert had first of all to be crossed, and the thirst-stricken carriers only just crawled into Taveta

[1] *Joseph Thomson, African Explorer*, by J. B. Thomson, 1897.

with its cool shade " beside the majestic mass of Kiliman-jaro ". Thomson failed in his first attempt to penetrate the Masai country, but later he joined a large trading caravan and proceeded to Lake Baringo, situated in the Rift Valley, which he was the first European to view, and which he proved to have no connection with the Nile system. On December 10 he finally reached Victoria Nyanza, which was the goal set him on this expedition. On his return journey he visited Mount Elgon. Thus ended two journeys of exploration, during which many important discoveries were made and the direct route from Mombasa was explored, Thomson thereby becoming the pioneer of the Uganda railway. Apart from his geographical discoveries, Thomson also rendered valuable services to the elucidation of the geological problems of Africa.

We have now reached the period in which Africa was being rapidly partitioned among the rival European states, and surveys undertaken primarily for the delimitation of boundaries, such as those made by Close and Boileau be-tween Lake Nyasa and Tanganyika in connection with the Anglo-German boundary in 1898, were of the greatest value. They marked a new epoch in scientific accuracy.

The successors of Livingstone in Nyasaland were John-ston and Sharpe, whose activities in establishing that protec-torate included much exploration; while Lugard, through-out his distinguished career, in Nyasaland, Uganda and Nigeria, explored a great deal of country and amassed much valuable information.[1]

In 1891 Macdonald commenced his important survey for a railway from Mombasa to Uganda, in which he traversed much imperfectly known, and some unexplored, country. Work was started in 1895, before the conquest of Uganda was completed, and, in view of the desert nature of part of the country, the unhealthiness of other parts, the hostility of various tribes and the depredations of lions, its comple-tion constitutes a monument to British determination and tenacity of purpose.

In 1899 Mackinder [2] led an expedition to climb Mount Kenya, which, rising to an altitude of 17,040 feet, gives its name to the colony. He camped on the site of the future capital, Nairobi, and after serious troubles with the Kikuyu porters, who attempted to desert in a body, and from feuds

[1] *The Rise of our East African Empire*, by Captain F. D. Lugard, 1893.
[2] " A Journey to the Summit of Mount Kenya ", by J. Mackinder, *G.J.*, May 1900.

between the tribes, the expedition moved very slowly towards its objective. Indeed, it took about three weeks to cover 100 miles to the plateau of Laikipia at the western foot of Kenya. The forest belt was traversed in one day, thanks to the axes of the Swiss mountaineers, but meanwhile two Swahilis were killed in the vicinity of the base camp, which caused delay. The peak was extremely difficult to climb, but, on September 14, Mount Kenya was conquered —a great feat of mountaineering.

The Ruwenzori Range had been examined by more than one traveller, but although British mountaineers, Freshfield and Mumm, with a Zermatt guide, had attempted to scale its peaks in 1905, uninterrupted rains had forced them to abandon the attempt. In 1906 the Duke of the Abruzzi, who undoubtedly ranks among the most distinguished of Italian explorers, appeared on the scene at the head of an important expedition, which included Swiss guides and porters.[1] The account of the ascent to the highest peak makes thrilling reading, and the Duke in true knightly fashion named the highest twin peaks of the range Margherita and Alexandra. In due course the entire range was examined. This brief account of the exploration of the " Mountains of the Moon " fitly closes discovery in Central Africa.

To turn to West Africa, in 1896 Trotter, as the British representative of an Anglo-French Boundary Commission, penetrated to the source of the Niger through a malarial jungle. The natives declined to point it out, " assuring us that it was the seat of the devil. . . . They believe that anyone who looks on the Niger source will die within the year, and they regard the water as poisonous." [2]

In 1887, the French traveller Binger explored the country to the south of the great bend of the Niger, and discovered that, contrary to the general belief, the Niger Valley was comparatively narrow. In 1892 he explored the Southern Sudan to ascertain the boundary between the Gold Coast and the Ivory Coast, travelling mainly in the hinterland of the latter area.

The commercial development of the Lower Niger was conducted by British firms, established on the Oil Rivers, which partly form the delta of the Niger and are partly independent creeks. In 1879 British interests were amalgamated

---

[1] *Ruwenzori*, by Filippo de Filippi, 1908.
[2] " An Expedition to the Source of the Niger", by Colonel J. K. Trotter, *G.J.*, Vol. X, September 1907.

into the United African Company, and, under the influence
of that great Englishman, Sir George Goldie, the Royal Niger
Company was founded.

In 1899 Nigeria was transferred to the Crown, and, under
Sir Frederick Lugard, the country was systemmatically explored. In 1902-3 valuable surveys were made in connection with the Anglo-French Niger and Chad Boundary Commission, and in 1904 the Boyd-Alexander expedition proved
that Lake Chad consisted of two shallow lakes connected by
a number of smaller ones.[1] In 1884 Germany declared a
protectorate over Togoland and the Cameroons, with the
result that both countries were thoroughly explored and
scientifically surveyed, mainly by surveyors attached to the
military expeditions that effected the German occupation.

Boundary commissions followed one another in rapid succession, accompanied by scientific surveys, and to-day, with
the possible exception of some parts of Liberia, West Africa
is a comparatively well-known country.

No account of the country would however be complete
without a reference to Mary Kingsley.[2] This intrepid Englishwoman travelled mainly in the French Congo, which at
that time was but little explored. Landing at Gabon in
1895, she voyaged up the Ogowe in a canoe and explored
the country. The Fans, who were cannibals, were unfriendly,
but she managed to travel among them in the rôle of a trader,
although she undoubtedly ran serious risks. Her description
of the tropical forests runs :

" One hundred and fifty feet above you there is a dense canopy,
formed by the interlaced crowns of the trees, and then infinity of bush-
ropes and parasitical plants, that shuts out all the sky ; around you on
all sides in the green gloom are countless thousands of grey bare trees
—columns, straight as ships' masts, and between them a twisted medley
of great bare black bush-ropes, looking as if they were some Homeric
battle of serpents that at its height had been fixed for ever by some magic
spell, while beneath you and away into the shadowed vastness lay the
stagnant currentless dark waters, making a floor for the forest, a floor
whose face is like that of a mirror seen in gloom—dimly showing you
the forms outside it, seeming to have in it images of unknown things."

But Mary Kingsley, who painted this wonderful word-
picture, will chiefly be remembered for her insistence that
the customs and point of view of the native should be studied
and understood and that institutions should be administered

---

[1] *From the Niger to the Nile*, by Lieut. Boyd Alexander, 1907.
[2] *The Life of Mary Kingsley*, by Stephen Gwynn, 1932.

by native rulers under the direction of Europeans. To prove the impression made by her personality, when she died, a "Mary Kingsley" hospital was founded for the study and treatment of tropical diseases, and a "Mary Kingsley Society of West Africa" for the systematic study of native customs and institutions. Wilberforce and Buxton had abolished slavery, Livingstone on land and the British Navy at sea had carried this abolition into effect, while Mary Kingsley showed the world how to govern the negro with justice based on understanding and mercy.

To turn to the Congo region, the French explorer De Brazza explored the Ogowe, founding Franceville on its upper reaches, and discovered many of the northern tributaries of the Congo River, reaching the main river at a point where he founded Brazzaville. He was the able pioneer of what is known as the French Congo. His rival was Stanley, who in 1879, acting as the representative of King Leopold of Belgium, staked out what is now known as the Belgian Congo. Other explorers in this area were Von Wissmann, who discovered the great Kasai tributary, and George Grenfell, who also discovered many of the tributaries of the Congo. These explorers gradually surveyed the enormous Congo area.

In Abyssinia and surrounding countries many explorers have appeared on the scene. In 1885, Teleké, a Hungarian explorer, started from Zanzibar with the object of discovering a lake situated in North-East Africa, which was called Sumburu by his Arab informants. In face of constant difficulties, he was able to make a partial ascent of Mount Kenya and explored the country of the Kikuyu. He reached Lake Baringo, and, continuing northwards, made the important discovery of Lakes Rudolph and Stephanie, situated in the volcanic region of the Rift Valley.

From 1899 to 1904, British officers, Gwynn and Austin, executed valuable surveys between the Blue Nile and the Sobat. Again, Butter and Maud, starting from Abyssinia in 1902, passed to the west of Lake Stephanie, and, travelling along the eastern side of Lake Rudolph, reached the Rift Valley. During this journey important surveys were made. Nor must Wellby, who had already won his spurs in Asia, be forgotten. Starting from Abyssinia, he reached Lake Rudolph by the Omo Valley—the Niam-Niam of early explorers. He then explored the Sobat, and finally reached Fashoda.

In 1903, during the Somali expedition, Beazeley surveyed

many thousand square miles of British Somaliland, while Gwynn, in 1908, delimited the southern frontier of Abyssinia.

The last area to be explored in Africa was the enormous Sahara, the dead heart of North Africa. To continue the account of its penetration from Chapter XXII, Flatters, who was commissioned to survey a route for a trans-Saharan railway, was murdered by Tuaregs in 1881. His successor was Foureau,[1] who, beginning in 1890, made repeated journeys to In Salah, towards Temassinim and the Tademait plateau. He thus gained the necessary experience of the nature of the country and its fanatical inhabitants. Success was finally achieved by the Foureau-Lamy Mission of 1898–1900. Marching due south from Biskra the explorers, supported by a strong escort, passed through Agades and reached Lake Chad, where they met Meynier from the Niger and Gentil from the Congo. Foureau completed his journey at the mouth of the Congo. Geographical and geological discoveries of great value were made—more than 500 places were fixed by astronomical observations—and upon the results of this journey were based the subsequent military and scientific expeditions despatched by the French Government.

In 1912, Commandant Tilho attacked the fanatical Senussis at Tibesti, and later he explored Borku and Ennedi, finally travelling through Wadai to Darfur. As a result of these journeys, undertaken by French explorers, a chain of astronomically fixed positions was forged from the Niger to Lake Chad and thence to the Nile.

In 1922, and again in 1927, an intensive study of Aïr and Damergu was undertaken by Rodd.[2] Particularly interesting is his account of the Tuaregs: "A man's status in Aïr, as elsewhere among the Tuareg, is determined by the caste and allegiance of his mother. Survivals of a matriarchal state of society are numerous among the People of the Veil. They colour the whole life of the race." Explanation of the veil, which is not worn by women, the author can offer none, but he states: "In this veil the men live and sleep. They lift the *imawal* up to eat, but in doing so hold their hand before the mouth. When the veil requires refixing, a man will disappear behind a bush to conceal his features even from his own family."

The French are gradually completing the conquest of the historical Atlas Mountains. To the south of this dividing

---

[1] *D'Alger au Congo*, by F. Foureau, 1902.
[2] *People of the Veil*, by F. Rennell Rodd, 1926.

range the oasis of Tafilelt was occupied in 1932, and before long the Sahara, conquered to some extent by the agency of the motor-car and the aeroplane, will have yielded up the last of its many secrets.

To complete the story in North-East Africa, the grim Libyan Desert has been penetrated—of recent years by motor-car in expeditions led by Bagnold—while on the right bank of the Nile, Hume and Ball have done work of considerable geographical importance.[1] Moreover, during the Great War valuable information was gained in connection with military operations and with missions, especially on the western frontier of Egypt.

In Chapter XXII reference was made to Rohlfs, who in 1879 was robbed in the neighbourhood of the Kufra Oasis. In 1920 Rosita Forbes[2] and Hassanein Bey determined to attempt a journey to Kufra. Hassanein Bey, an Egyptian of good family, had served as secretary to the Italo-British Mission to *Sayyid* Idris, the head of the religious order of the Senussi, in 1916. He had mentioned his desire to penetrate to Kufra to Idris, who provided letters of recommendation, without which the enterprise would have been courting certain disaster. As it was, the explorers ran considerable risks of being attacked by bandits, through reports of their presence being known or through treachery, apart from the equally serious risk of losing their way and dying of thirst.

All went reasonably well until nearing the Kufra Oasis, when the guide, intentionally it would appear, missed the route, and the party ran out of water. They were in a dangerous situation, which was saved by their arrival at Buseima to the west of the direct route. Upon arrival at Hawari, owing to the treachery of the guide, they were threatened by the fanatical tribesmen, but upon entering the oasis they were welcomed by the representatives of *Sayyid* Idris. They had reached Kufra after a trying journey of more than 400 miles.

After visiting the villages that composed the oasis of Kufra or " the Infidels ", so called from the pagan Tebus, who were its original owners, the explorers made for Jaghabub across another section of the desert. Here, at the headquarters of the Senussi, they were welcomed, and were permitted to visit the college buildings and the mosque. Shortly after

---

[1] " The Egyptian Wilderness ", by W. F. Hume, *G.J.*, Vol. LVIII, p. 247, and " Problems of the Libyan Desert ", by J. Ball, *G.J.*, Vol. LXII, p. 21.
[2] *The Secret of the Sahara: Kufra*, by Rosita Forbes, 1921.

leaving Jaghabub, the explorers met a British patrol, and this successful expedition ended at the Siwa Oasis.

In 1923 Hassanein Bey, encouraged by the success of this journey and the support of King Fuad, undertook a still greater enterprise.[1] Returning to Kufra he was well received, but he wrote about the suspicions he excited: "I finally discovered the real basis of the antagonism of those who live in the desert to the coming of persons from the outside world. It is not religious fanaticism; it is merely the instinct of self-preservation. If a single stranger penetrated to Kufra, the cherished centre of the life of their tribe, it would be as the Beduins say, 'the camel's nose inside the flap of the tent'."

The original plan of Hassanein Bey had been to proceed to Wadai across unexplored country, but hearing of two "lost" oases, Arkenu and Owenat, lying to the east of the Wadai route, he determined to find them. It was extremely difficult to engage guides and camels for the enterprise. However, the blessing of *Sayyid* El Abid helped matters, and at last the caravan started off south. After eight long marches "suddenly mountains rose before us like mediaeval castles half hidden in the mist. These were the mountains of Arkenu. . . . The sight of them so gripped me that for a while I dreamed that I was not in the desert any more." The oasis was temporarily inhabited for grazing by Goran tribesmen, who brought sheep and milk to the caravan, while the grazing was excellent and the water supply abundant, though not good.

A sorely needed halt was made and the journey was resumed. After a long night's march the Owenat Mountains were sighted, and in the oasis rock carvings of lions, giraffes and ostriches were discovered. The chief of the Goran agreed to act as guide to Erdi, from which camp the country was hilly. A herd of ostriches was sighted before reaching Enebah, where there was a well of good water and a large encampment. Here the explorer was seen by a *Shaykh* opening the instrument case, and "I could see in his cruel dark face with yellow eyes like those of a fox set close together that he believed I had gold in the box".[2] However sentry-go was ostentatiously instituted and no attack ensued.

Finally the expedition reached Darfur, where the Badawi, delighted with the dancing of the women, performed the ceremony of "singeing the girl's slippers" with their powder

---

[1] *The Lost Oases*, by Hassanein Bey, 1925.

[2] Similarly in Persia, the beautifully kept brass telegraph instruments were believed to be of gold by the ignorant tribesmen, who, on this account, time and again besieged the British Telegraph Offices.

play. These two important journeys, which lay almost entirely through unexplored country, not only linked up Egypt with the Sudan, but supplemented the explorations of Tilho, thus practically completing the exploration of North-East Africa.

So we complete the story of the exploration of Africa down the ages. Herodotus travelled in Egypt and drew the course of the Nile to correspond with the Danube. Later great Ptolemy, whose influence dominated geographers down to modern times, gave a remarkably accurate description of its sources. Idrisi and Ibn Battuta were followed by the Portuguese, but it was not until the nineteenth century that the heart of Africa was penetrated. Here Livingstone will remain for all time the central figure, not only for his wonderful discoveries, but for showing how to cope with the infamous slave-trade on land.

Europe had wronged Africa, inflicting unspeakable miseries upon her, but, led by Livingstone, heroic parties of missionaries settled in the country. They, in their turn, were supported by a magnificent band of British officers, who hoisted the British flag and abolished slavery over large portions of Africa. Other nations undertook the same task, and to-day the great continent knows such peace and security as never before. We sinned grievously, but repented, and, thanks to our great explorers and administrators, we have atoned for our sins.

CHAPTER XXVIII

THE EXPLORATION OF CENTRAL ASIA IN MODERN TIMES

"Oxus forgetting the bright speed he had
In his high mountain-cradle of Pamere.

. . . . . .

But the majestic river floated on,
Out of the mist and hum of that low land,
Into the frosty starlight, and there moved
Rejoicing through the hush'd Chorasmian waste,
Under the solitary moon."

MATTHEW ARNOLD.

"The locality is the surviving portion of reality of an event
that has long passed by. . . . It often restores to clearness
the picture which history has preserved in half-effaced outlines."

HELMUTH VON MOLTKE.

THE exploration of Central Asia in modern times has been
accomplished by Russia, advancing from Siberia in the north
and from the Caspian Sea in the west, while the British, based
on India, have also played a leading part in discovering and
surveying this immense area, which was first discovered by
Alexander the Great. The advance of Russia began with the
foundation of Sergiopol to the north-east of Lake Balkash in
1831. From this base, Semirechia was explored in 1840, and
a decade later Kulja, situated in the upper valley of the Ili,
was reached. Southwards Vyernyi was founded on the route
to Kashgar.

In 1857 the Tian Shan was explored by Semenov, who,
from the Balkash area, travelled south-east to Issyk Kul, crossing the Ala Tau. He then penetrated the main range of the
Tian Shan. Other explorers followed, and, in 1871, Fedchenko
crossed the Alai Range to the edge of the Trans-Alai Mountains, where he named the highest peak Mount Kaufmann in
honour of the Russian Commander-in-Chief. This magnificent mountain was sighted by me from the neighbourhood
of the great Kara-Kul Lake in 1915, when its austere beauty
was enhanced by a mantle of freshly fallen snow.[1]

[1] *Through Deserts and Oases of Central Asia*, p. 134.

We next come to the Russian advance on Central Asia from the Caspian and the Sea of Aral.[1] Survey operations were started in the Caspian under Muraviev, who in 1819 crossed the desert to Khiva. Twenty years later, a Russian expedition from Orenburg attempted to traverse the steppe and attack Khiva, but retreated before reaching the Ust-Urt plateau, mainly owing to lack of forage. Indeed, it was not until 1873 that the great desert oasis of Khiva was annexed and explored.

Russia reached the Sea of Aral in 1844, and the mouth of the Syr Darya was occupied in 1847. In 1849 the advance up the Syr Darya was commenced, and four years later Ak Masjid, some 220 miles up the river, was captured. In 1865 Tashkent was stormed, and before long Khojand, the site of Alexandria *Eschate*, and the rich provinces of Khokand and Farghana were annexed and explored. It was at this period that Vambéry made his celebrated journey in disguise across Persia to Bokhara and Samarkand. Russia completed her annexation of this vast area from her bases on the Caspian Sea. The Tekke Turkoman were crushed in 1881 at Geok Teppe, and the Turkoman of Merv submitted shortly afterwards.

The earliest British explorer of this period was Wood, who accompanied Burnes to Kabul in 1835. From that city he made a most important journey up the valley of the Oxus, following in the footsteps of Hsuan-tsang and Marco Polo, and on February 19, 1838, " we stood, to use a native expression, upon the *Bam-i-Dunia* or ' Roof of the World ', while before us stretched a noble but frozen sheet of water, from whose western end issued the infant river of the Oxus. This was Lake Sir-i-Kul." [2]

From India the Karakoram Pass, known from its height as the " Ridge-pole of the World ", was crossed in 1857 by the Schlagintwert brothers; [3] while in 1865 Johnson, an officer of the Survey of India,[4] travelled from Leh to Khotan, and fixed the position of the " City of Jade ". In 1868 Hayward, travelling by the Karakoram Pass, explored the Yarkand River and the Karakash and reached Kashgar. In a second journey, with the Pamirs as his objective, this intrepid explorer was murdered.

The first Englishman to gain accurate information about Chinese Turkestan was Robert Shaw, who, while living in

---

[1] This question is fully dealt with in Chapter LXXIX of Sykes, *History of Persia.*
[2] *A Journey to the Source of the Oxus*, by Captain John Wood, 1872, p. 232. The actual source of the Ab-i-Panja, the main Oxus stream, is in the Wakhjir Pass.
[3] *Proc. R.G.S.*, old series, Vol. II, p. 301.
[4] " Journey to Ilchi Khotan " (1866), *J.R.G.S.*, Vol. XXXVII (1867).

Ladakh, met an agent of Yakub Beg, the ruler of the country, and was invited to visit his master's domains. Shaw was well received by the *Atalik*, who cordially invited the British to despatch a mission to his court. In 1870, and again in 1873, Forsyth was entrusted with this task, and with him, in the later Mission, were Gordon, Chapman and Trotter, all of whom distinguished themselves as explorers. In addition to important surveys executed by the main body, Gordon led a party which crossed the Pamirs to the Oxus; while Trotter shot an *ovis poli* during this journey.[1] The "Pandits" who did such valuable survey work in Tibet, accompanied this Mission, and contributed considerably to its success. A Moslem, "The Munshi", left the party at Kala Panja and followed the Oxus through the unexplored districts of Shignan and Roshan.

Ney Elias began his distinguished career as an explorer by examining the new course of the Hwang-Ho in 1868, and two years later he surveyed its old channel. In 1872 he made an important journey across the Gobi to Uliassutai in North-West Mongolia, whence he travelled across Asia to Nijni-Novgorod. During this journey he ran great risks owing to the unsettled state of the country. In 1885 Elias made a second journey. Starting from Chinese Turkestan, which he had already visited, he travelled by the Little Kara-Kul Lake, which he discovered, to the Pamirs, where he visited the confluence of the Murghab and Panja Rivers, and indicated the true source of the Oxus. He then crossed Badakshan and reached the camp of the Afghan Boundary Commission near Herat. I first met Ney Elias at Meshed, where he was Consul-General. He taught me much about Central Asia, and it is my view that, owing to his disinclination to publish books on his journeys, the importance of his explorations, on which he invariably took astronomical observations, was not realized by the general public.

Among the greatest explorers of Central Asia was Prjevalsky,[2] who, starting from Kiakta in 1871, crossed the Gobi to Kalgan. He then explored North-East Mongolia. In the following year he travelled through Kansu to the lake of Kuku Nor, and the marshes of Tsaidam. Returning from Kuku Nor, he recrossed the Gobi to Urga. This journey lay

[1] Sir Henry Trotter, the first Englishman to shoot the *ovis poli*, gave me an account which I embodied in *Through Deserts and Oases of Central Asia*, p. 326. In this work I have also described the rise and fall of Yakub Beg—the *Atalik*—and the Forsyth Missions.

[2] *Vide* "Prjevalsky's Journeys and Discoveries in Central Asia," *Proc. R.G.S.*, new series, Vol. XIX, p. 214.

mainly through unexplored country, and in the course of it a fertile, well-watered range had been discovered in Kansu.

In 1876 Prjevalsky, on his second journey, started from Kulja, and crossed the Tian Shan to the Tarim River, following its course down to Lob Nor, which he surveyed. He also discovered the Altyn Tagh, but was unable to cross it in mid-winter. The Russian explorer thereby proved the connection existing between the Nan Shan range [1] to the east and the Kuen Lun to the west, the three ranges holding up the great plateau of Tibet on the north as the Himalayas buttress it on the south.

In 1879 Prjevalsky made Zaissansk his starting-point for a third journey. Traversing Zungaria to Hami, he crossed the Altyn Tagh, and passing to the east of the Tsaidam marshes, penetrated North Tibet. Refused permission to enter Lhasa, he returned northwards, and skirting the Hwang-ho, crossed the Gobi to Kiakta. In his fourth journey, the great Russian explored the sources of the Hwang-ho. He then marched to the south of Tsaidam and crossed the Altyn Tagh to Lob Nor and so to Khotan. During this journey, Prjevalsky explored the mighty Kuen Lun. He will certainly be remembered as one of the greatest explorers of Central Asia and Tibet. Among his many discoveries were " Prjevalsky's horse " and the wild camel.

In 1886, Younghusband accompanied an Indian civilian, H. E. James, on a journey to Manchuria. From Mukden the valley of the Sungari was ascended to its source, and other exploration was undertaken in this little known country.

In 1887, Younghusband [2] started off from Peking with the intention of traversing the Gobi to Chinese Turkestan, and, from that outlying province of China, crossing the Himalayas into Kashmir. From Peking, the Mongolian frontier was reached at Kalgan, and at Kara-Khoto, arrangements for crossing the Gobi were made, with the valuable assistance of a British missionary. Starting on April 26, an unexplored route across this great desert was followed, and, during this trying march, the *equus Prjevalsky* was sighted, while tracks of the wild camel were also observed. Traversing hilly country, the mighty Tian Shan was seen from afar, and, on July 4, Hami was reached—a distance of 1,255 miles from Kara-Khoto, mainly across the great desert.

From Hami, Younghusband followed the caravan route

[1] *From Kulja across the Tian Shan to Lob Nor*, by Colonel N. M. Prjevalsky, 1879.
[2] *The Heart of a Continent*, by Captain F. E. Younghusband, 1896.

248

skirting the Tian Shan to Kashgar. He then proceeded to Yarkand, where he decided to follow an unexplored route across the Mustagh Pass into Skardu. By good fortune he found some Baltis at Yarkand, who knew the route (which had only been closed by the Chinese some ten years previously), and who were willing to serve him as guides.

Starting off on the last section of his long and adventurous journey, his route ran to Kargalik. There the plain ended and the party entered the mountains. At the head of the Tisnaf River, the main caravan route across the Karakoram Pass to Leh was left, and a westerly course followed to the Yarkand River, which was crossed and recrossed continuously. Where it flowed through precipitous cliffs a pathway had to be made by throwing rocks into the water—a very serious task. Continuing the journey the Shaksgam River was discovered and K2 was sighted: " We could see it through a break in the mountains rising up straight, bold and solitary, covered from foot to summit with perpetual snow. The upper part, for perhaps 5,000 feet, was a perfect cone." This celebrated mountain, second only to Everest, is 28,250 feet in height, and as I sighted it from the Pamirs, it seemed like a giant among the pygmies.

The Mustagh glacier constituted a formidable obstacle for the ponies, while supplies were running short and there was no fuel to be found. Finally, Younghusband decided to leave the ponies in charge of three men, and, in the dark, he began to climb the glacier leading to the pass. Progress was terribly slow at the altitude of some 19,000 feet, but at noon the summit was reached. The descent was precipitous, and it seemed that failure was inevitable. However, led by a Balti, who cut steps across the steep icy slope, a cliff was reached, and finally the adventurous explorers found a dry spot where they bivouacked. On the following morning they struck the Baltoro glacier, surveyed in 1861 by Godwin-Austen, the first explorer of the Karakoram glacier system. Finally, on the third day after crossing the pass, Younghusband reached the little village of Askoli, where supplies were procured. A notable feat of exploration had been successfully accomplished.

During this period, thanks to the influence of Sir Mortimer Durand, the great boundary-maker, the northern frontiers of India were explored and laid down. Lockhart, making Gilgit his headquarters, visited the robber states of Hunza and Nagar, and, crossing the Hindu Kush, explored Wakhan, while

Younghusband surveyed the passes leading to the Pamirs, where he was arrested by a Russian force. Negotiations followed which led to the Pamir Boundary Commission of 1895, by the terms of which Wakhan was awarded to Afghanistan, to serve as a buffer between the two great powers.

The survey operations, undertaken before the Great War, by which the Indo-Russian triangulation connection was obtained, constitute a great achievement in the face of the gravest physical obstacles, and deaths by lightning and disease. When travelling in the Pamirs in 1915, I met the Russian Survey officers who had co-operated in this most important task, and they spoke in the most appreciative terms both of Bell, who died during the survey from illness aggravated by exposure, and of Kenneth Mason.[1]

During the latter half of the century explorer after explorer has penetrated into the fastnesses of the Himalayas. Their names, which appear on the roll of honour of the Royal Geographical Society, include Conway, Bruce, Longstaff, the Dukes of the Abruzzi and of Spoleto, De Filippi and Wood. Unfortunately space will not allow me to do justice to the skill and courage shown by each explorer.

Longstaff's discovery in 1909 of the Siachen glacier, the longest and most important in the mighty Karakoram system, led to the expedition of De Filippi. It was carried out by a body of Italian experts, whose explorations were aided by Wood and by Indian surveyors.[2] The chief geographical results included the complete delineation of the last great glacier system of the Karakoram. To this may be added the discovery of the source of the Yarkand River in a tongue of the Rimo glacier, which overflows northwards across the water-parting. The Great War brought the expedition to a premature close, but even so the results that were obtained were of the greatest importance.

From one point of view, Mason's exploration of the Shaksgam Valley[3] was a continuation and completion of the De Filippi expedition. Its important results included the survey of the main features of a portion of the divide between the drainage flowing to the Indian Ocean and that flowing into Central Asia.

[1] " The Indo-Russian Triangulation Connexion", by Lieut. Kenneth Mason, *G.J.*, Vol. XLIII, January 1914.
[2] *The Italian Expedition to the Himalaya, Kara Koram and Eastern Turkestan* (1913–1914), by Filippo de Filippi, 1932.
[3] *The Exploration of the Shaksgam Valley and Agil Ranges*, by Major Kenneth Mason.

LOADING UP THE YAKS ON THE PAMIRS

(From Through Deserts and Oases of Central Asia)

During the expedition of the Duke of Spoleto,[1] the gap which existed between the farthest point reached by Younghusband and by Mason, was bridged. To come to still more recent exploration, Dainelli,[2] in 1930, crossed from the Siachen glacier by a new pass on to the Rimo glacier, thus making the passage of the main range of the Karakoram between the Mustagh and the Sasir Pass. This he named the Italia Pass.

Many explorers have visited the vast country of Mongolia in recent years. Among the most important expeditions were those undertaken by Kozlov, who, in journey after journey, completed the exploration of the Altai. He then surveyed the upper reaches of the Yang-tse-kiang. Later he took soundings in the Kuku Nor. Throughout, he made valuable collections of animals and plants, and his journeys were perhaps as valuable from the geological as from the geographical point of view.

In 1908, Carruthers explored the Tian Shan, and two years later he made a systematic study of the upper basin of the Yenesei. The last of the important expeditions in Mongolia is that of Chapman Andrews, who, utilizing motor-cars as well as camels, has not only added materially to knowledge of the geography of the country between Kalgan and the Altai, but has been responsible for the striking discovery of the eggs of prehistoric reptiles, which was a result of studies in which all biological sciences were represented.

During the present century, Sir Aurel Stein has played the leading part on the stage of Central Asia.[3] In his first journey, undertaken in 1900, he crossed the Himalayas to the Sarikol Valley. He camped on the Little Kara Kul Lake, whence he climbed the spurs of mighty Mustagh Ata and viewed the Qungur Alps, which were explored by Skrine in 1922.[4]

Reaching Khotan in the autumn, he set to work on its ancient site of Yotkan, and on Dandan Uilik, " the ancient city Taklamakan ". In the Taklamakan Desert, towns and villages which had been watered by rivers flowing down from the great Kuen-lun range had been abandoned, owing to failure of the water supply, and this constituted an ideal hunting-ground for the archaeologist.

[1] " The Italian Expedition to the Kara Koram in 1929 ", by H.R.H. the Duke of Spoleto, *G.J.*, Vol. LXXV, No. 5, May 1930.
[2] " Italia Pass in the Eastern Kara Koram ", by Giotto Dainelli, *American Geographical Review*, July 1932.
[3] Stein's works include *Sand-buried Cities of Khotan*, 1903 ; *Ruins of Desert Cathay*, 1912 ; *Sèrindia*, 1921 ; and *Innermost Asia*, 1928.
[4] " The Alps of Qungur ", by C. P. Skrine, *G.J.*, Vol. LXXVI, No. 5, November 1925.

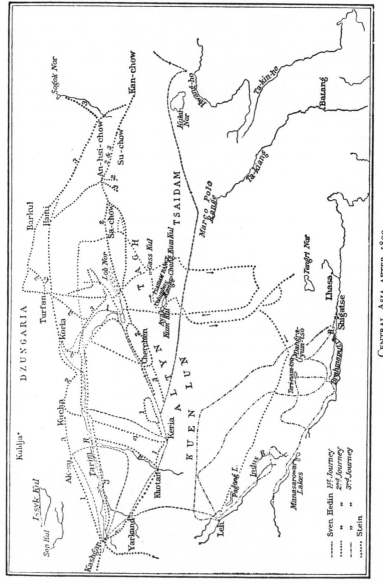

CENTRAL ASIA AFTER 1899.

Sogok Nor
Kan-chow
An-hsi-chow
Su-chow
Barkul
Ulini
Sa-chow
Turfan
Korla
Kucha
Ak-su
Kulja
Issyk-Kul
Son-Kul
Kashgar
Yarkand
Khotan
Keria
Tarim R.
Lob Nor
Cherchen
Gass Kul
A L T Y N T A G H
DZUNGARIA
TSAIDAM
Kürlik Nor
Hwang-ho
Ta-kin-ho
Batang
Ta-kiang
Marco Polo Range
Tengri Nor
Lhasa
Shigatse
Dahbra-yum-tso
Tar-nam-tso
Potala
Tsangpo
K U E N L U N
Manasarowar Lakes
Indus R.
Patong L.
Leh

Sven Hedin 1st Journey
    „   „   2nd Journey
    „   „   3rd Journey
Stein

During the winter many sites were visited, a stupa with colossal statues in stucco of Buddha representing the most striking discovery, and, after what may be described as a most successful reconnaissance, Stein reached England with his treasures in good condition.

Stein's second expedition of 1906–8 was of a far more ambitious nature. He travelled to Chitral and, by special permission of the Amir, was allowed to cross Wakhan. Everywhere copying inscriptions and noting Buddhist remains, Stein crossed the Hindu Kush by the Baroghil Pass, "where the watershed between Indus and Oxus drops to only 12,400 feet". Fording the "stripling Oxus", he writes : "laving my hand in it as a pious salute to a great river, touched at last after many years' waiting".

Passing through Khotan, Stein examined the Lob Nor region. Here his finds included documents sealed with clay seals representing Hercules, Eros and Pallas *Promachos*. He then crossed the Gobi, following in the footsteps of the early Chinese pilgrims and of Marco Polo. In this area he was rewarded by the discovery of the ancient fortified wall with its watch-towers and stations, which he explored for a distance of 200 miles, reaping a rich harvest of early Chinese and other records of historical interest. The epoch-making discovery of the great archaeologist was made at Tun-huang, the chief oasis at the western extremity of the ancient wall. Close by is situated the sacred site of the " Thousand Buddhas ", with its hundreds of cave-temples. Stein with amazing address gained access to, and possession of, "a great deposit of ancient manuscripts and art relics, which had lain hidden and perfectly protected in a walled-up rock chapel for about 900 years". A new chapter in the history of eastern art has been opened by these epoch-making discoveries of documents written in many tongues, known and unknown. Of especial general interest was " an excellently preserved roll with a well-designed block-painted picture as frontispiece, which had its text printed throughout, showing a date of production corresponding to A.D. 860. Here was conclusive evidence that the art of printing books from wooden blocks was practised long before the conventionally assumed time of its invention during the Sung period."[1]

Stein had convinced the guardian of the shrine of his sincerity by frequent references to his Chinese patron-saint Hsuan-tsang, and when the exquisitely beautiful banners were

[1] *Ruins of Desert Cathay*, Vol. II, p. 189.

discovered, he must have thought of the triumphal reception accorded to the explorer upon his return to neighbouring An-hsi, when, from every monastery, they met him with banners, carpets and rich palanquins in orderly procession.

During the summer of 1907, Stein explored some 20,000 square miles on the snowy Nan-shan, and in the winter of 1907–8, he crossed the " sea of sand " of the Taklamakan at its greatest width. The summer of 1908 was utilized for explorations in the mighty Kuen-lun. Here the intrepid explorer, at the very end of a most successful expedition, was surveying on the ice-clad crest of the main range when he was badly frost-bitten, and ultimately, after much suffering, all the toes of his right foot had to be amputated at Leh.

In 1913, Stein started on his third journey to Central Asia, and, owing to the favourable political situation, he was able to traverse the unexplored valleys of Darel and Tangir south of Gilgit, and, crossing the Darkot Pass, he returned to Chinese Turkestan. His first objective was again the Lob Nor area, where he made fresh discoveries of importance. He then proceeded to explore other portions of the fortified line of Han times.

Stein now penetrated to the ancient site of Kara-Khoto, first discovered by Kozlov, where he obtained a rich harvest of manuscripts in the Tangut and Tibetan languages. He thence made for Kan-chou, and, in spite of an accident to himself, his Indian assistant carried through the survey of the headwaters of the Kan-chou River. The untiring explorer then visited Zungaria, Turfan, and finally reached Kashgar in the summer of 1915.

In July 1915 Stein started on a new journey, which from the Pamirs led through Roshan and Shignan, where he made valuable studies, not only of the geography, but also of the types and languages of these unexplored valleys. He then travelled across Eastern Persia to Sistan, where, on the Kuh-i-Khoja, he discovered wall-paintings of the Sasanian period— the first to be brought to light in Persia.

This brief summary hardly does justice to a series of journeys which have embraced the whole heart of Asia. Throughout, the country has been scientifically surveyed, while almost every question, whether historical or scientific, has been dealt with in masterly fashion, so much so that Stein is undoubtedly the greatest archaeologist and explorer of Central Asia.

In a recent expedition Sven Hedin [1] made the remarkable

---

[1] *Across the Gobi Desert*, by Sven Hedin, 1931.

KASHGAR, SHOWING THE CITY WALL AND THE TUMAN SU

(From Through Deserts and Oases of Central Asia)

discovery that Lob Nor had wandered back to its ancient bed. This famous lake, known from early antiquity to the Chinese, was located by Prjevalsky in 1877, a degree farther south than the Chinese maps had shown it. Sven Hedin, who examined the question on the spot, made a most remarkable prediction : " I am convinced that in a few years' time the lake will be found in the locality where it was formerly placed by the Chinese cartographers." [1]   Nearly thirty years later the Swedish explorer was able to write :

> " A new and mighty swing of the pendulum has carried the flowing, as also the stationary waters back to the north again into their old beds in the Kum-darya and the lakes near Loulan.   Thereby there have been produced anew the same conditions as prevailed 2,000 years ago, and the old intimate connexion between Tun-huang and Loulan has at the same time been restored."

The great Swedish explorer may be congratulated not only on the fulfilment of his remarkable prediction, but also on being the first European to discover that fulfilment.

[1] *Central Asia and Tibet*, Vol. II, p. 174.

CHAPTER XXIX

MODERN EXPLORERS OF TIBET

" The Deserts of Tibet are certainly the most frightful country
that it is possible to conceive. The ground continuing to rise,
vegetation diminished as we advanced, and the cold grew
more and more intense. Death now hovered over the unfortunate caravan. The want of water and pasturage soon
destroyed the strength of our beasts. Each day we had to
abandon beasts of burden that could drag themselves no
further. The turn of the men came somewhat later."
Huc *and* Gabet *on the Central Plateau of Tibet.*

In Chapter XVII an account has been given of Ippolito de
Desideri, who in the eighteenth century raised a corner of
the curtain which concealed Tibet from the outer world.
After his great journey the curtain falls again for more than
a century, until it is lifted once more by French missionaries.

Early in the nineteenth century, the French mission in
China had been almost extirpated, when, to quote the Lazarist
Fathers Huc and Gabet :[1] " a great number of Christians
had sought peace in the deserts of Tartary . . . By dint of
perseverance the missionaries collected together these dispersed
Christians." While working as missionaries in Tartary, the
two Fathers decided to undertake an adventurous journey
across Tibet. Accordingly, in the autumn of 1844, to the
grief of their Chinese converts, they cut off their pigtails,
assumed the dress of Lamas and started off westwards. They
were particularly well qualified for the undertaking owing
to their knowledge of the Chinese and Mongol languages.
Moreover, their perfect adaptability and their excellent education enabled them to play the difficult part which they had
assumed with remarkable success. At first they crossed the
wide plains to Tolon Nor, where they reported the existence
of great foundries of the bells and idols which play such a
leading part in Tibetan worship. They then give a wonderful
description of the festival of the Loaves of the Moon among
the Mongols. Even in this remote part of the Chinese Empire,
news of the military operations of the English—the China War

[1] Huc and Gabet, *Travels in Tartary, Thibet and China, 1844–48* (Broadway Travellers),
1928. Colonel Ryder has read this and the following chapter and has made valuable
suggestions.

had ended in 1842—had leaked through. The English, called
" the Rebels of the South ", were described as " Sea-monsters.
They live in the water like fish. When you least expect them,
they appear on the surface, and hurl fire-bombs at you ; while
the instant your bow is bent to shoot them, down they dive
like frogs."

Upon reaching the banks of the Hwang-ho, the explorers
had great difficulty in transporting their camels across the
extensive inundated area, that animal being almost helpless
in marshy ground, while it cannot swim, although it can
float. Indeed, their experiences carried me back to marshy
Sistan with the Helmand in flood, where I was faced with
similar problems.

Travelling to the south-west, the French Fathers met the
King of the Alechan, who was bound for Peking to offer his
homage to the Emperor. The explorers, who had intended
to traverse his country, were warned of its utter sterility,
and so decided to avoid it by crossing into the Chinese
province of Kansu. There they were mistaken for Tartars,
and a mandarin attempted to oust them from the inn, but
finally explanations were offered, and " having saluted us with
his hand in a protecting manner, he retired like an ordinary
mortal to the small room which had been prepared for
him. . . . The triumph we had thus obtained in a country,
admission even to which was prohibited to us under pain of
death, gave us prodigious courage." Incidentally it proved
how perfectly the Fathers were playing their part.

Taking the road to Ili for a short distance, the explorers
reached the " Great Wall, which we passed over without
dismounting ". Their passports were demanded at a barrier,
or failing them a considerable sum of money, but they bluffed
the official with complete success. Traversing Kansu, which
is described as a very fertile province with " inexhaustible
mines of coal ", they met a Living Buddha.

> " When the inn had become tolerably clear, this strange personage
> gave full play to his curiosity ; he poked about all over the inn, going
> into every room and asking everybody all sorts of questions. . . .
> When he entered our chamber, we were gravely seated on the *Kang*;
> we studiously refrained from rising at his entrance. . . . Standing
> in the middle of the room, he stared at us intently, one after the other.
> We, like himself, preserving entire silence, exercised the privilege of
> which he had set us the example, and examined him closely."

Finally they became friends, and, at the return visit, the
" Living Buddha " said that his Lamasery was situated near

the Russian frontier, and that he had heard of the English and of Galgata or Calcutta.

In January 1845, "after crossing several torrents, ascending many hills, and twice passing the Great Wall, we arrived at Tang-Keou-Eul. . . . Nobody walks the streets without a great sabre at his side. . . . Not an hour passes without some street combat." At this turbulent town the difficulties of the onward journey loomed very large. "We should have to travel for four months through a country absolutely without inhabitants and should have to lay in all necessary provisions. The cold was so horrible that it often happened that travellers were frozen to death or buried beneath avalanches of snow. Moreover, there were hordes of brigands."

Realizing that they must await the annual Chinese embassy to Tibet, which had only just quitted Peking, before attempting to cross the elevated central plateau, the Fathers settled down to study Tibetan with a learned Lama. In due course they were invited to take up their quarters in the Lamasery of Kounboum, where they continued their studies in great comfort. Shortly after their arrival the famous Feast of Flowers drew crowds of pilgrims. "The flowers were bas-reliefs, of colossal proportions, representing various subjects taken from the history of Buddhism. The features were full of life and animation, the attitudes natural, and the drapery easy and graceful. The furs were especially good. The various skins of the sheep, the tiger, the fox and the wolf were so admirably rendered that you felt inclined to go and feel them with the hand." Yet everything was made from butter !

On the auspicious day of the festival—

"The Grand Lama walked in the centre of the principal dignitaries of the Lamasery, preceded by minor lamas, who cleared the way with great black whips. His costume was strictly that of our own bishops : he bore on his head a yellow mitre, a long staff in the form of a cross was in his right hand, and his shoulders were covered with a mantle of purple-coloured silk, fastened on the chest with a clasp, and in every respect resembling a cope."

After spending three months at Kounboum, the Fathers moved to a smaller Lamasery, "the country house of the Faculty of Medicine of Kounboum", where the mountain served "as an abode for five contemplative monks, none of whom seemed to know what it was that engaged their thoughts". When the summer came, with their "camels magnificently stout", the explorers travelled to Kuku Nor

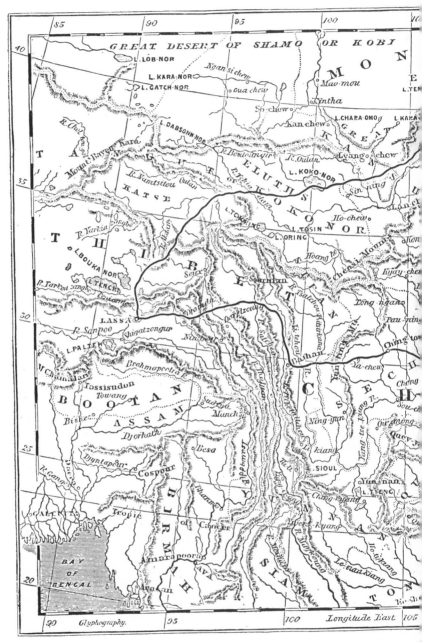

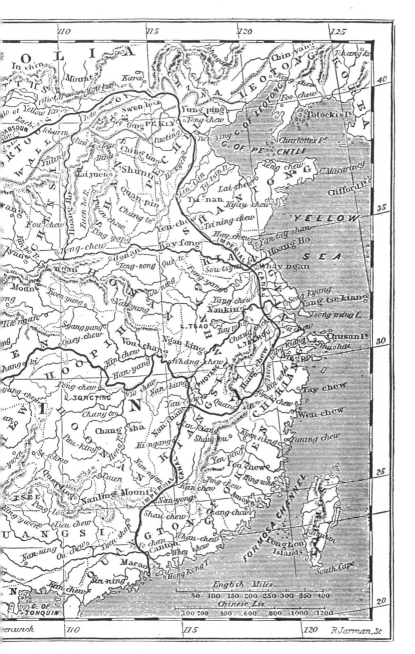

ROUTE OF THE TRAVELLERS, MM. HUC AND GABET.

TARTARY, THIBET, AND CHINA

or "Blue Sea", a vast body of salt water, surrounded by rich pasturage. There they remained until, in October, the Tibetan embassy accompanied by a great number of Mongol caravans arrived. Huc estimates the number of men at 2,000 and the various horses, yaks and camels at about 40,000.

From fertile Kuku Nor they traversed Tsaidam, "the soil, arid and stony, produces with difficulty a few dry, saltpetrous bushes". Then came the Bourhan-Bota Pass, which was not only steep and lofty, but dreaded because of its pestilential vapour. "Heavens! what wretchedness it was we went through; one's strength seemed exhausted, one's head turning round, one's limbs dislocated; it was just like a thoroughly bad sea-sickness." Presumably it was mountain sickness, in which connection Younghusband mentions that his Chinese servant thought that the air was poisonous when he was overcome by this distressing malady.

Yet another range—Mount Shuga—had to be crossed in bitter cold, with the result that "Poor M. Gabet had to deplore the temporary decease of his nose and his ears". These real hardships culminated in crossing the Bayen-Kharat, which runs from south-east to north-west. The point at which the range was crossed was near the source of the Hwang-ho. Fortunately the weather was warm, and plenty of *argol* or "dried dung", the only available fuel, was found on the camping-ground. Continuing the journey, they crossed the upper reaches of the Yangtze-kiang on the ice, seeing a heard of wild yaks which had been trapped in the ice and frozen to death. Many members of the caravan died during the crossing of the high plateau, which lies at a general elevation of 16,000 feet above sea level. Geographically it is of great importance, as from it flow the upper waters of the Yangtze, the Salwin and the Mekong. After twelve days on the plateau came the descent, and the goal of the expedition was reached at Lhasa.

At first the Lazarists were suspected of being surveyors, but when their property had been examined, they were taken into favour and were able to give a wonderful account of life at the capital of Tibet. "There exists a very touching custom at Lhasa. . . . Just as day is verging on its decline, all the Tibetans meet together, kneel down and chant prayers." The sacred formula runs: "*Om mani padme houm*," which signifies, "O the gem in the Lotus, Amen." This inscription, which may be seen on hundreds of stones in Tibet, possesses a mystical meaning, about which many books have been written.

The Chinese Ambassador at Lhasa feared that, if it was reported at Peking that he permitted French missionaries to preach at Lhasa, his life would be forfeit. Consequently he decided to send Huc and Gabet back to China under escort. The Fathers behaved with much dignity under trying circumstances, and, after an affecting farewell with the friendly Regent—the Dalai Lama was only a child—they marched off eastwards towards China on March 15, 1846. Thanks to the arrangements made by the authorities the journey was performed in comfort so far as the accommodation was concerned, but although this was the main route between Lhasa and China, it was merely a track passing through a very difficult belt of mountains. They crossed the watershed of Lha-ri with the greatest difficulty, but, in accordance with the custom which prevails in High Asia, the yaks went first to make the road and they, following in their wake, reached the summit.

The descent mainly consisted in a rapid slide down a glacier in which the yaks led the way, followed by the horses and then by the men. " We sailed over those frozen waters with the velocity of a locomotive." The crux was the journey to Alan-To. To quote Huc :

" Travellers are obliged to pass these deep abysses by following at a great height so narrow a ledge, that the horses frequently find only just enough room to plant their feet. As soon as we saw the oxen of the caravan making their way along this horrible path, and heard the low roar of the waters rising from the depths of those gulfs, we were seized with fear. . . . Lest we should get giddy, we kept our heads turned towards the mountain, the declivity of which was sometimes so perpendicular that it did not even offer a ledge for the horses to plant their feet on."

One more danger, well known to skiers, was a mountain where " you must abstain from even uttering a word, otherwise the snow and ice will fall upon you in abundance, and with astonishing rapidity ". Nearing the end of the journey there was civil war in one district, but, to obviate risks, women were placed in charge of the transport, as " men who would have the cowardice to fight with women, and take the animals confided to their care, would be despised by the whole world ".

At last the explorers reached the enchanting plain of Bathang. " We found ourselves all at once transported, as it were by magic. A delicious warmth gradually penetrated our limbs ; it was nearly two years since we had perspired." A few days later, in June 1846, the heroic French explorers reached China.

The successors of these French explorers were Indian surveyors, who, travelling under various disguises, carried out journeys of great geographical importance under conditions of extreme hardship and risk.[1] Nain Singh "the Pundit", an inhabitant of Kumaon, had already visited Gartok when he was commissioned to travel to the upper Indus Valleys and explore the region of the gold mines. In June 1867, he started from Badrinath, and, after examination by the suspicious Tibetan frontier officials, reached the mines at an altitude of 16,300 feet. The gold was worked by miners clothed in thick black garments who scratched up the soil into heaps with antelope horns, always guarded by their fierce mastiffs. In this custom, without much doubt, we have the origin of the gold-digging ants, guarded by their fierce dogs, about which Herodotus had heard.

Even greater than Nain Singh was Kishen Singh, who in 1871 penetrated to Shigatse and Tengri Nor, where he made a complete circuit of the great lake. Shortly afterwards he was attacked by a band of sixty armed robbers and only reached Lhasa with great difficulty. There, by pledging his instruments, he obtained money for his return journey to India.

In 1878, Kishen Singh undertook his most important journey. From Lhasa, which he reached *via* Darjeeling, he travelled north-east across Tibet, crossing the Altyn Tagh to Sa-chow. From this centre he crossed Eastern Tibet to Ta-tsien-lu and Batang on the Ta-kiang. He was not able to enter Assam, so he returned to Lhasa, and finally reached Darjeeling in 1882. "In this journey", to quote Baker, "he had linked areas where the British were active to those reached by the Russians, while his visit to Ta-tsien-lu connected up Indian and Chinese route traverses."

I cannot refrain from giving one more story. In 1879, a Chinese lama was trained and despatched to Lhasa with orders to follow down its great river as far as possible, and then to throw specially marked logs into it. For two years a watch on the river was maintained and was then abandoned. To quote Mason:

"Four years passed; Kinthup, who had been in the service of the lama, returned. He told his story; how the lama had failed in his trust; how he himself had been sold into slavery; how he had worked for freedom and made his way down the Tsang-po to carry out the work

---

[1] "Kishen Singh and the Indian Explorers", by Major Kenneth Mason, *G.J.*, Vol. LXII, p. 429; *Tibet the Mysterious*, by Sir Thomas Holdich.

allotted to his false master. He detailed the places he passed down the great river to a point within sixty miles of the plains of India. Finally, he reported how, being unable to proceed further, he had thrown the logs into the river."

Thirty years passed, Kinthrup's story was proved to be genuine, and at long last he received his reward. I have worked for many years with Indian surveyors, and I should like to add my tribute to the courage, capacity and enthusiasm of this very deserving body of men.

After this period, English explorers appeared on the scene, and in 1885 Carey, who is the oldest gold-medallist of the Royal Geographical Society alive at the time of writing, crossed Northern Tibet with Dagleish to Keria. He then visited Khotan, crossed the Takla Makan Desert, visited Lob Nor and travelled by Hami and Turfan to Kashgar.

During the last generation Lhasa has been the lodestone for traveller after traveller. Rockhill made two attempts. On his first journey in the disguise of a pilgrim, he approached Lhasa from Kuku Nor, but was refused permission to enter, and proceeded to Ta-tsien-lu, as did Bonvalot, who made a similar attempt from Kulja. In 1891, Rockhill travelled from Tsaidam, but was again refused permission. He thereupon crossed Tibet to Batang.

In 1891, Bower crossed Tibet, keeping to the north of Tengri Nor, and reached China after traversing 800 miles of unexplored country. In 1893 Littledale made a journey through Samarkand and Kashgar to Lob Nor. He then followed an unexplored route to Sa-chow. In 1895 he again travelled to Kashgar, and from Khotan made for Cherchen, thence marching south towards Lhasa. He had reached a point only some forty miles from the forbidden city, which he was refused permission to enter. He wrote to me from Leh that, but for the illness of Mrs. Littledale, he might have overcome the objections of the Tibetan officials. After Littledale came Wellby and Malcolm who, in 1896, travelled from Leh to Kuku Nor, and striking the Hwang-Ho, made for Peking. To complete the list of British explorers, Deasy surveyed the upper valley of the Yarkand River, called the Zarafshan, and large areas to the south of the Kuen Lun range, and also to the east of the Panggong.

In 1903, Rawling [1] entered Tibet to continue Deasy's explorations. He surveyed 35,000 square miles of unexplored country in North-West Tibet up to the southern slopes of

[1] *The Great Plateau*, by Captain C. G. Rawling, 1905.

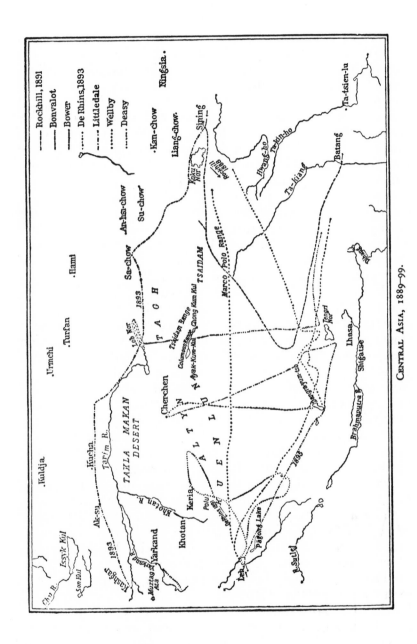

CENTRAL ASIA, 1889-99.

263

the Kuen Lun. He was prevented from visiting Rudok by Tibetans, but they gave him supplies for his return journey, of which he was sorely in need.

In 1904, a mission under Sir Francis Younghusband crossed the Tibetan frontier to insist upon the observance of the Treaty signed at Darjeeling in 1890. The Tibetans, however, were hostile, and finally, after some fighting, the mission dictated terms at Lhasa. Among the articles, it was agreed that a trade mart should be opened at Gartok ; and Major Ryder, who had been in charge of the survey party to Lhasa, and Captain Rawling led an expedition to explore the country westwards to Gartok. Captain Wood and Lieutenant Bailey, who had studied Tibetan, joined the expedition. At Shigatse a visit was paid to the Tashi Lama, whom Ryder describes as " an interesting personality, sixth holder of the office ; his face is one that would not pass unnoticed anywhere, still less in Tibet. He has clear-cut features, high cheek-bones, and a pale complexion ; his quiet dignified manner made a lasting impression on us." [1]

Rawling describes the sarcophagus of the first Tashi Lama : " It is of gold, covered with beautiful designs of ornamental work, and studded with turquoises and precious stones. Along the ridges at the side of the tomb stood exquisite old china vases and ancient cloisonné ware, whilst golden bowls and cups of the same material are placed in front of the base of the tomb." On the summit of the Kura La the explorers reached the watershed between the Ganges and the Brahmaputra basins. " Towering up thousands of feet, a glittering pinnacle of snow, rose Everest, a giant among pygmies, and remarkable not only on account of its height, but for its perfect form. It is difficult to give an idea of its stupendous height, its dazzling whiteness and overpowering size, for there is nothing in the world to compare with it."

This important journey resulted in the survey of the Tsang-po or Brahmaputra from Shigatse to its source. The Sutlej was also surveyed from its source to the Indian frontier, while the Gartok branch of the Indus was likewise explored. To Desideri belongs the honour of being the first European to travel along the Tsang-po to Lhasa, but it was reserved for British explorers, who were unaware of Desideri's journey, to survey this great area of southern and south-western Tibet under most trying physical conditions. To quote

[1] " Exploration and Survey with the Tibet Frontier Commission ", and " From Gyantse to Simla via Gartok ", by Major C. H. D. Ryder, G.J., Vol. XXVI, October 1905.

Younghusband: "This would have been a magnificent performance if it had been undertaken in the very best of weather; but it was done at the very worst season of the year."

Sven Hedin has undertaken more than one important journey in Central Asia and Tibet. In 1895 he traversed the Takla-Makan, discovering buried cities both in the desert and in the vicinity of Lob Nor, which discoveries were of considerable value to Stein. In 1906, Hedin devoted himself to the region lying between Shigatse and Leh, keeping north of the Tsang-po. His chief discovery was the existence of an important range of mountains parallel to the Himalayas.[1] In addition to his geographical discoveries, Hedin has always collected geological, zoological and natural history specimens. He is the last great explorer of Tibet on a large scale.

The recent attempts to scale Mount Everest have included a considerable amount of exploration, while Mallory and Irvine sacrificed their lives in a heroic attempt to reach its summit and perhaps were successful.

In June 1933, Everest was again attacked with better preparations of every kind. But, owing to the difficulties of terrain being intensified by storms and snowfall, success has not yet been achieved.

Meanwhile the Houston expedition has conquered "Nature's last terrestrial secret" After their arrival at Purnea, there was a long spell of bad weather, during which winds of 120 miles per hour were reported. But, on the morning of April 3, 1933, Lord Clydesdale, with Colonel Blacker as photographer, followed by the second Houston-Westland, piloted by Flight-Lieutenant M'Intyre, flew direct for Mount Everest. Crossing the brown plains of Bihar, they gradually rose across Central Nepal, sighting Kin-chinjanga to the east. At 19,000 feet Everest became visible above the haze, but a downward current of air over Lhotse, the south peak of Everest, caused a loss of altitude amounting to 1,500 feet, so that they only just managed to clear the summit of mighty Everest. Then, in spite of the gale and the great frozen plume of the mountain, into which they had flown, close-range photographs were taken, before returning to the aerodrome.

The results of this great feat include a mass of geographical material from which a map of a large unexplored area will be made. The southern face of Everest has never been seen before while the camera depicts the grave of heroic Mallory and Irvine.

[1] *Trans-Himalaya*, by Sven Hedin, 1909.

CHAPTER XXX

EXPLORATION IN ASIA—THE LAST PHASE

"Oh, who can hold a fire in his hand
By thinking on the frosty Caucasus?
Or cloy the hungry edge of appetite
By bare imagination of a feast?"

SHAKESPEARE.

"From India and the Golden Chersonese,
And utmost Indian isle Taprobane,
Dusk faces with white silken Turbants wreathed."

MILTON, *Paradise Lost.*

IN this chapter some account will be given of various countries in Asia which are not dealt with separately. To commence our survey from the west, the Caucasus was not unknown
to the Greeks. Some of their merchant-adventurers had
reached the Phasis, and had brought back accounts of gold
being secured by leaving sheep-skins in the mountain streams
to catch the sediment, which report must surely have originated the legend of the Golden Fleece. Aeschylus, too, made
its highest mountain the prison of Prometheus, who was chained
to its crags for stealing fire from heaven and giving it to
mortals. Curiously enough, the study of his great tragedy
brought Douglas Freshfield to the Caucasus, where, although
the Russians had surveyed the lowlands to some extent,
Elbruz, Kasbek and a number of other superb peaks had
never been scaled, from lack of initiative, from superstition
and from ignorance of the art of climbing with ice-axe and
rope.

In his attack on Kasbek, Freshfield and his companions,
starting from a camp 11,000 feet high, reached the base of
the peak of the mountain and were cutting steps in blue ice
covered with loose snow when the step-cutter slipped, placing
a severe strain on the climbers, who were just able to resist it.
After this narrow escape from disaster, the summit was reached
without great difficulty, and Kasbek was conquered.[1] This
magnificent peak, which dominates the landscape, rises to
16,540 feet.

[1] *Travels in the Central Caucasus and Bashan,* by Douglas W. Freshfield, 1869; also
The Exploration of the Caucasus, 1896.

LHASA: THE POTALA

(By permission of the Royal Geographical Society)

Elbruz, the scene of *Prometheus Bound*, which I sighted from the Black Sea, was next attacked. Pitching a camp near the snow-field, the cold was bitter. " Near the point where the snow began to slope towards the base of the mountain," writes Freshfield, " the crisp surface broke under my feet, and I disappeared, as suddenly as through a trap-door, into a concealed crevasse . . . and it cost us all a long struggle before I was hauled out."

The cold was intense, and frost-bite was imminent ; but the arrival of two porters, who had followed the explorers, encouraged them to persevere. A long climb up easy rocks restored their numbed limbs, and a few steps cut in an ice couloir, " the only approach to a difficulty on the mountain ", led to the summit at " one end of a horseshoe ridge ". Thus historical Elbruz, which rises to a height of 18,500 feet, was conquered.

Asia Minor was well known to the Greeks and Romans, but it was not until the beginning of the nineteenth century that it was scientifically explored. Leake and Kinneir both executed valuable surveys which were incorporated in Rennell's work, *The Comparative Geography of Western Asia*. In 1838 Ainsworth examined the country towards Sinope, and then visited Angora and reached the Euphrates. In the following year he travelled to Mosul. Of modern travellers, Wilson, Bryce, Ramsay and Hogarth have all left their mark on our geographical knowledge ; the two last-named were also famous archaeologists. Nor must we forget the Kieperts, father and son, who compiled a monumental map of the country.

In the Book of Genesis we read that " the ark rested in the seventh month, on the seventeenth day of the month, upon the mountains of Ararat ". It is no wonder then that Great and Little Ararat are among the most famous of mountains. Rising to an elevation of 17,000 feet, Great Ararat completely dominates the surrounding country. To quote Lynch : " Side by side stand two of the most beauteous forms in Nature, the pyramid and the dome. . . . On none of her works has she bestowed greater unity of conception, a design more harmonious, surroundings more august." [1] According to local belief, the sacred mountain could never be trodden by mortal foot. However, it was first climbed by Parrot in 1829, and since that date has been scaled by many travellers, including Bryce and Lynch.

[1] *Armenia*, by H. F. B. Lynch, 1901.

Palestine was surveyed by officers of the Royal Engineers, among whom Kitchener may be mentioned, in the interests of the *Palestine Exploration Fund*. They also studied its archaeology, geology and natural history. To-day the country is being examined with scientific minuteness, and the potentialities of the Sea of Lot, misnamed the Dead Sea, will probably prove a source of great wealth to the country.

Mesopotamia, now known as Iraq, has attracted many explorers and archaeologists. Rich spent many years as Resident at Baghdad and surveyed widely. But it was the Euphrates expedition under Chesney which surveyed that historical river with scientific accuracy. After Chesney came Rawlinson, who held the post of Resident at Baghdad from 1843 to 1855. With his support surveys were extended, while during this period Botta and Layard excavated ancient Nineveh. At the outbreak of the Great War there was, generally speaking, a distinct lack of accurate geographical information as regards Iraq. This, however, was remedied both during the progress of operations and after the Armistice, more especially in connection with the Boundary Commissions. To-day, thanks to the Survey of India, Iraq has been accurately surveyed—one of many benefits conferred on the country by the British.

Persia was visited by many travellers during the sixteenth and seventeenth centuries, who have been mentioned in previous chapters. In the middle of the eighteenth century an attempt was made to follow in the footsteps of Jenkinson and to reopen trade with Persia across Russia. At that time Nadir Shah, the Napoleon of Asia, who had sacked Delhi and conquered Khiva and Bokhara, was ruling the country with an iron hand, which provoked constant rebellions. Jonas Hanway,[1] the leading figure in this venture, decided to land his goods at Bandar Gaz and proceeded to Astrabad. His objective was Meshed, which was at that time the capital. Unfortunately a rebellion broke out at this juncture, during which Hanway lost his goods and barely escaped slavery. In a destitute condition he traversed the Caspian Provinces to Langar Rud, where he met Elton, the originator of the scheme, who supplied him with clothes and money. Thus re-equipped, he reached the royal camp at Hamadan, and gives an admirable account of Nadir Shah and of the tyranny exercised by that ruler. Hanway returned to Astrabad provided with an order for the restitution of his goods or for payment

[1] *Historical Account of British Trade over the Caspian*, by Jonas Hanway, 1753.

of their value. There he was a witness of the merciless punishments meted out to the rebels and saw two pyramids composed of their skulls.

At the beginning of the nineteenth century, the fantastic strain in Bonaparte's character brought Persia within the orbit of world politics. In conjunction with Paul of Russia he contemplated an invasion of India, in which the Persian army was to be utilized as an instrument of his far-reaching schemes.[1] To meet this peril, the British despatched Malcolm on missions to Persia in 1800 and again in 1810, which resulted in much discovery.

Notable explorers sent out by Malcolm were Christie and Pottinger. They travelled together in disguise as far as Nushki, whence Christie penetrated to Herat and thence reached Yezd and Isfahan. Pottinger traversed the whole of Baluchistan, of which he gave a most valuable description, and passing through Kirman, rejoined Christie at Isfahan. These two explorers, to quote Baker, " did much to reveal the essential geographical facts of Eastern Persia and Western Afghanistan ".

The first Afghan War, that ill-considered campaign, which lasted from 1838 to 1842, saw British troops marching in the footsteps of Alexander the Great from Kandahar to Kabul and beyond. During this period the country was explored to a considerable extent and much geographical information was collected.

The British maintained a mission at Herat from 1839 to 1841, and from that city Shakespear was despatched across the desert to Khiva to open up relations with the *Khan*. Not only did he induce that potentate to release his Russian slaves, but he actually conveyed them himself across the steppe to Orenburg—a great feat which should never be forgotten.[2]

Among the most fascinating books of travel of the middle of the nineteenth century is that written by Layard,[3] describing his wanderings among the Bakhtiaris and Lurs. Visiting Petra and Baalbek on his way eastwards, he inspected the ruins of Nimrud opposite Mosul, the excavation of which, later in his career, gave rise to the saying that " Nineveh had found Layard ". He then crossed the Persian frontier, and

---

[1] This question is dealt with in Sykes, *History of Persia* (3rd ed.), Chap. LXXV. The German plan for the invasion of India in the World War, utilizing the Turkish army for the purpose, was based on Bonaparte's scheme.

[2] In the *Journal of the Royal Central Asian Society*, Vol. VIII, 1921, there is an account of this memorable journey, together with a facsimile of the letter of the *Khan* of Khiva.

[3] *Early Adventures*, by Sir Henry Layard, 1887.

passing through Luristan reached Kermanshah. He joined the camp of Muhammad Shah, which he accompanied to Hamadan, and thence travelled to Isfahan by way of Burujird. His objective was the site of Shushan, and, making the acquaintance of a Bakhtiari, brother of Muhammad Taki, the Chief, he accompanied him across the Bakhtiari Mountains to Kala Tul, the residence of Muhammad Taki at that time. After curing one of his sick children, Layard was treated as an honoured guest, and was consequently in a position to visit the ancient ruins and to amass a vast store of valuable information. At this period lions—now practically extinct—were numerous, and Layard took part in more than one hunt. Later Layard travelled to Shuster, and explored the Hawizah district and other parts of Khuzistan.

No mention of Persia would be complete without reference to Sir Henry Rawlinson, who not only copied but deciphered the trilingual inscription at Behistun or Bisutun, and thereby furnished the key to the knowledge of the ancient civilizations of Babylonia, Assyria and Persia. Originally sent to Persia as a member of a Military mission in 1833,[1] Rawlinson marched Persian troops through Luristan in 1836 and was the first explorer of that province. He was the leading authority on Persia and Central Asia for many years.

In 1858 Russia despatched an important mission to Central Persia under Khanikoff. His expedition, which included a surveyor and a number of scientists, explored far and wide in Eastern Persia and penetrated into the Lut. It was the most important expedition despatched by Russia, and gained much valuable information.[2]

The construction of the Indo-European telegraph line which ran across Persia, and from Jask traversed Baluchistan, led to much exploration and to more than one Boundary Commission. Sir Frederic Goldsmid fixed the frontiers between British and Persian Makran, and later between Persian and Afghan Seistan, thereby inaugurating the modern Boundary Commission. The present writer owes much to this great pioneer's work. Nor must his officers Lovett and St. John be forgotten. Among their chief discoveries was the existence of a water-shed in Baluchistan at about 100 miles from the coast, which defined the area of Makran, and cut it off from the valley of the Helmand.

Among other travellers of this period was that distinguished

[1] *Vide* Sykes, *History of Persia* (3rd ed.), Vol. II, p. 327.
[2] *Memoir on the Southern Part of Central Asia*, by N. Khanikoff, 1883.

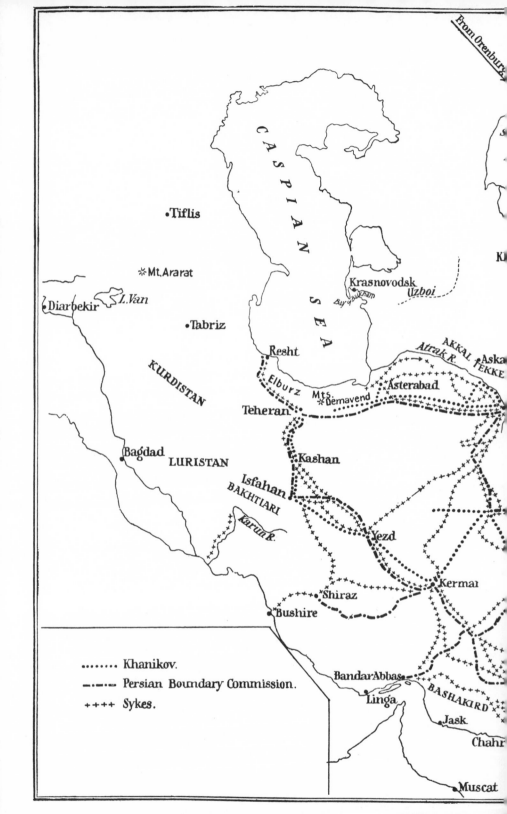

CASPIAN SEA

•Tiflis

✳Mt.Ararat

•Diarbekir   L.Van

Krasnovodsk
Bay of Balkham   Uzboi

KURDISTAN

•Tabriz

Resht

Elburz   Mts.

✳Demavend   •Asterabad

Teheran•

Afrak R.   AKKAL   Aska
TEKKE

Baǵdad   LURISTAN

•Kashan

Isfahan
BAKHTIARI

Karun R.

•Yezd

Kermai•

•Shiraz

•Bushire

.... Khanikov.

-.-.-.- Persian Boundary Commission.

++++ Sykes.

BandarAbbas•

•Linga

BASHAKIRD

•Jask

Chahr

•Muscat

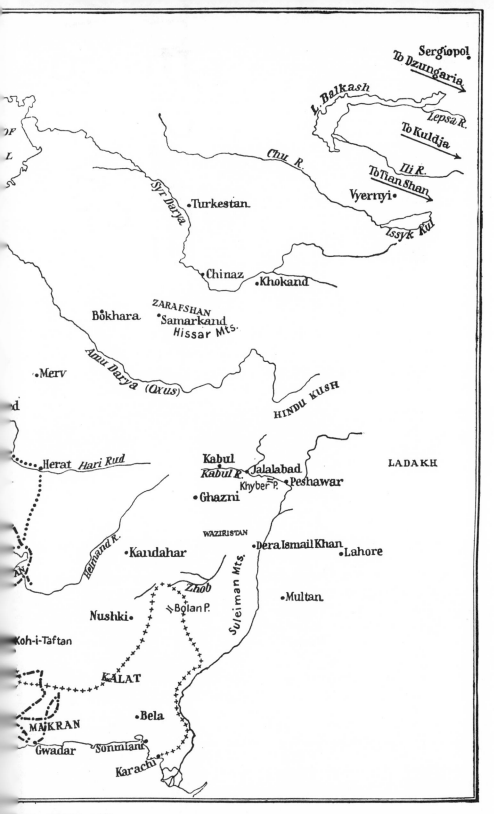

soldier Sir Charles MacGregor, who travelled extensively in Eastern Persia and Baluchistan. Through his insistence on the importance to India of gaining accurate geographical and political knowledge of trans-frontier countries, an Intelligence Division was gradually founded, and officers were encouraged to travel. In memory of this great pioneer a MacGregor Memorial Medal was instituted for exploration possessing military value.

At the end of the nineteenth century, Holdich was the leading explorer of the frontiers of the Indian Empire. Not only was he a scientific surveyor of distinction; he was also an artist of merit, and he wrote books which contain excellent descriptions of the countries which he surveyed.[1]

Holdich started his career with a survey of the country between the Bolan and the Khyber Passes during the Second Afghan War. Of greater importance was his work on the Afghan Boundary Commission, which stayed the advance of Russia so far as North-West Afghanistan was concerned, albeit not before the Panjdeh incident, in 1885, brought Great Britain to the brink of war with the Northern Power.[2]

In 1893 Durand, that great boundary maker, persuaded Amir Abdur Rahman to cede Roshan and Shignan to Russia, and thus made the Oxus the frontier from the point where the Afghan Boundary Commission terminated its labours. Farther east, in 1895, Holdich was chief surveyor on the Pamir Commission referred to in Chapter XXVI. To quote his description of Makran[3]: "A dead monotony of laminated clay backbones, serrated like that of a whale's vertebrae, sticking out from the smoother outlines of mud ridges which slope down on either hand to where a little edging of sticky salt betokens that there is a drainage line when there is water to trickle along it; and a little faded decoration of neutral-tinted tamarisk shadowing the yellow stalks of last year's forgotten grass along its banks." In the same year the boundary between Afghanistan and British Baluchistan for the settlement of which McMahon was British Commissioner, was also carried to Kuh-i-Malik-i-Sia, where the Indian Empire meets Persia and Afghanistan.

In Western Persia De Morgan, best known in connection with his epoch-making discoveries at Susa, explored in Kurdi-

---

[1] *The Indian Borderland*, 1901; and *The Gates of India*, 1910.
[2] This mission is fully dealt with in the present writer's biography of *Sir Mortimer Durand*, Chap. X.
[3] Holdich served as Chief Commissioner on the Perso-Baluch Boundary Commission, in 1896.

stan and in the Caspian provinces in 1889–91. Stahl, who gained valuable geographical information, also explored in Northern Persia. Vaughan made two important journeys, in one of which he travelled from Linga across the Dasht-i-Kavir and so almost to the Caspian, while Sawyer in 1890 explored a considerable new area in the Bakhtiari country.

To turn to my own journeys, in 1893 I travelled up the valley of the Atrek to Kuchan. I then crossed the Lut to Kerman, following in the footsteps of Marco Polo, and discovered a high range in its vast waste. In 1893–4 I explored in Persian Baluchistan, and was the first European to climb the volcano of Taftan, which is in the *Solfatara* state, and also the extinct volcano of Bazman.

In 1895 I founded the British Consulate for Kerman and Persian Baluchistan, and in the following year served under Holdich on the Perso-Baluch Boundary Commission. In the same year I visited the valley of the Karun on a special mission. In 1897 I took part in an expedition in Persian Baluchistan against the murderers of a British telegraph official, and in connection with it, in 1898, crossed an unexplored tract between Minab (close to the Harmozia of Nearchus) and Ramishk. In the autumn of that year King Wood and I travelled across Persia to Seistan to discover the best route for the Central Persian telegraph line to follow. There I founded the British Consulate for Seistan and Kain, and surveyed a large part of that little-known area.[1] Later when serving as Consul-General for Khorasan, I undertook journeys in the classical Parthia and Hyrcania. Thanks to the invaluable assistance of Indian surveyors, during the twenty-six years I spent in Persia, I was able to fill in many blanks on the map of that historical country.

Boundary Commissions have generally if not invariably been fruitful in valuable surveys, and that for the Turco-Persian Boundary has proved no exception to this rule. In 1848, British and Russian Commissioners appeared on the scene, among them being Colonel Williams, who was later to win fame as the defender of Kars. On this occasion " the Turkish salute of welcome at Erzerum included a gun charged with round shot carefully aimed at, and only just missing, the British Commissioners ".[2] Thus the Turks welcomed their future defender! The leisurely labours of this Commission occupied four years, and were interrupted by the Crimean

---

[1] For these travels *vide* Sykes, *Ten Thousand Miles in Persia*, 1902.
[2] " The Demarcation of the Turco-Persian Boundary in 1913–14," by Col. C. H. D. Ryder, *G.J.*, Vol. LXVI, p. 227.

War, after which many years were spent in the production of a *Carte Identique*, which was both inaccurate and probably more or less obsolete.

In December 1913 a new Commission met,[1] which, by October 1914, " had travelled from the Persian Gulf to Mount Ararat, and demarcated practically the whole 1,180 miles of the frontier. . . . The first pillar, set up where the frontier leaves the Shatt-al-Arab, a few miles above Mohammerah, was erected with such zeal by the masons that they built themselves in and a hole had to be made for their release." Crossing the desert, the Commissioners reached the Karkheh River, " the drink of none but Kings " of Milton, and continuing north-wards, near Qasr-i-Shirin struck the ruins of a great wall running in a dead line across country, and said to be over 100 miles in length. May not this have been one of the *Firdaus* or hunting parks of the Sasanian monarchs ? The last pillars were placed on the col separating Mount Ararat from Lesser Ararat, and the Commission broke up a day before Turkey declared war. It remains to add that, during the Great War, important surveys were made in various parts of Persia.

The scientific exploration of India was begun by James Rennell.[2] He commenced operations in 1764 with the Ganges valley, and in due course his surveys extended to the great boundary range which he named the Tartarian Mountains, now known as the Himalayas. Working incessantly year after year, Rennell was able to hand over to Lord Clive a map of Bengal, Bihar, and Orissa, and the Moghul Empire as far north as Delhi. In addition to the above, he had made a chart of the Ganges. This great survey was published in the *Bengal Atlas* in 1779. Rennell left India in 1777, and during the next fifty years he was the leading geographer in Europe, influencing almost every field of exploration, and fully earning the title of " Father of English Geography ".

After Rennell came the Great Trigonometrical Survey of India, which reached the Himalayas, and was extended to Kashmir in the middle of the nineteenth century. As mentioned in Chapter XXVI, it was joined up to the Russian Survey in 1911. Throughout the long period of its existence, many explorers who have already been referred to, or will be mentioned later, pushed beyond the borders of the Indian Empire. Indeed, no body of men has done more for

[1] Chief British Commissioner, A. C. Wratislaw, Captain Arnold Wilson, Assistant-Commissioner, and Col. Ryder, Chief Survey Officer. M. Minorsky was Chief Russian Commissioner.
[2] *Major James Rennell*, by Sir Clements Markham, 1895.

scientific exploration in Asia than the officers of the Survey of India.

Continuing our survey eastwards, one of the problems which had long been exercising the minds of explorers was whether the Tsang-po, which had been successfully explored in its upper reaches by Ryder, joined the Brahmaputra. The Abor country was explored by a punitive expedition in 1911, but still the problem remained unsolved.

In 1913 Moorshead and Bailey [1] were despatched to survey the basin of the Dibang River. From it they crossed into the district of Po-me, where they were received with much suspicion at first owing to the recent destruction of its capital Showa by the Chinese. From Showa they descended the Tralung, an important tributary of the Tsang-po, and finally struck the main Tsang-po at an altitude of 9,680 feet. The results of this adventurous journey included the survey of some 400 miles of the Tsang-po. Of greater importance was the proof that the enormous sudden fall in that river was caused by a series of rapids, and that it became the Brahmaputra in its lower course.

Burma was visited by Marco Polo and Varthema, but was not fully explored until the Burmese Wars. However, before the annexation of the country by Great Britain, Margary, in 1874, travelled from Shanghai up the Yangtse-Kiang, and crossing Yunnan, reached Bhamo—a great exploit.

Siam was visited by the Portuguese, who established a colony in the country ; but its chief explorer was McCarthy, who, entering the service of the King of Siam, started his survey operations in 1881. For many years he explored the country especially in the north and, before 1893, its main features were well known, while his work was continued by a Survey Department which he founded. In 1889–90 the Anglo-Siamese Boundary Commission delimited the boundary between Burma and Siam.

In French Indo-China the most noted explorer was Garnier, who in 1866 ascended the Mekong hoping to find a waterway suitable for commerce leading into Yunnan. Using gunboats and then native boats as far as possible, Garnier was soon forced to the conclusion that his scheme of diverting the trade of Yunnan to Indo-China was impracticable. With much difficulty, owing to rapids, Bassak in the Laos country was reached and selected as the headquarters of the expedi-

[1] " Exploration on the Tsangpo or Upper Brahmaputra ", by Captain F. M. Bailey, *G.J.*, Vol. XLIV, p. 341.

KUH-I-TAFTAN

(*From Frontiers of Baluchistan by G. P. Tate*)

tion, and from this centre the country was explored in every direction, while its inhabitants and resources were carefully studied. The French mission accomplished much, surveying the course of the Mekong, noting the volume of its water at various seasons, exploring the Laos and Shan States and penetrating into South China as far as Ta-li-fu. Garnier had many successors who completed the exploration of Indo-China.

The exploration of Yunnan was scientifically undertaken by Major Davies and Captain Ryder [1] who surveyed considerable portions of the country in 1898–99. A reference to the map will show that many affluents of the Irrawaddy, the Salwen, the Mekong, the Yangtse-Kiang and the Red River all flow through, or take their rise in, this high-lying province, and this is the most noticeable feature of the plateau. During the course of their travels many thousands of miles were covered, and the two explorers produced maps that were of far greater value than those of their predecessors, while they studied the numerous tribes with which they met.

Some years later, in 1920, Professor Gregory and his son made a remarkable journey across Yunnan. As a result of this journey they discussed the mountain system and the parallel rivers with authority.[2]

In 1921 Kingdon Ward, who had started his journeys in 1909, continued his explorations in this area. Primarily a botanist in search of new plants, he has surveyed much of the country and obtained a deep insight into its inhabitants.

> " It is a strip of crumpled crust averaging about 75 miles wide, over a length of 150 miles, as measured off the map, and may be regarded as a huge breach in the Asiatic divide. The western portal of the gap is framed by the broken end of the Himalaya, where a great bluff overlooks the plain of Assam. The eastern portal is formed by a tangled skein of mountains in Western China, flanking the gorges themselves. The two are connected by an arc of lofty mountains which form the rim of the Tibetan Plateau and envelop the sources of the Irrawaddy. Thus four rivers, whose sources lie hundreds of miles apart, come charging down from the north, converge, rush side by side through this narrow gateway, and swing apart again to flow to different seas." [3]

When he reached Salween, the explorer found that there had been a devastating flood, with the result that the cliff path was " simply pulverized ". The going was dangerous, and a " monkey bridge " proved to be more difficult to cross

---

[1] " Exploration in Western China ", *G.J.*, Vol. XXI, p. 109.
[2] " The Alps of Chinese Tibet and their Geographical Relations ", *G.J.*, Vol. LXI, p. 153.
[3] " From the Yangtse to the Irrawaddy ", by F. Kingdon Ward, *G.J.*, Vol. LXII, p. 6.

unaided than a Tibetan rope bridge. After many adventures
the western branch of the Irrawaddy was reached at Myitkyma.
The photographs taken by Kingdon Ward are beautiful. In
another expedition to the Burma-Tibet frontier, undertaken
in 1930,[1] the explorer looked over the Tamai Pass into Tibet.
Recently this indefatigable explorer has left England, determined to add to his laurels by exploration in Eastern Tibet.

In *Alastor*, Shelley describes a journey in Asia:

> " The Poet wandering on, through Arabie
> And Persia, and the wild Carmanian waste,
> And o'er the aerial mountains which pour down
> Indus and Oxus from their icy caves,
> In joy and exultation held his way;
> Till in the vale of Cashmire, far within
> Its loneliest dell, where odorous plants entwine
> Beneath the hollowed rocks a natural bower,
> Beside a sparkling rivulet he stretched
> His languid limbs."

"Explorations on the Burma-Tibet Frontier ", *G.J.*, Vol. LXXX, p. 465

CHAPTER XXXI

ARABIA—FROM NIEBUHR TO DOUGHTY

"The Beduins' old cruel rancours are often less than the golden piety of the wilderness. The danger past, they can think of the defeated foemen with kindness, having compassion of an Arab lineage of common ancestry with themselves."

DOUGHTY.

"Allah created the Beduin for the camel, and the camel for the Beduin."

Arab Proverb.

THE "Island of the Arabs", as Arabia is termed by its inhabitants, is the westernmost of the three peninsulas of Southern Asia. Situated among sterile lands, the Red Sea on the west and the Persian Gulf on the east are too narrow to influence its continental climate, and the only areas approaching fertility in this huge peninsula, which exceeds India in its extent, are Yemen, the neighbouring Hadramaut and the valleys lying on both sides of the Oman Mountains, the *Arabia Felix* of the classical writers, which benefit by the life-giving monsoon rains. Yet, in spite of its sterility and its entire lack of perennial rivers, few countries have played a greater part on the stage of history than Arabia.[1]

In the book of Genesis we read of the journey of Abraham, an Arab *Shaykh*, from the neighbourhood of Ur, whose marvellous past has been revealed to us by Woolley, to Harran, where Crassus, many centuries later, was slain by the Parthians. Later, we read of the Patriarch at Sichem, at Bethel, at Hebron, at Gerar and at Beersheba. A famine compelled him to seek refuge in Egypt and, on his return to Canaan, we read that amazing piece of history known as the battle of four kings with five, which is given in the fourteenth chapter of Genesis.

In Chapter IV I have given a sketch of the ancient history of Arabia and have referred to the expedition of Gallus, on which Ptolemy based his description of *Arabia Felix*. To this Idrisi added, so far as the west and south-west coasts of Arabia

[1] Sir Percy Cox has read these three chapters on Arabia and made many valuable comments and suggestions. Colonel T. E. Lawrence has rendered me valuable help in this chapter and in part of the following chapter.

are concerned. But the first great explorer of Arabia was Ibn Battuta, early in the fourteenth century, whose journeys are dealt with in Chapter X. Two centuries later, Varthema describes the pilgrimage which he accompanied from Damascus. He also travelled in Yemen and visited Dhufar and Maskat. Not long after, the Portuguese failed to capture Aden, but succeeded in occupying ports on the coast of Oman, albeit they were unable to penetrate into the interior. In their track followed the English adventurer, Henry Middleton, who, touching at Mocha in 1610, was trapped by the Turks and taken to Sanaa, which he described as " somewhat larger than Bristol, well built of stone and lime ". He was finally sent back to Mocha, and, escaping on a barrel to his ships, he promptly bombarded the port, with excellent results.

We now come to the expedition of Niebuhr,[1] which, consisting of five scientists, was despatched by the King of Denmark in 1761 and reached Jedda in the autumn of the following year. After a visit of two months, during which they were not permitted " to pass through the gate that opens towards Mecca ", the Danes coasted to Lahiya, and from this port began making numerous short journeys into the interior. Reaching Bait-al-Fakih, the coffee emporium, they were so little interfered with that the party broke up and explored the coastal area in various directions, Forskal making a valuable collection of plants in the mountains. In 1763, they reached Mocha, where their Arabic scholar Von Haven died. They had much trouble with the authorities at this port, but finally were summoned to visit the *Imam* at Sanaa.

Niebuhr was well received by this potentate.

"The *Imam* sat upon the throne between cushions, with his legs crossed in the eastern fashion; his gown was of a bright green colour, and had large sleeves. On each side of his breast was a rich filleting of gold-lace, and on his head he wore a great white turban. We were first led up to the *Imam*, and were permitted to kiss both the back and the palm of his hand, as well as the hem of his robe. It is an extraordinary favour when the Mahometan princes permit any person to kiss the palm of the hand."

Niebuhr gave a good description of Sanaa with the battery of guns lying derelict and a German mortar with the date 1514. He refers to the ill-treatment of the considerable Jewish colony, and mentions that " the *Banians* in Sanaa are reckoned to be about 125. They pay 300 crowns a month for permission to live in the city." The Mission had indeed been well received

[1] *Travels Through Arabia*, 1792.

at Sanaa, but knowledge of the *Imam's* avarice, joined to the facts that Forskal had died on the way up and that the sudden change of climate—Sanaa is situated at 7,250 feet above sea level—was injurious to their health, made Niebuhr think seriously of sailing for India with the English.

Consequently the explorers returned to Mocha and sailed for India, but finally, Niebuhr alone survived to return to Europe overland by the Persian Gulf route. Well indeed had he carried out his task of exploring Yemen, while he had compiled a mass of valuable information about other parts of Arabia.

The rise of the Wahabi religion in Central Nejd was an important event, which had repercussions not only throughout Arabia, but in neighbouring lands. The origin of this militant sect was as follows.[1] Among the petty chiefs of Nejd was Muhammad, a member of the noble clan of Anaza, whose stronghold was Dariya. Muhammad, the third or fourth in descent from his eponymous ancestor Saud I, was surrounded by powerful neighbours, who were always fighting with one another and with him for supremacy in Nejd. About 1744, an Arab, Muhammad ibn Abdul Wahab, who had studied at Baghdad and Damascus, returned to his home at Ayaina with a message, the gist of which is given in the following lines :

> " Hear what said the Prophet of God—
> ' Behold Jewry, it is divided into seventy and one divisions ;
> And lo ! the Nazarenes, into two and seventy divisions be they divided ;
> Verily, I say unto you, this people of mine shall be divided into seventy and three divisions ;
> They be, all of them, for the flames of Hell—except one '."

Suffering the usual fate of a prophet among his own people, Ibn Abdul Wahab betook himself to Dariya, where he was welcomed by its chief, Muhammad, and, under his patronage and that of his successor Abdul Aziz, the Wahabi religion was founded. Muhammad ibn Abdul Wahab lived to the great age of eighty-nine, and when he died in 1792, the Wahabi sect was successfully fighting its way to empire. " The Wahabi seer seems to stand out as a politician of amazing astuteness," writes Philby, " appealing to just that embryo of fanaticism innate in the hedonistic materialism of the Arab race."

The fighting Wahabis had no easy task in their rise to power, year after year passing without any striking success until, in 1773, they became masters of Nejd. The next generation was one of expansion gained by constant fighting, and

[1] *Arabia*, by H. St. J. B. Philby, 1930.

among the provinces that were annexed to the growing kingdom was Hasa. Karbala was captured in 1801, and, two years later, Mecca was added to the growing empire. Abdul Aziz was assassinated, but his successor Saud captured Medina in 1804. He followed up this success by adding both Oman and Yemen to his dominions.

Turkey was now awake to the menace of the new religion, and Muhammad Ali Pasha was appointed to Egypt with instructions to overthrow the Wahabis. In 1812, the first action was fought in the passes between the coast and Medina, in which the Wahabis were victorious. They withdrew from Hejaz, however, before the Egyptian troops, but in the winter of 1813–14 inflicted another defeat on the invaders at Turaba. In 1815, the situation changed and the Egyptians defeated Abdulla the ruling Chief near Taif and raided the Wahabi homeland from Medina, forcing the Wahabi chief to accept an unfavourable truce.

In 1818, Dariya was invested and taken. Abdulla was beheaded at Constantinople and a general massacre of the defenders was made. The Government of Bombay were deeply interested in the success of this campaign against the Wahabis, since the coastal tribes, notably the Jowasmi pirates, were ruining the valuable trade of the Persian Gulf and the rich pearl fisheries of Bahrein. Accordingly, it was decided in 1819 to despatch a special envoy to congratulate Ibrahim *Pasha* on the capture of Dariya and " to concert the necessary arrangements with a view to the complete reduction of the Wahabi power ". Upon his arrival at El-Katif Captain Sadleir, who had been selected for this important task, was informed that Ibrahim was evacuating Arabia. However, he decided to carry out his instructions and started on the first journey across Arabia made by a European. Upon reaching Hofuf in the oasis of Hasa, Sadleir found Ibrahim's troops preparing to evacuate the country, and accordingly he decided to march with them. He entered Nejd by Yemama, and passing to the north of Riyadh, he visited the devastated oasis of Dariya. He then followed in the tracks of the Egyptians, who had destroyed as they retired, and traversing Al-Washm, he reached Anaiza. At Rass he overtook the main body of the Egyptian army, but its leader had gone on to Medina.

Sadleir finally met Ibrahim in the vicinity of this sacred city. He was received politely, but was informed that the policy of Egypt was settled by his father, and that he could not treat with the Government of Bombay. The British

MECCA: PILGRIMS PRAYING TOWARDS THE *KAABA*

(*From Dr. J. Snouck Hurgronjes' Bilder aus Mekka*)

Envoy was not permitted to enter Medina, and had to be content to view its minarets from afar while travelling to the port of Yanbo. Sadleir, throughout this important journey across unexplored country, made a careful compass route survey, and his report contained notes on the tribes and on the oases which he visited. He was the first English explorer in Arabia, and deserves a niche in the Temple of Fame.

Among the chief pioneers of exploration in Hejaz was Burckhardt,[1] who had already travelled widely in Nubia and had discovered Petra. Owing to his profound knowledge of Arabic and of the Koran he was able to pass as a Moslem. Landing at Jedda in 1814, he visited Muhammad Ali Pasha, whom he already knew in Egypt, at Taif. After several interviews with the *Pasha* no objection was raised to his taking part in the ceremonies of the pilgrimage at Mecca, of which he gave a most accurate and detailed account. In the following year he travelled to Medina by the coast. The caravan was mainly composed of Malay *Hajis*, who, he notes, although they reviled the British, " never failed to add ' but their government is good ' ". Burckhardt gave an excellent description of Medina, although he was suffering from illness, and he ended his important journey at Yanbo.

Among the successors of Burckhardt in the Hejaz was Burton. His journey to Mecca in the disguise of a Moslem made him famous, but he merely confirmed what his predecessor had so ably described, and added little to geographical knowledge. Burton, as Hogarth points out, hoped to be able to cross the heart of Arabia as a *Haji*, but, upon making inquiries, he abandoned the scheme as impracticable.

Burton's claims as an explorer in Arabia were to arise after his great journey to the heart of Africa. In 1877 he led an expedition into the land of Midian from the port of Muwailah, mainly in search of minerals. He explored the coastal area to a point half-way up the Gulf of Akaba, thereby supplementing Moresby's survey. After exploring Northern Midian, Burton returned to Muwailah, and, passing through the coastal range, penetrated to the inner plateau. As a result of this expedition the land of Midian was scientifically surveyed. Burton's chief interest was Arabia, and by his translation of the *Arabian Nights* and his amazing studies on the manners and customs of the Arabs, he perhaps did more than any other explorer to draw the attention of the world to the " Island of the Arabs ".

[1] *Travels in Arabia*, by J. L. Burckhardt, 1829.

We now turn to the charting of the Arabian coast and especially to Wellsted,[1] an officer of the Indian Navy, who, in 1830, took part in the survey of the Red Sea in the " Palinurus " under Moresby. In addition to his arduous survey duties Wellsted landed at Tor, and, proceeding inland, visited cells hewn out of the rocks which had formerly been occupied by Christian hermits. Close to Tor, he visited the Jabal Nakus or " Mountain of the Bell ", and gives an early account of singing sands. He also travelled by land to Suez. His interesting description of the survey of the Gulf of Akaba shows with what dangers navigation in unknown waters is attended.

In 1834, Wellsted, who was now surveying the southern coast of Arabia, sighted some ruins on a " lofty, black-looking cliff " termed Hasan Gorab. Visiting the site, he discovered the first Himyaritic inscriptions, and, realizing the importance of the discovery, " three separate copies were taken by different individuals, all of which have subsequently been examined and compared ". In the following year, landing at a point some eighty miles east of Aden, Wellsted made an adventurous journey of some fifty miles up a long valley where he discovered the still more important ruins of Nakab-al-Hajar.[2] Situated on a hill rising out of the centre of the valley, a massive wall from thirty to forty feet in height, flanked by square towers erected at equal distances, encloses the fortress. A hollow square tower stands on either side of a ruined building in which the inscriptions, with letters eight inches in length, were discovered. The wall and the towers were carefully cemented with hard mortar. The discovery of these inscriptions, now numbered by thousands, created a new epoch in the history of Arabia.

Wellsted made further explorations under the protection of the *Imam* of Maskat[3] and landing at Sur, explored that part of Oman which lies behind Ras-al-Had. Although the tribes inhabiting this area had embraced Wahabi tenets and had been severely punished for supposed acts of piracy by a British force less than a generation before, Wellsted was received most hospitably. He thence travelled north-west towards the central range of Oman, passing a chain of fertile oases, which were fed by Persian *Kanats*, this system of underground irrigation channels having been introduced when Oman was a Persian province. Exploring the Jabal Akhdar, the great central range of the peninsula that is visible far out to

---

[1] *Travels in Arabia*, by Lieut. J. R. Wellsted, 1838.
[2] *J.R.G.S.*, 1837, p. 21.   [3] *J.R.G.S.*, 1837, p. 102.

sea, Wellsted wrote : " From the summit of the Jabal Akhdar
I had an opportunity during a clear day to obtain an extensive
view of the desert to the south-west of Oman. Vast plains
of loose drift-sand, across which even the hardy Beduin dare
scarcely venture, spread out as far as the eye can reach. Not a
hill, nor even a change of colouring in the plains occurs to
break the unvarying and desolate appearance of the scene."
Such is the *Rub' al Khali*, the great central desert of Arabia,
which exceeds in its utter aridity the Lut, that dead heart
of Persia. Nearly a century was to elapse before its austere
desolation was to be explored by another Englishman.

Wellsted subsequently surveyed the fertile Batina, a coastal
area to the north of Maskat, and attempted to penetrate farther
west towards Nejd, but the Wahabis were hostile, and he had
to content himself with exploring the northern end of the
range which terminates in Ras Musandam or " the Anvil ".
I shall never forget this black sombre peak rising sheer from
the sea for thousands of feet, when I first entered the Persian
Gulf at full moon. Wellsted's explorations, which are not all
included in this brief sketch, were of the greatest importance
from the geographical point of view, while his knowledge of
the languages and of the ancient history of the country, his
sympathy for the wild tribesmen, and his calm courage mark
him out as one of the great explorers of Arabia. Among
the successors of Wellsted were Colonel Miles, who crossed
the Jabal Akhdar to the Dhahira district and penetrated to
Baraimi, and Sir Percy Cox, who in more than one journey
supplemented the work of his predecessors.

Nejd, inhabited by the virile Shammar tribe, was still
unknown to Europe, in spite of the excellent description given
by Ibn Battuta, when a Swede, George Wallin, a distinguished
Arabic scholar, decided to explore it. He was singularly well
equipped for collecting information on many subjects, but made
no attempt at even a compass route survey. Leaving Cairo
in 1845, Wallin penetrated to Maan, situated to the south-east
of the Dead Sea. He thence crossed the *Hamad* to Jauf, where
he lived for two months. From this northern oasis he undertook the passage of the dreaded *Nafud*, travelling by night
across a waterless stretch which took eighty-seven hours of
marching to accomplish. His account of the Jabal Shammar
with its capital Haïl are of great importance. He pronounces
an eloquent eulogy on Abdulla ibn Rashid, of whose hospitality,
justice and kindness to the poor he speaks in the highest terms.
From Haïl Wallin proceeded to Medina and Mecca.

In a second journey Wallin landed on the coast of Midian and made for Tabuk, situated a considerable distance to the south of Maan. From this centre he marched south-east to Talima, and thence reached Haïl, where he found that Abdulla was dead. From Haïl Wallin marched north-east across the desert to Meshedi Ali in Iraq, thus winning an honourable position in the roll of explorers of Arabia.

The search for Himyaritic texts brought Arnaud to Sanaa in 1843. He visited the ruins of Marib and of its famous dam, whose destruction early in the Christian era caused the migrations of Arab tribes. His journey in the Jauf district and his discovery of Himyaritic texts in number too great to cope with, brought Joseph Halévy to Yemen some thirty years later. This Jewish traveller explored towards Jauf. He was also the first European to visit Nejran since Gallus. He discovered the ancient city of Negrana in the ruins of Medinet-el-Khudud.

In Central Arabia, in 1862, Palgrave started on a journey into the interior from Maan. Of Jewish extraction on his father's side, he had served in the Indian army. He then became a Jesuit on Mount Lebanon, and not only learned Arabic well, but was able to hold his own with any *mulla* by quoting passages from the Koran and other authorities. The French Government, anxious for information as to the political situation in Central Arabia, supplied the funds for this important journey, during which Palgrave travelled as a learned doctor who was a Syrian Christian.

The explorer crossed the desert to the oasis of Jauf, and gives a vivid description of the dread simoom :

> " So dark was the atmosphere and so burning the heat, that it seemed that hell had risen from the earth, or descended from above. But we were yet in time, and at the moment when the worst of the concentrated poison-blast was coming around, we were already prostrate one and all within the tent, almost suffocated indeed, but safe ; while our camels lay without like dead, their long necks stretched out on the sand awaiting the passing of the gale."

On continuing his journey from Jauf, he describes the *Nafud.* " We were now traversing an immense ocean of loose reddish sand, unlimited to the eye, and heaped up in enormous ridges running parallel to each other from north to south, undulation after undulation each well two or three hundred feet in average height, with slant sides and rounded crests furrowed in every direction by the capricious gales of the desert." At Haïl, the pseudo-physician was received most kindly by Telal ibn Rashid, the Shammar Amir, to whom he, in due course, revealed his identity. After amassing much valuable information on political and other subjects, Palgrave, with marked courage, decided to continue his journey southwards to Riyadh, the capital of the fanatical Wahabis. At Buraida he found a large caravan composed of Persians and Indians returning from Mecca, whom the Wahabi governor Mohanna was engaged in blackmailing in the most outrageous manner. Palgrave told the story of a former caravan which had been taken into the desert and left to die of hunger and thirst by the treacherous Arabs under the son of the governor, who ultimately gained possession of the whole of their property. After this atrocious act of perfidy, no Persian or Indian had ventured to follow the route across Central Arabia for two years, and the treatment which the " enemies of Allah ", as the Wahabi fanatics termed them, were now suffering must have acted as a strong deterrent to future pilgrims.

By good fortune Palgrave met a caravan leader, Abu Isa, who was bound for Riyadh and Hasa. Their party was completed by the Persian *Naib* of the caravan, who was visiting the Amir Feisal " to state by word of mouth grievances too many and too serious to be entrusted to pen and ink ". While crossing the *Nafud* Palgrave writes :

> " A little before noon, and just as the sun's heat was becoming intolerable, we reached the verge of an immense crater-like hollow, certainly three or four miles in circumference, where the sand-billows receded on every side, and left in the midst a pit seven or even eight hundred feet in depth, at whose base we could discern a white gleam of limestone rock, and a small group of houses, trees, and gardens, thus capriciously isolated in the very heart of the desert."

This was the little village and oasis of Wasit. The subsequent ascent was a matter of extreme difficulty. " Camels and men fell and rolled back down the declivity," but at last the *Nafud* was crossed and " the wall-like steeps of Jabal Tuwaiq came into sight, the heart and central knot of Arabia ".

To take up the story of the Wahabis, as Palgrave found them, Feisal, who was a grandson of Abdulla the defender of Dariya, had restored the fallen fortunes of the Ibn Saud family and had made Riyadh his capital. To quote again from Palgrave's breezy narrative, " Christians, heretics, polytheists and infidels were surely enough to call down fire from heaven". As a preliminary measure to meet this menace, *Amir* Feisal " left the castle by the secret gate and buried himself in the recesses of a secluded garden ". The *Amir*, at first, decided to get rid of the physician, " packed with post-horse up to heaven ". However, gifts of *ood*, the famous scented wood of the eastern poet, judiciously distributed, resulted in a decision that Riyadh "did seriously stand in need of an Aesculapius ". Consequently Palgrave was able to commence a practice which brought him into close touch with various important personages. Indeed, as at Haïl, he amassed much valuable and interesting information. Finally, he made a deadly enemy by declining to give strychnine to Feisal's son Abdulla, with which he wished to poison his half-brother Saud, and he was glad to leave suddenly for Hasa, after spending fifty days at the Wahabi capital.

Palgrave reached Hasa without incident, and there, in a friendly society of citizens who detested the puritanical tyranny of Wahabism, we may take our leave. In view of the extent of unexplored country that he crossed, and the great risks he ran, taking also into consideration his profound knowledge of Arabic literature and of the language, Palgrave certainly ranks as one of the greatest of Arabian explorers. His brilliant literary talents may have to be set against his undoubted lack of accuracy in geographical matters, but it is only fair to remember that he was primarily sent on a political mission.

In 1875, Doughty, who had already travelled far and wide in Syria, appeared on the scene at Maan. There he heard of the existence of ancient monuments at Madain Salih, some 300 miles to the south on the pilgrim route. Unable to venture alone, he proceeded to Damascus and arranged to join the annual pilgrim caravan. In this manner he travelled to Madain Salih, along the route described by Varthema, and examined the rock-hewn tombs with Nabathean and Himyaritic inscriptions as far south as the oasis of Al-Ala. He then, in the guise of an English doctor, joining a tribe of Beduins, set out on his leisurely wanderings, making in the first instance for Teima. He wrote :

> "Delightful now was the green sight of Teima, the haven of our desert ; we approached the tall island of palms, enclosed by long clay orchard-walls, fortified with high towers. . . . Those lighthouse-like turrets, very well built of sun-dried brick, are from the insecure times before the government of Ibn Rashid. . . . We entered between grey orchard walls, overlaid with blossoming boughs of plum trees ; of how much amorous contentment to our parched eyes."[1]

In due course Doughty, known to the Arabs as "Khalil", found his way to Haïl. There he was received by Abdulla ibn

[1] *Arabia Deserta*, 1888. This edition was published by the Cambridge University Press, but permission for quotation has been given not only by that body but by the author's executors and by Messrs. Jonathan Cape.

Rashid, brother of Telal, who had protected Palgrave. The *Amir* was suspicious, and to test the explorer, he was given a great historical work, dealing with *Isa bin Miriam* or " Jesus the Son of Mary ", and was asked to read a certain line chosen at random. The passage happened to run : " The King slew all his brethren and kindred." At this " the *Amir* was visibly moved, and with the quick feeling of the Arabs, he knew that I regarded him as a murderous man ".

Doughty was expelled from Haïl with such intense hostility that he feared the worst. However, the *rafiq* [1] to whom he had been confided was trustworthy, and the explorer was able to make his way towards Khaibar. Upon approaching this district, he crossed a range of volcanic stones at an altitude of 6,000 feet.

On the following day he writes : " The vulcanic field is a stony flood which has stiffened ; long rolling heads, like horse-manes, of those slaggy waves ride and over-ride the rest : and as they are risen they stand petrified, many being sharply split lengthwise, and the hollow laps are partly fallen down in vast shells and in ruinous heaps as of massy masonry."

Upon reaching Khaibar, where he found that the Jewish colony mentioned by Varthema had disappeared, Doughty was arrested by the Turkish officer of the post and his books and papers were despatched to the Governor of Medina, who gave strict orders for his release and good treatment. After this experience, Doughty again started on his wanderings, but on arriving once more at Haïl, he was received with marked hostility and expelled. His conductors tried to murder him, and then to desert him, and at Buraida he was assaulted and robbed, but his property was restored.

Doughty found it advisable to leave Buraida for Anaiza, but his treacherous *rafiq* abandoned him on the way. However, he secured transport, and, upon reaching Anaiza, he was befriended by the Governor Zamil. There he remained, not without danger, until the annual " butter caravan " started for Mecca. Doughty, with remarkable courage, joined the caravan, but when he reached the last stage before Mecca, whence he proposed to make for Jedda, he was threatened by a fanatical *sharif* or " descendant of the Prophet ". He was in serious danger, but thanks to his calm courage and ready tongue, although robbed and beaten, he managed to reach

[1] *Rafiq* actually means your (camel) pillion-rider and so your friend who will loyally defend and guide you. From another point of view a *rafiq* may be described as a living passport to his own tribe.

Taif, where he was received most hospitably. His great journey was now coming to an end and, in August 1878, he bade farewell to Arabia in these words : " I beheld the white sea gleaming far under the sun, and tall ships riding, and minarets of the town ! In this plain I saw the last worsted booths of the Ishmaelites."

Doughty was not only a great explorer, but, better than any other European of his generation, he understood the mentality of the Arab. To read his *Arabia Deserta* is to travel with him, to learn much about its unstable, fanatical people, and to realize the truth of the saying quoted at the beginning of this chapter ; it will remain a classic for all time.

The last notable traveller of the nineteenth century in Arabia was the Frenchman Huber. Travelling from Damascus to Haïl, Huber not only secured the famous Teima stone, which Doughty had reported, but the copying of many inscriptions and his geographical work were of the greatest scientific value. Indeed we are still dependent on Huber's observations for certain centres and on his maps for large areas which have not since been revisited. From Haïl the explorer made for Anaiza and Jedda. When travelling into the interior from Rabegh, the gallant Huber was murdered. Well wrote the Arab poet :

> " I read the history of man, age after age
> And little find therein but treachery and slaughter.
> No pestilence, no fiend could inflict half the evil
> Or half the desolation that man brings on man."

CHAPTER XXXII

ARABIA—THE MIDDLE PHASE

" The Beduin could not look for God within him : he was too sure that he was within God. He could not conceive anything which was or was not God.

      *   *   *   *   *

The Bedu were odd people. They were absolute slaves of their appetite, with no stamina of mind, drunkards for coffee, milk or water, gluttons for stewed meat, shameless beggars of tobacco."

LAWRENCE.

AFTER the great period comprised in the previous chapter, there was a lull, which was but the prelude to a still greater period. In 1909, Carruthers [1] set out from Damascus to visit the blank that existed between the Hejaz Railway and the area to the east. His main object was to stalk that rare quarry, the Arabian oryx. Accompanied by a capable camel-dealer, he joined the Beni Sakhr tribe, and, while accompanying them on their migration, he purchased some dromedaries. Securing a *rafiq* of the Sherarat tribe, not without difficulty, he rode off to the south-east.

Entering the oasis of Teima, Carruthers was ordered by the Governor to quit it, and " escaping by night ", he rode due north, skirting the western edge of the *Nafud*. Then, marching north-west again, he found at the well of Bayer the ruins of a large *Khan* on the ancient route between Basra and Egypt. Desiccation had apparently caused this route to be abandoned. The explorer then returned to the tents of the Beni Sakhr, after having succeeded in his quest of the oryx, which Aristotle mentions as having but one horn and which is possibly the unicorn of the medieval legend. He had also made valuable additions to the geography of Arabia.

In 1913, Gertrude Bell,[2] already an experienced traveller, made an adventurous journey from Damascus to Haïl, traversing the country east of the Medina railway. She called in at Ziza, now the starting-point of the air route between Palestine and Iraq, where her faithful servant rejoined her, and then made for Tuba, to visit a palace of the Omayyid Caliphs.

[1] *G.J.*, Vol. XXXV., No. 3, March 1910.   [2] *G.J.*, Vol. LXII, No. 1, July 1927.

She was travelling in a land where raids were the order of the day, and was thankful to be able to avoid the wells, owing to the abundance of rainwater. Upon reaching Tubaiq, she was well received, and made her plans for the onward journey. She was advised to avoid Teima and to make for Haïl, cutting across the south-west corner of the *Nafud*. The party was held up by tribesmen, whose ungallant *Shaykh* demanded a revolver and a pair of Zeiss binoculars, and, having received them, tried to induce her *rafiq* to desert her and to halve the spoils. However, matters were arranged satisfactorily during the night, the *Nafud* was crossed in favourable weather, heavy rain hardening the sand, and in due course Haïl was reached.

At that time the Shammar tribe had been weakened by frequent assassinations in the Chief's family, and the Amir who was then ruling was absent on a raiding expedition. At first the English explorer was treated somewhat as a prisoner, and, as she wrote in her diary, " the place smells of blood ". However, in due course the period of forced seclusion came to an end, and Gertrude Bell was permitted to inspect the fortress and town of Haïl. There was, however, no question of her continuing her journey to Riyadh, and she returned north-east to the Euphrates.

Geographically, her journey was important, and later, during the Great War, to quote Sir Percy Cox, " the great experience she had of Arab traditions and Beduin customs, and the knowledge of individuals which she had gained in this and previous journeys, was an enormous asset to us all ".

Among the noted pre-war explorers of Arabia, Leachman [1] holds an honoured place. Possessing a remarkable gift for making friends with the Beduin, in 1911 he joined a section of the great Shammar tribe, which had crossed the Euphrates into Iraq, and accompanied them on their return migration to the neighbourhood of Hail. His section of the Shammar was attacked by the Roalla, owing to a misunderstanding, but Leachman managed to escape. At that time the great Anaza tribe was marching on Haïl to attack the Shammar. " Looking from an eminence, the desert as far as the eye could reach was a moving mass of Arabs . . . while in the middle on a picked dromedary was the ' Mirkab ' of the Roalla. This consists of a frame covered with black ostrich feathers, in which a maiden from the sheik's family rides in battle, exhorting the combatants to deeds of valour."

[1] " A Journey in North-Eastern Arabia ", by Captain G. E. Leachman, *G.J.*, Vol. XXXVII, March 1911.

On the march the road of Zubayda, mentioned by Ibn Battuta, was struck, and, some days later, the Anaza were surprised by the Shammar, who swept through their camp. Few casualties were inflicted, but Leachman wrote : " I was much struck by the fact that several Anaza women, in passing me in their flight from the camp, thrust upon me their silver ornaments for safe keeping, rather than entrust them to one of their own countrymen." Leachman, who was protected by a Shammar acquaintance, accompanied him to Ibn Rashid's camp and gave an account of the series of assassinations which had brought the Shammar tribe to a very low ebb. He was received by Saud, son of Abdul Aziz, who had been killed in battle by the Wahabi *Amir*, and writes : " Saud is a handsome little boy with beautiful features and very fair hair." He also comments on the lavish hospitality shown to guests, of whom there were seldom less than sixty or seventy. Leachman was not permitted to visit Haïl, and after accompanying the Shammar to the famous wells of Lina, situated on the pilgrim route between Medina and Najaf, he was ordered to leave the camp by the Regent Zamil and to join a caravan bound for Zobeir.

In 1912, Leachman undertook another important journey,[1] starting from Damascus with a party of " Ageyl ", privileged Arab traders of Kasim, who were returning to their homes, their privilege was soon proved, as, on being attacked near Dumeir, a village in the Damascus plain, by a section of the Roalla, the cry " Ageyl " saved the party.

In due course the explorer reached the wells of Lina for the second time and later saw the remarkable horse-shoe depression mentioned by Palgrave. Crossing the border between the Shammar and the Wahabis at Kusaiba, Saleh, his companion, ensured him a good reception at Ayun, where he posed as an inhabitant of Mosul. At Buraida, Leachman was not received too well, although he escaped the ill treatment suffered by Palgrave and Doughty. He then travelled to Shakra, the capital of Washm, and at Riyadh, Ibn Saud welcomed the English explorer. Leaving the Wahabi capital, Leachman was hospitably treated by the Turkish garrison of Hofuf and finally reached the coast at Oqair. The geographical importance of Leachman's journeys is evident, and the intimate knowledge he acquired of the politics and chiefs of Arabia were of the highest value to the British military authorities in Mesopotamia during the Great War.

[1] " A Journey through Central Arabia ", *G.J.*, Vol. XLIII, May 1914.

Among the well-equipped explorers of South-West Arabia was Wyman Bury, who surveyed the country to the east of the Aden protectorate, and also visited Sanaa. His book, *The Land of Uz*, contains a fascinating account of his many adventures and incidentally proves how intimately he knew the mentality of the various wild tribesmen among whom he travelled. He points out that no one of tribal origin may marry into non-combatant stock. There is an ancient saw: " Quoth Father Noah : the ploughman, the retainer and the slave, to each his female counterpart." Like most Englishmen, he appreciated the virile tribesmen and disliked the effeminate townspeople, while the hill girls " throw stones with a force and accuracy that commands respectful admiration ". There were few Englishmen who could rival the knowledge of " Abdullah Mansur," as he was termed, who certainly ranks among the noted explorers of South-West Arabia.

Among the explorers who perished in the Great War was Shakespear.[1] After serving at Bandar Abbas and Maskat, he was appointed Political Agent at Koweit in 1909, and for six years made journey after journey into the interior, filling up blanks in the map, making friends with the Chiefs and collecting information destined to be of the greatest value. Moreover, he discovered the first Sabaean inscriptions in North-East Arabia. These expeditions constituted admirable training for the journey he determined to make to Riyadh and thence across Arabia to the Gulf of Akaba.

Starting from Koweit in February 1914 with a well-equipped caravan, Shakespear marched south-west to the forty wells of Hafar, the site of the famous " Battle of the Chains ".[2] Following up the great valley, " old wells and traces of buildings " were noted, and traversing the sand-belts of the *Nafud*, the English explorer crossed the northern end of the Tuwaiq escarpment and looked down on Zilfi. From this important trade centre Shakespear rode to Riyadh, where he paid a visit to Ibn Saud, whom he already knew. From Riyadh he accompanied the Wahabi *Amir* on an expedition for some distance to the north. He then left the Wahabi camp and made for Shakra, the capital of Washm, where he struck Sadleir's route. At Anaiza, thanks to Ibn Saud, Shakespear had a most friendly reception by *Amir* Saleh, the son of

[1] " Captain Shakespear's Last Journey ", by Douglas Carruthers, *G.J.*, Vol. LIX, No. 5, May 1922.
[2] *Vide* Sykes, *History of Persia* (3rd ed.), Vol. I, p. 490.

Doughty's protector Zamil, and he notes that everyone spoke well of "Khalil". From Anaiza, Buraida was visited. There he made arrangements that enabled him to follow a new line to Jauf, and, during this section of twenty-nine days' travelling, he saw no village. At last he reached the edge of an escarpment and looked down upon Jauf, the most northern of the Arabian oases.

From Jauf, situated midway between Baghdad and Akaba, some 300 miles had to be crossed to the Sinai frontier. Serious troubles now began, each chief determining to pluck the traveller. Huweitat *rafiqs* promised safe escort to Akaba for £10, and then shamelessly guarded Shakespear only to the next section of their tribe. Auda, chief of the Abu Tayy section of the tribe, who was later Lawrence's stout henchman, proved the most avaricious of all, but he kept his word, and, under his guidance, Shakespear crossed "a smooth black basalt expanse, without a vestige of growth", for fourteen hours. Then came the storm-swept Tubaiq, where Gertrude Bell had preceded him. He struck the Hejaz railway south of Mudawara, later a scene of Lawrence's exploits, and avoiding a Turkish frontier patrol, the Egyptian police post of Kuntilla on the Gulf of Akaba was reached, after a journey which included 1,200 miles of unexplored country. Shakespear was killed in 1915 during an engagement between Ibn Saud and Ibn Rashid. But for his untimely death, he would have rendered more valuable services. In any case he was a great explorer of Arabia, and a worthy descendant of Sir Richmond Shakespear of Khiva fame.

No account of Arabia would be complete without mention of Lawrence, who, although his military exploits throw his geographical discoveries into the shade, yet travelled far and wide in Hejaz.

Lawrence had served under Hogarth, the eminent archaeologist and geographer, at the excavations of Carchemish on the Euphrates, and there gained his marvellous insight into the mentality of the Arabs which he turned to such good use when the Great War broke out. "Some Englishmen, of whom Kitchener was chief, believed that a rebellion of Arabs against Turks would enable England, while fighting Germany, simultaneously to defeat her ally Turkey." [1] Thus were laid the foundations of the revolt of the Arabs against the Turks. Lawrence as a junior member of the staff in Egypt visited Jedda, and was sent to examine the position of affairs at Feisal's

[1] *Seven Pillars of Wisdom*, by T. E. Shaw, 1926.

camp. Landing at Rabegh, he started off into the interior. He finally reached *Wadi* Safra and met *Amir* Feisal, now King of Iraq, for the first time. At this juncture the Arabs, badly equipped and fed, were demoralized by the artillery of the Turks. Munitions and supplies had been sent to Rabegh by the British, but the local chief had made up his mind that the Turks would be victorious and had appropriated them.

Lawrence returned to Feisal's camp only to see the Turks carry his position, and the whole demoralized force retreated to the coast at Yenbo, followed by the enemy. This port was hastily fortified and the Turks, alarmed by the number of warships and the searchlights, "turned back: and that night, I believe the Turks lost their war".

Lawrence realized that "if the revolt was to endure, we must invent a new plan of campaign at once". With British naval support, the base was removed north to Wejh, which was captured, and attacks were made on the Hejaz railway. Before long, Auda abu Tayyi, "came down to us like a knight-errant . . . The port of Akaba was naturally so strong that it could only be taken by surprise from inland." Lawrence and Auda decided to make the attempt, and started off on their great adventure. Their plan was to enrol tribesmen in Auda's neighbourhood for the operation. Crossing the railway, the adventurers reached Auda's area, where some 500 men were enrolled. Then recrossing the line, " we ruined ten bridges and finished our explosive ".

A Turkish battalion, which held the pass leading to Akaba, broke under a charge of camelry and surrendered, and finally " we raced through a driving sandstorm down to Akaba, four miles further, and splashed into the sea on July the sixth, just two months after setting out from Wejh ". This magnificent exploit brought the Arabs into contact with the British by land. Equally, it prevented the Turks from the railway at Maan using this port to threaten the right flank of the British.

Lawrence, needless to say, traversed much unknown country, and he discovered that the large *Wadi* of Taif, which starts from hills to the south-west, passes to the east of Mecca and keeping close to Medina, joins the *Wadi* Hamdh, which reaches the sea to the south of Wejh. Incidentally this proved that the main divide of the peninsula was situated inland from Taif. Much of the survey connected with this expedition was executed by Newcombe who had already in 1913–14 carried a survey across the Sinai Peninsula to Beersheba and connected it with surveys undertaken from Egypt. Woolley and

Lawrence were attached to this expedition as archaeologists. The old adage that connects progress with the powder-cart was certainly exemplified, so far as exploration was concerned, in Arabia, as in the neighbouring countries of Iraq and Persia, during the Great War.

CHAPTER XXXIII

ARABIA—THE FINAL PHASE

" And Ophir, and Havilah, and Jobab : all these were the
sons of Joktan. And their dwelling was from Mesha, as thou
goest unto Sephar, a mount of the east."

Genesis x. 29–30.

" C'est la désolation absolue, le grand triomphe incontesté
de la mort. Et là-dessus, tombe un si lourd, un si morne
soleil, qui ne parait fait que pour tuer en desséchant. . . .
Nous n'avions encore rien vu d'aussi sinistre ; on est là comme
dans les mondes finis, dépeuplés par le feu, qu'aucune rosée ne
fécondera plus."

PIERRE LOTI, *Le Désert.*

THE final period of exploration was the greatest. It is
dominated by two British explorers, Philby and Thomas.
The former may be said to have owed the first opportunity
vouchsafed to him for exploration in Arabia to the fortunes
of the Great War. In October 1917, the British being then
in occupation of Baghdad, it was decided to despatch a small
mission to Ibn Saud to study the actual situation in Central
Arabia, and to report, after conferring with him, as to the
manner and direction in which that potentate could render
us the most serviceable co-operation. Philby, then serving on
the Staff of Sir Percy Cox, was deputed to lead the mission, and
proceeding *via* Bahrein landed in November with Lieut.-Col.
Cunliffe-Owen and Lieut.-Col. Hamilton, at Oqair, the port of
the Hasa Province, bound for Ibn Saud's capital at Riyadh.[1]

Like other successful explorers Philby had a competent
knowledge of the language and of the country ; he had also
.made the most of his opportunities for studying the manners
and customs of the Arabs during his two years' service in
Mesopotamia. On quitting Hofuf, the capital of Hasa, for
the onward journey, Arab clothes were donned, " designed
at once for comfort and dignity ", as Pierre Loti once remarked,
and surveying the route as they proceeded, the Mission
reached Riyadh without incident.

Philby describes how, after the death of *Amir* Feisal, his
sons, Abdulla and Saud, as Palgrave foresaw, fought for the

[1] Vide *The Heart of Arabia*, by H. St. J. B. Philby, 1922.

throne. The former called in Muhammad ibn Rashid, the Shammar chief, who defeated and killed Saud in 1885, and then annexed the country, Abdulla dying a guest-prisoner at Haïl without issue. For some years Riyadh remained under the Shammar, Muhammad ibn Rashid dying and being succeeded by his nephew during this period. The usurpation was, however, challenged in 1900, when, supported by *Shaykh* Mubarik of Koweit, Abdur Rahman, a younger brother of *Amir* Feisal, attacked the Shammar Chief, and was defeated. Abdul Aziz, the eldest son of Abdur Rahman, thereupon decided to venture all on a desperate hazard. In 1901, with only 200 men whom he had gathered round him in Hasa, he approached Riyadh secretly, and, with a picked band of fifteen, he seized the house of the Governor close to the fort, where that individual slept for greater security. At dawn when the massive gates of the fort were opened, the daring adventurers killed the Governor and his guard, and Abdul Aziz was acclaimed by the astonished populace lord of the land of his fathers.

Ibn Rashid, who was supported by Turkish troops, was not prepared to accept the position uncontested, but in 1906 a decisive battle was fought in which the Shammar chief was slain. The descendants of Saud were found cowering among their baggage. Their lives were spared, but, with the Arab genius for nicknames, they were called *Al Araif* or " Lost Property recovered ", and by this name they are known to this day. Thus the victor, who had been trained by adversity and had learned much about British justice and power while residing at Koweit, re-established himself in the position of his forbears as ruler of Southern Nejd. As a religious leader, he has encouraged the spread of a stricter and more fanatical element of the Wahabi movement known as *Ikhwan* or " Brethren ", whom he specially utilizes as colonists on his frontiers. They are not agreeable neighbours, as, contrary to the Arab custom of sparing women and children in their raids, they massacre men, women and children, and glory in these cruel deeds.

During the course of his negotiations Philby speedily realized that the relations between Ibn Saud and King Husayn of Hejaz constituted the chief difficulty to any concerted action between the two rivals. He had expected that an officer representing the High Commissioner for Egypt would have joined him at Riyadh, from Hejaz. However, while residing at Riyadh Philby heard that King Husayn had refused to allow any British to enter Nejd from the west, on the grounds that the routes were unsafe. He thereupon decided to cross Arabia and to bring back the British representative to Riyadh.

On December 9, with a picked party of Ibn Saud's men and camels, Philby started on his journey, and visiting the ruins of Dariya, he lamented over its fall. The difficult Jabal Tuwaiq was crossed by the Sagta Pass, " between whose beetling crags and tumbled boulders a rough and narrow path descended precipitously to the plain below, zigzagging from ledge to ledge ". Philby studied his companions closely, and before long he learned their ideas on many subjects. One of the leaders of the party told him " in all seriousness and simplicity, that thunder is caused by the angels shouting and beating on their gongs among the clouds to precipitate the rain on places selected by God ".

The explorer was following the pilgrim route to Mecca and was travelling steadily to the south-west, surveying the country as he passed, marking its ranges and its drainage. He sums up his views : " While the main slope of the peninsula is from west to east, that is to say from the Hejaz Mountains towards the Persian Gulf, a central ridge running, so far as we can judge, in a north-easterly direction . . . creates a diversion."

Continuing the journey, on one occasion seeing distant riders, the guides marked " the brand-signs of Ibn Saud in the sand ; such is the simple desert method of communication . . . sufficient to proclaim the identity of travelling parties ". At last Taif was reached, with its striking four-storeyed buildings, and Philby was greeted with the good news of the capture of Jerusalem by Allenby. He then sat down to his Christmas dinner served on " a metal tray, whose snowy whiteness contrasted strangely with the brown mess of dusty rice boiled in dirty water to which we had grown accustomed in the desert ". Philby proceeded to Jedda, where he met King Husayn, but that monarch utterly declined to co-operate with Ibn Saud, and some six years later the Wahabi *Amir* conquered Hejaz and King Husayn fled with his treasure.

Philby returned to Arabia *via* Bombay and Basra, and gives an interesting account of his visit to the somewhat unreliable Arab chiefs to the west of Basra, who were being paid by the British to prevent supplies reaching the enemy. The party then turned towards Riyadh, and on the way met a party of the mysterious Saluba, "a race apart, assimilated by environment to the Arabs, but not of them. . . . They are not ashamed of the current myth, which regards them as the surviving relic of some Christian tribe of the past. They are the tinkers and smiths of the nomad community, and as such indispensable." Crossing Summan and the Dahana, which had already been traversed in the former march to Riyadh, Philby finally, on April 11, 1918, reached the camp of Ibn Saud, and in due course accompanied him back to his capital.

In the spring of 1918, Philby started off on a journey to the unexplored districts of Southern Nejd. Passing the ruins of Manfuha, once the rival of the early Wahabi *Amirs*, he entered an arid *Wadi*, which, according to local tradition, was formerly dotted with fertile oases, and Philby inclines to the theory that a devastating flood was the probable cause of the change from fertility to sterility. Actually he heard of a recent flood in the Dawasir *Wadi*, which had carried away 150 human beings and countless sheep.

On this journey the first stage was Hair, with its palm groves cultivated by Bani Khodhir of negro extraction. Thence he came to the district of Kharj, where he saw the Persian *kariz* [1]; he also found the Persian name Firzan. Some miles to the east lay the once important city of Yamama, now a struggling village which was undoubtedly destroyed by flood action. From Kharj three days' journey due south led to Aflaj, with Laila its chief centre, and here were not only six great pools, but also a lake, " the like of which probably exists nowhere in Arabia ". In this oasis the local tradition recognizes the ruins as " one of the great cities of the kingdom of Ad, son of Shaddad ". The most southern point of the journey was reached at Sulaiyil in the *Wadi* Dawasir, famous for its beauty. From this centre Philby was informed that it was only seven days' travel to Najran in Yemen. During this journey fanatical hostility was only displayed at the village of Tamra, but fortunately there was no bloodshed, the " irreconcilables headed by the Wahabi prelate retiring temporarily into the desert ". Philby reached the edge of the *Rub' al Khali*, some 300 miles south of Riyadh, and, as Hogarth put it, " thanks entirely to his journeys, Southern Nejd, a very large area, is now about as well known to us as was any part of Arabia before the war ".[2]

Among the unexplored areas of Arabia was the district of Asir, which roughly stretches along the coast of the Red

---

[1] A *kariz* is an underground irrigation channel.
[2] *G.J.*, Vol. LV, No. 6.

Sea for some 250 miles north of Hodeida, while inland its boundaries are formed by the ranges of mountains that constitute the watershed of Hejaz. In November 1922 Rosita Forbes [1] landed at Jizan, after fourteen days' sail in a *dhow* from Port Sudan, to make a reconnaissance in Asir. She found herself among a fanatical population : "No strangers, whether Moslem, Christian or Jew, are allowed in Asir, and under its *Amir*, the puritanical precepts of the Senussi are observed most rigidly."

Thanks to an introduction to the *Amir*, Sabya, which, with the surrounding villages, has a population of 20,000 inhabitants, was visited, and the new quarter, containing some large houses, was inspected. The founder of the Idrisi sect, *Sayyid* Ahmad-al-Idrisi, is buried at Sabya. Later the journey was continued southwards to Hodeida. The English explorer was able to describe the guard of the *Amir*—" picked men from Abu Kish and Sabya . . . small of stature, lithe and hipless, olive-skinned, fine regular features with long noses and good foreheads. . . . Further inland the features coarsen, and we saw men from Jabal Huras who were like savages of Central Africa. . . . The intense hatred of strangers, which made our journey from village to village a succession of minor fights," must have constituted a serious state of affairs, and a tribute is certainly due to the gallant Englishwoman who raised a corner of the curtain concealing Asir.

No account of Arabia would be complete without some mention of Eldon Rutter, who, after studying among the Arabs of Malaya, and later in Egypt, felt himself prepared to undertake the pilgrimage to Mecca. [2]

In 1925, garbed as an Egyptian *Effendi*, Rutter took a passage in a *dhow* at Massawa. Mixing with fellow-pilgrims, with whom he was perfectly at home, he landed at the tiny port of El Gahm in Asir. The direct route was closed at this period owing to the fact that Jedda was being besieged by Ibn Saud. Crossing an unexplored section of the *Tihama*, Rutter in due course reached Mecca, and gives a most vivid description of the religious ceremonies, of the *Kaaba* and of its slave-market. He spent several months in Mecca, where he was received with courtesy by Ibn Saud, and his descriptions of that virile conqueror and of the Wahabis are among the most valuable in his book. After a residence of seven

---

[1] "A Visit to the Idrisi Territory in Asir and Yemen", *G.J.*, Vol. LXII, 1923, p. 271.
[2] *The Holy Cities of Arabia*, by Eldon Rutter, 1928.

months at Mecca, Medina surrendered to Ibn Saud, and Rutter, in spite of illness, completed the objectives of his journey by a visit to Medina. To quote one of his word pictures : " To the Badawi the empty desert is as full of interest as the English countryside is to ourselves. He rides hither and thither in it all his life, searching among the hot stones for pasturage for his camels."

In 1922, Philby, who was then in political charge of Trans-Jordania, and Holt,[1] who was anxious to examine the North Arabian desert with a view to ascertaining its possibilities for railway construction, visited Jauf. In a first attempt made with cars, they reached Kaf, situated near the head of the *Wadi* Sirhan, hoping to be able to arrange for camels and an escort for the onward journey. Philby was desirous of investigating the political situation at the great northern oasis, which was especially interesting owing to the fact that Ibn Saud, who had slain the Shammar Chief and annexed Haïl, had determined to add Jauf to his conquests.

Philby's first attempt ended in failure at Kat, but in May, upon receipt of an invitation from the grandson of Nuri ibn Sha'lan, the Ruler of Jauf, the explorers returned to Kat. There, after much hard bargaining, the party resumed its march ; albeit the situation at Jauf was distinctly unsettled with a rebel holding one part of the oasis in the interests of Ibn Saud. Actually, the travellers just missed a Wahabi force which, camping at a neighbouring well, attacked the Sha'lan near Kat only to be decisively beaten. Having " by a series of flukes missed several opportunities of disaster ", Philby entered Jauf on May 20, where the " slave governor was one of the most attractive personalities I have ever met in Arab lands ". He refused a cash present, but was anxious to be provided with a good poison !

From Jauf, the explorers decided to cross the desert to Karbala, and after visiting Sakaka, where the siege was being pursued in the leisurely Arab fashion under the grandson of Nuri, they left Jauf without regret on June 2. Throughout this stage of the journey there was imminent risk of attack, although actually they were the attackers on the only occasion in which Beduin were sighted. Finally, Karbala was reached, after an adventurous journey, and, early in July, Ibn Saud took possession of Jauf.

[1] " Jauf and the North Arabia Desert ", by H. St. J. Philby ; and " The Future of the North Arabian Desert ", by Major A. L. Holt, *G.J.*, Vol. LXII, No. 4, October 1923.

We now come to the conquest of the *Rub' al Khali*, the greatest feat of exploration in Arabia. The " Empty Quarter " of Arabia signifies the immense desert which lies between Oman and Yemen. The huge unexplored area of some 300,000 square miles has hitherto been protected by its aridity, but even more perhaps by the fanatical hostility of the Beduins, determined to prevent the curtain of their beloved land from being raised, and ready at all times to die in defence of its brackish water-holes and scanty grazing-grounds.

Among the recent travellers in Arabia to reach the *Rub' al Khali* is Cheesman,[1] whose main object was to investigate the distribution of resident birds and the movement of migrants through the Great Sand Desert. He had already made a journey along the coast from Oqair to the ruins of Salwa. Thanks to Sir Percy Cox, an invitation from Ibn Saud was secured and the explorer landed for a second time at Oqair; on this occasion, while searching for specimens, " a series of mounds strewn with a litter of blue pottery reminded me of the ruin-fields of Babylonia. . . . Mounds of rubble and lines of mounds radiated in all directions." Here then was the probable site of the ancient port of Gerra. Nor does the modern name Oqair, pronounced Ojair, fail to support this identification.

After a somewhat long delay at Hofuf, waiting for news of rain having fallen in the south, in February 1924 the expedition marched off under the guidance of a Murra tribesman, Saleh by name, whose knowledge of desert craft was amazing. Two short stages brought the caravan to the Zarnuga wells, an important centre of the Murra, who were a tribe of pre-Arab origin and recent converts to Islam. Six waterless marches southwards were now crossed to Jabrin. Along the route were sand-dunes, which could, however, be generally avoided by keeping a little to the west, where there was a bare gravel plain.

Cheesman was received with politeness owing to the orders of Ibn Saud, albeit the Murra chief, being a recent convert to the fanatical Ikhwan sect, naturally disliked entertaining a Christian. Saleh, who referred to the desert as *Al Rimal* or " The Sands ", stated that his tribe wandered as far as Maqainma some 120 miles to the south, and that he knew of tribesmen who had traversed the desert to Najran

---

[1] " The Deserts of Jafura and Jabrin ", by Major R. E. Cheesman, *G.J.*, Vol. LXV, p. 112.

in Yemen, which was considered to be a month's journey. Cheesman had blazed the trail for his successors.

At long last the *Rub' al Khali* was destined to be crossed by one British explorer, Bertram Thomas,[1] from south to north, and by another, Philby, in part, from east to west. Thomas had served for thirteen years in Iraq, Trans-Jordania and Oman, and had studied the language, the dialects and the customs of the dwellers in the desert. At this period, he had served for six years as *Vizier* to the progressive Sultan of Maskat, and had thus gained indispensable contact with the Chiefs of his kingdom. Owing to the constant support of His Highness, coupled with his own deep knowledge of and sympathy for the Arab point of view, a spirit of tolerance towards the Christian *Vizier* had gradually been created, without which exploration off the beaten track would have been impossible. Thomas also realized that although Dhufar belonged to Maskat, the tribesmen beyond the Qara Mountains were as wild as hawks and that this state of affairs was the normal position at any distance from the capital.

Thomas started on his first journey, in which, as was his invariable rule, strict secrecy was observed, in December 1928, and landed at a little port to the south of Ras al Had with the intention of marching through the southern borderlands to Dhufar. His only predecessors had been Wellsted and Bent, who had visited the Dhufar Mountains in the early 'nineties. "Between lay a stretch of 500 miles untrodden by a European. Assuming Arab dress, wearing a beard, foregoing tobacco and alcohol and sharing the life of my Badawi, these were I knew the most hopeful paths."[2] Thomas was well received by the *Amir* of the Beni Bu Ali, whose predecessor had also treated Wellsted hospitably. The tribesmen are of the Wahabi faith, and used a currency struck by local Persian governors in the eighteenth century.

After meeting numerous objections the *Amir* arranged a party to escort the explorer as far as Khaluf, situated one-third of the distance to Dhufar. At this little port the inhabitants were, at first, hostile, but gradually, by tact and by gifts, camels and escort were forthcoming for the onward journey. In due course the frankincense country was approached, and in the *Wadi* Andhaur some rude Himyaritic characters were found, scrawled upon stones. A party from Dhufar now

---

[1] *Arabia Felix*, by Bertram Thomas, 1932.
[2] "The South-Eastern Borderlands of *Rub' al Khali*", by Bertram Thomas, *G.J.*, Vol. LXXIII, No. 3, March 1929.

appeared, and at Salala, its capital, this preliminary journey came to a most successful conclusion.

In 1929, thanks to the presence of the Sultan in Dhufar, Thomas was able to organize an expedition to the fringe of the sands of the *Rub' al Khali*.[1] Under the guidance of the chief of the Kathir tribe, who provided an escort of twenty-five camelry and three *rafiqs*, the explorer crossed the well-watered Qara range, and in the desolate *wadi* beds to the north found the frankincense tree. "In appearance it is a young sapling having almost no central trunk, but from near the ground there springs out a clump of branches which grow to a camel's height and more, with ash-coloured bark and tiny crumpled leaves. . . . It is found growing as a commercial crop, only in Central South Arabia between 2,000 and 2,500 feet in a region which happens to be identical with the territorial limits of the Qara tribe." This then is the region from which came the celebrated gum, and, as Thomas states: "it was burned before the tabernacle of the Israelites in the days of Moses, the hill of frankincense is mentioned in the *Song of Solomon*, and it was brought as a gift, with gold and myrrh, to our Infant Lord". In view of this priceless product, belief that Dhufar was the Ophir of antiquity and the mart for ivory and peacocks' feathers is much strengthened. In any case, the peacocks must have been imported from India, and on this account a port is clearly indicated.

Upon reaching the vicinity of Ar-Rimal, or "The Sands", as the desert is termed by its inhabitants, there was much fear of raiding parties, but Thomas had exceptionally good luck throughout. At the springs of Al Ain sandgrouse were bagged and mosquitoes became a pest, and from this stage a short excursion was made into the desert.

During the return journey near Aduwab, "the neighbourhood provided us with a mixed bag of fossils and snakes. There were nests of large sandstone oysters, all presumably of the same kind." Bertram Thomas had thus prepared the ground not only by undertaking these two journeys but also by the relations he established with the Kathiri and Rashidi Beduin.

Bertram Thomas landed once again at Dhufar in October 1930. In his second journey he had given a rich reward to Sahail the Rashidi, who had secretly pledged himself to meet the explorer with a camel party, ready to guide him into the

[1] "A Journey into. *Rub' al Khali*", by Bertram Thomas, *G.J.*, Vol. LXXVII, No. 1, January 1931.

"Empty Quarter". But of Sahail there was no news, whereas there was war between the Rashidi and the Sa'ar of the Northern Hadramaut. The outlook was thus most gloomy, and the only hope lay in two Rashidi tribesmen, who had arrived at Dhufar for the frankincense harvest. Accordingly Thomas unfolded his plans to these men under their sworn oath and, to gain a rich reward, they promised to seek out the Rashidi and give the message.

Six weeks were spent in exploring the Qara range when one morning after his return to Salala "forty dainty riding camels and as many ragged Beduins" appeared on the scene at Dhufar. After many days spent in negotiations, *Shaykh* Salih their leader, who stated frankly that only avarice had brought his men, swore to accompany the explorer throughout his journey and to work to ensure the co-operation of the neighbouring Murra, whose territory extended to the northern limit of the desert, as Cheesman had proved. This weighty question having been settled, rations were arranged for forty men in four relays, and on December 1, 1930, Bertram Thomas started from Dhufar on a journey of 700 miles across Arabia. The direction at first lay northwards over the Qara range to Shisur, six marches to the north. So far Thomas was following his former route; he now marched north-west. Salih had already gone ahead to enlist the services of the Murra *rafiq*, Hamid bin Hadi, who alone knew the route through the heart of the sands. Shortly afterwards, "we were floundering through heavy dunes when the silence was suddenly broken by a loud droning on a musical note. I was startled for the moment, not knowing the cause. 'Listen to the cliff bellowing, Sahib!' and a man at my side pointed to a sand cliff a hundred feet or so high. . . . The noise continued for about two minutes and, like a ship's fog signal, ended as abruptly as it had begun." This was, of course, another instance of the famous "music of the sands".

The route then ran through the Uruq Dhaheya, "a great immensity of dune country. Vast ridges rise to towering heights; about them are precipitous gorges. Again and again we were driven to dismount and to scoop footholds with our hands in the soft yielding slope, so that the camels could climb." At the Khor Dhahiya, *Shaykh* Salih was not to be found, but, on the following day, "the footmarks of the Murra guide and his camel were identified in the sands by the Badus, and a little later those of other Rashidis, including *Shaykh* Salih. A *Badu* knows the impression of every man and camel of his tribe and many of his enemies'. . . . . The sands are a public diary."

Changing his camels and escort at the grazing-ground, under the guidance of Hamad bin Hadi, Thomas marched due north to the sands of Dakaka, lying at an average altitude of 900 feet—the invaluable Salih going ahead to arrange for a third relay of camels and men to be ready at Shanna, a deep waterhole in Western Dakaka. To quote again : " Lying inside the great dune bulwark of the southern borderlands, Dakaka consists of these wide, sweeping red sandscapes of hardest sand with low dunes running in all directions. It falls in altitude from probably 1,100 feet in the south to 785 feet hereabouts, and its long axis runs east-north-east for a seven days' march."

At Shanna, thanks to rains of the previous year, Thomas was able to secure good camels for the last stage. He also recruited a valuable guide, who had already crossed the sands from Qatar that year, and who knew the grazing grounds of the *Ikhwan* in the Jiban, the coastal area at the neck of the Qatar peninsula. Shanna was the most southerly stage reached by Philby in 1932.

After Dakaka came Suwahib, " one of the most extensive regions in the sands ". Here a route was followed to the north-east to escape massacre at the hands of fanatical *Ikhwan* tribesmen. For similar reasons of prudence, contact with travellers or with grazing patties was also avoided.

At Banaiyan the northernmost limit of the desert had been reached, and the explorer had only a section of 100 miles to traverse. Fortunately the *Ikhwan* had retreated to distant oases " to observe the fast of Ramazan in the bosom of their families ". Thus the way lay open to the sea, and, at Doha, in the peninsula of Qatar, Bertram Thomas reached the Persian Gulf on February 5, 1931, having crossed the *Rub' al Khali*.

It is difficult to express adequately the greatness of this achievement. The thoroughness of preparation included not only a knowledge of surveying, of geology, of photography and of natural history, but a long study of the language and its dialects, its history and that of the tribes, the manners and customs of the Arabs. Above all, the physical fitness and hardihood of the explorer were remarkable. Bertram Thomas owed much to the support of the Sultan of Maskat, but, once he had entered the *Rub' al Khali*, the success of the expedition depended on his being able to keep the Arabs loyal to the oath sworn by Salih. Unless he had displayed qualities that the Arabs

A SMALL AL-MURRA ENCAMPMENT

(From Bertram Thomas's Arabia Felix, by permission of Messrs. Jonathan Cape & Co.)

admired, they would, in all probability, have murdered him for his wealth, all the more so, as he never concealed the fact that he was a Christian, and was thus liable to be killed as a *Kafir*. No living explorer has prepared himself more thoroughly for a great task and none has achieved greater success.

"Few men", writes Lawrence, "are able to close an epoch. We cannot know the first man who walked the inviolate earth for newness' sake: but Bertram Thomas is the last; and he did his journey in the antique way, by pain of his camel's legs, single-handed, at his own time and cost."

Apart from his feat as an explorer, Thomas discovered "the entire southern borderlands of the Great Desert stretching between latitude 57° 45′ E., and latitude 52° 00′ E., and the mountains of the central south, to be peopled by a 'bloc' of ancient pre-Arab remainders, troglodytes for a large part, speaking pre-Arab languages. Ancient quarries in their mountains, the mountains of Dhufar (also the great frankincense country), are traditionally held to be ancient gold diggings."[1] Not content with his own observations, he made systematic measurements which, on the authority of Sir Arthur Keith, proved "that they represent a residue of the population of South Arabia before the familiar Arab came in".

With this extremely important discovery to guide us, it would perhaps be convenient to discuss the passage quoted from Genesis. It is clear that Dhufar is the biblical Ophir, the Sephar of the motto and the Supphur of Ptolemy. Ophir and Havilah are mentioned together, while "the land of Havilah, where there is gold", is referred to in Genesis ii. In view of the gold diggings in the Qara Mountains, it may be accepted that Havilah was also situated in the south of Arabia. Finally Hazarmaveth, described as a son of Joktan, is undoubtedly Hadramaut, and Mesha is the Mesech of Ezekiel.

Again, Thomas proves by reference to Qazwini and Yakut, who flourished in the thirteenth century, that this great southern tract was known as Ubar, a later form of which is Philby's Wabar. Finally, Thomas suggests with much force that Ubar and the Hebrew Ophir are identical.

To approach the question from the ethnological side, "the sons of Joktan" may be identified with the Shahara tribe, considered to be the most ancient in Arabia. To-day a mere remnant inhabits the Qara Mountains, but among its

[1] "Ubar—The Atlantis of the Sands of *Rub' al Khali*", by Bertram Thomas, *Journal of the Royal Central Asian Society*, Vol. XX, Part II, April 1933.

divisions we find Qutun and Jabob which may perhaps be identified with Joktan and Jobab.

The *Rub' al Khali* had been crossed by one great British explorer, and on January 7, 1932, Philby,[1] who had long prepared himself for the expedition, started from Hofuf with a picked party of men and camels. The power and influence of Ibn Saud were at his back, and the instructions of the Governor of Hofuf to his guide ran : " You will go to Wabar if you can find it. And you will do as this man wishes as you value your life, and you will answer to me for him. Now go in the keeping of Allah." I would add that Philby was a convert to Islam, which fact strengthened his position among the fanatical Arabs.

At the wells of Dulaiqiya outside Hofuf, Philby found thirty-two picked camels in the pink of condition, and nineteen men, six of whom belonged to the Murra tribe in whose territory the journey lay throughout. The expedition then crossed the Jafura Desert in bitter cold, and, following in the tracks of Cheesman, reached the oasis of Jabrin. The unknown country was struck south of Jabrin, which was left on January 31, and in three stages, the well of Maqainama, situated in a strip of gravel dividing the limestone steppe from Ar-Rimal, or " The Sands," was reached. Near this well Philby found a bronze arrow-head, while the deeply-scored caravan tracks running westwards and eastwards suggested the ancient caravan route which may have run from Gerra to Mecca. Continuing the journey eastwards to Bir Fadhil and then southwards, freshwater shells and flint implements were collected " from a vast deposit which evidently represented the site of an old Neolithic period and date back to a period when there was permanent water in this arid desert ".

For years Philby had heard of Wabar, the capital of King 'Ad, which, according to the Arab belief, had been destroyed by fire from heaven as a punishment for wickedness. The modern Beduin had reported an iron block " big as a camel ".

To quote Philby :

" I had resolutely persuaded myself that at the very best we should possibly find the remains of such broken-down forts as are still to be seen at Jabrin. But what I did see from that hill-top simply took my breath away, and I scarcely knew whether to laugh or weep. . . . I looked down not on the ruins of a city, but into the open mouth of what I took to be a volcano with twin craters side by side surrounded by low walls of what looked like outpoured slag and lava. And that

---

[1] " *Rub'-al-Khali* ", by H. St. J. Philby, *G.J.*, Vol. LXXXI, No. 1, January 1933.

was the Wabar of which I had heard and dreamed so much all these many years." [1]

Actually Philby had discovered two distinct craters, the larger circular in outline with a diameter of some 300 and a depth of some 30 feet. Isolated patches suggested the existence of other craters buried beneath the sand. The piece of iron " as big as a camel " proved to be a much rusted mass of meteoric iron weighing only twenty-five pounds. Wabar, as he found it, was caused by the impact of a shower of meteorites. In view of the exaggeration to which Arabs are especially prone, it is not difficult to realize how the fall of a huge meteorite would in due course become a legend of the dramatic destruction by fire from heaven of the city of Ad. On the other hand Thomas, whose informants were perhaps more reliable, spoke of *Umm al Hadid* or the " Mother of Iron ".

From Shanna, Philby's " Farthest South ", he made the decision to cross the unexplored waterless desert to Sulayil in the Dawasir Oasis—a distance of some 360 miles. On February 22 the march westwards was begun, but the country was drought-stricken and the camels broke down. To proceed would have been madness, and so it was decided to retreat, the camels being given doses of water through the nose for the sake of economy. Then the situation was suddenly changed by a providential fall of rain

With grim determination Philby induced his discouraged Arabs to make another attempt, and, on March 5, the venture was undertaken with picked men and camels For six days they marched long stages, and again the camels were exhausted : " It was pitiable to see their ugly pessimistic faces as they stood or sat round us without making the slightest effort to prospect for forage." On March 11, the camels were driven from 2 a.m. to 9 p.m. " Never had I seen Arabs drive camels as they drove that day, never have I seen camels on the borderland of starvation march as those camels marched."

The worst was now passed, the uplands of Tuwaiq were sighted, grazing was found and animal life began to reappear. At last the *Wadi* Dawasir was reached. The *Rub' al Khali* had been crossed for the first time, in its most waterless section from east to west, and a journey of 1,800 miles had been accomplished in ninety days—a magnificent achievement.

---

[1] " *Rub' al Khali* ", by H. St. J. Philby, *Journal of the Royal Central Asian Society*, Vol. XIX, October 1932. I have also consulted *The Empty Quarter*, 1933, by the same author, which was published after this chapter had been printed.

By the journey of these two great British explorers, the veil that hid the *Rub' al Khali* from the world has been rent not once but twice, and the word *Finis* has been written on land exploration in the old sense of the world. The last of the great unknown areas of the inhabited globe has been conquered. Furthermore it is a subject of intense satisfaction that both explorers, after training for long years, have earned success while travelling on camels and using Beduins as their guides. Finally, it is remarkable that Southern Arabia, which is described in the motto from the book of Genesis, should have been the last country in the world to be explored.

CHAPTER XXXIV

THE EXPLORERS OF THE ARCTIC

" Beyond this flood a frozen continent
Lies dark and wild, beat with perpetual storms
Of whirlwind and dire hail, which on firm land
Thaws not, but gathers heap, and ruin seems
Of ancient pile ; all else deep snow and ice,
A gulf profound as that Serbonian bog
Betwixt Damiata and Mount Casius old,
Where armies whole have sunk ; the parching air
Burns frore, and cold performs th' effect of fire."
MILTON, *Paradise Lost.*

THE heroic attempts of English and Dutch navigators to discover the North-East and North-West Passages to the Spice Islands during the sixteenth and seventeenth centuries have been described in Chapter XVI. The commercial and political necessity for these efforts ceased with the decay of Spain and Portugal and the consequent opening up of the ocean routes to India and the Spice Islands by England and Holland. However, the discovery by Bering in 1728 that the continents of America and Asia were divided by the Strait referred to in Chapter XIX, reawakened British interest in possible Arctic routes.[1]

Consequently Captain Cook in his third voyage was instructed to continue the quest for the North-West Passage, and he penetrated beyond Bering Strait eastwards to Icy Cape. Later, towards the end of the eighteenth century, Vancouver's surveys proved that there was no North-West Passage to be found below the Arctic Circle.

The final victory of Great Britain in the Napoleonic Wars released a number of highly experienced naval officers, and, thanks to the support of the far-sighted Secretary of the Admiralty, Sir John Barrow, the quest of the North-West Passage was resumed as a scientific exploration to be conducted on systemmatic lines. Frobisher, Davis, Hudson and Baffin had already penetrated far into the Arctic and pointed the way. The latter navigator, more especially, sailing across

---

[1] The author has merely crossed the Arctic circle as a passenger, and consequently Mr. J. M. Wordie's help in this chapter has been especially valuable.

Baffin Bay, had discovered Lancaster Sound, and had thus marked out the true route to be followed.

The first explorers of this great period were John Ross and Parry. The latter reached Lancaster Sound in 1818; and Ross had concluded, without due examination, that it was landlocked, but Parry did not agree. In 1819, selected to command a new expedition in the *Hecla* and *Griper*, Parry reached Lancaster Sound in August and discovered a wide channel leading to the west between lofty cliffs. Discovery followed discovery, and, naming a great strait after Barrow, the explorers, sailing ever westwards, coasted the south edge of Melville Island, where the bounty of £5,000, promised by the British Government for crossing longitude 110° W., was won. In September the ice began to form, and the expedition wintered at Melville Island. In the following summer Parry led the first naval land party with its supplies loaded on a cart which broke down. However, unlike the lifeless Antarctic, game was abundant and, after a journey lasting a fortnight, the explorers returned to their base. When the ice broke up, Parry continued his voyage westwards but, meeting with impenetrable ice-fields, he returned to England, having practically proved the existence of a connection between the two oceans. This expedition ranks among the greatest of Arctic voyages.

It was followed by almost annual voyages to the Arctic, and slowly but surely the huge area lying to the North-West was explored, Parry himself making three more voyages. In 1829, Ross and his nephew James Clark Ross—the latter had accompanied Parry—penetrated to Prince Regent Inlet, and, sailing southwards towards an unexplored land, named it Boothia. There winter quarters were established, and, by the help of Eskimos, who supplied him with dog teams, James Ross made a great journey. He first crossed the Isthmus of Boothia, and then, turning northwards across unexplored country, which was named King William Land, he termed its northern point Cape Felix. On a second journey he hoisted the British flag at the magnetic pole. Unable to extricate the ships, after spending four winters in the Arctic, the party made their way to Lancaster Sound, where they were rescued by the *Isabella* whaler. John Ross thus retrieved his reputation, while James Ross won distinction and promotion.

To turn to land journeys, the exploration of the Coppermine and Mackenzie Rivers to the Arctic Ocean has already been described in Chapter XXI. In 1819 Franklin, with

Richardson as naturalist and Hood and Back as midshipmen, sailing from England in a merchant-vessel, landed at York Factory in Hudson Bay, and proceeded to Fort Chipewyan early in 1820. Thence, following in Hearne's track, the party reached the mouth of the Coppermine River, and in their frail bark canoes explored the coast eastwards for nearly 500 miles to Cape Turnagain. Franklin decided to land at a river, which he named Hood River, and, after a tragic struggle with starvation, the lives of Franklin and Richardson were saved by Back, who met some Indians and sent them to rescue his comrades.

In 1825 the intrepid Franklin, Richardson and Back undertook a second expedition. Starting their land journey from New York they made for the Great Slave Lake and then proceeded to the Mackenzie River. Descending it to Fort Norman, situated in latitude 65°, Back went east to build winter quarters on the Great Bear Lake, while Franklin followed down the Mackenzie to its mouth and then returned to Fort Franklin for the winter. Starting off again in June 1826, the party descended to the delta of the Mackenzie River, where Franklin and Back explored the coast westwards for some four hundred miles.

At this time Beechey, following Cook, had reached Point Barrow, about 150 miles beyond Icy Cape. The two explorers were 160 miles apart, and consequently did not meet. Meanwhile Franklin's second party under Richardson travelled eastwards to the Coppermine River, sighting Wollaston Land to the north. The expedition returned to England in 1827, after an absence of over two years, during which they had surveyed more than 1,000 miles of coast-line. No other explorer has two such magnificent journeys to his credit.

In 1833 Back led a party to succour the Ross expedition, of which there had been no news for some years. From the Great Slave Lake the explorers proceeded down the Great Fish River, with its numerous falls and cascades involving constant portages. Back built two boats, to meet the special conditions, and reached the estuary of the river, which is also known as Back's River. Hearing the good news that the Ross expedition had been rescued, he explored the coast westwards to Cape Richardson, thus completing the exploration of that section of the coast of Northern Canada.

Such was the position in the Arctic when, in 1845 Franklin, no longer young, was appointed to lead an expedition of about 120 men in the *Erebus* and *Terror* to complete the task of previous explorers, and navigate the North-West Passage. The winter of 1845–6 was spent on Beechey Island, and, when free from the ice, he sailed south down Peel Sound. To quote Markham :

> "It was all open to the south. If they had continued on their southerly course, the two ships would have reached Bering Strait. . . . But alas ! the chart-makers had drawn an isthmus (which only existed in their imagination), connecting Boothia and King William Island. . . . They altered course to the west and were lost, for they were soon beset in that mighty ice-pack which flows down from the great polar ocean and impinges on the north-west coast of King William Land." [1]

After spending a second winter locked in the pack ice, in the spring of 1847 a land party under Graham Gore advanced towards Cape Herschel and thus forged the last link in the North-West Passage. Franklin's expedition ended in tragedy ; the ships were abandoned in 1848, and the parties which made for Back's Fish River all perished.

The nation was moved at the disaster when it was too late. Expeditions were sent out, and returned to report failure in their search for their lost comrades. But the quest, mainly thanks to the efforts of Lady Franklin, was not abandoned, and in 1850 no less than twelve vessels were searching for the Franklin expedition. Among them were the *Assistance* and *Resolute* under Austin's command, with the tenders *Pioneer* and *Intrepid*. Wintering in Cornwallis Island, sledge journeys were organized along the southern and western coasts of Melville Island, and along the eastern coast of Bathurst Island. During these expeditions, McClintock came to the front, travelling 770 miles in eighty days and exploring a large area. Clements Markham, who served as a midshipman, gives an account of the experiences of the *Intrepid* in the following year :

> "She was making a rendezvous in August when the ice closed round, and she was obliged to make fast to a floe. Soon the floe was in motion and moving rapidly towards a large grounded iceberg. Before the vessel could be extricated, she was driven with a frightful crash against the berg. The vessel rose to the heavy pressure and soon the vessel's taffrail was forty feet and her bow thirty feet up the side of the berg, the masses of ice rising nearly ten feet above the bulwark. Then the pressure ceased, the piled-up masses sank from alongside, and the ship was left suspended on the side of the berg. It seemed inevitable that she must fall over on her broadside and be smashed. . . . The pressure began again, but ceased quite suddenly, and the ship shot down into the water, and was safe."

Such are the risks of Arctic explorations !

[1] *The Lands of Silence*, by Sir Clements Markham, 1921.

In 1854 definite news of Franklin's fate was received from Dr. Rae of the Hudson Bay Company, who had been surveying the West coast of Boothia. He had met Eskimos, who had seen thirty men dragging a boat southwards over the ice, and later they had seen several dead bodies near the mouth of a great river. The Eskimos had picked up silver plate and other articles belonging to officers of the *Erebus* and *Terror*. In 1857 a final search expedition was sent out under McClintock, who commanded the screw yacht *Fox* of 177 tons. He wintered in Bellot Strait. Eskimos were met with, many of whom had acquired articles from the ill-fated expedition. Travelling in winter the great explorer completed the discovery of the coast-line of North America. He also discovered the only possible north-west passage for ships between Boothia and King William Island. In a second year's journeys, complete success was obtained. A letter was found at Point Victory in King William Land, which contained the information that the *Erebus* and *Terror* had been abandoned in April 1848 and that the objective of the survivors was Back's Fish River. An Eskimo woman reported that " they fell and died as they walked ". Thus these heroic British explorers " forged the last link of the North-West Passage with their lives ".

During the search for Franklin, in 1850 Collinson in the *Enterprise* and M'Clure in the *Investigator*, after sailing through Bering Strait, separated. Collinson explored the Beaufort Sea, and reached the Prince of Wales Strait in 1851. In the following year he passed through Coronation Gulf to Cambridge Bay and made a sledge journey across Victoria Strait, between Victoria Land and King William Island. M'Clure reached Prince of Wales Strait and his land parties discovered the insularity of Banks Island. In 1853, after having been frozen in for eighteen months, the party was rescued, " and the crew crossing the ice of Melville Sound by sledge was the first party to make the North-West Passage ".

Collinson's voyage is one of the most remarkable and successful in Arctic records. To quote Greely : " He sailed the *Enterprise* for more than ten degrees of longitude through narrow straits along the northern shores of Continental North America, which never before or since has been navigated, save by small boats and with excessive difficulty." [1]

The first explorer who actually sailed a ship through the

[1] *The Polar Regions in the Twentieth Century*, by Major-General A. W. Greely, 1929.

North-West Passage was Amundsen.[1] Starting in the summer of 1903, the winter was spent on King William Island, where the exact position of the magnetic pole was determined. During the summer of 1904, survey and other scientific work was undertaken, while the explorers made friends with the Eskimos and learned much about their customs. " We were suddenly brought face to face here with a people from the Stone Age : we were abruptly carried back several thousand years."

In August 1905 Amundsen resumed his voyage through the North-West Passage. Queen Maud's Sea was full of ice, and there were dangerous shallows : " It was just like sailing through an uncleared field." There were many ice floes in Victoria Strait, and the coast was flat and monotonous, but on August 17 the explorer wrote : " We had now sailed the *Gjöa* through the hitherto unsolved link in the North-West Passage ". He had now reached waters charted by Collinson, and finally the North-West Passage was accomplished.

*   *   *   *   *

In Chapter XVI an account is given of early attempts to discover the North-East Passage. Willoughby, Chancelor, Burrough, Barents and Hudson all joined in this quest, but penetrated no further than the River Ob by sea. During this period Russia was rapidly crossing Asia to the Pacific, and her explorers not only reached the Arctic Ocean at more than one river-mouth, but Deshnev sailed from the mouth of the Kolyma River round the extreme north-eastern point of Asia. Consequently there were known rivers and explored portions of the coast when in 1875 Nordenskiöld, who was already a noted explorer of Greenland, made a voyage to Novaya Zemlya and the Yenisei. His next voyage was also to the mouth of the Yenisei in 1876 ; he was, however, not the first navigator to reach the Kara Sea, having been preceded, in 1874, by Captain Wiggins. These were pioneer voyages.

In July 1878 the Swedish explorer started on his great voyage of discovery in command of the *Vega*[2] and the *Lena*. Fog hindered their progress after passing the Yenisei, and the explorers anchored off Taimur Island, but scientific investigations of the contents of the dredger, of the dust on the ice and of all forms of life never ceased in this truly scientific expedition. On August 19 Nordenskiöld fired a salute off Cape Chelyuskin where " for the first time a vessel lay at

[1] *The North-West Passage*, by Roald Amundsen, 1908.
[2] *The Voyage of the " Vega " round Asia and Europe*, by A. E. Nordenskiöld, 1881.

anchor off the northermost cape of the old world ". Continuing the voyage eastwards, fog and ice again hindered progress and a northerly course was steered for an opening. They were sailing over what was marked as land on the map, and were able to make very important corrections. On August 27 the *Lena* parted from the *Vega* and sailed up the River Lena to Yakutsk. The *Vega* now steered for the New Siberian Islands, which had been discovered by Russian explorers in the eighteenth century. The weather was beautiful until September 3, and the Bear Islands off the mouth of the Kolyma were reached. Here the explorers had their first fall of snow, and ice forced them to make towards the mainland, where a narrow channel was found.

There were no signs of any inhabitants until, off Cape Shelagskoi, they were boarded by two large skin boats loaded with " chattering natives, men, women, and children, who indicated by cries and gesticulations that they wished to come on board . . . they acknowledged the name of *Chukch* ". Upon landing, the explorers were able to secure some walrus tusks and various articles and dresses from these friendly natives. At the end of September the *Vega* was somewhat unexpectedly frozen in while anchored in Kolyuchin Bay, which is situated at a short distance from Cape Deshnev.

During the winter an expedition was made to a reindeer camp, where in the morning " we saw all the reindeer advancing in a compact troop. At the head was an old reindeer with large horns, that went forward to his master, and bade him good morning by gently rubbing his nose against his master's hands. While this was going on, the other reindeer stood drawn up in well-ordered ranks . . . and the owner saluted every reindeer."

On July 18, 1879, the *Vega* steamed clear of the ice, and two days later Nordenskiöld wrote : " These were the mountain summits of the easternmost promontory of Asia, East Cape, an unsuitable name, for which I have substituted on the map that of Cape Deshnev, after the gallant Cossack who for the first time 230 years ago circumnavigated it." And again : " Thus finally was reached the goal towards which so many nations had struggled, all along from the time when Sir Hugh Willoughby . . . ushered in the long series of North-East voyages." Thus ended the quest for the North-East Passage, the achievement of which has given the gallant Swede Nordenskiöld a place among the great explorers of the world.

*   *   *   *   *

The discovery and colonization of a part of South-West Greenland has been described in Chapter VI, and its sighting by Frobisher and Davis is mentioned in Chapter XVI. In the latter part of the nineteenth century the interior of Greenland, an unexplored area of 700,000 square miles, exceeding that of the " Empty Quarter " of Arabia, was considered to constitute one of the greatest Arctic problems. During the nineteenth century, Polar explorers added to the knowledge of the coast. Among them was Inglefield,[1] who, in his screw yacht *Isabel* of 149 tons, passed Baffin's " Farthest North " in 1852. He was the first explorer to enter Smith Sound and named Ellesmere Land (now Ellesmere Island).

On the east coast, Scoresby the younger roughly charted some 200 miles north from Scoresby Sound in 1822, while Clavering a year later surveyed from latitude 73° to 75° N. on the same coast. In 1870, and again in 1883, Nordenskiöld attempted to cross Greenland from the West.

It was however reserved for Nansen, who had first visited the east coast in 1882, to accomplish this difficult task. He was accompanied by five companions, including Otto Sverdrup, all of whom were good skiers and accustomed to the use of snowshoes. Starting from Umivik in the middle of August 1888, the general direction followed was north-west, but the hauling of the sledges uphill, the danger of breaking through the snow-bridges and the storms made the adventure a perilous one. Crevasses also were so numerous that the direction had to be changed time and again, to avoid them. The highest elevation to be crossed was 8,920 feet, and, after forty strenuous days, the explorers, who finally turned towards the south-west, reached the head of the Ameralik Fjord. There they were some sixty miles to the north of Gotthaab, which they reached after a journey altogether of some 350 miles.

Exploration in the north was carried on by Rasmussen, who, in 1912, crossed Greenland to Danmark Fjord and re-crossed it to the west. He added to geographical knowledge by this and by later journeys, as was also done on two other crossings, De Quervain in 1912, and by J. P. Koch in 1913.

Large areas, however, remained to be discovered, and the Cambridge Expeditions of 1923, 1926 and 1929, under the leadership of Wordie,[2] explored in East Greenland. After

---

[1] *A Summer Search for Sir John Franklin*, by Commander E. A. Inglefield, 1853. I have to thank his son, Rear-Admiral Sir Edward Inglefield, who has reproduced the frontispiece of this book as a memorial to his distinguished father.
[2] *G.J.*, Vol. LXX, p. 225, and Vol. LXXV, p. 481.

conducting pendulum experiments on Sabine Island, to verify and add to those made by Captain Sabine in 1823, an intensive study was made of the island. On the mainland this intensive study, geographical, geological and archaeological, was continued and an expedition was made inland with Petermann Peak, the highest mountain in Greenland, as its ultimate objective. This virgin peak was conquered after a very difficult climb in a raging gale, with considerable risk of frostbite, and its height was finally settled to be 9,650 feet.

An account must now be given of the Canadian Arctic Expedition led by Stefansson, who depended almost entirely on game for his food and thus obviated the necessity of transporting heavily laden sledges. Commencing operations in 1913, for five years the Beaufort Sea and the Arctic Ocean to the east and west of Prince Patrick Island were surveyed, while new islands were discovered to the north of Melville Island. All this was accomplished after a preliminary disaster. The *Karluk*, under Captain Bartlett, which had been caught in the ice and was drifting westward, was suddenly crushed and sank in January 1914. Wrangel Island, distant some eighty miles, was reached with much difficulty. Bartlett then started off with a sledge and one Eskimo on a hazardous journey to Siberia to arrange for the shipwrecked party to be rescued. It says much for Stefansson that he achieved so much in the next four years with seriously diminished resources.

We now come to Spitsbergen. In Chapter XVI the discovery of this island in 1596 was described. Other voyages followed, but " the Basques were then the only people who understood whaling ", and the English had, at first, to be content themselves with walrus, bears and deer. However, in 1612 the Muscovy Company engaged a Basque, and " there was not one whale killed with one boat alone, save ours, with all English, save the Baske aforesaid, which slue three without the helpe of any other boate ".[1] None of these whale hunters left the coast, and consequently the interior of the island remained unknown until the late nineteenth century.

In 1896 Conway, who has won fame as an explorer in three continents, appeared on the scene. Accompanied by Gregory and Garwood, he started inland from Advent Bay on the west coast and found the whole country covered with thawing snow, beneath which lay a bog. However, nothing daunted by the bad going or unsuitable equipment, the explorers

[1] *No Man's Land*, by Sir Martin Conway, 1906, p. 48.

" crossed overland from Advent Bay to Klok Bay, from Klok Bay to Sassen Bay, and from Sassen to Agardh Bay, on the east coast, and back to Advent Bay ".[1] This was the first crossing of Spitsbergen.

An honoured place in the history of Spitsbergen must be given to Isaachsen and Hoel, who have spent twenty years surveying the coast; and also to the Scottish explorer, W. S. Bruce, who made nine visits in all to explore the country and its coal resources.

In 1924 Binney [2] led an Oxford University Expedition to examine neighbouring North-East Land. He conceived the idea of utilizing a seaplane for survey and photography and, after being nearly drowned owing to engine breakdown, he was able to make considerable use of it. The achievements of the expedition include the east to west crossing of North-East Land by a sledging party in face of unfavourable weather conditions, while not only was much valuable survey work accomplished, but many of the technical difficulties of carrying out a survey with the assistance of an aeroplane were overcome.

Expeditions to the west of Greenland had hitherto been despatched mainly to find the North-West Passage, but in the search for Franklin, Inglefield explored the coast and was followed by Kane who penetrated to Cape Fraser in Ellesmere Island. In 1875 Nares was appointed to command a British naval expedition, and following Hall, who had penetrated to the Polar Ocean in 1871–3, the *Alert* reached her winter quarters at 82° 27′ N., near a low beach facing the Polar Ocean. The North Pole was now the main objective.

Sledge expeditions were despatched, but, most unfortunately, scurvy broke out and Albert Markham was obliged to return after reaching " Farthest North " in 83° 20′ N. Pelham Aldrich's party explored the north coast of the Grant Land portion of Ellesmere Island, while Beaumont explored the north coast of Greenland. In spite of failure to reach the North Pole, the expedition discovered much new country and made important discoveries, together with magnetic, meteorological and tidal observations.

In 1881 Lieutenant Greely,[3] of the United States Army, was despatched to Lady Franklin Bay with the object of

---

[1] *The First Crossing of Spitsbergen*, by Sir Martin Conway, 1897.
[2] " 7   Oxford University Arctic Expedition ", by F. G. Binney, *G.J.*, Vol. LXVI, p. 9.
[3] *Three Years of Arctic Service*, by Adolphus W. Greely, 1886.

establishing a station for scientific observations, and for geographical discovery. In the following spring, Lockwood led an expedition along the north coast of Greenland and reached Lockwood Island in latitude 83° 24′ N. The relief vessel twice failed to reach the expedition which, in August 1883, left the ship and retreated southwards in boats towed by a steam launch. Upon reaching Cape Sabine it was ascertained that the relief ship had foundered. The English food depot was found and the expedition settled down to a winter of starvation. Greely describes one tragedy after another until, upon the arrival of relief in June 1884, " the seven survivors—out of a party of twenty-four—realized that the agony was over, and the remnant of the Lady Franklin Bay Expedition saved ".

In 1893, Nansen sailed north with the deliberate intention of allowing his ship, the *Fram*, to be frozen in and drift towards the Pole. This actually occurred north of the New Siberian Islands. After drifting to latitude 85° 57′ N., the *Fram* under Sverdrup as captain remained in the ice for nearly three years, and finally emerged north of Spitsbergen. Nansen himself meanwhile had attempted to reach the Pole with sledge and *kayak* and actually reached 86° 12′ N. He then entered Franz Josef Land, where Jackson was exploring, and had the good fortune to meet Jackson, who brought him home. The voyage of the *Fram* made the most important discovery that the North Pole was a deep ice-covered sea, and, without doubt, Nansen's voyage in the *Fram* is the greatest of all Arctic voyages.

The conquest of the North Pole was claimed both by Dr. Cook and by Peary.[1] Cook's claim, however, has never met with general acceptance. Peary, like the majority of great explorers, had trained himself for the task by long years of endeavour, gaining experience alike in success and failure. After preliminary journeys in North Greenland, during which he conclusively proved its insular nature, Peary determined to devote his life to the great quest. He realized that his only chance of success was to live among the Eskimos, to learn their methods of hunting and fishing, on which they entirely depended for their existence, and their other arts ; to make friends with them and thereby to secure their willing service. In short, with their help and that of their dogs, he hoped to reach the North Pole.

Sailing in 1908 in the s.s. *Roosevelt*, commanded by Captain Bartlett, the noted Newfoundland navigator, the explorer

[1] *The North Pole*, by Robert E. Peary, 1910.

reached Cape York in August. Continuing the voyage northwards, Eskimos were recruited making a total of sixty-nine
men, women and children; there were also 250 dogs. Part-
ing from the *Erik* at Etah, which served as an advance base,
the *Roosevelt* " was kicked about by the floes as if she had
been a football ", but at last Cape Sheridan in Grant Land
—the winter quarters of the *Alert*—was reached, and the
Roosevelt was unloaded of its sledges, coal and stores. During
the autumn a depot was formed at Cape Columbia, the most

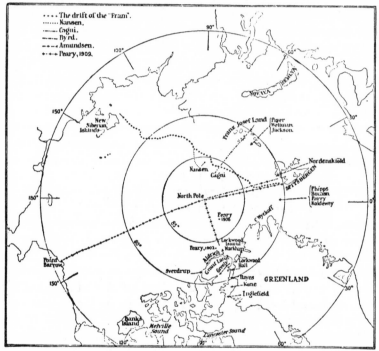

THE NORTH POLAR REGIONS—II: THE ADVANCE TO THE NORTH POLE.

northern point of Grant Land, some ninety miles to the north-
west. At the same time a large number of musk oxen, with
a few deer and bear, provided fresh meat and healthy
excitement. On February 22, 1909, Peary, who had sent
Bartlett on a week ahead with the advance parties to Cape
Columbia, started on his march to the North Pole. The
greatest difficulty consisted in the lanes of open water, which
caused a delay of six days early in March. But, upon the
weather clearing up, the open water froze over and the journey
was resumed. Peary was favoured by the weather, so much

so that one of his Eskimos sagely remarked that the devil must be asleep or having trouble with his wife!

Bartlett made the trail up to 87° 47′ N., and Peary then pushed on with four Eskimos and a negro till his record shows that on April 6, 1909, he reached the North Pole, a distance of 540 miles from the *Roosevelt*. He thereby accomplished the dream of Arctic explorers, and his name will never be forgotten.

The year 1914 saw the first aeroplane flights in the Arctic, and, as mentioned above, Binney used the first seaplane specially equipped for photographic surveying. In 1925 Amundsen, with two flying-boats, attempted to reach the North Pole. A forced landing was made in 87° 43′ N., and after super-human efforts to prepare a runway on the ice, the party flew back in one machine to Spitsbergen about a month later. The first airman to reach the Pole was Byrd, who, flying from Spitsbergen on May 9, 1926, reached the North Pole and returned in fifteen hours, thus demonstrating the wonderful possibilities of mechanical flight. Two days later Amundsen, Nobile and Ellsworth left Spitsbergen in the Italian semi-rigid airship *Norge* and reached the Pole in sixteen hours, making Point Barrow in Alaska some thirty hours later. Ever aspiring to outdo his predecessors, Wilkins, who had covered much unexplored country in Alaska while making preliminary flights, in 1928 flew from Alaska to Spitsbergen in twenty hours—a distance of 1,200 miles. In this year the airship *Italia* under Nobile flew to the North Pole *via* Cape Bridgeman, the northernmost point of Greenland, traversing a large unexplored area. The Pole was safely reached, but on the return journey a disaster occurred. Amundsen lost his life flying to the rescue, thus closing a career which Baker aptly terms "an epitome of Polar exploration".

Owing to the development of flying, it was decided in 1930 by Watkins, then a Cambridge undergraduate, to examine the possibility of organizing an air route from London to Canada *via* Iceland and Greenland. The main settlement of Eskimos on the east coast of Greenland was at Angmagssalik, and it was decided to despatch an expedition which should have its base within fifty miles of this settlement and study the country by means of land journeys across Greenland. It was also especially important to study meteorological conditions.[1] The work of this expedition was remarkable. Long

[1] " The British Arctic Air Route Expedition ", by H. G. Watkins, *G.J.*, Vol. LXXIX, pp. 353 and 466.

land journeys were undertaken, aeroplanes were employed for the reconnaissance of unknown country and for the support of sledging parties, while Watkins himself led a voyage in a small boat round the south coast of Greenland. In order to hunt alone with reasonable safety, Watkins and his companions learned to roll right round with the *kayak* and come up on the other side, an accomplishment rare among Europeans.

Alas! after receiving the Gold Medal of the Royal Geographical Society in 1932, Watkins returned to Greenland and lost his life while hunting from a *kayak*. Thus, in the flower of his youth, perished the greatest of the younger generation of Arctic explorers. To him the poignant lines of Sir Thomas More especially apply :

> " He that hath no grave
> Is covered by the sky."

CHAPTER XXXV

THE EXPLORERS OF THE ANTARCTIC

" Had we lived, I should have had a tale to tell of the hardihood, endurance, and courage of my companions which
would have stirred the heart of every Englishman. These
rough notes and our dead bodies must tell the tale."
ROBERT FALCON SCOTT.

THE great pioneer of Antarctic exploration was Captain Cook,
and it was not until the second decade of the nineteenth century that the *Siege of the South Pole*,[1] as Mill aptly describes
his classic, was resumed by the despatch of a Russian Antarctic expedition under Admiral Bellingshausen in 1819. Calling at Rio de Janeiro, the first objective was South Georgia,
where a running survey was undertaken to complete Cook's
survey of the north coast. Resuming the voyage to the
south, three small islands, one of which was an active volcano, were sighted to the north of the Sandwich group.
After passing this group and identifying islands seen by Cook
from the west, Bellingshausen crossed the parallel of 60°, where
his way was barred by a solid ice-pack. Again and again
attempts were made to force a passage southwards, but with
scant success. Supplies ran low, and the gallant Russian, who,
since leaving the Sandwich Islands had kept south of Cook's
track, shaped his course for Sydney.

The winter of 1820 was spent in exploring the South
Pacific, where Bellingshausen Island marks his route. After
revisiting Sydney, Antarctic exploration was resumed, and the
parallel of 60° was crossed in longitude 163° E. in December
1821. Icebergs and later pack ice barred the further progress of the explorers, who cruised along its edge south of
New Zealand, and on January 1, 1822, the " Farthest South "
was reached at 69° 52' S. in longitude 92° 10' W. The heroic
efforts of Bellingshausen under the most trying conditions were
finally rewarded by the discovery of Peter I Island, the first
land to be discovered within the Antarctic Circle. Farther

[1] Lady Hilton Young has not only read through this chapter and made valuable
suggestions, but has selected the illustration, which shows her late husband, Captain
Scott, preparing to start on his journey to the South Pole. Dr. Hugh Mill has also
given me much valuable help.

east a distant island was viewed and named after Alexander I. Reaching the South Shetlands, the Russian Admiral met British and American sealers at anchor, and completed his remarkable voyage of circumnavigation at South Georgia. " The voyage ", wrote Mill, " was a masterly continuation of that of Cook, supplementing it in every particular, competing with it in none."

We now come to Weddell, a sealer, who in 1819 commenced the exploration and survey of the South Shetlands in his own ship. On a second voyage he surveyed the South Orkneys. By a happy chance in open water he reached latitude 74° 15′ S. and longitude 34° 16′ W., which area is known as Weddell Sea.

The Enderby brothers were ship-owners interested in exploration, and, in 1831, under exceptionally trying conditions, Captain Biscoe in one of their ships discovered Enderby Land. A year later he saw Adelaide and Biscoe Islands off Graham Land. Another important discovery was made by Captain John Balleny, who, sailing from New Zealand in 1839, reached the islands named after him, the first land to be discovered within the Antarctic Circle south of Australia.

These discoveries excited deep interest in Europe, and, in 1838, D'Urville led a French expedition which surveyed the Straits of Magellan and then explored the Antarctic to the south of Cape Horn, finding Louis Philippe Land. In 1840 the French explorer was still more fortunate in discovering Adélie Land to the south of Australia. At the same time Lieutenant Wilkes of the United States led a poorly equipped expedition with great courage, and discovered land close to Adélie Land. He actually sighted D'Urville's ships, but through a regrettable misunderstanding the two explorers did not meet. His name is commemorated in Wilkes Land, and he deserved more credit than he received at first either in America or in Europe.

We now come to Captain James Ross, whose services in the Arctic have already been mentioned.[1] His main object on this expedition was to improve the knowledge of magnetism, in which science he was already an expert ; he also made most important discoveries. In September 1839 the *Erebus* and *Terror* sailed for the Antarctic, setting up magnetic observatories at St. Helena, the Cape of Good Hope, and Kerguelen Island, where simultaneous obser-

[1] *Voyage in the Antarctic Regions*, by Captain Sir James Ross, 1847.

vations proved that "every movement of the needle at Kerguelen was simultaneous with a similar movement in Toronto
almost at its antipodes".

In July 1840 the explorers sailed to Hobart Town, where
they were welcomed by Sir John Franklin. Here Ross heard
of the discoveries of D'Urville and Wilkes in the very regions
to which he was bound. He promptly decided to avoid
these areas and to follow the 170° E. meridian for his attempt
to reach the magnetic pole. The report of Balleny, who had
mentioned an open sea at 69°, influenced this wise decision.

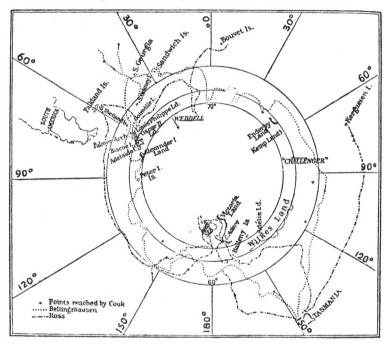

THE SOUTH POLAR REGIONS—I : NINETEENTH CENTURY.

Ross was the first explorer in the Antarctic whose ships
had been especially strengthened to resist ice pressure. Consequently, in January 1841, his ships both crossed the Antarctic Circle and were steered into the pack ice. Land was
sighted, and soon two great ranges were distinguished, with
peaks ranging up to 10,000 feet. The first notable promontory of the new coast-line was named Cape Adare, and, landing on a neighbouring island with considerable difficulty, the
Union Jack was hoisted in the presence of innumerable pen-
guins who were ranged along the ledges. The country was
named Victoria Land, and the island Possession Island. Sail-

ing south, snow-clad mountains rising to 14,000 feet were sighted and named, while to complete the voyagers' amazement, two great volcanic peaks, aptly named Erebus and Terror, were sighted. The highest latitude was reached at 78° 4' S. After following the great Southern Barrier for a continuous length of 250 miles, Ross, unable to find a possible site for a winter camp, or indeed for a landing-place, decided to sail north, and, passing within sight of Balleny Islands, he reached Tasmania, after accomplishing a very great feat of exploration.

Ross had been fortunate in his first voyage into the Antarctic, but in the second luck was against him. In January 1842—

> "a violent gale from the northward compelled us to reduce our sails to a close reefed main-top-sail and storm-stay-sails, the sea quickly rising to a fearful height. Breaking over the loftiest bergs, we were driven into the heavy pack under our lee. Our ships were involved in an ocean of rolling fragments of ice, hard as floating rocks of granite, which were dashed against them by the waves with so much violence that their masts quivered, and the destruction of the ships seemed inevitable from the tremendous shocks they received."

This storm was successfully weathered, but an even greater danger was the collision of the two ships, which, but for a display of magnificent seamanship, must have ended in utter disaster. Finally, in 1843, the expedition returned to England. Ross, apart from his scientific observations, had made far greater discoveries than any other explorer, and deservedly occupies a leading position among the heroes of the Antarctic.

This great period of exploration was followed by one which Mill terms an era of "averted interest", the quest of the North-West Passage again turning the eyes of the world to the Arctic regions. Valuable work was however accomplished by Larsen, who in 1895 made the first landing in the Antarctic Continent. In 1898 Gerlache organized a Belgian expedition, which included several scientists. From the South Shetlands he sailed south, and discovering the Strait that separated Palmer Archipelago from the mainland, collections of geological and natural history specimens were made. Gerlache was caught in ice in 71° 30' S. and drifted about with it during the first winter that was spent in the Antarctic. From 80° 30' W. to 102° W. longitude and about a degree of latitude were covered during the thirteen months of imprisonment, but, when the ship escaped, the expedition returned to Europe where the importance of the duration and regularity of the routine scientific observations and the completeness of the collections won great credit for all concerned.

In 1898 Borchgrevink, a member of Larsen's expedition, thanks to the financial support of Sir George Newnes, sailed south to Hobart and succeeded in getting through the pack. He landed a hut, stores, and instruments, and, despatching the ship to winter in New Zealand, a party of ten settled down to scientific work, no land exploration being found possible.

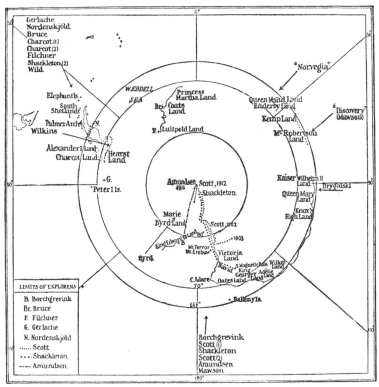

THE SOUTH POLAR REGIONS—II : TWENTIETH CENTURY.

In the spring the *Southern Cross* came back and, after making the first landing on the Barrier and setting up a " Farthest South " record, the expedition returned to Europe, having accomplished a valuable piece of work.

The twentieth century produced great explorers, and, thanks mainly to the personality and untiring efforts of Sir Clements Markham, an expedition to the Antarctic was organized to follow up the work of Sir James Ross and winter on the coast of Victoria Land. Commander Scott, R.N., was appointed leader, with Armitage as second in command and Koettlitz, who had served on the Jackson-Harmsworth expedition; Wilson, who was later to share in the tragedy of the *Terra Nova* expedition, Charles Royds as First Lieutenant, Shackleton and Bernacchi. The *Discovery* was specially built to cope with ice conditions in all circumstances.

Scott sailed from England in August 1901, and, after coasting the great Barrier eastwards, and discovering King Edward VII Land, anchored at the south of Ross Island in February 1902, where the ship was frozen in for two years. Huts were erected on shore and short excursions were made.

In the spring long sledge journeys were undertaken. Scott, Shackleton and Wilson, travelling south and then south-west, reached 82° 17' S., at a distance of 380 miles from their winter quarters. The return journey was a terrible effort for the half-starved party. The dogs collapsed, and gallant Shackleton, who, like the others, suffered from scurvy, broke down but struggled on. The smoke of Mount Erebus was sighted at a distance of over a hundred miles, and the final food depot was reached, with its abundant store of food. At last the pioneer journey ended, and the entry runs : " If we had not achieved such great results as at one time we had hoped for, we knew at least that we had striven and endured with all our might." Scott's motto to this chapter runs :

> " How many weary steps
> Of many weary miles you have o'ergone
> Are numbered to the travel of one mile."

The results of this voyage were of great importance. Two sledge-journeys into the interior had revealed the existence of a great plateau rising to nearly 10,000 feet beyond the coast mountains, and had afforded experience of value to future explorers. The work of the scientific staff was also fruitful.

In 1901 Professor von Drygalski headed a German expedition to the Antarctic, co-operating with that in the *Discovery*, during the course of which Kaiser Wilhelm II Land was discovered and valuable scientific results were obtained. At the same time Nordenskiöld led a Swedish expedition to the east of Graham Land (later proved to be a group of islands), while Bruce in the *Scotia* explored the Weddell Sea and passing Weddell's " Farthest South ", discovered Coats Land.

In 1903, and again in 1908, Charcot, an enthusiastic French

THE *EREBUS* PASSING THROUGH THE CHAIN OF BERGS, 13th MARCH, 1842

(From Voyage in the Antarctic Regions, by Sir James Ross)

From a photograph by Herbert G. Ponting

SCOTT AND HIS COMPANIONS STARTING FOR THE SOUTH POLE

(With Mount Erebus in the background)

yachtsman and scientist, made important discoveries on the
west coast of Graham Land and further to the south-west,
naming new lands after his father and after presidents of the
French Republic.

The siege of the South Pole was continued by another
great explorer, Ernest Shackleton,[1] who in 1907 started from
England in the *Nimrod* as leader of an expedition, which included an exceptionally good staff of scientists. Landing at
Cape Royds on Ross Island, in February 1908, winter quarters
were established and the active volcano of Mount Erebus
was scaled at a height of 13,700 feet. On the ascent the explorers were caught in a blizzard, but it cleared up on the
second day, when they reached the summit, to find themselves on the "brink of a precipice of black rock, forming
the inner edge of the old crater".

By October 29, supplies had been laid out and Shackleton started on his adventurous attempt to reach the South
Pole, using ponies for transport. The weather conditions
were extremely good upon the whole, and, on November
26, Shackleton writes : "A day to remember, for we have
passed the 'Farthest South' previously reached by man."
Early in December a great glacier was reached in the Western
Mountains, and on December 7 the last of the four ponies
fell into a fathomless crevasse, but the sledge was most fortunately saved. On December 16 the record runs : "We have
now traversed nearly 100 miles of crevassed ice and risen
6,000 feet on the largest glacier in the world." Their position was 84° 50' S. Upon reaching 88° 7' at a height of
10,000 feet on the plateau, the explorers were overtaken by
a raging blizzard, but, when it cleared on January 9, 1909,
they marched to 88° 23', where they hoisted the Union Jack
and a brass cylinder containing documents. The Pole could
easily have been reached if provisions had sufficed. The
return journey looked like disaster owing to dysentery, but
at last the heroic explorers with "death stalking from behind ",
reached their ship, just as approaching winter compelled her
to leave. They had accomplished a great land journey in
the Antarctic and proved that the South Pole could be reached.
Nor was this the only result, for Professors David and Mawson had made their way with infinite difficulty to the magnetic pole which, as calculated by Mawson, was reached in
latitude 72° 25' S., longitude 155° 16' E., with the temperature
exactly at zero Fahrenheit. Their journey was a great feat.

[1] *The Heart of the Antarctic*, by E. H. Shackleton, 1909.

The South Pole was conquered, but not by a British explorer.[1] Amundsen, who first sailed a ship through the North-West Passage, as described in the last chapter, left Norway in August 1910 with the intention of reaching it. On the voyage he was favoured by climatic conditions, the pack being sighted on January 2, 1911, and traversed in what he termed a "four days' pleasure-trip". Ross Sea was also free of icebergs, and, reaching the Great Barrier, the members of the expedition landed at the Bay of Whales and had the courage to make winter quarters on the ice. The laying out of supplies was executed with much promptitude and, before the arrival of winter, three tons had been collected in depots, the farthest of which was situated in latitude 82° S.

On October 19 the start for the great enterprise was made, Amundsen having four companions and four sledges, each drawn by thirteen dogs. From latitude 85° S. it was decided to make the final attempt to reach the Pole—a distance there and back of 683 English miles. On November 17 the explorers began the passage of the Western Mountains south of Shackleton's pass ; the peaks rising to 15,000 feet. But, favoured by the perfect weather, they made good progress until a blizzard forced them to rest for five days. Their onward progress was then hindered by crevassed ice, but once on the plateau the South Pole was reached on December 14, 1911, by Amundsen, who thus accomplished one of the greatest feats of world exploration. All honour to the splendid qualities displayed by the Norwegian explorers, who traversed entirely unknown country all the way.

We now come to Scott's second expedition. After a farewell luncheon given by the Royal Geographical Society, in June 1910 the explorers shaped their course for New Zealand and then sailed south to the Antarctic. Entering the pack, after weathering a dangerous storm, the *Terra Nova* forced her way through 370 miles of ice, and on January 4, 1911, winter quarters were established at Cape Evans, on Ross Island, fourteen miles north of the *Discovery's* winter quarters. On November 1, 1911, after supplies had been laid out, Scott started on his last great journey. On November 15, One Ton Camp was reached, situated 130 geographical miles from Cape Evans, and a day's halt was decided upon. As the journey progressed, the ponies were killed to feed the explorers and the dog teams, but Scott wrote : "Our luck in the weather is preposterous." On December 5, a blizzard

---

[1] *The South Pole*, by Roald Amundsen.

necessitated a halt of four days. When the journey was resumed, the deep soft snow made the situation serious. The remainder of the ponies were slaughtered on December 9 at the entrance of the Beardmore Glacier. The ascent of the glacier proved terribly difficult, as Shackleton had found it, and on December 14 the diary runs : " We are just starting our march with no very hopeful outlook." It was on this day that Amundsen reached the South Pole! On December 22, the plateau had practically been reached, and the third stage of the journey opened with good promise after an affecting farewell to the last returning supporting party. Crevasses constituted a danger until the top of the plateau was reached, as Shackleton had also found, and on Christmas Day an Alpine rope had to be requisitioned to pull a member of the party out of a crevasse 50 feet deep and 8 feet across.

On January 4 1912 the explorers reached latitude 87° 32' at an altitude of 10,000 feet, and the party, consisting of Scott, the naval officer, Wilson, doctor and artist, Bowers, the officer of the Indian Marine, Oates, the cavalry officer, and Petty Officer Evans, R.N., said good-bye to the second party and started on the last stage to the South Pole, distant 140 miles. On January 9 Shackleton's " Farthest South " was passed ; new ground was entered, and on January 16, 1912, the South Pole was reached, but a black flag tied to a sledge-bearer proved that the Norwegians had forestalled them. Small wonder that Scott wrote: " Great God! this is an awful place, and terrible enough for us to have laboured to it without the reward of priority."

The return journey of 800 miles was commenced, and, on February 9, some thirty-five pounds weight of fossils were collected, which shed important light on the geology of the continent. On February 16 Evans collapsed in mind and body, dying the following day. The survivors reached the Middle Barrier depot on March 6, but were faced with a shortage of oil. The tragedy deepened when, in the middle of March, Oates, realizing that he was an encumbrance to the survivors and was lessening their chance of winning through to safety, said: " I am just going outside and may be some time." Thus died a very gallant British officer. The three survivors struggled on to within a few miles of One Ton Depot and there died. Scott's Message to the Public, quoted at the head of this chapter, is graven on his statue, and is one of the most moving ever penned by a dying explorer. It will stimulate unborn generations of his race to deeds of adventure and to knightly unselfishness.

In the space at my disposal I cannot do more than mention the valuable work accomplished by other parties, which in the face of extraordinary difficulties executed a geological survey extending some thirty miles inland, and made important observations.

The next great explorer to appear on the scene of the Antarctic was Mawson, who had gained experience and signal distinction when, serving under Shackleton, he not only reached the Magnetic Pole, but wrote many of the scientific reports. In 1911 he led an expedition to examine the area between Victoria Land and Kaiser Wilhelm II Land.[1] Four bases were to be established, expeditions were to be made inland and scientific research of every description was to be undertaken. The expedition started in December 1911, and, a month later, Mawson's party established the main base at Cape Denison. Journeys inland were then undertaken. That of Mawson himself with two companions reached a distance of 300 miles, when Ninnis, one of his companions, fell into a deep crevasse and was killed. On the return journey, Mertz was too ill to move, and Mawson risked all reasonable chances of safety by nursing his comrade until he died. He then, endowed with superhuman strength, which enabled him to climb out of a crevasse and to continue on his course, reached Cape Denison. As he wrote : " The long journey was at an end—a terrible chapter of my life was finished." The Mawson expedition added to the map King George V and Queen Mary Land, which was explored by his western party under Wild, and accomplished especially valuable oceanographic work.

In 1913 Shackleton decided to attempt a journey across the entire Antarctic, a distance of 1,800 miles. His plan was to establish a main base on the Weddell Sea and to travel to the geographical pole, and thence, following Scott's route, to McMurdo Sound. This main party, which he would lead in person, would be supported by a party which would, from a base in the Ross Sea, lay out supplies for the main party from Beardmore Glacier to the coast.

The expedition spent a month at South Georgia in November 1914, and in January 1915 Shackleton reached unexplored land, which he named Caird Coast. The *Endurance* was then caught in the ice, and for eight months was transformed

[1] *The Home of the Blizzard*, by Sir Douglas Mawson, 1914.

" into a wintering station ". The ship had drifted ninety-five miles in a north-westerly direction by March 31, 1915, and on August 1 the ice pressure was serious. The danger passed, but only temporarily, and finally, on October 27, Wordie wrote : " The floes, with the force of millions of tons of moving ice behind them, were simply annihilating the ship." After this disaster, Ocean Camp was established on a thick floe and the wreck was salvaged for supplies and equipment with considerable success, until, on November 21, the good ship *Endurance* sank. The expedition then camped on a floe keeping three boats ready to be launched. With the disintegration of the ice pack, the crisis approached ; on April 10, 1916, the whole party embarked, and on April 13 they made a course for Elephant Island, where they landed on April 15, everyone being worn out from thirst and lack of sleep.

Shackleton, whose power of rising to the most difficult situations was amazing, realized that it would be impossible to transport the entire party to South Georgia. He thereupon decided to lead a forlorn hope and to sail some 840 miles to that island with a picked party of five sailors. On April 24 Shackleton started. The seas were so rough that nearly everyone was seasick, while they were constantly soaked and cold. Apart from the raging seas, they now suffered from thirst, the second breaker containing brackish water. A fortnight after starting on their hazardous voyage, South Georgia was sighted. A gale then nearly drove the boat on to the rocks, but at last they were able to land in a cove with a stream of fresh water.

It now remained to cross the island to Stromness, a dangerous task for the tired men, across unknown mountains and glaciers, but it was successfully accomplished. To quote Mill's eulogy : [1] " If his return to the *Nimrod* on the Plateau, the Glacier and the Barrier, seven years before, had been a race with death on his pale horse, Shackleton's return from the *Endurance* over the Floe, and the Ocean, and the Mountains, had been one long wrestling bout with the same grim adversary." The three men left with the boat were promptly fetched in a whaler while, after more than one failure, " the party of twenty-two men was rescued and found all well ", after spending over four months on Elephant Island. The supporting party in the Ross Sea accomplished their assigned task of transporting supplies to the Beardmore Glacier. The effort was tremendous and cost three lives. The *Aurora* also,

[1] *The Life of Sir Ernest Shackleton*, p. 227.

after being frozen in, was carried out to sea in a blizzard and was nearly lost, but just managed to reach New Zealand, in a battered condition, in April 1916. Finally the supporting party was rescued by the *Aurora* in December 1916.

Thus this ambitious adventure ended in failure, but it was an heroic failure. Shackleton has been greatly honoured by the Royal Geographical Society, his statue being placed in a niche in the exterior wall of their premises. There, clad in his Antarctic clothing, he stands as a symbol of the spirit that has made the British Empire first in the field of exploration.

We now come to the use of aeroplanes in the Antarctic. Wilkins, as already stated, had a splendid record in the Arctic. As a result of two seasons' work, his most important discovery in the South was that Graham Land, instead of being a peninsula, was in reality a series of islands. He had also added Hearst Land to the map. After Wilkins came Admiral Byrd, who had also won fame in the Arctic. Leading a splendidly equipped expedition, Byrd, on Amundsen's recommendation, selected the Bay of Whales, and with teams of dogs speedily formed his base inland and erected his well-found station with its wireless permitting communication with New York, its three houses, its aeroplanes and its gymnasium.[1] Byrd's main objective was the South Pole, a distance of 800 miles, and by way of preparation a depot of petrol was laid out, the range of his aeroplane not exceeding 1,700 miles.

On November 28, 1929, having received a message from an advance aeroplane that the weather conditions in the mountains were excellent, Byrd started at 3.29 p.m. The chief difficulty was the crossing of the pass in the Queen Maud Range, which rose to about 10,000 feet. This was only effected by the sacrifice of 250 pounds of food, which gave the necessary gain in altitude, and the aeroplane duly reached the plateau. As Byrd wrote: " It was difficult to believe that in recent history the most resolute men who had ever attempted to carry a remote objective, Scott and Shackleton, had plodded over this same plateau, a few miles each day, with hunger—fierce, unrelenting hunger—stalking them every step of the way." Byrd, on the contrary, reached the South Pole in a few hours, and having circled over it recrossed the range, refuelled, and in nineteen hours the flight to and from the South Pole had been safely accomplished. Apart from this spectacular flight the expedition did useful exploring work

[1] *Little America*, by Rear-Admiral Richard Evelyn Byrd, 1931.

by air to the east of King Edward VII Land, and brought in an important geological collection by dog-sledge.

The work of exploration in the Antarctic continues steadily. The *Norvegia* under Riiser-Larsen, while primarily concerned with the whaling industry, has discovered Queen Maud Land to the west of Enderby Land; in 1931, it completed the circumnavigation of the Antarctic. The *Discovery* has also added new lands to the map, including Princess Elizabeth Land to the east of McRobertson Lands. Both expeditions have carried out oceanic research of great value.

There still remain more than 2,000 miles of unexplored coast to be charted, and it is just possible that Antarctica may be severed by a broad channel connecting the Weddell and Ross Seas, those two huge gulfs which point towards each other. By the use of aeroplanes this problem can be solved without a tithe of the risk or toil involved in the old heroic days.

$$* \quad * \quad * \quad * \quad *$$

In this work I have attempted to describe the course of exploration down the ages. But what of the future? In a recent lecture Mason said : "I have hinted that the world is discovered, but I doubt whether a hundredth part of the land surface of the globe is surveyed in sufficient detail for modern requirements. If the pioneer's day is nearly over, the specialist-explorer's dawn is only breaking."[1] This clearly indicates that in the future, expeditions with specialists intensively studying a limited area will be the order of the day.

Richard Hakluyt, the leading geographer of the sixteenth century, wrote : "I have greatly wished there were a Lecture of Navigation read in this Citie for the increase and generall multiplying of sea-knowledge in this age, wherein God hath raised so general a desire in the youth of this Realme to discover all parts of the face of the earth, to this Realme in former ages not knowen."

Could he return to earth, Hakluyt would surely be delighted with the progress that has been effected since generation after generation of explorers have gone forth to discover, each generation, generally speaking, being better trained and having benefited by the experience of its predecessors. And what of the future? I firmly believe that the youth of to-day are as adventurous as their forbears, and they are certainly

---

[1] *The Geography of Current Affairs*, an Inaugural Lecture delivered by Kenneth Mason. Professor of Geography in the University of Oxford, on November 15, 1932

better educated and better equipped. There is thus every hope that they will ever hand on the torch; and, on this note, I conclude my task with a verse of Robert Browning:

> Then welcome each rebuff
> That turns earth's smoothness rough,
> Each sting that bids nor sit nor stand but go !
> Be our joys three-parts pain !
> Strive, and hold cheap the strain,
> Learn, nor account the pang; dare, never grudge the throe.

APPENDIX

EXPLORATION

IN RECENT TIMES

" Here is a crucible, where human kind
Was scorched and buffeted by sun and wind,
Until the dross was shattered and the gold
Repaid God's alchemy an hundred fold. "
LORD LATYMER, " *Downland Songs* ".

BASHAKARD AND COASTAL MAKRAN

AMONG the scientific explorers of Persian Baluchistan J. V. Harrison, D.Sc., occupies a leading position. Working for the Anglo-Iranian Oil Company, in 1918, he travelled in Biyaban and, in 1937, he explored barren Bashakard. Its inhabitants were primitive and feuds were a curse, while raiders harried villagers, shepherds and travellers.

Anguran, the capital, is described as a village, consisting of some mat huts overlooked by a mosque and a ruined fort, set on a terrace fifty feet above it. Its inhabitants lived on the fruits of some date palms. They also kept a few camels, donkeys and goats. The pish-palm played a leading part in their economy, being utilized for making harness, shoes and maps. Moreover, a fire can be kindled by an expert, who twirls one stick against another with the aid of pish strings for perhaps twenty minutes.

In the winter of 1922-23, an expedition was made by Harrison accompanied by N. L. Falcon to explore coastal Makran.[1] Jask was the selected base and, until recently, had constituted an important centre of the Eastern Telegraph Company.[2] In due course wireless was installed and now Jask, which I recollect as a busy telegraph centre, has ceased to function.

Makran, as Harrison points out, is still emphatically the home of the Ichthyophagia, since not only do the natives live on fish, but so do their cattle, dogs and hens. Sun-dried fish, a malodorous product, is even exported to Ceylon, where it is utilized as manure for the tea shrubs. He describes the people as suspicious and " guns sometimes went off—due rather to sudden surprise than to malice aforethought ".

Harrison's task was to map geographically a strip along the coast to the border of British Baluchistan. Using plane-tables, " our programme involved ascending the range by one

[1] " Coastal Makran ", by J. V. Harrison, *Geographical Journal* for January, 1941.
[2] Jask was still operating in 1932 as a telegraph cable office and indeed, in December, 1937, it was still only the land line which was working. At that date the wireless mast was installed, but there was no transmitter nor staff to keep it in commission.

river, crossing a suitable pass to the next, and returning by this one."

Along the coast a low-lying plain extends some twenty miles in width with a rich growth of camel-thorn which not only affords good grazing, but also, probably due to its saltness, cured the mange from which all the camels suffered farther inland. In this area, a monster mud volcano, 180 feet high, was seen. The central cone was " steep-sided and is composed of individual flows of thick mud ".

The journey ended at Chahbar, once an important telegraph station, but now abolished. To-day it is the terminus of a motor road to the Jaz Murian and to Khwash, in Sarhad. Chahbar possesses the best harbour in Makran.

*　　*　　*　　*　　*

In 1934–35, Harrison and his colleagues were deputed to study the general features of the Jaz Murian depression.[1] He points out that " a striking feature in most of Western and Central Asia is the number of enclosed basins with no drainage outlet to the sea ", and that the Jaz Murian is a typical instance of this. The waters of the Bampur River from the north-east and the Halil Rud from the north-west strive to enter the central sump and unite, but achieve this only in years of exceptional rainfall. A curious feature of the basin was the sweetness of the water in the wells. To quote the author : " We have to think of a much more fertile basin than exists now. This can be visualized on the assumption that the Jaz Murian had experienced a long period of stable government and planned public works some two thousand three hundred years ago, and without any wetter climate than now exists." To-day the ruined villages on the northern side are the haunt of big game, including the wild ass.

[1] *Vide* " The Jaz Murian Depression", Persian Baluchistan, R.*G.S. Journal* for May 1943. I was informed that Jaz Murian signifies " The haunt of birds ".

II

FROM MECCA TO THE INDIAN OCEAN

" —my travel's history :
Wherein of antres vast, and deserts idle,
Rough quarries, rocks and hills, whose heads touch heaven,
It was my hint to speak—— "

Othello, Act I, Sc.3.

MORE than one of St. J. Philby's journeys in Arabia, which
rank among the greatest that have been carried through in that
historical land, have already been recorded in this work. I
now propose to give some account of his important exploration in South-West Arabia in 1936–37.[1]

During this journey he traversed that last great unexplored
area of Arabia, which lay between Najran and Shabwa. This
latter ruined city, which flourished in Himyaritic days, although
included in the Aden Protectorate, had never been visited by
a British official or explorer.

Starting from Mecca on the first stage of his journey in two
cars, and without using camels in this comparatively fertile
area, his first objective was Khurma, which was situated on the
edge of the immense lava-field with its numerous volcanic
cones and absolute lack of life.

From the vicinity of Khurma, the route to Shabwa ran
approximately due south. Passing through Raushan and
Nimran with their weekly markets, the explorer noted that the
Wadi Bisha divided the two great tribes, the Shahran and
Qahtan, the country belonging to the former extending nearly
to the Red Sea.

Keeping well to the east of the Wadi Misha, to avoid
mountainous country unsuitable for wheeled transport, Philby
struck the celebrated " Road of the Elephant ". It marks the
route followed by an Abyssinian army under its general Abraha,
which, in A.D. 570, marched north from the Yemen with Mecca
as its objective. The campaign was unsuccessful, but the elephants, which accompanied it, struck the imagination of the
Arabs.

[1] *Vide* " The Land of Sheba ", reprinted from the *Geographical Journal*, vol. XCII, nos.
1, 2, July and August 1938. Also his work *Sheba's Daughters*, 1939.

Continuing the journey, the relatively fertile oasis of Khaibar, consisting of six small hamlets set in palm groves, was reached. At Najran, camels had been collected and " a bodyguard of eight Nejdi henchmen of the Amir, who were responsible for my safety ", completed the expedition. Philby himself and his staff continued to travel by car. At Nejran he noted that, up to one thousand years ago, it was the see of a Christian bishop, but he saw no traces of a cathedral. There is, however, a small but very ancient Jewish community, whose members were traders.

Continuing the journey, with the addition of fifteen Arabs, who were representatives of the tribes to be met with, at Khadra, the last well in the Najran Valley, the friendly Wahabi governor wished Philby a prosperous journey.

Cars had reached Najran before this, but whether it would be possible for them to reach Shabwa and beyond, constituted a problem, as was also the petrol question. Keeping along the western boundary of the Rub'-al-Khali, we learn that, in a waterless area, a large flock of white sheep with attendant shepherds was passed. To his surprise Philby was informed that white sheep could go without water indefinitely if they were kept away from it ! Black sheep, on the other hand, had to be watered regularly. The shepherds, it was noted, drank the sheeps' milk.

To continue, skirting the barrier of hills, which form the eastern frontier of Yemen, it was found that the cars could travel without any serious difficulty. From Abr to Shabwa, distant some eighty miles, a broad belt of sand-dunes was crossed in a sandstorm and, on the following day, Shabwa, the goal of the journey, was reached.

Philby was naturally anxious as to his reception, since on approaching the tomb of Muhammad bin Buraik, he sighted a number of armed men drawn up in line. To quote from his account:

" I observed one or two important-looking persons and went forward to greet them. One of them, a fierce-looking, fork-bearded individual, I seized by the hand, but he pressed me back firmly, but gently, towards my companions. . . . As we stood there in any sort of order, I observed a movement among our hosts. The long line turned to the right, wheeled left, and wheeled left again to pass before us, and, as they passed, each man shook each one of us by the hand ! "[1]

The famous ruins of Shabwa proved to be disappointingly small and insignificant, but were carefully examined. It was,

[1] *Sheba's Daughters*, p. 80.

however, proved that there had been one temple of supreme magnificence. It was probably dedicated to Astarte.

Sabota, as Pliny termed the city, owed its importance to being the centre of the incense trade. This highly esteemed gum was collected on the northern slopes of the range behind Dhafar,[1] the Ophir of the Bible. To quote Pliny's interesting description:

> "The incense, after being collected, is carried on camels' backs to Sabota, of which place a single gate is left open for its admission. To deviate from the high road while carrying it, the laws have made a capital offence."

He goes on to detail the various charges which included

> "a tenth part in honour of their god".

Before leaving Shabwa, it remains to note that a German, Hans Helfritz by name, had penetrated to the ruined city in 1935. He and his party had arrived in the night, and in the morning when it was known that a "Farangi" was in their midst, intense hostility was displayed. Taking his camera, Helfritz pluckily took some photographs of the ruins and then escaped with his escort through a hail of badly aimed bullets. He was thus the first European to reach Shabwa and deserves credit for his initiative. The above account also proves that Philby, himself a Moslem, who was travelling under the patronage of Ibn Saud with eight guards provided by one of his governors, mainly, if not entirely, owed his friendly reception to these important factors.

Philby was determined to cross Arabia to the Indian Ocean. He was also in need of fresh tyres and supplies. Making for Shibam, he passed through two of the outlying villages of the Hadhramaut whose inhabitants were at war with one another. On the following day he reached a third village which was divided into two hostile sections "living only one hundred yards apart". The "English Peace" had not penetrated to the outlying villages !

To conclude, upon entering the Hadhramaut, Philby was welcomed with friendly hospitality and reaching the port of Shihr, he had completed the last great journey to be made in Arabia, and deserves immense credit for the manner in which he carried through a most arduous task.

[1] *Vide* for a full account of this gum, *Arabia Felix*, by Bertram Thomas, p. 122.

EXPLORATION IN SOUTH-EASTERN TIBET

AMONG the explorers of the present generation, Ronald Kaulback has already won a high position. Coming down from Cambridge, he was elected a fellow of the Royal Geographical Society and decided to make his mark as an explorer. Not only did he study to become a scientific cartographer, but he also gradually ascertained what important areas in Asia were still unexplored.

At that period, as it chanced, Captain Kingdon Ward, the great explorer-botanist, if I may so term him, had decided upon undertaking yet another journey[1] in Asia. He heard of Kaulback's ambition and, after due consideration, decided to take him on it. Kaulback was indeed fortunate to have the privilege of accompanying such an experienced explorer, while Kingdon Ward fully appreciated Kaulback's qualifications. The third member of the expedition was B. R. Brooks Carrington, whose task was to make a natural colour film of the journey.

Starting in 1933, on what proved to be Kaulback's preparatory journey[2] from Sadiya, the last town in Assam, where the British colony gave the explorers every assistance, the Lohit-Brahmaputra valley, inhabited by Mishmi tribesmen, was first followed.

During this section of the journey the amazing steepness of the mountains which rose almost sheer from the river and the dense undergrowth, made marching fatiguing. Added to these natural difficulties, were the attacks of leeches, sandflies and blister flies. The Mishmis were also unfriendly, but Kingdon Ward who knew the country and its primitive inhabitants was able to engage coolies to carry the baggage, albeit not without considerable trouble.

In due course, the expedition reached the Boundary Stone, a large rock which marks the boundary with Tibet. It bears two inscriptions. That in English runs : " 5th Coy., 1st Batt. K.G.O. Sappers and Miners, 1912." The other inscription is in Chinese.

---

[1] Vide " Zayul and the Eastern Tibet Border Country ", in the *Journal of the* R.G.S., Vol. XXI, Part III, for July 1934.

[2] It is described in *Tibetan Trek*, published in 1934. The second and far more important journey was published, in 1938, under the title of *Salween*.

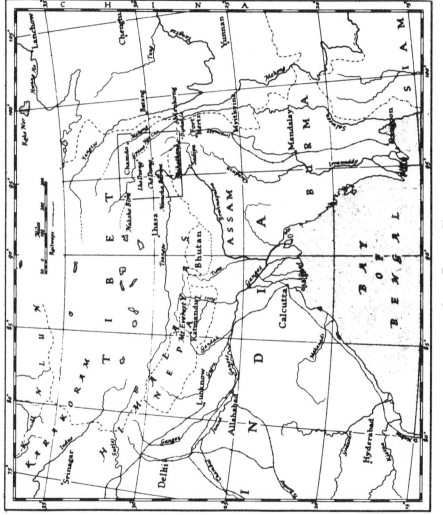

SOUTH-EASTERN TIBET

The explorers had now entered the province of Zayul and the lofty mountains of Tibet were visible in the distance. At Shigatang the Chinese Governor received the explorers in a friendly manner, presenting them with rice, barley flour and eggs when he paid his call. Throughout the journey, food was always a difficulty, since by the religious law of Tibet the abundant game could not be shot. Indeed Kaulback and his companions wisely did not bring firearms into the country.

In Zayul polyandry was the fashion, one woman marrying all the brothers of a family. I had noticed its existence many years ago in Ladakh and had been informed that it was adopted to keep down the population in a barren country.

From Shigatang no progress was possible until a new bridge, consisting of a single rope made entirely of twisted bamboo, was ready. It was then crossed by means of a wooden slide. The Rong To Valley was found to be easily traversed through lofty pine forests. From the village of Rongyul the explorers came to the Ata Chu, which river flows down in a continuous cataract through a superb narrow gorge. In this area, the path ran along insecure galleries of wood pegged into the rocks.

All was going well for the crossing of the main range, when, suddenly, a letter from the India Office, which had been intended to reach the expedition at Sadiya, was received. It laid down that as Kaulback was not expressly mentioned by name on the pass, he could not be allowed to enter Tibet. Actually he had already been in that country for some two months and, with the permisssion of the Tibetan authorities, he was able to accompany Kingdon Ward to the summit of the Ata Kangla. There, at an altitude of 16,000 feet, the two men parted. Kaulback was naturally bitterly disappointed. On the other hand, he had already surveyed some unexplored country and had gained valuable experience in managing the various peoples that inhabit it.

Kingdon Ward had advised him to travel back by the difficult Diphuk La, a pass rising to 14,250 feet and thence to make for Fort Hertz. This journey was accomplished safely by the two Englishmen and, at hospitable Fort Hertz, Kaulback wrote that " it was September 24th, just two hundred days since we had left Sadiya ". The young explorer had gained most valuable experience in this expedition and his motto undoubtedly was : *reculer pour mieux sauter.*

* * * *

In 1935, Kaulback started on his second journey with the

exploration of the Upper Salween and, if possible, the discovery of its source as his main objectives in South-Eastern Tibet.

His companion, Mr. John Hanbury-Tracy, had served in the Sudan and was a trained surveyor.[1] The two explorers, while stopping for a few days at Calcutta, secured the services of two veterans of the Everest quest and, with a carefully selected mass of equipment and stores, they boarded the Burma train, and Myit Kyina, the railhead in Upper Burma, was reached in April, 1935. To Fort Hertz, the two hundred and twenty miles were traversed without difficulty by the use of a car and of mules. No survey work was needed in this area, and so a start was made in collecting insects and reptiles. At Fort Hertz, preparations were completed for the march northwards up the Nam Tamai valley with its very steep banks and dense forests. On May 13th, the snow-clad mountains of Tibet were again sighted and it was feared that the depth of snow on the Diphuk La would prove an insurmountable obstacle. However, the plucky coolies rose to the occasion and, although without boots, fortunately escaped frost-bite when crossing the pass. At Shigatang, the explorers were warmly welcomed with presents of food by old friends and halted until a new bridge had been made. Survey work had been commenced from the Diphuk La and, in view of the routes followed by Captain Bailey in 1931, and by Kingdon Ward in 1933, the only unexplored area was in the Lepa area. At Lepa they were stormbound for eleven days, since survey was out of the question without clear weather. It was a village of ten houses, producing wheat and barley. There were also cattle and sheep.

On July 4th, Lepa was left in fine weather, and for three days the explorers mounted through pine forests with clumps of bamboos and rhododendra to the Duk La, at 13,990 feet. Two days later, after a very stiff climb, the summit of the La Sar was reached at 14,930 feet. This pass consisted merely of a cleft in a knife-edged ridge barely six feet wide at the top and extremely steep on both sides. Since it was blocked by a cornice of frozen snow which overhung for some twenty feet, it seemed to constitute a hopeless obstacle, but the plucky coolies attacked it with their knives. For over an hour there was no sign of progress when, suddenly, the snow cornice fell and there was sufficient width through which to lower the animals and the baggage on to the path below.

[1] *Vide* " A Journey in the Salween and Tsungpo Basins, South-Eastern Tibet ", by Ronald Kaulback, in *The Geographical Journal* of February 1938. He also published his adventures in *Salween*, in 1938. Mr. Hanbury-Tracy published *Black River of Tibet* in the same year.

Later it was decided that the two explorers should divide and explore the different sides of the range and should meet again at Dashing. This plan worked out successfully, as did others, but the growth of a beard by Hanbury-Tracy resulted in his being considered to be a Russian. Reference was made to Lhasa and three months later the reply was received confirming the British nationality of both of the explorers. But this delay made it impossible, if only from lack of funds, to complete the plan of travelling to the source of the Salween. Accordingly, it was decided to concentrate on the Salween lower down and on the Salween-Brahmaputra watershed to the south. Actually this range was crossed by one or the other of the industrious surveyors no less than six times. Winter was now at hand and the explorers, a great task accomplished, returned to Sadiya. To conclude this brief summary, the two explorers, in twenty-one months, had surveyed an area of unexplored country measuring 25,000 square miles, which is practically the size of Ireland.

IV

THE VALLEY OF THE ASSASSINS—LURISTAN AND THE HADHRAMAUT

" The Old Man . . . had caused a certain valley between two mountains to be enclosed, and had turned it into a garden, the largest and most beautiful that ever was seen . . . And there were runels too, flowing freely with wine and milk, and honey and water ; and numbers of ladies and of the most beautiful damsel in the world."

YULE's *Marco Polo*, Vol. I, pp. 139–40.

FREYA STARK has won her laurels as an ardent and fearless explorer in Persia and also in the Hadhramaut. To deal with her journeys in the former country, they fall into two parts, the first of which was a journey to the famous " Valley of the Assassins " in 1930. The second part deals with her exploration in the Pusht-i-Kuh of Western Persia, consisting of two journeys, undertaken in 1931 and 1932 respectively.[1] Her visits to the Hadhramaut included some unexplored country and the last journey was made in 1938.

To describe her first journey, starting from Kazvin, she marched north-east, stopping at the villages of Dastgird and Chala in the plain. Later, crossing a pass and climbing down a steep descent, she reached the point at which the Alamut and Talagan streams united to form the Shahrud river. The village called Shirkuh constituted the " Western Gate " of the Valley of the Assassins, the steep path being guarded by a fortress, of which the traveller heard only when it was too late to visit it.

The Rock of Alamut, the stronghold of the famous " Old Man of the Mountain ", is described as rising 3,000 feet above the valley and the castle of Nevisar Shah situated " on a pyramid of rock 3,000 feet above the Alamut ", constitutes the " Eastern Gate ". To this latter ruined castle the explorer climbed and found it to stand at about 10,000 feet. It is most satisfactory to have this question definitely settled, since Marco Polo[2] wrote of " a certain valley between two mountains ".

The next objective of the explorer was another stronghold

---

[1] *Vide* " The Assassins' Valley and the Salambar Pass ", in *The Geographical Journal*, January 1931 ; also *The Valleys of the Assassins*, 1934.
[2] *Vide* Yule's *Marco Polo*, Vol. I., p. 139.

of the Assassins at Lamiasar, which had not previously been visited by a European. Crossing into the thickly wooded district of Rudbar, this fortress was also climbed. Its chief building covered a space of 100 feet by 85 feet and there were numerous ruined cisterns. Among the various tribes met with were the Jangalis,[1] who had given the British much trouble during the first World War.

A break in the journey was caused by the explorer succumbing to the malarious climate of Muzanderan. Treated with much kindness by everyone, she was carried back to the Alamut Valley where, most providentially, a Persian doctor appeared on the scene and took her to a neighbouring village where she speedily recovered. With considerable courage she returned to malarial Mazanderan and ended her journey on the shores of the Caspian Sea.

* * * * *

In the autumn of 1931, Freya Stark, lured by the find of mysterious bronzes of an ancient civilization in the Tazhan area east of the Saidmarreh River in north-western Luristan, attempted to reach that area, but was prevented from doing so " by the solicitude of the Persian police ", as she puts it.[2]

On a second occasion, the determined explorer fared better. She secured a *visa* for Persia without any restrictions, and engaging two muleteers (who were probably smugglers), with their two mules, on the Irak frontier, she avoided a Persian town and a Persian police post successfully and reached a small encampment of Lurs, who were kinsmen of the muleteers. Her guide was an aged quilt-maker, who was a Lur, and who gained respect by his frequent prayers !

The position at the time was that the *Vali* of Pusht-i-Kuh had left the country and was living in exile at Baghdad, while the Persian Government was attempting to stop smuggling and to impose a most unpopular " new order " on the recalcitrant inhabitants. For example, the import of sugar and tea, the only luxuries of the tribesmen, together with cotton stuffs, was strictly forbidden, as was the export of charcoal.

Passing the Customs Post of Mansurabad, the explorer arrived in the Pusht-i-Kuh and a north-east direction was followed across a desolate belt of country without inhabitants to Pir Mohad. There a shrine with four blue minarets and a dome was occupied by Sayyids, who claimed to be of Arab

[1] For the Jangalis *vide* my *History of Persia*, 3rd ed., Vol. II, p. 489.
[2] *Vide* " The Pusht-i-Kuh ", in *The Geographical Journal* of September 1932 ; also *The Valleys of the Assassins*.

descent. At dusk Arkwaz was reached, where the result of a drought was such that the villagers, as soon as their store of flour was exhausted, were reduced to living on acorns ground and kneaded into bread, which was fatal for the children in many cases. It was also noticeable that, owing to the disarmament of the tribes, wolves and boars were increasing in numbers, much to the detriment of flocks and crops.

Not far from Kabir Kuh, a ruined city, apparently dating from Sasanian days, was examined. Not long after, the energetic explorer, who had dug up two graves and had found some pottery and a skull, was overtaken by a lieutenant of the Police, under whose escort she was taken to the town of Husainabad which had recently been founded as the new capital of the country. Everywhere she was treated with politeness, but, nevertheless, she was escorted back to the Persian frontier.

Among other objects of interest, she mentioned the construction of a motor road, which joined the Karind-Kerman road, and was nearly completed. Before recrossing the frontier, she wrote : " Nothing can mitigate the surrounding nakedness and the impression of desolation increases as one rides hour after hour through the shadeless chaos." Such were her final impressions of the Pusht-i-Kuh.

*   *   *   *   *

Freya Stark travelled in the Hadhramaut on more than one occasion. On her last journey,[1] in the Spring of 1938, she was accompanied by Miss Caton-Thompson, who laid bare a temple dedicated to the Moon God, and by Miss Gardener, who examined the geology of the district.

The important exploration of the Hadhramaut carried out by Mr. Ingrams is described on p. 358. Miss Stark mainly followed in his footsteps, but I will now deal with her journey from Hureida to the coast, which, to some extent, lay across unexplored country. In the first section of her journey, the Wadi 'Amd was found to be inhabited by the Jada tribe. Its Chief, " a fine grey-beard with six old bullet wounds scattered about him ", was advised by a Council of Elders. As to the representative of the Qu'aiti Government, he was a stranger and a slave, and the English visitor was asked " whether I would advise sending a deputation to Mr. Ingrams or murdering him first ! "

Further on, the explorer suffered from an attack of fever,

[1] " An Exploration in the Hadhramaut and Journey to the Coast ", *The Geographical Journal*, January 1939.

but, with the courage which she invariably displayed, she decided to continue the journey and chose the Azzan route, which was largely unexplored and ran across the healthy uplands that were free of malaria.

Miss Stark was especially anxious to trace the ancient frankincense route with its Himyaritic inscriptions, and considered that it probably ran to the west of the great fortress of Nakab-al-Hajar [1] to Shabwa. Of especial interest was the fact that the local tribesmen retain the ancient name of Beni Himyar. They proved to be somewhat hostile but, after a skirmish with her guard, became relatively friendly.

A few days previously the R.A.F. had landed at Azzan and the local Sultans were hoping to establish the " English Peace ", as they termed it. To conclude, the Arabian Sea was reached at Balhaf, a miserable roadstead, situated on the edge of a bare volcanic range. It consisted of three towers and a few huts, and the nearest water supply was distant some eight miles. One of the last incidents was a demonstration of hostility against the family of the local Sultan. From this most inhospitable coast, a dhow bore the explorer to Mukalla.

To sum up, Freya Stark has proved herself to be a most courageous and determined explorer in little-known countries ; her powers of observation and writing are remarkable, as is also her gift of establishing friendly relations with their inhabitants. More especially in the Hadhramaut, her knowledge of Arabic helped her. Finally, her illustrations are admirable.

[1] *Vide* p. 282 for Wellsted's discovery, in 1834, of this ancient fortress and of the first Himyaritic inscriptions. For Shabwa *vide* Philby's *Sheba's Daughters*, p. 60.

V

THE GOBI DESERT

FEW travellers have undergone greater hardships and risks than Miss Mildred Cable and her devoted companions Miss Francesca and Miss Eva French. Distinguished members of the China Inland Mission, for twenty-one years they had worked with remarkable success to build up a system of schools in the distant province of Shansi.

One day, they received orders to fight the good fight for Christianity in the dreaded Gobi Desert.[1] To hear was to obey ! Accordingly, leaving their headquarters at Hwochow, their first objective was Kanchow, one of the principal cities of the province of Tangut. With Suchow, as the second important centre, the province has been aptly named Kansu.

Travelling through bandit-infested areas in a cart drawn by mules, and occasionally guarded by truculent soldiers, who invariably attempted blackmail, the party was welcomed by Dr. Kao, a capable Chinese medical missionary, whose influence in Kansu was remarkable. It is of especial interest to note that Marco Polo was the governor of this.city for some time and described the population as consisting of " Idolators, Saracens and Christians ".

The Kansu province touches the borders of Tibet and, ever anxious to preach Christianity to the Tibetans, a special journey, which involved crossing a " muddy, roaring, tumultuous " river, was undertaken. Upon reaching the Lamaserai, " red-robed lamas " and " Living Buddhas " welcomed the ladies, as did a number of Tibetan women.

Miss Cable's comment on the weird rituals which she witnessed ran : " One felt oneself to be in the presence of very old and very evil influences." She also noted that the acolytes of the " Buddha Incarnate " chose among the girls the goodliest to do his pleasure.

From Kanchow the important city of Suchow was the

---

[1] *Vide* " The Bazars of Tangut and the Trade Routes of Dzungaria ", in the *Journal of the* R.G.S., July 1934 ; and " A New Era in the Gobi ", ditto, November-December 1942. Also *Through Jade Gate and Central Asia*, by Mildred Cable and Francesca French, 1927 ; and *The Gobi Desert*, by Mildred Cable and Francesca French, 1943.

next objective. Here, seeking Cathay, Bento de Goes [1] found heaven, as his biographer writes. Miss Cable discovered and photographed his grave.

At Suchow, some time was spent in making careful preparations for the arduous task ahead. It was of great importance to make the acquaintance of the citizens who traded or who owned transport, in addition to the necessity of collecting information as to the stages, the supplies and, above all, the water. The atmosphere, as Miss Cable puts it, was rather that of Central Asia than of China.

Suchow is proud of not possessing a Western Gate and, in reply to a puzzled traveller, will exclaim : " Kiayukwan is the western gate of our city." To-day this " Barrier of the Pleasant Valley ", as the name signifies, has three gates, that opening on to the Desert of Gobi being termed the " Gate of Sighs ". Travelling was made especially arduous by the long distance between wells or streams which necessitated travelling by night, since the mules could not support the long stages, if made in the heat of the day.

The Gobi has many ruined cities, owing to war, and perhaps even still more, to desiccation. Yet at Tunhwang, the travellers visited the great " Tower of the Thousand Buddhas ", whose artistic and historical wonders have been described by the late Sir Aurel Stein. [2]

The population of the Gobi, which depends mainly on supplying the needs of wayfarers, is hard, but yet they are not dullards, and an inscription on the wall of a filthy inn ran :

" Jewels and gems are but stones ;
" Barley and beans strengthen your bones."

The history of this great trade route, known also as the Silk Road, has been dealt with fully in this work, [3] and Miss Cable is at her best in describing the many races she met and lived among. With the Chinese there was a background of more than twenty years of sympathetic understanding. Again, with the Moslems, thanks partly to the gifts of sections of the Bible and to her medical skill, it was understood, by the women at any rate, that the visitors were " people of Allah ", to give them the name by which they were called. Also Moslems, living with Mongols and Chinese, are much less fanatical than in purely Moslem countries.

---

[1] For the journey of Bento de Goes, *vide* pp. 160, 161.
[2] *Vide* pp. 253 and 255 of this work.
[3] *Vide* pp. 21 and 48.

Before quitting the Chinese Empire, an insight into the extraordinary character of its inhabitants is revealed in the following note : " In one place the splintered rocks have been so handled as to present the effect of armed men ready for defence, and a perfect illusion has been secured with the minimum of trouble."

From a geographer's point of view, the province of Turfan merits especial attention, since it represents the deepest portion of a great fault trough, which descends to a thousand feet below sea level. To mark the contrast, the neighbouring snow-covered peaks of Bogda-Ola rise to 22,000 feet. The fertility of the oasis is amazing and, to quote Miss Cable : " The productiveness depends on underground supplies connected with the eternal snows which have never been known to fail."

Turfan also possesses another interest, for its ruins, termed Dakianus and also Apsus, were definitely the work of Persian architects. Some fifty years ago, I visited ruins, situated some sixty miles inland from Bundar Abbas, a port on the Persian Gulf, which bore a similar name. In reply to my enquiries, it appeared that " Dakianus " was the Roman Emperor Decius and that owing to his persecution of the Christians of Apsus or Ephesus, seven of them, followed by a dog, took refuge in a cave. Here we undoubtedly have the legend of the " Seven Sleepers ", who, according to Moslem belief, await the call of Allah on the Day of Judgement to quit this sanctuary.[1]

Miss Cable gives some valuable information on the benefits of this great trade route which have been granted to humanity. To it China owed the grape vine, the walnut and lucerne clover and it gave to Europe the silkworm, the peach, the apricot and many medicinal plants.

To conclude, this book gives us much valuable information and, for many years to come, will remain the leading work on the *Gobi Desert* and its interesting inhabitants.

[1] *Vide* Sykes, *Ten Thousand Miles in Persia*, p. 267.

THE HADHRAMAUT

" Thou from the first
Wast present, and with mighty wings outspread
Dove-like sats't brooding on the vast abyss,
And madest it pregnant."

MILTON.

THE shores of the Hadhramaut can claim an almost immemorial antiquity and, in the Book of Genesis, Hazarmaveth, described as a son of Joktan, is undoubtedly Hadhramaut. To-day its inhabitants also proudly claim to be descendants of Joktan.

The exploration and establishment of order in this historical land was the task assigned to W. H. Ingrams, C.M.G., O.B.E.,[1] who was aided by his gifted wife throughout.

Ingrams had held appointments at Zanzibar, Mauritius and Aden. At Zanzibar he met natives of the Hadhramaut, many of whom had amassed considerable fortunes in Malaya and the Dutch Indies. In their old age they, generally speaking, returned to end their days in the Hadhramaut, in spite of its entire lack of modern communications, the incessant tribal warfare and private feuds. They built magnificent fortified houses, imported motor cars with great difficulty, using camel transport, and were naturally anxious to secure something of the civilization which they had learned to prize. Appeals were consequently made to Sir Bernard Reilly, the Governor of the Aden Protectorate, who instructed Ingrams to explore and report on this little-known portion of his charge.

Before describing his adventurous Mission, it is desirable to refer to an Agreement which had been negotiated in 1918 between the British Government and the Qu'aitis and Kathiris, the two principal tribes of the Hadhramaut. By its terms, these two rulers declared that the Hadhramaut constituted an appanage of the British Empire. The Qu'aiti Sultan, it was declared, ruled the whole country, but the Kathiris were to manage their own domestic affairs.

In 1934, Mr. and Mrs. Ingrams landed at Mukalla, the

---

[1] *Vide* his *Arabia and the Isles*; also his "Hadhramaut: A Journey to the Sei'ar Country and through the Wadi Maseila" in *The Geographical Journal*, Vol. LXVIII, No. 6, December 1936.

capital of the Qu'aiti Sultan, where the various activities of the Government, which included an armed force of 400 Yafa'i mercenaries, and a cadet force of slave boys were inspected. Schools and a hospital were also inspected.

In due course, camel transport was engaged and the travellers started off into the interior with the Wadi Duan as their first objective. On the way a chief object of interest was the Tomb of Mola Matar, a giant and prophet of the tribe of Ad. This recalled the well-known " There were giants in the land in those days ! " In view of the sanctity of the tomb, the inhabitants or travellers handed over their property to be kept for them, without any fear of robbery.

Ingrams was deeply impressed by his first view of the Wadi Duan. Standing on the edge of a thousand foot precipice, he sighted date palms set in green crops with towns and great castles of the same colour as the sand-coloured cliffs in the distance. The descent into the valley took over an hour and the reactions of the author ran : " Sleep brooded over the place . . . the eternal sleep of a distant past which has never known an awakening."

The notables of Duan welcomed the party warmly and they soon sighted the white pillars, which, by a curious custom, marked the boundaries within which the bedouin may not raid each other. The main water supply is drawn from deep wells, the canals serving for the distribution of flood water, on which the crops mainly depended.

The palatial forts, whose interiors of purely Arab design were of peculiar beauty, were visited, and the hospitality of their owners was princely. Duan, it is interesting to note, has been identified with the Thabane of Ptolemy and the Thoani of Pliny.

One host was asked whether floods were not dangerous. His reply was : " Yes, in the time of Father Nuh (Noah), the whole land was covered with water. Nuh and his family built a great ship and lived in it while the flood lasted ! "

The Wadi Hadhramaut, which was now entered, is described by the explorer as " the key feature " of the geography of the country, to which it owes its name. North and south of it, the land rises to extensive plateaux which form watersheds. The one to the north, about 3,500 feet above sea level, has a series of wadis draining north into the sands, and another series draining south into the Wadi Hadhramaut. The watershed to the south, consisting in the same way of plateaux, is higher than that to the north, for it rises to some 6,000 feet.

From it, the wadis drain north into the Wadi Hadhramaut and south to the sea ".[1]

Continuing the journey, Shibam, described as the " eye and backbone of the Hadhramaut ", was next visited. The bulk of its trade came from Mukalla, but it was also the chief market for the surrounding tribes. The Sei'ar, the most important of these nomads, described by Ingrams as " the wolves of South Arabia ", interested him and he decided to visit their unexplored territory.

Starting with a small caravan of Sei'ar and Harizi tribesmen, he marched north-west to the Wadi Ser. On the following day he visited a tomb of the Prophet Saleh, on which a Himyaritic inscription was copied. Later, turning into the Wadi Ser, he marched north, following in the footsteps of the Bents to a tomb with another Himyaritic inscription.[2] The Sei'ar country was now entered, and caravans with charcoal and timber for the Shibam market were met, with whom the customary greetings were exchanged. Farther on, a small party of men on riding camels approached the party. They dismounted, but made no responses to the greetings. This, at first, appeared to be ominous, but, in due course, it was explained that these camel-riders had a feud in the neighbourhood and therefore wished to pass through *incognito*!

Later, the son of a Sei'ar Chief, " anxious to obtain our bounties ", met the party, and a height of 3,600 feet was reached. It was the highest ridge on the plateau to the north of the Wadi Hadhramaut. This was the farthest point to which Ingrams penetrated, but the return journey through this desolate country was made by the Wadi Maseila. The last lap was covered in a car.

Seiyun, which was visited more than once, is the capital of Kathiri land, and was ruled by the Sultan Ali bin Mansur, whom Ingrams describes as " one of the most delightful and perhaps the most lovable of the chiefs of the Protectorate ". Possessing an ample fortune, derived from property in Singapore, he spent the scanty revenue on the public service. He was also the leading Moslem figure in supporting Ingrams, whose crowning achievement was to carry through a " Three Years' Truce ".

The last section of this important journey to the port of Seihut, a distance of 200 miles, lay mainly down the Wadi Maseila, through entirely unexplored country. At some of the

[1] " Hadhramaut : A Journey to the Sei'ar Country and through the Wadi Maseila ", *Royal Geographical Journal*, No. 6, December 1936.
[2] *Vide* Mrs. Bent's *Southern Arabia*, p. 129.

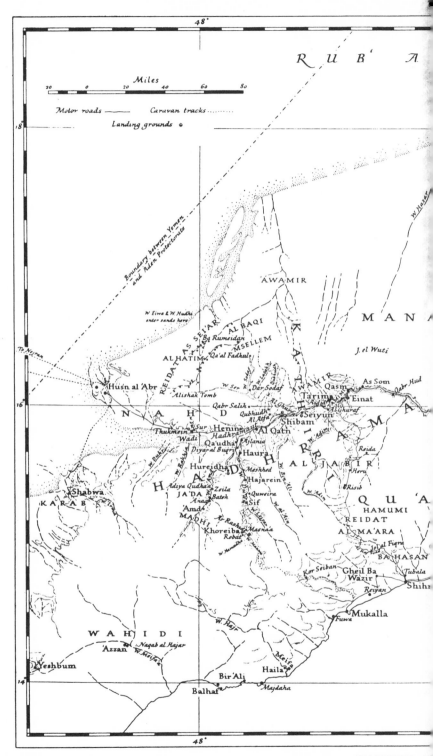

EASTERN A[

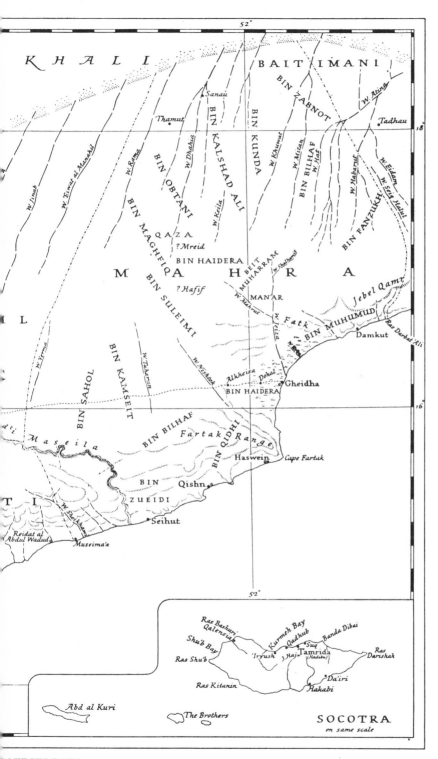

stages there was no water, at others it was very bad. At the little village of Hudhafa a *Siyar*, who may perhaps be described as "a walking passport", was engaged as representing the Bin Sahal clan of the Mahras. A lad of sixteen, at night he would climb the cliff and loudly proclaim that the caravan was under his protection! The Mahras occupy a wide tract of country and their Sultan now resides in Sokotra. The Bin Zueidi, whom the explorers met later on, also belonged to the Mahra tribe. Much of the country is volcanic, with hot sulphur springs.

Nearing the coast, a youthful Zueidi *Siyar* was engaged and the journey towards the coast continued. However, at a village on the estuary, men of the Bin Zueidi threatened to shoot the explorers as being *Nasara* or Christians. They also claimed that the Siyar system was not intended to cover *Nasara*. The situation was tense for a while and loaded rifles were aimed at Ingrams. Fortunately the *Siyar* declared that he would fight to defend him, as did the caravan drivers, who opportunely appeared on the scene in strength. The explorers accordingly were permitted to pass on to the stage at Darfat, close to Seihut, which port was entered early on the following morning.

Sultan Saud, the Governor, was a very sick man, who explained that the Zueidis had descended from their mountains a few years previously, and had seized the port. They even levied the taxes. However, no further difficulties were experienced, a dhow of twenty tons burden was engaged and, touching at the port of Shihr, the travellers landed at Mukalla, after accomplishing a journey of the greatest importance.

I have not hitherto mentioned the valuable rôle that was played by the Royal Air Force in the establishment of law and order in the Hadhramaut, but I cannot refrain from giving a brief mention of their work. When murders or other outrages were proved against lawless members of the community, they and their chiefs were generally assessed in live-stock. The defendants were further informed that if the tribe had not submitted by a certain date, the Royal Air Force would bomb their village and, when the bombing was imminent, they were warned to quit it. Somewhat naturally the tribesmen would not believe that anything would really happen, but, on the first occasion, five aeroplanes flew over the guilty village and dropped two smoke bombs, followed by a real bomb which fell in the fields. Finally, big bombs were dropped on the houses with the result that the Hadhramaut suddenly realized that law and order would be established. The defendants indeed said : " You did well to bomb us and we thank you. If we had given in before, people would have said that we were cowards."

To conclude, Ingrams was rightly proclaimed " Father of the Hadhramaut ".

VII

THE YEMEN

" The multitude of camels shall cover thee, the dromedaries of
Midian and Ephah ; all they from Sheba shall come ; they shall
bring gold and incense."

Isaiah LX., v. 6.

To the north of the port of Aden with its forbidding rocks,
rises a great mountain mass. Its tablelands, to quote Hugh
Scott, F.R.S., Sc.D.,[1] average 8,000 feet in height, while the
higher peaks, as yet incompletely surveyed, tower to more than
12,000 feet. The heavy rainfall of the south-west monsoon,
strikes these mountains and, by assuring their fertility, renders
the neighbouring country of Yemen, with Aden included,
to have been appropriately named *Arabia Felix* by the
Romans.[2]

The chief object of Messrs. Scott and Britton was to form
representative collections, comparable to those already made by
Scott in Abyssinia. Although the insects of the region were
their principal object, bats, reptiles and frogs were not passed
by, while 600 specimens of flowering plants and ferns were
collected.

While awaiting the permisssion of the *Imam* to enter Yemen,
a journey was undertaken to the heights of Jabal Jihaf, rising
to 7,800 feet in the vicinity of Dhala, which is situated some
90 miles inland from Aden. It proved to be a great massif of
igneous rock and a profitable month was spent on its heights,
the bag including " fairy shrimps ", the most primitive of all
small crustaceans and solifugids, who possess powerful shears
on either side of the mouth, with which they kill insects. It
remains to add that, as was appropriate, in the Land of Ur, a
shrine venerated by the Arabs as the tomb of Eyyub, the
Patriarch Job, was shown to the travellers.

In due course, the important permission was received
from the Imam of the Yemen. It announced that the travellers
would be welcomed at Tai'izz, the southern capital, on the
condition that their movements were strictly supervised.

[1] *Vide* " A Journey to the Yemen ", in *The Geographical Journal* for February 1939 ;
also *In the High Yemen*, by Dr. Scott, 1942.
[2] *Vide* p. 279 of this work.

Scott and his companion were quick to take advantage of this permission. They soon crossed the frontier and entered Tai'izz, the most beautiful city of Yemen, which lies at an altitude of 4,500 feet. The walls that enclose it on three sides run at either end up the slope of the range, on which is situated the residence of the Governor-General of southern Yemen.

A second permission was now granted to visit San'a. Accordingly, from Tai'izz, the journey was continued by motor transport to Sayani. At this town, the heavy baggage was loaded on camels and, crossing a pass at an altitude of 8,000 feet, Ibb, situated at 6,700 feet was reached. Described by Scott as " one of the very kernels of the East ", with its sixty mosques and teeming population, the city stands on the spur of a mountain which rises behind it to over 8,000 feet. Eastwards again rises a still higher range. Scott mentions that pots on roof gardens were everywhere seen, and he was informed that sweet basil was universally grown to be stuck in turbans at marriages and other festivities.

To resume the journey, the travellers now passed through a high-lying area, 9,700 feet being registered at one point on the road. Indeed the collecting of beetles was ended for the present owing to the cold. The last stage before San'a was Yarim, where " a very military reception was accorded us ". Scott notes that Forskal, the botanist in Niebuhr's Mission, had died at this city.[1]

The last long stage to San'a was made in a car, with a halt at Dhamar, where a police officer, " who spoke some English ", said that our arrival would be telephoned to the capital. However, on knocking at the gate of San'a late at night, entrance was denied until a note written in Arabic, handed through a chink in the wooden gate, " finally caused the gates to be swung back."

San'a, lying at the altitude of 7,900 feet, did not rise to its present importance until the destruction of the famous dam of Marib[2] ruined that ancient capital. Under its earlier name of Bir al Azal, it is traditionally connected with Uzal, the son of Joktan, who appears in the Book of Genesis as the brother of Hazarmaveth.

The buildings resemble those of the Hadhramaut, rising to a considerable height. The Turkish occupation, which indeed only ended in 1918, left considerable traces, in particular in its mosques which were built in the sixteenth or early seventeenth century.

[1] *Vide* pp. 278–9 of this work.　　　[2] *Vide* p. 284 of this work.

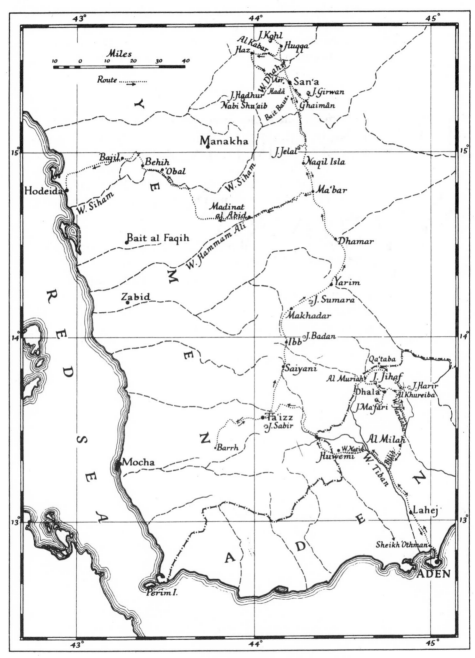

THE YEMEN
(Showing the routes taken by Dr. Hugh Scott)

365

The Jews, who were to be seen everywhere, wore long curls, while the dress of the women was distinctive. The San'a silver filigree work which they make is well known. As elsewhere, they occupy a separate quarter and their houses are only two storeys high.

The English visitors were, after a long delay, received by the *Imam* Yahya, who was immersed in his work, which he apparently controls to the smallest administrative detail, possibly mistrusting the honesty of his staff. Interrupting his labours, he " asked us many questions about our motive for visiting his country and the practical uses of our work ". Soon, however, he returned to his accounts. At a later interview with the *Imam*, after some explanation of his work, Scott, after thanking him, asked for permission to take his departure and to travel by the old Manakha mule track to Hodeida. This he was most anxious to do, owing to the high altitude traversed, but to his annoyance this reasonable request was refused.

The journey to Hodeida was, however, successfully accomplished, and finally Scott with his collections packed in forty-seven packages, once more landed at Aden. He had accomplished useful geographical work in the Yemen, quite apart from the valuable collections he had made. His book will long remain the standard work on the subject.

VIII

A JOURNEY THROUGH CENTRAL ASIA

ONE of the greatest trade routes in Asia, that connects China with Sinkiang (Chinese Turkestan) and the West, had been followed by illustrious Marco Polo and by his successors whose journeys across the Gobi Desert have been recorded in this work.

In 1935, Major Peter Fleming and Miss Ella Maillart, travelling at the time when the Chinese Empire was in a disturbed condition, gallantly decided to explore a route to Sinkiang *via* the Tsaidam Swamp, and, as we shall see, successfully carried through this very difficult enterprise.[1] The route to be followed lay through Lanchow and, thanks to the enterprise of Miss Maillart, valuable guides up to the Tsaidam were found in the shape of White Russians, Stepan Smigunov and his wife, " who had lived and traded in the Tsaidam for several years ", and were anxious to return there. The expenses of the journey were offered to, and accepted by them. Smigunov spoke Mongoli, Turki and a little Chinese, while Russian was the language they had in common.

The adventurers, as they might certainly be termed, left Peking on February 15, 1935 and, in due course of time, reached Sian, the terminus of their railway journey. General Chiang Kai-Shek, the Commander-in-Chief of the Nanking armies and his equally distinguished wife, had recently visited Sian and had launched a campaign for the social regeneration of China; it is certainly interesting to hear of their beneficent activities at this period.

The next stage of the journey to Lanchow was made on an overcrowded lorry. Loaded up with passengers and freight by 8 a.m., it only started off at dusk, owing to the application of official pressure. There were actually three lorries and, after their falls through bridges and other mishaps, the owner of the convoy stated that they were held up indefinitely for repairs. However, another lorry was finally engaged, which started off with twenty-seven passengers and, on February 27, Lanchow, the capital of Kansu, was reached.

[1] *Vide* " A Journey through Central Asia ", by Peter Fleming, in *The Geographical Journal* for August 1936 ; also *Forbidden Journey*, by Ella Maillart, 1937.

The city was under martial law—at any rate as far as foreigners were concerned—and, in spite of six days' hard work, " Ma and Fu " alone were permitted to continue their journey, and the unfortunate Smigunovs were ordered to be deported back to the coast.

The next section of the journey to Sining was accomplished by employing three hired mules. On the second day, the Yellow River was crossed by ferry and Sining was reached in five stages. At this centre it was declared by the Chinese authorities that their passports were out of order, but, pending orders from Nanking, the travellers were permitted to visit the famous monastery of Kum-bum.' Upon returning to Sining, a passport was issued to them authorizing a visit to the Koko Nor.

Quitting Sining for Tangar, the last Chinese village on the edge of the Tibetan plateau, they were befriended by Mr. and Mrs. Urlep of the China Inland Mission. Indeed, thanks to their influence, on March 28, they were able to continue the journey with four camels. They also carried an introduction to the Prince of Dzun,[1] the chief of one of the four tribes in the Tsaidam area.

In due course they joined the camp of the Prince who " received us kindly, but did not know quite what to make of us ". The real journey now began, in the sense that relatively well-known China had been left behind. The Tsaidam which politically formed part of China, and, geographically, was part of Tibet, is inhabited by Mongols, who actually wear Tibetan dress.

Travelling along the southern shore of the Koko Nor at an altitude of 10,000 feet as members of a caravan of men and camels over a mile long, at the halts an addition to the larder was usually made by bagging a goose or a hare or, on one occasion, an antelope. On April 5, a steep pass at the altitude of some 12,000 feet was crossed. At Dzunchia, the Prince had reached his headquarters, consisting of a dilapidated monastery, around which a trading post had sprung up.

Continuing the journey with fresh camels, at Teijinat, by good fortune, the travellers found Borodishin, a friend of the Smigunovs, whose home it had been. Invited to visit the young Prince of the Mongols, who was acting for his father, the explorers were not received with the usual laws of hospitality in the form of a roast sheep. Nor would their host in any way

[1] The word signifies " left " and also appears in Dzungaria, the country to the North-West of Sinkiang.

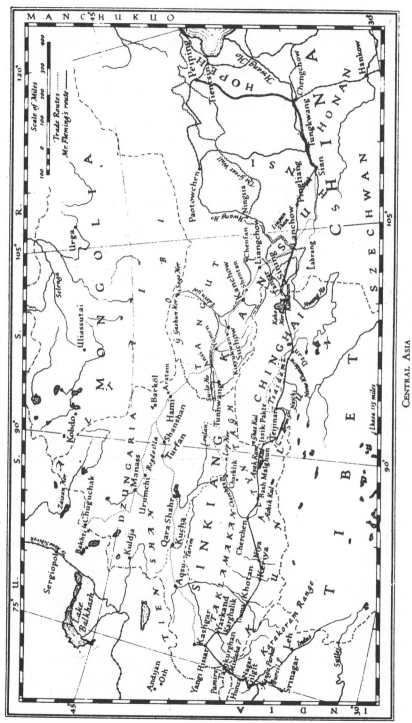

CENTRAL ASIA

(Showing the route of Major Fleming and Ella Maillart)

help to find camels for the onward journey. It was also unfortunate that from no source could they learn anything as to the political situation in Sinkiang, there being no contact whatever with that province. Borodishin, however, advised them to follow a track through the mountains. This they did under the guidance of their Cossack friend and camping the first night in the gorges of the Boron Gol and then crossing a desert country 14,000 feet above sea level, in four stages they reached a Turki encampment at Issik Pakte. Once again there was no news whatever about the situation in Sinkiang, the few Turki families living entirely cut off from their fellows. Their Cossack friend here quitted them, since, as Fleming put it : " White Russians have a very low survival value in Sinkiang."

Before leaving, however, he arranged for the Turkis to provide two guides and, on May 29, the journey was continued. For two days the route lay along the northern shore of an immense salt lake, the Ayak Kum Kul, where water of bad quality was obtained by digging in the shingle. On June 1, a low pass had to be crossed ; the camels had already shown signs of distress and one of them now collapsed. That night a halt was made in a waterless gully at the elevation of 15,000 feet. The barley was finished and there was no other forage. On the next day a second camel collapsed. About the same time Ella Maillart's pony also collapsed at a river called Tornksai. The explorers were now working round the northern slopes of the Achik Kul Tagh, and a very long march was made to yet another waterless camp. At last, however, on June 8, Bash Malghun, a small Turki encampment was reached where they were told the distance to Cherchen and hired two donkeys. Finally, on June 13, the last range separating the explorers from the Takla Makan basin was crossed and, on the following day, they camped within sight of the oasis of Cherchen.

Upon their arrival in this paradise, as it seemed to them, they were arrested and their passports were taken from them, but were duly returned with the necessary visas. Indeed there were no signs of hostility, and they were soon thrilled by the sight of the Union Jack flying over the house of the British Agent or *Aksakal*,[1] whose influence had, in all probability, secured this happy solution to a question which, for long, had been the cause of serious anxiety.

The onward journey lay for some few stages across deserts but, at the oases, supplies were abundant. In due course

---

[1] *Aksakal* signifies " White Beard " and is the invariable title given to British Agents in Sinkiang.

Khotan,[1] the headquarters of the Tungan army, was reached and a visit was paid tʋ the Commander-in-Chief of the Tungans. Badruddin, the elderly Aksakal[2] was still holding the post, but the greatest interest was excited by meeting an Armenian who took in *The Times*, which was delivered by a donkey-man wearing " a leather belt with a metal plate inscribed ' British Indian Postman ' ". In due course, Yarkand was reached and, finally, the explorers were warmly welcomed by Colonel and Mrs. Thomson-Glover at the British Consulate-General, Kashgar.

After enjoying the delights of this historical city, the explorers followed the usual route *via* Gilgit to Srinagar, the capital of Kashmir, which they reached on September 12. Thus ended an adventurous and exhausting journey of 3,500 miles, covered in seven months. In exploring unknown country where supplies and water were hard to come by and where life was held cheap, Peter Fleming and Ella Maillart had accomplished a remarkable feat.

[1] Khotan, more correctly Yu-tien, signifies " Kingdom of Jade ".
[2] He rendered invaluable service to the late Sir Aurel Stein.

THE SOUTHERN LUT

THE exploration of the Lut, so termed from the Patriarch Lot, owes much to the courage of Dr. Alfons Gabriel [1] and his gallant wife. He lays down that "we must distinguish two great belts of desert, which are separated by the East Persian mountains. . . . The one belt lies completely within the boundaries of Persia. This belt begins immediately outside Teheran and stretches for over 600 miles right into the heart of Persian Baluchistan".

In his first journey, landing in the Persian Gulf, Dr. Gabriel visited Bashakard and, entering the Lut, first investigated its great northern swamps. Four years later, several months were spent in the salt-swamps of northern Persia and the *Rig-i-Jinn* or "Sand-desert of the Jinns" was also explored. He then travelled in the Sarhad of Persian Baluchistan. In a third journey a tract of the size of Belgium was examined in the southern area of the Lut.

In February 1937, the explorer started from Fahzy (a village on the edge of the desert east of Bam) and made for Nasratabad (Sipi) which is situated on the caravan route to Sistan. From Nasratabad, he marched due north through a mass of sand dunes, "a waste of giant waves sculptured in sand". Along the route he saw camel-dung and was informed that Afghan rifle smugglers used this desert route, thereby avoiding centres at which the Persian authorities might seize their contraband goods.

The expedition was caught in one of the terrible sand-storms and the author writes: "The storm seized us with its full force. For several anxious hours, we lay motionless and helpless, outstretched on the ground." Upon resuming the journey, the chief obstacle was the "notorious Kalut", a continuous wall of even height consisting of one wild range of hills behind another.[2] Finally, with broken-down camels and utterly worn out, the oasis of Keshit was reached.

[1] "The Southern Lut", by Dr. Alfons Gabriel, in *The Geographical Journal*, September 1938. I have retained the term Persia and have not used Iran.

[2] The term Kalut was meant to signify "the Cities of Lot", as these curious formations were termed in other quarters of the immense desert. It is of interest to note that the Arabs term the Dead Sea *Bahr-al-Lut* or "Sea of Lot".

In his final journey, Dr. Gabriel ascended the Kuh-i-Bazman and the Kuh-i-Taftan, the latter being a volcano in the solfatara stage of its existence. Finally, travelling to Sistan, he crossed southern Afghanistan to Kandahar and so to Quetta. He has certainly added materially to our knowledge of this forbidding dead heart of Persia.

X

IN THE NEW HEBRIDES AND DUTCH NEW GUINEA

AMONG British women explorers Miss Evelyn Cheesman holds a high position. Her chief object is the collecting of insects, but she also explores in little-known countries. Their inhabitants are sometimes cannibals and, generally speaking, live in malarious surroundings, with blackwater fever and yaws prevalent in the case of the New Hebrides.

I propose to give brief accounts of two journeys, the first dealing with the island of Malekula[1] in the New Hebrides, and the second the Cyclops Mountains of Dutch New Guinea[2].

*   *   *   *   *

Malekula, the second largest island of the New Hebrides Group, is densely forested throughout. The trees are not lofty, but climbing plants make the undergrowth dense. Only on, or near the coast is there cultivation. To quote: " The interior is a medley of short, low ranges with small valleys between." There is also a low-lying marshy area. In the north-west, on the other hand, " the whole of that side has been raised again and again, forming remarkable series of coral plateaux ".

The inhabitants are Melanesians and most primitive. They are hostile to one another and are rapidly dying out. Compared with the natives of the Society Islands, who are good-looking Polynesians, with a friendly attitude to everybody, the Melanesians are squat with repellent manners, incapable of showing gratitude or affection and are dominated by terror of the supernatural. It must, however, be noted that they have suffered much injustice at the hands of sandalwood traders and recruiters and, even to-day, little, if any, attempt has been made to govern the tribes in the interior. The work of missionaries has been rewarded with some success.

Collecting was started at Unua, working for five miles along the coast and three miles inland. The beach was composed of pumice-stone from the volcano of Ambrym, distant

[1] *The Geographical Journal* for March 1930; *Backwaters of the Savage South Seas*, by Evelyn Cheesman, 1933.
[2] *The Geographical Journal* for January 1938; *The Land of the Red Bird*, by Evelyn Cheesman, 1938.

some fifteen miles to the east. While Miss Cheesman was residing on Malekula a fissure eruption of this volcano took place with serious destruction of property.

Miss Cheesman's next collecting station was on Atchin, a small island off the north-east coast. There, while collecting

aquatic insects at a little lake on the mainland, she, one morning, found a native on guard with a gun, since, on the previous day, one of his relatives had been murdered by a hillman. The fearless Englishwoman dismissed her boy to avoid reprisals and worked on alone !

The interior of the north of Malekula is owned by two cannibal tribes termed the Big Nambas and the Small Nambas, and Miss Cheesman owed her safety when travelling in their country mainly to being considered a " medicine woman ".

This reputation was won by carrying "a box of tubes of methylated spirit attached to my belt for preserving ants, and this was looked upon as ' magic medicine.' "

The paramount Chief of the Big Nambas was Ringapat who welcomed the explorer on the beach. After entertaining her at a meal, under his escort, she climbed five terraces to the top of the plateau, on which was the village of Tumaru with its well-kept gardens of yams. It was surrounded by a bamboo fence some six feet high, the canes being planted close together and " strengthened by transverse bundles bound together by creepers."

As to his wives, " when he called them, they put out their heads from low doorways of the huts just like some strange wild beasts looking out of their lairs." Ringapat was a remarkable man and, upon the last celebration of the initiation ceremonies of boys to manhood status, he abolished the immemorial custom of human sacrifice and substituted a pig. This step of supreme importance was clinched by a message which he wished Miss Cheesman to take to H.M. King George. It ran as follows : " Ringapat, King of the Big Nambas, wishes King George to know that he will never eat man's flesh, white man or black boy ; that he will never kill man, either white man or black boy ; and that he will be good to all white men, so long as they are good to his boys and do not steal them." He also sent a gift to His Majesty consisting of " a carved spear which had been in his family for generations ". The explorer was warned that the tip was poisoned and, when tested before presentation, strychnine was suggested. It remains to add that His Majesty graciously accepted the gift.

* * * * *

Miss Cheesman, in 1936, spent a year in Dutch New Guinea to collect for the British Museum in the Cyclops Mountains, a coastal range with peaks rising to some 6,000 feet. In 1768, Louis Antoine de Bougainville had named its two conspicuous peaks *les deux Cyclopes*.

This coast, long before the arrival of the Dutch, who now own it, was known to Chinese and Malay traders who dealt especially in the plumes of the beautiful bird of paradise. *Saprop Mani*, the ancient name for the district, signifies " the Land of the Red Bird ", whence the title of Miss Cheesman's book. She, however, explains that the colour of this beautiful bird is rather chestnut, and that the epithet " red " actually signifies " of good omen ".

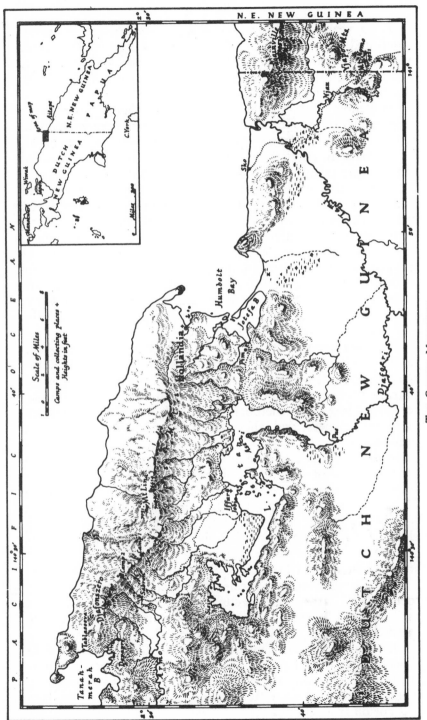

THE CYCLOPS MOUNTAINS

Long years ago, Malay hunters, in quest of the plumage, penetrated into the interior of New Guinea, keeping to certain bush tracks, some of which can still be traced by Malay words that are, even to-day, in current use by the natives far inland. This trade has now been forbidden.

Hollandia is described as a very small village, governed by a Controller of the Dutch Government. That Government had also constructed a good road from Humboldt Bay to Tanah Merah Bay. In its vicinity, the natives were taxed, whereas the tribes living inland were practically uncontrolled.

The rainfall at Hollandia was registered at 110 inches and there were terrific thunderstorms in the mountains where the fall was considerably higher, the atmosphere thus created being extremely damp. Insect pests were ubiquitous, among them mosquitoes with large blue wings. There were also flies and midges, but the red ants are described as " the real inhabitants of Saprop Mani ". They do not hesitate to attack and are quite fearless. Moreover, there are stinging plants which grow thickly up to 4,000 feet. Their sting is severe and the effects last for over twenty-four hours.

Diseases are numerous, one of the chief pests being the jigger flea which attacks the bare-footed natives. We learn that, in 1910, the Dutch representatives who formed the exploring party for the boundary between Dutch and German territory, lost one member by death, another contracted sleeping sickness and they all suffered from malaria and beri-beri.

Indefatigable Miss Cheesman started collecting insects at the base of one of the Cyclops Mountains, cutting a path through the scrub to about 1,000 feet above her camp and there creating a clearing for her purpose. The site of the camp was on a precipice, thereby, as the fearless traveller explained, making clearance easy, since trees felled above it brought down others and thus a comparatively safe open platform could be constructed on which to camp! Collections made rapid progress, and on a single log ten species of insects, one frog and two species of lizards were secured. On another occasion, a thrilling fight between a big digger wasp and its victim, one of the hairy nocturnal spiders, was witnessed.

In the mountains, a visit was paid to Lake Sentani, some sixteen miles long by four miles wide. It is especially interesting in that, among the fish, is a shark, which has apparently " become adapted to a fresh water existence since the lake was cut off from the sea ".

The villagers depend largely on fishing and, to quote our traveller, " a square tray-shaped net is held between the women's arms. . . . They swim after the fish with these trays and scoop them up, then, with a very deft movement, fold the net back against their breast with a struggling fish inside ".

On this note, I conclude a brief epitome of two remarkable journeys by a highly qualified, indomitable explorer.

XI

THE REINDEER-RIDING TUNGUS OF MANCHURIA

" AND when you leave Caracoron and the Altai . . . you go North for forty days till you reach a country called the Plain of Bargu. The people there are called Mescript; they are a very wild race, and live by their cattle, the most of which are stags, and these stags, I assure you, they used to ride upon."

This quotation from Yule's third edition of *Marco Polo*[1] is most interesting, as it gives a reasonably accurate description of the home of the tribe, which in his eulogy of the illustrious explorer he terms " Reindeer-Riding Tunguses ".

Miss E. J. Lindgren, Ph.D., visited this tribe during the course of three journeys into North-Western Manchuria, which were accomplished between 1929 and 1933. She was no ordinary traveller, but thanks to special tuition at Cambridge, her study of this fast-vanishing race was that of an expert,[2] who spoke the Russian, Pekinese and Mongol languages. She had, moreover, undertaken many important journeys on the northern frontiers of Sweden and Finland.

She states that, at the beginning of the nineteenth century, the Reindeer-Tungus, as she terms them, who were then inhabiting the Yakutsk Government in Siberia, were gradually being ousted from their hunting grounds by a more powerful tribe, the Yakuts, who were also better traders. Consequently, many sections of the Tungus migrated towards the Valley of the Amur and finally settled in the almost inaccessible forests of North-West Manchuria. Their only neighbours were Cossack settlers, who had left Siberia during the Russian Revolution, and had occupied land on the Manchurian side of the border. There they had resumed their agricultural and hunting life, keeping horses, cattle, sheep and pigs. In the spring, their special quarry was the male wapiti, whose antlers in velvet fetched high prices owing to their important medical value in

---

[1] *Vide* Vol. I., p. 269 ; *vide* also p. 83 of this work. I would add that Caracoron is Karakoram, and that the Mescript are now termed Merkit, while Bargu is still used for the home of the Bargut nomads.

[2] *Vide* " North-Western Manchuria and the Reindeer-Tungus ", in *The Geographical Journal* for June 1930. *Vide* also " The Reindeer-Tungus of Manchuria ", by E. J. Lindgren, in the *Journal of the Royal Central Asian Society*, April 1935.

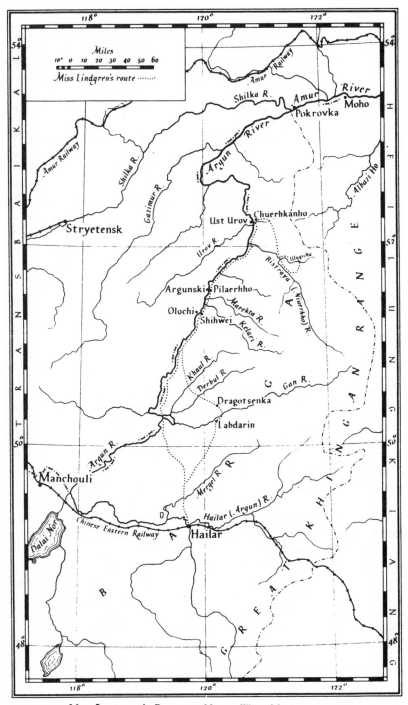

MISS LINDGREN'S ROUTE IN NORTH-WEST MANCHURIA

the eyes of the Chinese. They also hunted squirrels and other fur-bearing animals.

These Cossacks traded with the Reindeer-Tungus, bringing flour, cloth, tea, tobacco, gunpowder, lead, alcohol and sugar on their sledges to points previously agreed upon by both sides. For these commodities the Tungus bartered squirrel and other skins.

In Doctor Lindgren's first journey to this area, in 1929, the explorer followed the right bank of the Argun River through unsurveyed country to Chuerhkanho, a village of Cossacks, who were late arrivals in the country. She then travelled eastwards through dense forests and finally came upon two families of Reindeer-Tungus, who were living on tributaries of the Bystraya River. This first visit was curtailed by shortage of food, but made the explorer anxious to study their activities at other seasons.

Two years later, benefiting by information gathered from Tungus and Russians, the explorer took a more direct route, starting from a village in the Three Rivers District and crossing to the Bystraya basin from one of the sources of the Gan. No accurate survey of this area has as yet been made.

She found two Reindeer-Tungus tents, in one of which lived a *Shamaness*, Olga by name, who was quite willing that Doctor Lindgren should be allowed to accompany her party, provided that the pack-horses of the visitor travelled far ahead of the reindeer, who would otherwise be frightened.

The squirrel hunting season was at its height and necessitated frequent movement of the Tungus. The procedure was to collect the reindeer—not always an easy task—to load them, to make a march to the next camp and there to unload and to pitch the camp. The cold was intense with the thermometer sometimes registering 48°F. below zero at sunrise. As was only to be expected, the Reindeer-Tungus suffer severely from rheumatism.

During the course of Miss Lindgren's visit, Olga decided to *Shamanize*, in order to ascertain from the spirits whether her husband would soon kill an elk and also whether a Cossack trader, imprisoned by the Chinese, was still alive. To mark the importance of the occasion, a reindeer was slaughtered and the partly-cooked meat was placed on a platform as an offering to the spirits. This was all done by the men. The *Shamaness* then, wearing a head-dress surmounted by heavy iron antlers with small sleigh bells—these latter representing spirit animals—danced, drummed and sang. Questions were put to her through her assistants and were answered by means of a curved stick, which she threw on the ground. If the concave side came uppermost, the reply was interpreted as favourable.

Olga's brother was a smith and women were not allowed to approach the smithy, which was set up behind the tents " where the spirits are believed to reside ". The professions of *Shaman* and smith are closely associated. Indeed, Olga's grandmother was a *Shamaness*.

It is of special interest to learn that negro metal-workers in Africa have magico-religious associations to such an extent that smiths sometimes rank as *Shamans*. And to go back to early European mythology, was not the god Hephaestus, or Vulcan, a smith who possessed an anvil with twenty bellows which worked simultaneously ?

To conclude, it is very sad to note that this interesting tribe, which alone has kept its reindeer and its typical cultural elements, material and social, numbers less than two hundred and fifty families and is undoubtedly dying out. But this fact only increases the great debt that we owe to intrepid and accomplished Doctor Lindgren.

XII

THE EXPLORATION OF THE NILE-CONGO DIVIDE

"Content can soothe where'er by fortune placed,
Can rear a garden in a desert waste."
                                        KIRKE WHITE.

IN 1919, Great Britain and France signed a friendly convention for settling the western boundary of the Anglo-Egyptian Sudan, where it marches with French Equatorial Africa. The boundary was defined in the treaty as being the water-parting between the basins of the Nile and Congo Rivers, " until it shall reach the eleventh parallel of northern latitude ".[1] From that point the boundary was to divide the tribes of Darfur from those of Wadi. It extended to 1,600 miles in length and included different types of country, from dense forest to waterless desert. Much of it was unexplored.

Starting from Khartum, the French and British parties reached the scene of their labours at the end of 1921. Colonel P. K. Boulnois, O.B.E., M.C., first surveyed northwards from Andrei, which village incidentally is situated exactly in the centre of Africa. The boundary ran in a northerly direction to the Wadi Howa, passing the remarkable Lake of Undur on the way. Some two miles in length and half a mile broad, even in summer it is full of water, but when it dries up, no digging will reveal water.

Wadi Howa was relatively fertile and the camel grazing was excellent. Upon continuing the journey, north of the wells of Sendia, an attempt was made to complete the survey along the 24th meridian to the turning point of the boundary where it intersects with latitude 19° 30'. Twelve camels had been specially trained to march for nine days without water but, even so, there was nearly a disaster. The expedition had reached a point eighty miles from the Sendia wells in an absolutely waterless country and perforce marched back, but failed at first to find the wells on which their lives depended.

The task for the second season was to discover and survey the Nile-Congo watershed from " the 11th parallel of northern

[1] *Vide R.G.S. Journal* of June 1924.

latitude ", to the point where the Belgian Congo and French
Equatorial Africa met at latitude 5°. In this densely wooded,
uninhabited area, donkeys and bulls took the place of camels.
No food was procurable locally, and supplies, some forty
tons in quantity, had to be arranged for at regular intervals by

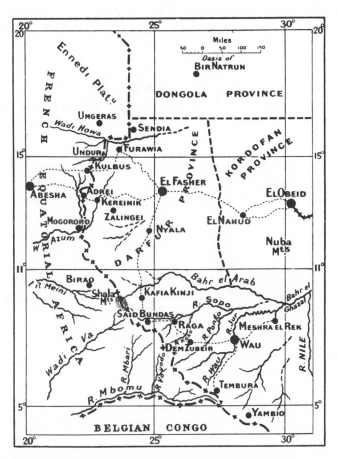

WESTERN FRONTIER OF THE ANGLO-EGYPTIAN SUDAN

the various local officials of the Anglo-Egyptian Sudan. Since
it was out of the question to fix an exact spot in a pathless
forest, everything depended on striking the track made by the
supply convoy. On one occasion, no sign of a path appeared
and although native scouts were sent out in every direction to
make a big circular cast, they failed to find the dump. Supplies
had come to an end and the rains had begun. Finally another
big circular cast was made and soon the cry of " sicca "—the

path—ended a terribly anxious experience. To quote: "And so our life went on. Six months in uninhabited forest—never a road, never a path encountered; no eggs, no milk, no butter, no fresh vegetables."

From the survey point of view it was extremely difficult to find the watershed between the two rivers. One surveyor on each side undertook to discover the source of streams which flowed into the Nile or the Congo respectively. This was accomplished by striking out and continuing for perhaps a day's march on a compass bearing and, on reaching a stream, the surveyor would have to carry his wheel and compass traverse up to its actual source and that of its tributaries. Even then, the sources of the streams were merely marshes as a rule. When each of these two "source discoverers" had reached their goals, the control point was found by astronomical latitude and by wireless longitude and their work would be adjusted. These men, needless to say, ran serious risks of being lost in the foodless forests.

The expedition also suffered severely from malaria and from the complete lack of suitable food. Moreover, the thunderstorms were "a revelation in their intensity; and casualties among the native porters were twice caused by lightning".

As might be supposed, the country was a paradise of game and Boulnois describes that on one occasion when bathing he counted within sight a giraffe, four Jackson's hartebeest, one eland, two bush-buck and a dozen buffalo. He writes that his only dangerous experience was "when a very large herd of buffalo stampeded ahead of the convoy and came round, threshing in an ever-widening circle that on its last ring missed us by only a very few yards".

To conclude, Colonel H. G. Pearson died of blackwater fever at the start of the expedition. Malaria and fever also attacked most of the members of the Commission during the eighteen months of exhausting travel. The delimitation, however, was finally completed and a beacon was erected and suitably termed "The Three-Boundary Point". As the successful leader in this truly Herculean task, Colonel Boulnois certainly joins the ranks of the great explorers of Africa.

ANTARCTIC EXPLORATION

In 1933–35, Admiral Byrd, determined to add to his laurels, undertook a second expedition.[1] which included some fifty scientists, assistants and mechanics. The scale of the equipment of aeroplanes, tractors and radio communications was unprecedented.

Based again on the Bay of Whales, the main discovery made was that the Ross Barrier or Shelf Ice was surrounded by high land on the east, west and south, thus proving that there was no sea-level communication with the Weddell Sea. Finally, a new approximation to the coast line between the Falkland Islands Dependency and Ross Dependency was given, while a large extent of Marie Byrd Land, east and south of King Edward VII Land, was explored.

John R. Rymill, who had accompanied Watkins in his two expeditions, was the experienced leader of the Graham Land Expedition of 1934–37. His party, which sailed on the *Penola*, a small sailing ship fitted with auxiliary power, was commanded by Lieutenant R. E. D. Ryder, R.N., with W. E. Hampton as second-in-command of the expedition, which also included A. Stephenson and Quintin Riley.[2]

Starting from England in September 1934, the Falkland Islands were duly reached. The next objective was Deception Island, a disused whaling station, and a wintering harbour for the *Penola* was established on the Argentine Islands ; a landing ground for the aeroplane was also constructed and, in 1936, the second winter base was formed. In view of the whole distribution of land and sea to the south, as viewed from an aeroplane, being totally different from the reports of previous explorers, it was decided to explore the " new " country under the leadership of Stephenson. To describe his journey : travelling with two teams of dogs, he accompanied Rymill's party to the edge of the shelf-ice south of Cape Berteaux. He then

---

[1] *Antarctic Discovery, The Story of the Second Byrd Antarctic Expedition*, by Rear-Admiral Richard Byrd, 1936.

[2] *Vide The Geographical Journal* for April and May 1938 ; also *Southern Lights*, by John Rymill, with two chapters by A. Stephenson and an " Historical Introduction ", by Dr. R. Mill, 1938. *Vide* also " King George VI Sound ", by Alfred Stephenson and the Rev. W. L. S. Fleming in *The Geographical Journal* for September 1940.

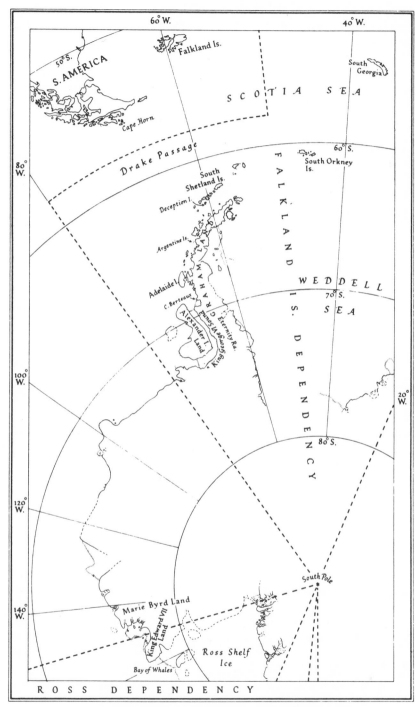

THE ANTARCTIC—ROSS AND FALKLAND ISLES DEPENDENCIES

climbed a col to the height of 2,700 feet and, when the stormy weather cleared, he advanced southwards to latitude 72°, thereby discovering an important waterway of unknown length which, in due course, by His Majesty's permission, was named " King George VI Sound ". The explorers, furthermore, were the first to land on Alexander I Island, which Bellingshausen had discovered and named.[1] Lack of supplies forced them to retrace their steps.

Rymill himself, on the summit of a 3,000 foot pass near Cape Berteaux, met the returning party, and, hearing that there was no possible route across Alexander I Island to the west, he decided to march east across Graham Land. In thirteen marches, the range on the coast was reached and the explorer camped at the height of 7,500 feet.

This completed the work in which the use of the aeroplane, the wireless and the tractor, aided by the dog teams, materially helped to win important success.

To conclude this Antarctic section, during the years 1939 -41, Admiral Byrd organized yet a third expedition[2] which worked in two divisions. One party under Dr. Siple, based also on the Bay of Whales, widely extended the surveys of the second expedition by an air survey.

The second party, under Admiral Byrd himself, from a base south of Adelaide Island, made a complete survey of King George VI Sound and the whole coast of Alexander I Island, following the Eternity Range on the mainland of Antarctica far to the south. The survey was extended across the Graham Land plateau into the south of the Weddell Sea and concluded the valuable discoveries of Admiral Byrd, who ranks high on the roll of Antarctic explorers.

[1] *Vide* pp. 325–26 of this work.
[2] *Vide* " Preliminary Account of the United States Antarctic Expedition 1939-1941 ", *Geographical Review*, Vol. 31, 1941.

INDEX

ABBAS, Shah of Persia, 152
Abbasid, 48 ; dynasty, descent of, 47, 48
Abdul Aziz, 279, 291, 297 ; assassination of, 280
Abdul Malik, Caliph, 47
Abdulla, ruling Wahabi chief, defeat by Egyptians, 280 ; beheaded, 280
Abdulla, son of Amir Feisal, 286
Abdulla Ibn Rashid, *Amir*, 286, 287
Abdulla Ibn Rashid, Wallin's eulogy on, 283 ; death of, 284
Abdulla Khan, King of Shirwan, 151
Abdur Rahman, 47, 297 ; *Amir*, 271
Abraham, an Arab *Shaykh*, 277 ; rescue of Lot by, 2 ; journeys of, 277
Abruzzi, Duke of, naming of peaks in Ruwenzori Range by, 238 ; Himalayan explorer, 250
Abu Bekr, Caliph, 45
Abu Isa, caravan leader, 285
Abu Kish, 300
Abu Said, last of Ilkhan rulers of Persia, 87
Abuna, River, 200
Abydos, 13
Abyssinia, 83, 100, 240, 241 ; mission of Covilham to, 228 ; exploration of, 240
Acbaluc Mongol word, 79 (footnote)
— Manji, 78
Achaean Confederacy, capital of, 6
Achaeans, 4
Achaemenian monarchs, tombs of, 149
Acre, 69, 85
— area of Bolivia, 200
Actium, Battle of, 36
Adaluja, 88
Adamawa, 218
Adam's Peak, 81
Adams, William, in Japan, 169
Adelaide, 205, 206, 207
Adelaide Island, 326, 389
Adélie Land, 326
Aden, 38, 87, 104, 112, 113, 229, 278
— protectorate, 292, 343
Adrianople, 97
Aduwab, 304
Advent Bay, 319, 320
Adventure, Capt. Cook's ship, 179
Aegean area, favourable for navigation, 3
— Sea, 7
Aelana, 22
Aelius Gallus, 39
Aeroplane, use of, in discovery in Africa, 242
Aeschylus, *Prometheus Bound* of, 266
Afghan Boundary Commission, 271 ; camp of, 247

Afghan War, 269
Afghanistan, 16 ; Herat province of, 16 award of Wakhan to, 250
— Northern, 15
— North-West, 271
— Western, 269
Aflaj, 299
Africa, 39, 40, 41, 49, 211, 212, 213, 216, 218, 219, 220, 223, 224 ; expedition round coasts of, manned by Phoenicians, 5 ; north and west coasts of, trading posts established by Phoenicians, 5, 16 ; Phoenician cities built along coasts of, 6 ; northern coast of, little known to Herodotus, 8 ; coast of, 53 ; west coast of, 64 ; east coast of, 87 ; trade-routes, 97 ; completion of exploration of, 236 *et seq.* ; partition among rival European states, 237 ; discovery in, aided by motor-car and aeroplane, 242 ; abolition of slavery in, 244
— East, discoveries in, 229 ; delimitation of Anglo-German boundary in (1898), 237
— North, 37, 46, 60, 84, 241
— North-East, information gained through military operations and missions in, during Great War, 242 ; completion of discovery in, 242 ; exploration of practically completed, 244
— West, sketch map of, illustrating Ibn Battuta's travels, 93 ; exploration in, 238, now practically completed, 239
African Association founded 1788, 213, 215
Africans, Sudanese, how differing from negroes, 94
Agades, 217, 218, 241
Agardh Bay, 320
"Ageyl", 291
Agra, 154, 155 ; described by Fitch, 154
Agriculture, probable site of origin of, 1
Ahmadabad, 155
Ahmad-al-Idrisi, 300
Ahwaz, 14
Ainsworth, in Asia Minor, 267
Ainus, hairy, 170
Ăir, 96, 241
Ak Kuyunlu (White Sheep) dynasty, 148
Ak Masjid, 246
Akaba, 293, 294 ; Gulf of, 22, 281
Akkad, 2 ; dynasty of, founder of, 2
Ala Tau Range, 245
Alabaster unguent vase, discovery near Rudbar, 18 ; possibly property of Alexander, 18
Alai Range, 245

391

INDEX

INDEX

INDEX

INDEX

NABATHEAN inscription, rock-hewn tombs with, 286
Nabopolassar, capture of Nineveh by, 3
Nachtigal, G., in Africa, 218
Nadir Shah, Napoleon of Asia, 268
Nafud desert, Arabia, 283, 285; description of, by Palgrave, 284, 285
Nagar, 249
Nagarahara, 26
Nahavand, 45, 47
Nain Singh, "The Pundit", in Asia, 261
Nairobi, 237
Najaf, 86
Najran, 299, 302, 343
Nakab-al-Hajar, ruins of, discovered by Wellsted, 282, 354
Nalanda, 27
Nambas tribe, Big, 375
—— Small, 375
Nansen, F., 318, 321
Nan-shan, range of, 254
Nan-shan range and Kuen Lun range, connection between, 248
Naples, 59
Napoleon I, Emperor, 192, 268, 269; invasion of Egypt stimulating French activity in valley of Nile, 228
Naram-Sin, conqueror of Lulubi, 2
Narbo, Martius, 41
Narbonne, 47
Nares, in the Arctic, 320
De Narvaez, Pamfilo, in North America, 130, 131, 182
Nassaw Mountains, 209
Natal, 109
Navidad, 139
Navigation, Aegean area favourable for, 3
Near East, manufactures used as means of barter by Sumerians, 2
Nearchus, 31, 72, 82; voyage of, westward on Indian Ocean, 17, 18
Nechako River, 190
Necho, King of Egypt, sailing expedition manned by Phoenicians sent by, 5
Negrana, ancient city, discovery of, 284
Negro Lands, 92
Negroes, right management and government of, 240
— Sudanese Africans differing from, 94
Nejd, 86, 280, 283; capture by Wahabis (1773), 279
— Central, rise of Wahabi religion in, 279
— Southern, 297, 299
Nejran, Halévy first European to visit since Gallus, 284; Philby visits, 344
Nepal, Central, 265
Nerchinsk, 166
Nero, 37
Nestorian Christians, 67, 74, 105
— Church, missionaries of, explorations by, 31, 32
Nestorius, sect of, spread among Eastern races, 32
Neva River, 54
New Amsterdam, 184
— Brunswick, 183

New England, 183
— France, 192
— Guinea, 171, 172, 173, 209, 374; discovery of, 139
— Hebrides, 375
— Holland (Australia), 175
— Orleans founded in 1717, 192
— Plymouth, 183
— Siberian Islands, 317, 321
— South Wales, 207
— Wales, 177
— York, 184, 313, 336
New York Herald, proprietor of, despatch of Stanley to discover Livingstone, 228
New Zealand, 173, 174, 178, 179, 199, 207, 208, 209, 211, 325, 326, 329, 332, 336
New Zealand Company, 208
Newbery, John, in India, 153, 154
Newcombe, Col. S. F., Survey of Sinai Peninsula, 294
Newfoundland, 125, 146, 321; Vikings' discoveries of, 56
Newnes, Sir George, 329
Ngami, Lake, 222
Niagara Falls, 182
Niam-Niam, 240
Nicaea, 61, 62, 88
Nicobar, 83
— Islands, 30, 155
Nicollet, Jean, 182
Nicopolis, battle of, 97
Niebuhr, G., in Arabia, 278, 279
Niger, 49
— River, 94, 95, 211, 212, 213, 214, 215, 216, 217, 218, 219; acquaintance of Herodotus with river identifiable with, 10; mistaken for Nile by Ibn Battuta, 95; delta of, 238; source of, 238; valley of, exploration, 238
—— Lower, 238
—— Middle, caravans trading across Sahara reaching, 16
Nigeria, 237; systematic exploration of, 239; transference to Crown, 239
Nijni Novgorod, 150, 246
Nil-al-Sudan, 49
Nile River, 212, 228; description of Egypt as "gift" of (Hecataeus), 8; Niger mistaken for, by Ibn Battuta, 95; source of, Livingstone's last attempt at discovery of, 226; source of, problem of, 228 *et seq.*; problem of, solution of, producing great band of explorers, 255; conception of course of, by Herodotus, 244; right bank of, exploration, 242; sources of, accurately described by Ptolemy, 246
—— valley of, 39, 40, 218
—— valleys of, 1
— Egyptian, 49
— and Euphrates valleys, trade connections between, how proved, 2
Nile-Congo Divide, 384
Nimrod, 31, 335; in Antarctic, 331
Nimrud, 269

413